Field Studies, **10**, (2002) 207 - 531

CW01082995

BRITISH PLANT GALLS
IDENTIFICATION OF GALLS ON PLANTS AND FUNGI

MARGARET REDFERN
2 Victoria Road, Sheffield S10 2DL
AND
PETER SHIRLEY
72 Dagger Lane, West Bromwich, West Midlands B71 4BS
ILLUSTRATED BY
MICHAEL BLOXHAM
1 St John's Close, Sandwell Valley, West Midlands B70 6TH

With major contributions from Tom Preece, Brian Spooner, John Southey and Keith Harris

DEDICATION

To Fred Stubbs and John Pearson, the founding fathers of the British Plant Gall Society and inspiration for this work; with regret that they did not live to see it come to fruition.

ABSTRACT

Galls are abnormal growths formed from tissues of a plant or other host, due to the parasitic activity of another organism. Fully illustrated keys are provided to the *galls*, with the causal organism included only where necessary for identification. Included are galls on plants caused by insects, mites, nematodes, fungi and bacteria, and galls on fungi caused by insects (galls on fungi may also be caused by other fungi; see Spooner, 2002). Like all guides in the AIDGAP series, these keys have been extensively tested prior to publication.

CONTENTS

Preface

Many naturalists are familiar with the bizarre and often colourful oak apples, marble galls, robin's pin cushions, rosettes and bean galls on oaks, wild roses and willows, and wish to discover more about them. In 1986, the fledgling British Plant Gall Society produced an aid to identification of galls found in Britain – *Provisional Keys to British Plant Galls*, edited by Fred Stubbs.

The present work is an extension of those keys, more comprehensive and bringing nomenclature up to date. Every effort has been made to keep technical terms to a minimum, and to explain them where they are used, thereby making the keys as easy to understand as possible. In addition, many galls and their inhabitants are illustrated. Our intention is that field naturalists will be able to identify (where this is possible) all common plant galls discovered in the field in Great Britain, as well as the majority of those less commonly encountered. The keys are as comprehensive as they can be, given that new discoveries continue to be made and taxonomic advances result in corrections to previous publications.

There are over 330 keys arranged, firstly, by groups of gall causers (arthropods, nematodes, fungi, bacteria, viruses and plants) and then, within these groups, mainly by host genera. In a few cases, hosts are treated by family (Apiaceae, Brassicaceae, Poaceae), or by larger group (Fungi). No keys are given to galls on animals or algae (see Introduction), and only one gall each on a lichen and a bryophyte is included (see Nematode Key, Section D).

In compiling these keys we have drawn, inevitably, on the work of others. Information has been used from many sources, including the classic keys of Houard (1908-1913), Docters van Leeuwen (1957, revised 1982) and Buhr (1964-1965), as well as the more recent guides of Coulianos & Holmåsen (1991), Redfern & Askew (1992, updated 1998), Dauphin & Aniotsbehère (1993, revised 1997) and Csóka (1997).

Introduction

Galls make ideal subjects for study by amateur naturalists, who can provide invaluable information on their distribution and natural history, and we hope that they, and professional ecologists, will find this work useful.

What are galls?

This question provokes argument and the answer evolves as more is discovered about how galls are formed. A gall involves an intimate association between two organisms which is largely parasitic, the gall causer being the parasite and the organism whose tissues form the gall being the host. Normally most advantage passes to the gall causer. The following definition is generally accepted, though it is narrower than some:

A gall is an abnormal growth produced by a plant or other host under the influence of another organism. It involves enlargement and/or proliferation of host cells and provides both shelter and food or nutrients for the invading organism.

This definition covers both swellings caused by increase in size or number of cells, and increases in vascular tissues stimulated, for example, by gall-causing aphids, adelgids and other insects.

Not all distortions of plants and other hosts are galls. Generalised herbivores, such as caterpillars, which remove pieces of leaf, are clearly not gall causers even though wounded

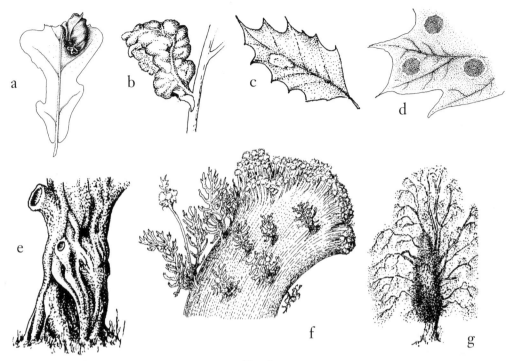

FIG. 1

Examples of distortions to plants that are not regarded as galls. (a) leaf roll of the beetle *Atellabus nitens* on oak, *Quercus* sp.; (b) distortion caused by the cuckoo-spit froghopper, *Philaenus spumarius*; (c) wounding of a holly, *Ilex aquifolium*, leaf by the holly leaf miner, *Phytomyza ilicis*; (d) a sycamore, *Acer pseudoplatanus*, leaf marked by the tar spot fungus, *Rhytisma acerinum*; (e) a gall-like callus developed as a result of mechanical damage; (f) fasciation of a ragwort, *Senecio jacobaea*, shoot; (g) a birch, *Betula*, tree showing the condition known as witches' broom. Various scales.

tissues may become thickened and distorted. Sometimes a caterpillar or beetle larva may fold or roll leaves and feed inside (Fig. 1a); these are not galls unless the leaf is also thickened. Similarly, wrinkling and curling of leaves, without any associated thickening, caused by many aphids, thrips and plant hoppers (Fig. 1b) are not regarded here as galls.

Most leaf mines and stem borings do not involve an increase in the number of cells; the miner is merely a specialised herbivore living in the thickness of the leaf or stem. Wounding by the holly leaf miner, *Phytomyza ilicis*, provokes callous tissue produced by cells bordering its mine, which may induce a distinct bulge in the leaf (Fig. 1c); the larva does not, however, feed on this tissue and so is not a gall causer. This is not true of all miners; some mining moths may be classed as causers of simple galls in leaves, and some stem boring beetle larvae and caterpillars cause true galls.

Some fungal growths may be confused with galls, e.g. the common tar-spot of sycamore leaves (Fig. 1d), caused by *Rhytisma acerinum*, does not involve enlargement or thickening of cells. Gall-like growths of callus may be caused by mechanical damage (Fig. 1e), problems during plant growth may result in fasciation (Fig. 1f) and witches' brooms (Fig. 1g); and chemicals and genetic abnormalities may cause growths. All may be difficult to separate from true galls.

Types of galls

Galls vary from single enlarged cells on algae to complex multicellular growths with well differentiated layers of tissue (structural, systemic and nutritive) on flowering plants.

Galls on algae require specialised techniques of study and are unlikely to be encountered by ordinary field naturalists*. They are not considered further here (for more information, see Spooner, 1994a and b). Other hosts include fungi, mosses, ferns and conifers, but it is on flowering plants that galls show their greatest diversity. They occur on all parts of plants: roots, stems, leaves, flowers, fruits and seeds. They appear as swellings and nodules, patches of hairs, rolls and folds of leaf margins and of whole leaves, dimples, blisters, pustules, discs and balls on leaf blades, and swellings of buds, flowers and fruits. Some are tiny, requiring diligent searching, while others are large, recognisable from the windows of a moving car or train.

Animals may have swellings or growths on them caused by other animals, perhaps analogous to galls. Some pycnogonids (marine arthropods related to spiders, Arachnida) live in cyst-like growths on sea firs (Cnidaria: Hydrozoa; Chinery & Spooner, 1998), and a few specialised worms (Annelida: Myzostomaria) and larval copepods (Crustacea: Copepoda) cause gall-like swellings on starfish, brittle stars and sea urchins (Echinodermata; Spooner, 1997). These, and swellings in mammals caused by parasitic warble-flies (Diptera: Hypodermatidae) and cancerous growths caused by viruses, are not included here.

All galls involve additional tissues, in the form of enlarged or additional cells or enhanced vascular tissues, which provide nutrients for the causer. They form in young, undifferentiated tissues, the cells of which can actively grow and multiply (such as shoot and root meristems), or in older tissues induced to de-differentiate so that their cells can actively grow, divide and multiply. Some galls have a relatively simple structure, e.g. the swellings, pouches, nodules and leaf rolls induced by bacteria, fungi, nematodes, mites, beetles and some aphids. Others are elaborate, with several layers of specialised tissues, linked to enhanced vascular tissues. These attract nutrients from elsewhere in the plant so that more of the plant is affected than the immediate site of the gall. The most complex galls are induced by insects, particularly by cecidomyiids (gall midges), tephritids (gall flies) and cynipids (gall wasps).

Ninety eight per cent of all known galls are found on flowering plants, with 90% on dicotyledons. Sixty five per cent affect leaves, 20% stems, 10% buds, and 5% all other organs (Dauphin & Aniotsbehère, 1993; 1997). In Britain the plant families with most species of arthropod galls are:

Asteraceae (daisies, thistles etc.); over 100 species
Salicaceae (willows and poplars); about 90 species
Fabaceae (legumes); about 90 species
Rosaceae (roses, brambles, cherries etc.); about 80 species
Fagaceae (oaks and beech); about 60 species

In terms of number of gall causers per plant species, however, the two native oaks (*Quercus robur*, English or pedunculate oak, and *Q. petraea*, sessile or durmast oak) are at the top of the league with about 50 species. Over half of these cause two different types of gall at different stages of their life cycle and on different parts of the trees.

Galls are known from fossils. The oldest known gall is from the roots of the tree *Lepidodendron*, found in rocks of Upper Palaeozoic-Triassic age from 300-200 million years ago (mya; Larew, 1992). This was probably induced by a fungus; similar galls are caused by

---

*except on the seashore, where nematodes of the genus *Halenchus* cause galls to form on the stipes of egg wrack, *Ascophyllum nodosum* and bladder wrack *Fucus vesiculosus*. Milford Haven can be added to the list of localities for *H. fucicola* (see Coles, 1958). (Ed.)

living *Physoderma* (= *Urophlyctis*) (Chytridiales) on roots of *Medicago* (Fabaceae (= Leguminosae)). Gall induction by insects is of relatively recent origin (Roskam, 1992). The oldest probable insect gall is a swelling in the cone stalk of the conifer *Aethophyllum stipulare*, from the early Triassic (225 mya; Larew, 1992). Structurally, this is a simple gall similar to present-day beetle, sawfly or some fly galls (it is not possible, though, to determine the type of causer). The majority of insect galls, including those of the cecidomyiids and the cynipids, evolved later, coinciding with diversification of the flowering plants in the Cretaceous (140-70 mya). Galls of agromyzids and tephritids seem to be among the most recent, being found on plants of Miocene age (34 mya; Scott *et al.*, 1994).

The gall causers

Gall-causing has evolved independently many times in insects (Roskam 1992) as well as in other groups. The variety of gall causing organisms is shown in Table 1.

In order to manipulate growth, gall causers must be closely adapted to the form, structure, development, seasonal changes and life cycle of their hosts. Most, therefore, are more or less host-specific and either monophagous (feeding on one host species only), or oligophagous (feeding on a group of related species, in the same genus or family). A few are polyphagous, feeding on a wide range of hosts in unrelated families; these tend to cause simple galls, without specialised layers of tissues, and often variable in size and form. Examples include crown gall caused by *Agrobacterium tumefaciens*, and swellings caused by mistletoe and nematode worms. The range of host species for each gall causer is included in the keys.

Ensuring that the offspring of each generation finds new hosts is hazardous and chancy, and has led to a wide variety of life cycles, some of them very complex. Production of large numbers of eggs, young or spores is common (e.g. in cynipids, gall aphids, rust fungi), ensuring that some, at least, survive to start the new generation. In addition, many species have several generations a year, on the same or on different host plants. Rust fungi and gall aphids may cause galls on one host but not another, while cynipid wasps on oaks usually have alternate generations, each causing distinct galls either on a different part of trees of the same species or on a second oak species. These alternate generations have, in turn, males and females and females only. The male and female (sexual) generation usually causes relatively short-lived galls in spring and summer. The all-female (agamic) generation usually causes more persistent galls in summer and autumn within which the causers overwinter. In Britain for some species this involves alternation between *Quercus robur* or *Q. petraea*, and the introduced *Q. cerris*.

For information on life cycles, see Wilson & Henderson (1966) for rusts, Mordue & Ainsworth (1984) for smuts, Redfern & Askew (1992, 1998) for selected mites and insects, and the volumes of edited papers listed in the literature review below.

Where to find galls

The simple answer is wherever the host organism is found. Galls on trees are the best known and often the easiest to find. Habitat and structure play a part – woodland edge usually provides more galls than enclosed woodland whatever the host species. For example, galls seem to be more numerous and found in greater variety on young scrub oaks than on large trees in ancient woodland. Old meadows, and chalk and limestone grasslands, with a rich variety of herbaceous plants, are usually productive. Hedgerows, heaths and vacant land can also be rich sites.

TABLE 1. Gall-causing organisms in Britain (modified after Coulianos & Holmåsen, 1991, Dreger-Jauffret & Shorthouse, 1992, Dauphin & Aniotsbehère, 1993, 1997, Spooner & Bowdrey, 1993, Hawksworth *et al.*, 1995, and Preece, Spooner and Southey, personal communication)

MAJOR GROUP / PHYLUM	CLASS	ORDER	SUPERFAMILY/ FAMILY/ SUB-FAMILY	COMMON NAME
Viruses				
Phytoplasmas				
Bacteria				crown gall
				root nodules
	Actinomycetes			root galls
Protoctista (= Protozoa)*				
Plasmodiophoromycota*	Plasmodiophoromycetes	Plasmodiophoromales	Plasmodiophoracaceae	
Chromista				
Oomycota	Oomycetes	Peronosporales	Albuginaceae	white blister
Fungi				
Chytridiomycota	Chytridiomycetes	Chytridiales	Synchytriaceae	
Ascomycota	Taphrinomycetes	Protomycetales	Protomycetaceae	
		Taphrinales	Taphrinaceae	
	Ascomycetes	Erysiphales	Erysiphaceae	
		Helotiales	Hyaloscyphaceae	
		Hypocreales	Clavicipitaceae	ergots
			Nectriaceae	
	Hyphomycetes			
Basidiomycota	Teliomyctes	Uredinales	Chaconiaceae	rusts
			Coleosporiaceae	
			Cronartiaceae	
			Melampsoraceae	
			Phragmidiaceae	
			Pucciniaceae	
			Pucciniastraceae	
			Sphaerophragmiaceae	
			Uropyxidaceae	
	Ustomycetes	Ustilaginales	Tilletiaceae	smuts
			Ustilaginaceae	smuts
		Exobasidiales	Exobasidiaceae	
Plants				
Magnoliidae	Rosiflorae	Santalales	Viscaceae	mistletoe
	Asteriflorae	Solanales	Cuscutaceae	dodder
Animals				
Nematoda	Secernentea	Tylenchida	Anguinidae	nematodes
			Meloidogynidae	
			Pratylenchidae	
		Aphelenchida	Aphelenchoididae	
		Dorylaimida	Longidoridae	
Arthropoda	Arachnida	Acari	**Eriophyoidea**	gall mites
			Tarsonemidae	tarsonemid mites
	Insecta	Hemiptera:	**Psylloidea**	psyllids
		Sternorrhyncha	**Aphidoidea:**	
			Adelgidae	woolly aphids
			Aphididae including	
			Pemphiginae	gall aphids
			Phylloxeridae	
			Coccoidea	scale insects

* Classification after Alexopoulos *et al.* (1996), Ingram & Robertson (1999)

Major Group / Phylum	Class	Order	Superfamily/ Family/ Sub-family	Common Name
		Coleoptera	Brentidae (=Apionidae)	weevils
			Cerambycidae	longhorn beetles
			Chrysomelidae	leaf beetles
			Curculionidae	weevils
		Lepidoptera	Cochylidae	
			Coleophoridae	
			Gelechiidae	
			Heliozelidae	
			Incurvariidae	
			Momphidae	
			Nepticulidae	
			Pterophoridae	
			Pyralidae	
			Sesiidae	
			Tortricidae	
		Diptera	Agromyzidae	leaf mining flies
			Anthomyiidae	
			Cecidomyiidae	gall midges
			Chloropidae	gout flies
			Platypezidae	
			Tephritidae	gall flies
		Hymenoptera	Blasticotomidae	sawflies
			Tenthredinidae	sawflies
			Chalcidoidea	chalcid wasps
			Cynipidae	gall wasps

Galls tend to be more common, with greater diversity, in southern England than further north (although this may reflect the distribution of cecidologists); there are, however, species typical of northern England and Scotland. Information on distribution is included sparingly in the keys and only when it is based on firm evidence. Field evidence of distribution is often patchy and absence of records may reflect under-recording rather than a real limited distribution. We hope to add such information when reliable records have accumulated. Time and length of appearance varies too. Leaf galls may be found only when the leaves first appear, or they may persist for several months and subsequently be found in leaf litter. Flower and fruit galls require that these stages are present, although some galls in fallen acorns remain for a few years before the inhabitants emerge. Other galls appear, mature and fall from the affected part in just a few weeks. Further information on when to find galls, where known, is included in the keys.

HOW TO USE THE KEYS

Like other AIDGAP publications, these keys are intended as introductions to the identification of a difficult group of organisms. We have attempted to include all galls that naturalists are likely to come across and, by also including hosts less commonly encountered, to encourage people to search for the more unusual galls.

The keys provided are for the identification of the *galls*, structures formed by a particular host under the influence of the named gall causer. Causers are therefore identified at second hand, often without being seen. This approach assumes that all galls are unique; that recognising the gall allows infallible determination of the gall causer. This is often true but, sometimes, it is misleading; notes are included in the keys when identification of the galls needs to be confirmed by rearing and identifying the gall causer.

The keys provided are to galls on plants and on fungi. The first task is to identify the host, as accurately as possible, using a flora or field guide (e.g. Fitter *et al.*, 1974, 1984,

Mitchell, 1974, Rose, 1981, Clapham *et al.*, 1987, Courtecuisse & Duhem, 1995, Stace, 1997). Looking up the genus or common name of the host in the index will refer you to the appropriate page in one or more of the sections:

A. Bacteria, Phytoplasmas and Viruses
B. Fungi
C: Plants
D. Nematodes
E. Arthropods: Insects and Mites

With experience you will often be able to recognise the right section (A, B, C, D, or E) and turn immediately to it. When you are uncertain, you will need to work through each of them, eliminating each in turn. In most cases, the choice will be between sections B (fungi) and E (arthropods). Hosts are cross-referenced between Section E and the other sections making it easy to move from one to another. In some cases, identification of the host to genus will allow accurate identification of the species causing the gall. Often, though, it will be necessary to identify the host species. This is essential if distribution records are to be kept or if work is to be done on the natural history of the gall and its inhabitants.

Many host plants, or other host organisms, have only one, or only a few, known galls. These are described in turn. For hosts with several or many galls, a dichotomous-style key is given (in a few couplets more than two choices are offered). The most appropriate option should be chosen, which will lead you step by step to the identity of your specimen. The keys to three genera with large numbers of galls, *Quercus*, *Populus* and *Salix*, are subdivided to make them easier to use. Most galls are illustrated. The figures are an integral part of the keys and should be referred to, where indicated; they add to the description of the gall, and often help to explain unfamiliar terminology. Most drawings include an indication of scale (the numbers alongside are millimetres). Technical terms have been kept to a minimum, but some have been included for brevity or when in frequent use. Consult the Glossary for explanation of terms used. Notes in small type appear under some couplets; these emphasise the need for caution in particular cases, especially where there is lack of knowledge of a particular species.

Keys are not infallible, and this work is no exception. The distortion you are attempting to name may not be included, perhaps because it is not thought to be a gall, or has not been found before. Some galls, particularly those caused by some gall mites and gall midges, are due to organisms not yet named; these have not been included. Some growths which are included may, when they have been adequately studied, turn out not to be true galls. It is hoped that future editions of the keys will include such corrections, adding or removing species as more is discovered about them.

The keys are designed for the identification of typical mature galls, which are not distorted by unusual growth or by the presence of inquilines (organisms other than the causer which feed on gall tissue) or parasitoids and predators (organisms which feed on causers, inquilines and other parasitoids). These and other organisms may confuse identifications (the keys assume that any organism in the gall is the causer). Parasitoids, predators and inquilines often occur in fresh galls, with mites, psocids, springtails, fungi etc. entering old galls after the causer has left. Recognising larvae or nymphs of gall causers will help (and figures are included with the keys). Redfern & Askew (1992, 1998) provide a key to 'other larvae' which will help to sort out the arthropod community, and experience of opening galls and examining their contents using a microscope will lead to familiarity with the communities characteristic of different galls.

Confidence in the keys, and your ability to use them, will increase with experience. In many cases, it should be possible to identify the gall on its host plant with the aid of a hand lens. If identification is in doubt, and if there is no shortage of specimens, it is worth collecting the gall in order to rear the causer, or to study it further. Its identity can be checked in a specialist key (e.g. the Royal Entomological Society's keys for adult insects, Wilson & Henderson, 1966; Ellis & Ellis, 1985; Preece & Hick, 1990 for fungi). Confirmation by experts should be sought for possible new records.

Although attempts have been made to include normal variation, it is sensible, if possible, to check the identification on a number of galls. If this means collecting specimens, do not take more than is essential, and never pick galls which you suspect may be rare. Never collect in nature reserves unless you have permission. If you need a specimen, search for one on the same host outside the reserve. Wardens and owners of nature reserves, however, will often readily give permission for limited collecting, in return for a list of the species you find. Try to use small cutters, such as secateurs, when removing small twigs and branches. This is aesthetically better, is less damaging to the plant and makes it easier to secure lightly attached galls than pulling and ripping vegetation. When searching for root galls, remember that the Wildlife and Countryside Act requires that you have the landowner's permission to uproot any plant, and some species are completely protected from such treatment. Examining tree roots is therefore generally in order, but uprooting herbaceous plants is not.

If a gall is suspected of being new to Britain, its causer must be identified (and the adult reared if possible), and confirmed by an expert, before it can be added to the British list. Identification of the gall alone is not sufficient for new records (see Bowdrey, 1999).

As more work is done on particular groups of gall-causing organisms and their taxonomy is revised it is often necessary to alter their names. The following works have been used for nomenclature in these keys:

Native plants	Stace, 1997
Exotic plants not in Stace	Mitchell, 1974; Clement & Foster, 1994
Bacteria and fungi	International Mycological Institute, 1964 onward; Henderson, 2000; Vánky, 1994
Nematodes	Southey, 1978, Krall, 1991, Brzeskí, 1998, Siddiqi, 2000
Eriophyids	Amrine & Stasny, 1994
Psyllids	Hodkinson & White, 1979; White & Hodkinson, 1982
Aphids, including adelgids	Blackman & Eastop, 1994
Weevils	Morris, 1991, 1993; Morris & Booth, 1997, Gønget, 1997
Agromyzids	Spencer, 1972
Cecidomyiids	Chandler, 1998
Tephritids	Chandler, 1998
Cynipids	Eady & Quinlan, 1963, Ambrus, 1974, Redfern & Askew, 1998
Sawflies	Liston, 1995
Other insects	Kloet & Hincks, 1964, 1972, 1975, 1977, 1978

Eriophyid mite nomenclature has, fortunately, been simplified in Amrine & Stasny's *Catalog* (1994). Most subspecies known previously by cumbersome trinomial (three word) scientific names have been elevated to full species.

There is no better way to improve your ability to identify galls accurately than to search for them in the company of more experienced cecidologists. Becoming a member of the British Plant Gall Society (BPGS), and joining its field excursions, will help considerably too (contact the Hon. Secretary: 1 Palfreyman Lane, Oadby, Leicester LE2 4UR).

Techniques for recording, collecting, rearing, preserving

The British Plant Gall Society is building up a data-base of species and welcomes records from anywhere in Britain and Ireland. Record cards, which list the common species, can be obtained from the Hon. Secretary (address above). Essential information to note with every record is date and grid reference (six-figure grid reference if possible) of the site, the host species, collector's name and, if necessary, the name of an expert who has confirmed the record. Confirmation is particularly important for naturalists new to the subject, for unfamiliar species and for species new to the country.

Field work

Bud galls on trees and shrubs can sometimes be more easily found by examining branches and twigs looking up against the light, rather than looking down on them against the ground. When searching for leaf galls both surfaces should be examined. Galls hidden inside plant parts (such as tephritid fly galls in the heads of thistles) will only be revealed by cutting open the parts concerned, although squeezing affected parts may indicate the presence of galls because of hardening of tissue.

Many galls can be identified on the host plant or fungus, with the aid of a hand lens (x10 is the most useful magnification). Collecting equipment is simple: polythene bags, specimen tubes or small containers (small compartmented anglers' boxes are very useful), a stout penknife or secateurs, plus a field notebook, pencils and spare paper for labels. A walking stick with a curved handle is useful for galls just out of reach (the most interesting ones always seem to be just out of reach!). In addition to these keys, a flora is essential, plus a fungal guide if your interests include these hosts.

Work at home, or in the laboratory

For identifying gall causers and their parasitoids and inquilines at home, identification keys (many are referenced here) and a stereomicroscope are necessary. Good second-hand instruments are often available; local natural history societies and museums may have information on sources. To be certain of the connection between causers and inquilines and their galls, specimens must be isolated from each other at the time of collection and be kept isolated thereafter.

Rearing insect gall causers and their parasitoids and inquilines is not difficult provided they are collected as fully fed larvae or as pupae. Galls can be kept in containers, preferably in an unheated outhouse, until adults emerge. Some species pupate in the soil, so their containers should contain a layer of sterile soil or sand/compost mixture which is kept damp. Problems may arise due to larvae or their galls drying out or developing mould if too damp; the containers need to be checked regularly. Identifying and rearing mites and fungal gall causers requires more specialist equipment and expertise; local natural history societies as well as the BPGS can often provide help.

For nematode galls, some species can be identified fairly reliably from the characteristic form of the gall, especially those due to *Anguina* and related genera. Otherwise, species identification by a specialist is needed, using a high-power microscope. Preliminary examination may be made by opening galls or teasing apart suspected tissue in water under a stereomicroscope. It should be noted, however, that the presence of nematodes does not in itself mean that they are the cause of any swelling observed. Free-living nematodes are frequently present in damaged or diseased plant tissue, and most of these are bacteria-feeding species, not gall causers.

To aid the process of recording, it is well worth building up a reference collection of galls and, perhaps, gall causers. Woody galls can be kept dry, those on leaves pressed and dried as in a herbarium, with adults and larvae preserved in 70% alcohol or mounted on pins or card, as in an insect collection. Soft and colourful galls, however, will lose these characteristics. Photographs of developing and mature galls provide an excellent record, particularly with drawings alongside showing characteristic features. Keep accurate and detailed records so that life cycles can be worked out. Often these are incompletely known, even for the commonest gall causers, such as the eriophyid mites that cause red pimples and pouches on sycamore and maple leaves (*Acer* spp.). Such information can be published in journals such as *Cecidology*, the journal of the BPGS. Like many organisms, abundance of galls may vary dramatically from year to year. A record of numbers from year to year at the same site or on the same tree can be of great interest and can also be published.

LITERATURE REVIEW

Interest in galls in Britain has fluctuated over the last one hundred years, as has the availability of up to date literature. The end of the 19th and start of the 20th centuries saw the publication of several books on gall identification (Adler & Straton, 1894; Connold, 1901, 1908, 1909; Houard, 1908-1913; Swanton, 1912), and papers on particular groups were published in various journals (e.g. Trail, 1888;, Bagnall & Harrison, 1918).

During the following 30 years galls were neglected. No more general texts appeared until the series on gall midges of economic importance by Barnes (1948-1956, the final volume being completed in 1969 by Nijveldt), and on the ecology of galls by Mani (1964). Interest in identification revived with the appearance of Felt (1940), Docters van Leeuwen (1957), Eady & Quinlan (1963), Buhr (1964-1965) and Darlington (1968). The last led a revival of interest for British amateur gall enthusiasts that has lasted to the present, and which resulted in the formation of the British Plant Gall Society.

With a few exceptions (Stubbs, 1986; Bevan, 1987; and Redfern & Askew, 1992, updated 1998) modern identification guides are in languages other than English. They include Ambrus (1974), Docters van Leeuwen (1982, an expansion of the 1957 edition), Coulianos & Holmåsen (1991), Dauphin & Aniotsbehère (1993, revised 1997), and Csóka (1997, including an English translation). They all, however, have good illustrations (drawings and photographs) of many British species. Meyer & Maresquelle (1983) and Meyer (1987) describe the structure of galls, and Gagné the biology of gall midges of North America (1989) and of the American tropics (1994), while Ananthakrishnan (1984), Shorthouse & Rohfritsch (1992), Williams (1994), Price *et al.* (1994) and Csóka *et al.* (1998) are compilations of papers on many aspects of gall biology, particularly of gall insects and mites.

Fungal galls, and those caused by bacteria and viruses, are included in many of the books mentioned, although amateur interest in them has lagged behind interest in arthropod gall causers. Good texts on the identification of fungi, and especially of rusts and smuts which cause the majority of fungal galls, are Wilson & Henderson (1966), Mordue & Ainsworth (1984), Ellis & Ellis (1985), Preece & Hick (1990) and Vánky (1994).

For references to nematode galls see Section D; and for information on selected fungal and arthropod galls, see the relevant key in Sections B and E.

Section A.
Galls on Plants caused by Bacteria, Phytoplasmas and Viruses
By Tom Preece

Bacteria

It is extremely likely that bacterial galls are much more widespread in natural vegetation than is at present recognised. The cause of any bacterial gall can only be proved by isolating the bacteria on agar and performing a battery of tests, mostly concerned with type of nutrient substrate utilised. Most important of all is the re-inoculation of pure cultures of the bacterium into the uninfected host and reproduction of the galling symptom. Where this latter step has been omitted, assumptions that a particular bacterium causes galling of a plant are not valid. Isolation of what is thought to be the pathogenic bacterium is not enough. This is best illustrated by an example. The widespread galls which occur on garden *Forsythia* (Fig. 2) are usually said to be caused by a bacterium in the genus *Corynebacterium*. Corynebacteria of various kinds are widespread in the natural environment. All attempts (in particular by Shattock at the University of Wales, Bangor) have failed to produce these *Forsythia* galls by inoculation of *Corynebacterium* isolated from such galls. The cause of this gall, therefore, is unknown. Similar growths occur on *Rosa* species.

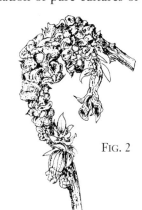

Fig. 2

In general, most bacteria affecting plants do not cause galls. Usually bacterial diseases of plants show symptoms such as dark spots on leaves and fruits. An example is common on walnut (*Juglans*), where the spots are jet black, caused by a *Xanthomonas* species. Another is the *Erwinia* infection of apples, pears and other members of the Rosaceae, known as fireblight. At the other extreme, *Rhizobium* nodules on the roots of clover are definitely galls, and are highly beneficial (see below).

Again generalising, the galling which occurs on plants caused by bacteria is of three kinds, two of which are of indefinite size and shape ('growths' and 'tufts') and the third of defined and characteristic shape as in many insect galls. Unlike fungal galls, bacterial galls do not produce at any stage a 'dust' of spores. The following describes the three types in more detail:

Growths produced by bacteria consist of a mass of irregular tissue, solid and lacking any organisation. An example is crown gall caused by *Agrobacterium tumefaciens* (Smith & Townsend) (Plate 8.8). Often found after damage to a plant provided a wet surface by which the bacteria could enter, these galls are usually, but not always, associated with soil. Thus they may be found on root crops, blackberry runners near mole hills, and many species of trees. Crown galls, e.g. of sugar beet, can be bigger than the organ in which they grow. In trees they can be enormous. *Agrobacterium* has the widest host range of any bacterial plant pathogen, occurring on hundreds of different species of flowering plants, in a wide range of genera and families. Almost all of these are dicotyledonous plants. Monocotyledons (in particular, grasses) are not normally infected with *Agrobacterium*.

A serious disease of ash *Fraxinus excelsior* in Britain produces dramatically disfiguring growths on the branches. This is caused by a *Pseudomonas*. This is an unusual symptom of a bacterial disease.

Tufts are bacterially-induced bundles of small shoots, usually occurring near the ground on, e.g. sweet peas, chrysanthemums, dahlias etc. These are caused by the bacterium *Corynebacterium fascians* (Tilf.).

Nodules are concerned with fixing of atmospheric nitrogen. Legumes (e.g. *Laburnum*, *Ulex*, *Lupinus*, *Medicago*, *Trifolium*, *Vicia*, *Lathyrus*, *Lotus* etc.) have small nodules on the roots containing bacteria in the genus *Rhizobium*. As with *Agrobacterium* growths, the number of plant hosts affected by *Rhizobium* nodules is enormous. There are, world-wide, about 10,000 species of legumes, though relatively few have been examined for nodules in the wild. It seems that recording these nodules on wild plants in Britain is unusual, presumably because the nodules are *root* nodules, below ground!

The other well-known nodule is that caused by the actinomycete *Frankia* on the roots of native alder, *Alnus glutinosa*, and introduced alders. Actinomycetes are filamentous bacteria. *Frankia* causes large, orange, 'lumpy' nodules and, inside them, fixes atmospheric nitrogen. It is becoming clear that other plants have root galls containing nitrogen-fixing actinomycetes in the genus *Frankia*, e.g. the native sweet gale, *Myrica gale*, sea buckthorn, *Hippophae rhamnoides* and mountain avens, *Dryas octopetala*; also introduced oleasters, *Elaeagnus* species and *Ceanothus* species.

Phytoplasmas and Viruses

Most phytoplasmas (formerly known as mycoplasmas) and viruses produce 'yellowing' symptoms, not galls, and so are not included in this book. It is difficult to consider anything produced by a virus infection of plants as a gall, except possibly for the grossly distorted catkins of willows, *Salix* species (Fig. 3, Plate 8.2). This was originally thought to be due to a mite, *Stenacis triradiatus* (Nalepa) (= *Eriophyes*), but detailed anatomical studies by Westphal & Michler (1975, reported in Meyer 1987) demonstrated the presence of virus particles. These may or may not be the cause of the gall (see comments above about *Corynebacterium* and *Forsythia*). The only common phytoplasma gall seen in Britain is the so-called clover phyllody (Fig. 4), transmitted by leaf hoppers.

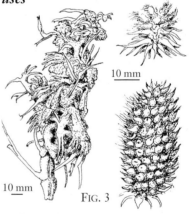

10 mm

10 mm

Fig. 3

Other growths

Unusual growths on plants can be induced by chemicals and other non-biotic agents. Chemical weedkillers (2-4-D type) produce growths on the roots of *Brassica* species which are strikingly like *Agrobacterium* galls, and there are 'genetical tumours', usually seen only by research scientists, on various plants such as tobacco, *Nicotiana*. The latter growths are due to a genetic change in plant cells, not caused by another organism.

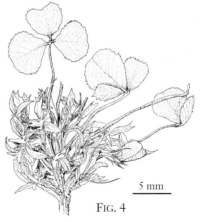

5 mm

Fig. 4

SECTION B.

GALLS CAUSED BY FUNGI
BY TOM PREECE AND BRIAN SPOONER

Fungi causing galls on plants are included here; those galling lichens and other fungi are not included (but see Spooner, 2002). Most are basidiomycetes, either rusts (Uredinales) or smuts (Ustilaginales), but numerous ascomycetes, such as the ergot-forming *Claviceps purpurea*, and the leaf- or fruit-galling *Taphrina* species, also cause galls, as do some members of the Chytridiomycota (e.g. *Synchytrium*), Protomycetales (e.g. *Protomyces*) and the Plasmodiophoromycota (e.g. *Plasmodiophora*). For classification, see Table 1 on page 212.

Most fungi affecting wild plants have not been microscopically examined *in situ* to see whether adjoining plant cells have been enlarged or have increased in number. Where this has been done it is sometimes found that slight 'galling' has occurred, not visible from the outside. An example of this occurs with the rust fungus *Puccinia buxi* on *Buxus sempervirens*, which is, therefore, included here.

It may be considered that more fungi should have been included here. In general, a rather conservative view has been taken as to which species cause galls, and some species such as *Synchytrium aureum* may gall hosts other than those given here. Not included are:

- Some smuts affecting seeds and anthers.
- Most downy mildews (Peronosporaceae) and powdery mildews (Erysiphales).
- Most of the enormous number of leaf-spot causing fungi, the majority of which are anamorphic fungi (asexual states, previously referred to as Fungi Imperfecti, mitosporic fungi or Deuteromycotina).
- Some rare or little-known species.
- *Epichloe typhina* and allied species (Hypocreales: Clavicipitaceae) which cause choke disease of grasses. Although commonly cited as gall-causers, these appear to cause thickening of stems due to the development of fungal tissue and do not induce true galls. The fungus encircles the stem and is white at first, turning yellow, with orange-coloured perithecia, the structures which contain asci and ascospores. These 'choked' culms do not produce flowers.

Further work may result in more fungi being recognised as gall causers and included in future editions of these Keys.

Beginners in mycology will find the guide for amateurs (Preece 1996) helpful, especially as regards rusts and smuts. Up to date details of other fungal groups and nomenclature can be found in the indispensable *Dictionary of the Fungi* by Hawksworth *et al.* (1995). In the keys that follow, references to more extensive information on particular fungi are usually listed by giving the page number in five sources in an abbreviated form:

MA	(Mordue & Ainsworth, 1984)
EE	(Ellis & Ellis, 1985)
PH	(Preece & Hick, 1990)
WH	(Wilson & Henderson, 1966)
CMID	(Commonwealth Mycological Institute Descriptions, 1964 to date)

In the case of rusts and smuts, the terminology used is complex and some explanation may be helpful here, especially as they contain the majority of gall-causing fungi.

Rusts and smuts are *basidio*mycetes and have *basidia* and *basidio*spores resembling those of mushrooms and toadstools. Rusts, however, have additional spore-bearing structures and spores, besides basidiospores. It seems likely that, amongst all living things, the rust fungi have the most complex life cycles and nuclear arrangements! Only a general outline necessary to understand the terms used in this work can be attempted here.

Roman numerals are internationally agreed to denote the spore-producing structures (sori) of rusts. These, which are used in this book, with plurals in brackets, are:

0 *spermogonium* (*spermogonia*), producing spermatia

I *aecium* (*aecia*), producing aeciospores (the stage concerned in most gall-causing rusts)II *uredinium* (*uredinia*), producing urediniospores

III *telium* (*telia*), producing teliospores (these in smuts are called ustilospores, and are characteristically black)

IV *basidium* (*basidia*), borne on the teliospore, producing basidiospores (borne on the ustilospore in smuts).

Smut fungi do not have stages 0, I or II, and their basidiospores are borne on the ustilospores (III). Smuts do not have alternate hosts.

In rust fungi, alternate hosts are common, but not universal. *Puccinia urticata*, for example, has stages 0 and I (I being the gall-causing aecia) on the nettle, *Urtica dioica*, and stages II, and III bearing IV, on a sedge, *Carex* sp. In some rusts, 0, I, II, III and IV are borne on one host.

In the following keys, genera of plants in the cabbage family are treated together under BRASSICACEAE. Similarly, genera of the mallow family are treated under MALVACEAE, the daisy family under ASTERACEAE, and grasses under POACEAE. Genera of the APIACEAE (= Umbelliferae), unlike in Section E, are considered individually in alphabetical order within the Key.

B1. *ABIES*

One rust gall (**Uredinales: Pucciniastraceae**) is found on European silver-fir, *A. alba* Miller, and, occasionally, on other species. All *Abies* species are introduced.

Mass of branched shoots forming a witches' broom which grows for many years, often several on one tree; spermogonia (0) and aecia (I) present; aecia on lower surface of needles in two rows, one on each side of midrib
.... ***Melampsorella caryophyllacearum*** Schroet.

EE75, PH59, WH43. Rarely aecia of *Pucciniastrum epilobii* Otth and of some fern rusts occur on *Abies* needles.

B2. *ADOXA*

Two rust galls (very rarely a third) (**Uredinales: Pucciniaceae**) occur on moschatel, *A. moschatellina* L.

1 Leaves and stems distorted, swollen and stunted, with a whitish appearance; chocolate brown telia (III) present; early spring; common .... ***Puccinia adoxae*** DC.

EE301, PH79, WH186

2 Leaves distorted with whitish to pale yellow spermogonia (0) and aecia (I), present March - April; leaves and stems not appreciably swollen or stunted
.... ***Puccinia albescens*** Plowr.

PH80, WH188. Very rarely uredinia (II) and telia (III) of *P. albescens* are found; also aecia of *Puccinia argentata* (C.F. Schultz) Wint., containing golden spores.

B3. *AEGOPODIUM*

Two fungus galls are found on the leaves and petioles of, the probably introduced, ground-elder, *A. podograria* L.

1   Both leaf surfaces with small, scattered yellow pimples with black telia (III); probably quite common but overlooked: **Uredinales: Pucciniaceae**
.... *Puccinia aegopodii* (Str.) Röhl.
EE301, PH80, WH144

2   Petiole or veins with small, yellow-white translucent mounds, often elongated; or bulges on upper side of blade with depression beneath; without black sori: **Protomycetales: Protomycetaceae** .... *Protomyces macrosporus* Unger
EE301. Also found on *Angelica sylvestris*, *Anthriscus sylvestris* (L.) Hoffm., and some other umbellifers, especially visible in early spring when emerging leaves may be completely distorted (see Preece & Hick 2001 for details).

B4. *ALCHEMILLA*

One rust gall (**Uredinales: Phragmidiaceae**) is found on lady's-mantles, *A. filicauli* Buser, *A. glabra* Neyg., *A. minima* Walters, *A. monticola* Opiz. and *A. xanthochlora* Rothm.

Leaves small, pale, often much deformed and with long petioles; in spring orange, yellow or whitish aecia (I) may cover the undersides of leaves, brown telia (III) develop later; infected rosettes do not flower .... *Trachyspora intrusa* (Grev.) Arth.
EE302, PH181,WH364

B5. *ALISMA*

One fungus (**Blastocladiales: Physodermataceae**) galls, the possibly introduced, ribbon-leaved water-plantain, *A. gramineum* Lejeune, and is known elsewhere in Europe on water-plantain, *A. plantago-aquatica* L.

Small, irregular, sometimes confluent pale pustules on leaves and stems
.... *Physoderma maculare* Wallr.

B6. *ALLIUM*

One smut (**Ustilaginales: Ustilaginaceae**) galls wild onion *A. vineale* L., and the introduced onion, *A. cepa* L., and leek, *A. porrum* L.

Leaves and bulbs often irregularly distorted, with conspicuous, often confluent, pustules, containing smut sori which rupture when mature to expose a black powdery spore mass; scarce .... *Urocystis magica* Pass.
CMID298, EE304, MA42 (all as *U. cepulae*).

B7. *ALNUS*

Three ascomycete fungi (**Taphrinales: Taphrinaceae**) gall alder, *A. glutinosa* (L.) Gaertner.

1 Leaves up to twice as large as normal, thickened, brittle and incurved, due to large blisters on both surfaces, covered with a white bloom
.... ***Taphrina tosquinetii*** (Westend.) Magn.
EE86

2 Leaves, also enlarged, with bright yellow spots, up to 1 cm across, on under surface
.... ***Taphrina sadebeckii*** Johansson
EE86

3 Female catkins with conspicuous red or purple tongue-like growths (Fig. 5, Plate 8.10)
.... ***Taphrina alni*** (Berk. & Br.) Gjaerum
(= *T. amentorum*)

This species was very rare, known only from Cornwall in the 1940s, but since 1999 it has been recorded in many parts of Britain (see Mix, 1949, Ellis, 2000, Jackson, 2000).

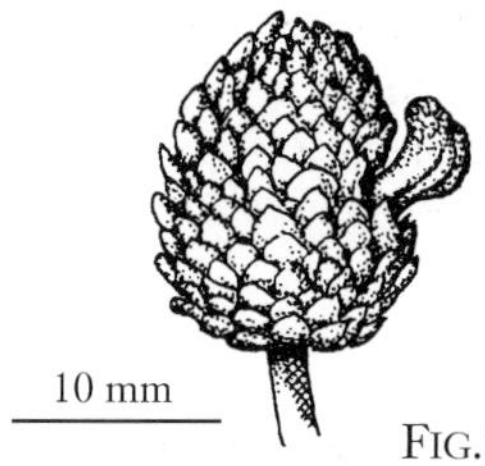

10 mm

FIG.5

ALTHAEA see MALVACEAE

B8. *ANCHUSA*

One rust (**Uredinales: Pucciniaceae**) galls bugloss, *A. arvensis* (L.) M. Bieb., and introduced borage, *A. officinalis* L.

Leaves with bright orange raised aecia (I) found in areas where rye *Secale cereale* L. is grown; spermogonia (0) also present .... ***Puccinia recondita*** f. sp. ***secalina*** Rob. & Desm.
EE306, PH161, WH288

B9. *ANDROMEDA*

One fungus (**Exobasidiales: Exobasidiaceae**) galls bog-rosemary, *A. polifolia* L.

Shoots slightly enlarged, leaves broader than normal, becoming reddened
.... ***Exobasidium karstenii*** Sacc. & Trott.

B10. *ANEMONE*

Five fungi gall wood anemone, *A. nemorosa* L., and cultivated garden anemones, *A. coronaria* L.

1 Any above-ground part of plant with hard black galls up to 0.5 mm across; on *A. nemorosa*: **Chytridiales: Synchytriaceae** .... ***Synchytrium anemones*** (DC.) Woronin
EE308

- Not like this; on leaves only 2

2   Blister-like swellings beneath epidermis, which rupture to produce black spores; on
    A. nemorosa; **Ustilaginales: Tilletiaceae** .... *Urocystis anemones* (Pers.) Winter
    EE307, MA42

-   Not causing blisters; spores white or brown: **Uredinales** **3**

3   Leaves long and narrow, pale green, with aecia (I); on *A. nemorosa*; rare:
    Chaconiaceae .... *Ochropsora ariae* (Fuckel) Ramsb.
    EE307

-   Leaves of normal shape, with rust galls on under surface: **Uropyxidaceae** **4**

4   White aecia and spermogonia (0) covering the under surface; on *A. coronaria*
    .... *Tranzschelia discolor* (Fuckel) Tranz. & Litv.
    CMID287, EE307, PH183, WH304

-   Powdery chocolate-brown telia (III) scattered on under surface; on *A. nemorosa*
    .... *Tranzschelia anemones* (Pers.) Nannf.
    EE307, PH182. Also rarely found on *Thalictrum flavum* L. and *T. minus* L.

B11. *ANGELICA*

Four rare fungi gall wild angelica, *A. sylvestris* L.

1   Leaves with irregular swellings and pustules, especially in spring: **Protomycetales:**
    Protomycetaceae .... *Protomyces macrosporus* Unger

2   Leaves with small, hard gregarious pustules <0.5 mm across: **Chytridiales:**
    Synchytriaceae .... *Synchytrium aureum* Schroet.

3   Leaf veins and petioles conspicuously thickened and distorted; aecia (I) up to 3cms
    long, preceded by spermogonia (0), and followed by uredinia (II) and telia (III):
    Uredinales: Pucciniaceae:

    Aecia cinnamon brown .... *Puccinia angelicae* (Schum.) Fuckel
    EE308, PH83, WH145. Very unusually the same spore stages are found on milk-parsley, *Peucedanum palustre* (L.) Moench, Cambridge milk-parsley *Selinum carvifolia* (L.) L., and pepper-saxifrage, *Silaum silaus* (L.) Schinz & Thell.

    Aecia bright yellow or orange .... *Puccinia bistortae* DC.
    EE308, PH88, WH160. Also occurs rarely on pignut *Conopodium majus* (Gouan) Loret.

B12. *ANTHRISCUS*

Two fungi gall cow parsley, *A. sylvestris* (L.) Hoffm.

1   Leaves and petioles swollen, sometimes twisted; yellow aecia (I) preceded by
    spermogonia (0) in early spring, followed much later in the year by dark brown
    uredinia (II) and telia (III): **Uredinales: Pucciniaceae** ..... *Puccinia chaerophylli* Purton
    EE309, PH103, WH148

2   Leaves with irregular swellings or pustules, especially in spring: **Protomycetales: Protomycetaceae** .... ***Protomyces macrosporus*** Unger
Also occurs on *AEGOPODIUM, ANGELICA* and other umbellifers.

B13. *APIUM*

Three fungi gall fool's water-cress, *A. nodiflorum* (L.) Lag., or wild celery, *A. graveolens* L.

1   Leaves distorted, with brownish blisters up to 1 mm across in brown discoloured areas; on *A. nodiflorum*: **Protomycetales: Protomycetaceae**
.... ***Burenia inundata*** (Dangeard) Reddy & Kramer
EE311. For further details, see Preece & Hick (2001)

2   Leaves with small, hard, gregarious pustules <0.5 mm across; on *A. nodiflorum*: **Chytridiales: Synchytriaceae** .... ***Synchytrium aureum*** Schroet.

3   Leaves and petioles with thickened, yellowish spots bearing aecia (I) ; on *A. graveolens*: **Uredinales: Pucciniaceae** .... ***Puccinia apii*** Desm.
CMID284, EE311, WH146

B14. *AQUILEGIA*

Two fungi gall columbine, *A. vulgaris* L. and introduced *A. amaliae* Heldr.

1   Leaflets with swollen blisters which rupture, exposing a black, powdery spore mass, whole leaf sometimes distorted; rare: **Ustilaginales: Ustinaginaceae**
.... ***Urocystis sorosporioides*** Körn.

2   Underside of leaves with swollen spots bearing rust aecia (I); uncommon: **Uredinales: Pucciniaceae** .... ***Puccinia recondita*** f.sp. ***agrostidis*** Oud.
PH105, WH278

B15. *ARCTOSTAPHYLOS*

One fungus (**Exobasidiales: Exobasidiaceae**) galls bearberry, *A. uva-ursi* (L.) Spreng.

Leaves with small, thickened, reddish-orange spots .. ***Exobasidium sydowianum*** Nannf.

B16. *ARUM*

A smut (**Ustilaginales: Tilletiaceae**) very rarely galls lords-and-ladies, *A. maculatum* L.

Leaves with large, deep, whitish blisters, containing black pepper-like spore masses (visible when held up against the light); in spring
.... ***Melanotaenium ari*** Cooke (Lagerheim)
Recorded in 1872 in Sussex; found recently (1990s) in Shropshire (see Preece *et al.*, 1994, and Vánky, 1994).

B17. **ASTERACEAE** (= Compositae)

This Key excludes *Bellis*, *Centaurea*, *Cirsium*, *Chrysanthemum*, *Taraxacum* and *Tragopogon*, which are treated individually

Four fungi gall various genera of the Asteraceae including hawkweeds, *Hieracium*, mouse-ear-hawkweed, *Pilosella officinarum* F. Schultz & Schultz-Bip., spotted cat's-ear, *Hypochaeris maculata* L., hawkbits, *Leontodon* spp., hawkweed oxtongue, *Picris hieracioides* L., saw-wort, *Serratula tinctoria* L. and, the possibly native, chicory, *Cichorium intybus* L.

1   Leaves are thickened and deformed with reddish-yellow spots; aecia (I) in spring, followed by uredinia (II) and telia (III): **Uredinales: Pucciniaceae**:

On all host plants listed above .... *Puccinia hieracii* Mart.
EE369, PH125, WH203

On *P. officinarum* only .... *Puccinia hieracii* var. *piloselloidarum* (Probst) Jørst.
EE369, PH125, WH203. These rusts need further study in the light of name changes and taxonomic revision of the Asteraceae.

2   All parts of shoot with white crusty blisters, very variable in size; on all host plants listed above: **Peronosporales: Albuginaceae**
.... *Albugo tragopogonis* (Pers.) Gray **white blister**
EE435

3   Leaves with small, gregarious, hard pustules <0.5 mm across; on *Hieracium* spp.: **Chytridiales: Synchytriaceae** .... *Synchytrium aureum* Schroet.

AZALEA see *RHODODENDRON*

BELLEVALIA see *MUSCARI*

B18. *BELLIS*

Four fungi gall daisy, *B. perennis* L. and cultivated *Bellis* spp.

1   Leaves yellowed with wavy edges and raised areas, often more erect than usual; petioles distorted by aecia (I) present April - November, sometimes telia (III) also present later in the year: **Uredinales: Pucciniaceae** .... *Puccinia distincta* McAlpine
This species has dramatically affected wild daisies in Britain since 1997, after occurring on cultivated species for many years. It is not included in the usual references; see instead Weber *et al.* (1998) and Preece *et al.* (2000).

2   Leaves with copper-coloured areas; spermogonia (0) present, also aecia (I) September – December; found where the alternate hosts, *Luzula* spp. (which are not galled) occur: **Uredinales: Pucciniaceae** .... *Puccinia obscura* Schroet.
EE317

3   Leaves with slightly thickened, yellowish or yellow-brown spots: **Protomycetales: Protomycetaceae** .... *Protomycopsis bellidis* (Krieger) Magnus

4   Leaves with small, hard, gregarious pustules <0.5 mm across: **Chytridiales: Synchytriaceae** .... *Synchtyrium aureum* Schroet.

B19. *BERBERIS*

Two rusts (**Uredinales: Pucciniaceae**) gall , the probably introduced, barberry, *B. vulgaris* L.; the first is very well known.

1   Fruits and undersides of leaves with raised areas, pale yellow at first, later orange, becoming purple-red; spermogonia (0) or aecia (I) present; rare
.... ***Puccinia graminis*** Pers.
    EE93, PH119, WH259. Also on *Mahonia*.

2   Undersides of leaves with raised areas; spermogonia or aecia present; may also cause witches' brooms; very rare
.... ***Puccinia brachypodii*** var. ***arrhenatheri*** (Kleb.) Cummins & Greene
    PH50, WH250. For certain identification the spores of these species should be examined under a microscope; spores of *P. graminis* are smooth or very finely punctate, and those of *P. brachypodii* are distinctly warted.

B20. *BETA*

Three fungi gall beet, *B. vulgaris* L. including the subspecies sugar beet and spinach beet.

1   Both surfaces of leaves with raised thickened areas, particularly noticeable on garden beetroot; all four spore types found: **Uredinales: Pucciniaceae**
.... ***Uromyces betae*** Kickx.
    CMID177, EE318, PH196, WH315

2   Leaves thickened and distorted, covered with downy mildew: **Peronosporales: Peronosporaceae** .... ***Peronospora farinosa*** f.sp. ***betae*** Byford
    CMID765

3   Leaves, stems and roots with marked swellings containing large, hemispherical sporangia: **Blastocladiales: Physodermataceae**
.... ***Physoderma leproides*** (Trabut) Karling
    CMID752

B21. *BETULA*

Two ascomycetes (**Taphrinales: Taphrinaceae**) gall birches, *Betula* spp.

1   Bunches of short erect shoots, with small swollen pale leaves, form witches' brooms (Fig. 6)
.... ***Taphrina betulina*** Rostr. (= *turgida*)
    EE94. Some witches' brooms on birches may be caused by a phytoplasma.

2   Leaves with yellow or reddish spots, up to 10 mm across .... ***Taphrina betulae*** (Fuckel) Johansson
    EE94

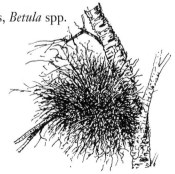

Fig. 6

B22. **BRASSICACEAE**

Four fungi gall crucifers, *e.g.* shepherd's-purse, *Capsella bursa-pastoris* (L.) Medikus, sea radish, *Raphanus raphanistrum* (Sm.) Thell., cabbages, *Brassica* spp., water-cress, *Rorippa nasturtium-aquaticum* (L.) Hayek and its hybrids, the probably native charlock, *Sinapis arvensis* L. and the introduced wall-flower, *Erysimum cheiri* (L.) Crantz, aubretia, *Aubretia* spp. and honesty, *Lunaria* spp. as well as other genera.

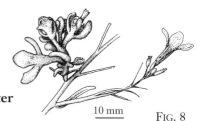

FIG. 7

1   On roots **2**

-   On above ground plant parts **3**

2   Large root galls, aptly called 'club root' or 'finger-and-toe' (Fig. 7); on *Brassica* spp., *Capsella bursa-pastoris*, *Sinapis arvensis*, *Erysimum cheiri*; common: **Plasmodiophorales: Plasmodiophoraceae** .... ***Plasmodiophora brassicae*** Woronin
    EE321

-   Roots shortened, thickened and distorted; on watercress *Rorippa nasturtium-aquaticum*: **Plasmodiophorales: Plasmodiophoraceae   crook root disease** .... ***Spongospora subterranea*** (Wallr.) Lagerh. f.sp. ***nasturtii*** Tomlinson
    EE391

3   White crusty blisters, very variable in size, on stem, leaves and fruits; on *C. bursa-pastoris* (Plate 8.1), *R. raphanistrum* (Fig. 8), and many other genera: **Peronosporales: Albuginaceae** .... ***Albugo candida*** (Pers.) O.Kuntze **white blister**
    EE326. The downy mildew *Peronospora parasitica* (Pers.) Fr. (**Peronosporales: Peronosporaceae**) is often found with *A. candida*; it may cause distortion and swelling of stems.

    10 mm   FIG. 8

-   Small, hard gregarious pustules, <0.5 mm across on leaves: **Chytridiales Synchytriaceae** .... ***Synchytrium aureum*** Schroet.
    EE94

BROTEX see MALVACEAE

B23. *BUNIUM*

One rust (**Uredinales: Pucciniaceae**) galls the rare great pignut, *B. bulbocastanum* L., which is restricted to the counties of Bedfordshire, Buckinghamshire, Cambridgeshire and Hertfordshire.

Leaves, petioles and stems swollen and curved, with both spermogonia (0) and aecia (I) present; black telia (III) develop later; rare .... ***Puccinia bulbocastani*** Fuckel
EE322, PH93,WH147

B24. *BUPLEURUM*

One rust (**Uredinales: Pucciniaceae**) galls slender hare's-ear, *B. tenuissimum* L., in southern England.

Plant deformed, with leaves narrow and slightly thickened, usually with abundant aecia (I) on the underside, uredinia (II) and telia (III) develop later; rare
.... ***Puccinia bupleuri*** Rud.
EE322, WH147

B25. *BUXUS*

One rust (**Uredinales: Pucciniaceae**) galls box, *B. sempervirens* L., but apparently only ancient specimens.

Leaves with yellow circular patches caused by telia (III), turning purplish brown as the teliospores mature (Plate 8.11); swelling scarcely visible to the naked eye but can be seen under a microscope .... ***Puccinia buxi*** DC.
EE100, PH94, WH135. For more details, see Preece (2000).

CALAMINTHA see MALVACEAE

B26. *CALTHA*

Three fungi gall marsh-marigold, *C. palustris* L.

1   Leaves with elongated swellings with yellow aecia (I): **Uredinales: Pucciniaceae**
.... ***Puccinia calthae*** Link or ***P. calthicola*** Schroet.
To separate these two species, teliospores should be collected and examined between August and December. Those of *P. calthae* (EE324, PH95,WH123) are smaller and apparently smooth-walled; those of *P. calthicola* (EE324, PH97,WH124) are larger, with distinct warts. Spermogonia (0), uredinia (II) and telia (III) are produced, but the aecia usually disappear before uredinia and telia appear.

2   Leaves with small, hard gregarious pustules, <0.5 mm across: **Chytridiales: Synchytriaceae** .... ***Synchytrium aureum*** Schroet.

B27. *CAMELLIA*

One species (**Exobasidiales: Exobasidiaceae**) causes remarkable leaf galls on the introduced camellia, *C. japonica* L.

Leaves greatly enlarged and thickened, forming 'gall-apples'; mostly in SW England
.... ***Exobasidium camelliae*** Shirai
For more information, see Ing (1994).

B28. *CAREX*

A smut (**Ustilaginales: Tilletiaceae**) galls glaucous sedge, *C. flacca* Schreb.

Leaves with elongated blisters parallel with veins; covered by epidermis which ruptures in June to produce black powdery masses of ustilospores
.... ***Urocystis fischeri*** Körn
MA44, EE523. Species of *Anthracoidea* (**Ustilaginales: Ustilaginaceae**) occur in the ovaries of various sedges, which may be quite prominently enlarged. Although sometimes described as gall causers, they do not appear to cause swelling of host tissue.

B29. *CARPINUS*

An ascomycete (**Taphrinales: Taphrinaceae**) galls hornbeam, *C. betulus* L.

Bunches of short thick twigs, with leaves which are paler than normal, form witches' brooms .... ***Taphrina carpini*** Rostrup
EE103

B30. *CENTAUREA*

Three fungi (and, perhaps, a fourth, although this may be extinct) gall common knapweed, *C. nigra* L.

1   Lower surface of leaves swollen, especially midrib, and petiole; spermogonia (0) and aecia (I) present: **Uredinales: Pucciniaceae**:

  More common .... ***Puccinia calcitrapae*** DC.
  EE327, PH94, WH191

  Less common .... ***Puccinia hieracii*** Mart.
  EE369, PH122, WH203. All stages of both rusts occur. The two species can only be distinguished by microscopic examination of the urediniospores in the uredinia (II).The possibly extinct species is *P. dioicae* Magn.

2   All parts of shoot with white crusty blisters, very variable in size: **Peronosporales: Albuginaceae** .... ***Albugo candida*** (Pers.) O.Kuntze
white blister

B31. *CHAEROPHYLLUM*

One rust (**Uredinales: Pucciniaceae**) galls the introduced golden chervil, *C. aureum* L.

Leaves and petioles swollen, sometimes twisted, bearing spermogonia (0) and yellow aecia (I); followed by dark brown uredinia (II) and telia (III)
.... ***Puccinia chaerophylli*** Purton
EE329, PH103, WH148

B32. *CHENOPODIUM*

One fungus (**Blastocladiales: Physodermataceae**) galls red goosefoot, *C. rubrum* L., in Britain, and occurs elsewhere in Europe on other species of *Chenopodium* and on *Atriplex*.

Gregarious, irregular, brownish pustules on leaves .... ***Physoderma pulposum*** Wallr.
CMID754

CHIONODOXA see *MUSCARI*

B33. *CHRYSOSPLENIUM*

A smut (**Ustilaginales: Tilletiaceae**) galls alternate-leaved golden-saxifrage, *C. alternifolium* L., and opposite-leaved golden-saxifrage, *C. oppositifolium* L.

Leaves with rounded swollen raised white spots, containing colourless ustilospores; rare .... ***Entyloma chrysosplenii*** (Berk. & Br.) Schröter
MA23, EE333. Not seen in Britain for 100 years until 1996 when found in Yorkshire (Preece *et al.*, 1999).

B34. *CIRCAEA*

Two rusts (**Uredinales**) gall enchanter's-nightshades, *Circaea* spp.

Stems and lower surfaces of leaves and veins with raised areas; only telia (III) present: **Pucciniaceae** .... ***Puccinia circaeae*** Pers.
EE334, PH105, WH141. The uredinia (II) of *Pucciniastrum circaeae* (Wint.) De Toni (**Pucciniastraceae**) is also rarely found.

B35. *CIRSIUM*

Three fungi gall creeping thistle, *C. arvense* (L.) Scop., and other *Cirsium* species.

1   Whole plant spindly, pale, does not flower; spermogonia (0) smell sickly in early spring; aecia (I) cover the whole of the lower surface of leaves, followed by uredinia (II) and telia (III); on *C.arvense*; very common: **Uredinales: Pucciniaceae** .... ***Puccinia punctiformis*** (Str.) Röhl.
EE335, PH158, WH210

2   Leaves with small, densely gregarious pustules; on *Cirsium* spp.: **Chytridiales: Synchytriaceae** .... ***Synchytrium sanguineum*** Schroet.

3   Stems and leaves with white blisters, sometimes crusty: **Peronosporales: Albuginaceae** .... ***Albugo tragopogonis*** (DC.) Gray
CMID458, EE336

CLINOPODIUM see *MENTHA*

B36. *COLCHICUM*

A smut (**Ustilaginales: Tilletiaceae**) galls meadow saffron, *C. autumnale* L.

Leaves with elongated, blister-like swellings, 0.5-1.0 x 2-10mm, parallel with the veins, which burst to expose dark brown ustilospores
.... *Urocystis colchici* (Schlecht.) Rabenh.
MA43, EE337

B37. *CONOPODIUM*

Two rusts (**Uredinales: Pucciniaceae**) gall pignut, *C. majus* (Gouan) Loret.

1   Leaf veins and petioles swollen, twisted, often pale coloured, bearing telia (III); urediniospores are found in the telia (other stages are not found)
.... *Puccinia tumida* Grev.
EE338, PH170, WH158.

2   Stems and petioles with bright orange, thickened areas bearing aecia (I); rare
.... *Puccinia. bistortae* DC
EE338, WH160. This rust more usually occurs on *Angelica sylvestris*.

B38. *CRATAEGUS*

Three fungi gall hawthorn, *C. monogyna* Jacq., and midland hawthorn, *C. laevigata* (Poir.) DC.

1   Leaves, petioles and fruits (Plate 8.6) swollen with groups of spermogonia (0) and aecia (I): **Uredinales: Pucciniaceae**:

Either .... *Gymnosporangium clavariiforme* (Pers.) DC.
CMID542, EE113, PH40, WH116. Found near to juniper, *Juniperus communis*, bushes affected by its tongue-like telia (III) (see *JUNIPERUS*).

or .... *Gymnosporangium confusum* Plowr.
CMID544, EE113, PH41, WH117. The alternate host is *Juniperus sabina*, but aecia seem to occur on *Crataegus* in areas without infected junipers. Further study of its life-cycle is needed. See also *CYNODON* and *MESPILUS*.

These species can only be distinguished by spore size and microscopic examination of the aecial walls. Under a dissecting microscope, the aecia of *G. clavariiforme* on *J. communis*, with reflexed aecial walls, look like small flowers. In 1675, Malpighi referred to them in an illustrated account of a tumour bearing 'flowers' on twigs of English hawthorn. This is one of the earliest references to a plant gall caused by a fungus.

2   Leaves blistered, swollen and folded, often yellow or reddish, shoots sometimes distorted: **Taphrinales: Taphrinaceae** .... *Taphrina crataegi* Sadeb.
EE114

CRUCIATA see *GALIUM*

B39. *CYDONIA*

A rust (**Uredinales: Pucciniaceae**) galls the introduced quince, *C. oblonga* Mill.

Leaves, petioles and fruits swollen with groups of spermogonia (0) and aecia (I)
.... ***Gymnosporangium confusum*** Plowr.
CMID544, EE116, PH7, WH117. See also *CRATAEGUS*.

B40. *CYNODON*

A smut (**Ustilaginales: Ustilaginaceae**) galls , the probably introduced, Bermuda-grass, *C. dactylon* (L.) Pers.

Inflorescence distorted, black powdery spore mass present when mature
.... ***Ustilago cynodontis*** (Pass.) Henn.
EE490, MA52

B41. *DIANTHUS*

Two rusts (**Uredinales: Pucciniaceae**) gall maiden pink, *D. deltoides* L., and introduced sweet-william, *D. barbatus* L., clove pink, *D. caryophyllus* L., and rainbow pink, *D. chinensis* L.

Leaves and stems with rounded or elongate swollen patches, bearing telia (III)
.... ***Uromyces dianthi*** (Pers.) Niessl
carnation rust
or ***Puccinia arenariae*** (Schum.) Wint.
CMID180, EE343, PH140, WH312 (*U. dianthi*); EE313, PH87, WH127 (*P. arenariae*). Microscopic examination of the teliospores is necessary to distinguish these species; teliospores in *U. dianthi* are one-celled, in *P. arenariae* they are two-celled. *P. arenariae* is also found on *Moehringia*.

B42. *DIPSACUS*

One fungus (**Chytridiales: Synchytriaceae**) occasionally galls teasel, *Dipsacus fullonum* L.

Leaves with small, gregarious pustules <0.5 mm across
.... ***Synchytrium succisae*** de Bary & Woronin
EE431

B43. *DRYOPTERIS*

Two fungi (**Taphrinales: Taphrinaceae**) gall narrow buckler-fern, *D. carthusiana* (Villars) Fuchs, scaly male-fern, *D. borreri* Newm., and male-fern, *D. filix-mas* (L.) Schott.

1   Pinnules with small, thickened, yellowish spots or blotches:

On *D. carthusiana* .... ***Taphrina filicina*** Rostrup
EE563

On *D. borreri, D. filix-mas* .... ***Taphrina vestergrenii*** Giesenh.
EE563 For further information see Mix (1949).

B44. *ELEOCHARIS*

Four fungi gall the few-flowered spike-rush, *E. quinqueflora* (Hartman) O. Schwartz, common spike-rush, *E. palustris* (L.) Roemer & Schultes, dwarf spike-rush, *E. parvula* (Roemer & Schultes) Bluff, Nees & Schau, and slender spike-rush, *E. uniglumis* (Link) Schultes.

1   On inflorescence or stems above ground **2**

-    On roots or underground rhizomes **3**

2   Inflorescence with projecting black ergots, over 10 mm long; on *E. palustris*, *E. uniglumis*; E. Anglia: **Hypocreales: Clavicipitaceae** .... *Claviceps nigricans* Tul. EE543

-    Stems with dark, thickened spots 2 – 6 mm long: **Blastocladiales: Physodermataceae** .... *Physoderma heleocharidis* (Fuckel) Schroet.

3   Roots with cylindrical, sometimes forked, whitish swellings, up to 20 x 3 mm, narrower at the point of attachment; contain yellowish brown ustilospores, turning purplish when mature; on *E.quinqueflora*: **Ustilaginales: Tilletiaceae** .... *Entorrhiza scirpicola* (Correns) Sacc. & Sydow MA20, EE542

-    Roots and rhizomes with yellow-brown to blackish tubercles or swellings, containing sticky spore masses; on *E. parvula*; very rare: **Ustilaginales: Ustilaginaceae** .... *Ustilago marina* Dur. EE542, MA54. Known in Britain from a single specimen collected in Dorset.

B45. *EPILOBIUM*

One rust gall (**Uredinales: Pucciniaceae**) occurs on great willowherb, *E. hirsutum* L., broad-leaved willowherb, *E. montanum* L., hoary willowherb, *E. parviflorum* Schreb. and square-stalked willowherb, *E. tetragonum* L.

Infected plants paler than normal, yellowish; leaves puckered, with yellowish raised areas bearing pale orange aecia (I) covering most of leaf surface, usually on underside; dark brown uredinia (II) and telia (III) develop later .... *Puccinia pulverulenta* Grev. EE346, PH155, WH143

B46. *ERANTHIS*

A smut (**Ustilaginales: Tilletiaceae**) galls the introduced winter aconite, *E. hyemalis* (L.) Salisb.

Leaves and petioles blistered, when blisters rupture black ustilospores are exposed .... *Urocystis eranthidis* (Pass.) Ainsw. & Sampson MA43, EE350

B47. *ERYNGIUM*

A smut (**Ustilaginales: Tilletiaceae**) galls sea-holly, *E. maritimum* L.

Leaves with fawn-coloured raised spots, 1-3 mm across, containing yellow-brown ustilospores .... ***Entyloma eryngii-plani*** C. Ferri
MA24, EE351. See Vánky (1994).

B48. *EUONYMUS*

A rust (**Uredinales: Melampsoraceae**) galls spindle, *E. europaeus* L.

Leaves with pale yellowish, slightly thickened, irregular spots bearing aecia (I)
.... ***Melampsora epitea*** Thuem.
EE120, PH50

B49. *EUPHORBIA*

Five rusts (**Uredinales**) gall sun spurge, *E. helioscopia* L., petty spurge, *E. peplus* L., wood spurge, *E. amygdaloides* L., and the, possibly native, caper spurge, *E. lathyrus* L., dwarf spurge, *E. exigua* L., cypress spurge, *E. cyparissias* L. The host species must be accurately identified in order to correctly identify the fungus.

1   On *E. amygdaloides*; stems elongated and deformed; leaves distorted, pale and narrow; with telia (III) preceded by spermogonia (0); very rare: **Pucciniaceae**
   .... ***Endophyllum euphorbiae-sylvaticae*** (DC.) Wint.
   EE353, WH308

2   On *E. exigua*; stems and leaves only slightly deformed; with spermogonia (0), aecia (I), uredinia (II) and telia (III); exceptionally rare: **Pucciniaceae**
   .... ***Uromyces tuberculatus*** Fuckel
   EE353, WH341

3   On *E. cyparissias*; leaves and stems deformed; very rare: **Pucciniaceae:**

   Leaves yellowish, with aecia (I); all other spore stages also occur
   .... ***Uromyces pisi-sativi*** (Pers.) Liro
   CMID58&59, EE353, PH209, WH330

   Uredinia (II) and telia (III) present, other spore stages absent; a few urediniospores may be found in the telia .... ***Uromyces scutellatus*** (Pers.) Lév.
   EE353, WH339. Microscopic examination of the spores is necessary to distinguish these two species. They have been found together on patches of *E. cyparissias*.

4   Usually on *E. helioscopia* or *E. peplus*; stems and leaves distorted, thickened and twisted, nearly covered by uredinia (II) and telia (III); very common: **Melampsoraceae** .... ***Melampsora euphorbiae*** Cast.
   EE353, PH51, WH67

FALLOPIA see *PERSICARIA*

B50. *FILIPENDULA*

Four fungi gall meadowsweet, *F. ulmaria* (L.) Maxim. or dropwort, *F. vulgaris* Moench.

1/2 Leaves twisted and distorted, with striking swellings bearing orange aecia (I), followed by uredinia (II) and telia (III): **Uredinales: Sphaerophragmiaceae**:

On *F. ulmaria* .... *Triphragmium ulmariae* (DC.) Wint.
EE354, PH187, WH112

On *F. vulgaris* .... *Triphragmium filipendulae* Pass.
EE354, PH185 WH112

2   Radical leaves with large swollen, irregularly shaped sori, up to 44mm long, sori erupt, revealing a mass of black ustilospores; on both *Filipendula* spp.: **Ustilaginales: Tilletiaceae** .... *Urocystis filipendulae* (Tul.) Schröter
MA44, EE354

4   Stems, leaves and shoots thickened and sometimes twisted or distorted, covered with thick, white mycelium (**Erysiphales: Erysiphaceae**) ...... *Sphaerotheca spiraeae* Sawada
EE356

FRANGULA see *RHAMNUS*

B51. *FRAXINUS*

One ascomycete (**Hypocreales: Nectriaceae**) galls ash, *Fraxinus excelsior* L.

Trunk or branches with large woody cankers, very variable in size
.... *Nectria galligena* Bres.
CMID147, EE164. Similar cankers on ash are caused by *Pseudomonas fraxini* (see p. 218).

B52. *GAGEA*

A smut (**Ustilaginales: Ustilaginaceae**) galls yellow star-of-Bethlehem, *G. lutea* (L.) Ker Gawler.

Leaves and pedicels with raised blisters, 1-10 mm long, covered by epidermis at first, later showing purple-brown ustilospores; April – May; rare
.... *Ustilago ornithogali* (Schmidt & Kunze) Magnus
MA55, EE359

B53. *GALIUM*

Four fungi cause galls on heath bedstraw, *G. saxatile* L., fen bedstraw, *G. uliginosum* L., lady's bedstraw, *G. verum* L., cleavers or goosegrass, *G. aparine* L. and hedge bedstraw, *G. mollugo* L.

1   Leaves with tiny, gregarious pustules; on *G. saxatile*: **Chytridiales: Synchytriaceae**
     .... ***Synchytrium aureum*** Schroet.

-    Stems (which may be distorted) and leaves with swellings, or whole plant stunted **2**

2   Whole plant stunted; swellings on leaves and stems rupture releasing black, dust-like
     spores which blacken the plant; on *G. mollugo, G. verum*: **Ustilaginales: Tilletiaceae**
     .... ***Melanotaenium endogenum*** (Unger) de Bary
     MA30, EE361

-    Stems swollen and distorted; swellings on leaves often red: **Uredinales:
     Pucciniaceae**... **3**

3   Cushion-like swellings on leaves, red and raised on upper surface, telia (III) in
     depression below, yellow when young, later brown; on *G. saxatile, G. uliginosum, G.
     verum*; common .... ***Puccinia galii-verni*** Ces.
     EE360, PH118, WH186. Very rarely found on crosswort *Cruciata laevipes* Opiz.

-    Swellings with yellow spermogonia (0) and aecia (I), followed by brown telia; on *G.
     aparine*; very rare .... ***Puccinia difformis*** Kunze
     EE360, WH184

B54. *GERANIUM*

Two rusts (**Uredinales: Pucciniaceae**) may gall cut-leaved crane's-bill, *G. dissectum* L.,
dove's-foot crane's-bill, *G. molle* L., meadow crane's-bill, *G. pratense* L., small-flowered
crane's-bill, *G. pusillum* L., herb-robert, *G. robertianum* L., round-leaved crane's-bill, *G.
rotundifolium* L., wood crane's-bill, *G. sylvaticum* L. and possibly native hedgerow crane's-
bill, *G. pyrenaicum* Burm.

1   Underside of leaves with swellings, up to 2 cm long, especially on veins, bearing
     orange spermogonia (0) and orange aecia (I) .... ***Uromyces geranii*** (DC.) Fr.
     CMID270, EE363, PH202, WH318.

2   Leaves with spots, pale greenish at first, later reddish, bearing aecia (I); on *G.
     dissectum*; very rare .... ***Puccinia polygoni-amphibii*** var. ***convolvuli*** Arth.
     EE403, PH98, WH164. Recorded once only in Yorkshire in 1946.
     Cultivated 'geraniums' (*Pelargonium* spp.) are often affected by *Puccinia pelargonii-zonalis* Doidge. Usually
     only uredinia (II) are present, rarely teliospores as well. The aecia (I) are unknown. First recorded in
     Britain in 1965.

B55. *GLADIOLUS*

A smut (**Ustilaginales: Tilletiaceae**) galls cultivated gladioli, *Gladiolus* spp.

     Leaves with dark brown blisters parallel to the veins, often several centimetres long;
     blisters rupture when mature to reveal dark brown ustilospores
     .... ***Urocystis gladiolicola*** Ainsw.
     MA45, EE364

B56. *GLECHOMA*

One rust (**Uredinales: Pucciniaceae**) galls ground-ivy, *G. hederacea* L.

Stems, petioles and underside of leaf veins with yellow, brown or black swollen, raised areas; only telia (III) present, each up to 1mm across, usually in groups up to 4 mm across .... ***Puccinia glechomatis*** DC.
EE365, PH118, WH178

B57. *HELLEBORUS*

A smut (**Ustilaginales: Tilletiaceae**) galls green hellebore, *H. viridis* L.

Leaves and petioles with blister-like swellings, often several cm long; blisters rupture to release black ustilospores .... ***Urocystis floccosa*** (Wallr.) Henderson
MA45, EE367

B58. *HEPATICA*

One very rare smut (**Ustilaginales: Tilletiaceae**) galls some cultivated liverleaf, *Hepatica*, species.

Stems, petioles and leaves with irregular swellings, rupturing to expose black powdery spore masses .... ***Urocystis syncocca*** (Kirchn.) Lindeb.
MA46 (as *U. hepaticae-trilobae*).   (= *U. hepaticae-trilobae*)

B59. *HERACLEUM*

One rust (**Uredinales: Pucciniaceae**) galls hogweed, *H. sphondylium* L.

Underside of leaves distorted by spermogonia (0) and aecia (I) which are densely crowded in thickened yellow areas, especially on veins; uredinia (II) and telia (III) develop later; often only young, small plants affected .... ***Puccinia heraclei*** Grev.
EE367, PH121, WH151

B60. *JUNCUS*

Three smuts (**Ustilaginales: Tilletiaceae**) gall roots or stems of sharp rush, *J. acutus* L., sharp-flowered rush, *J. acutiflorus* Ehrh. ex Hoffm., jointed rush, *J. articulatus* L., or toad rush, *J. bufonius* L.

1   Lower part of stems with swellings which rupture in summer to release blackish brown ustilospores; on *J. acutus*, *J. acutiflorus* .... ***Urocystis junci*** Lagerheim
    MA46, EE545

2   Roots with swellings, up to 1-3 cm across; contain yellow-brown ustilospores in summer; on *J. bufonius* .... ***Entorrhiza aschersoniana*** (Magnus) Lagerheim
    MA19, EE545

3   Roots with simple or bilobed swellings, up to 1 cm long; contain golden-yellow to brown ustilospores; on *J. articulatus*......... ***Entorrhiza casparyana*** (Magnus) Lagerheim
MA19, EE545

B61. *JUNIPERUS*

Two rare rusts (**Uredinales: Pucciniaceae**) gall juniper, *J. communis* L. (See also Keys for *CRATAEGUS, PYRUS* and *SORBUS*).

1   Branches with long raised swellings bearing orange 'tongues' of teliospores (III) which swell greatly when wet (Plate 8.5); commoner in N. England and Scotland than further south .... ***Gymnosporangium clavariiforme*** (Pers.) DC.
CMID542, EE150, PH40, WH116

2   Young branches and leaves with swellings bearing telia (III), chocolate-brown, later orange .... ***Gymnosporangium cornutum*** Kern
EE150, PH42, WH121.
Very rarely, two rust galls are found on the introduced *J. sabina* L.: *Gymnosporangium confusum* Plowr. with chocolate-brown telia (CMID544, EE150, PH41, WH117), and *G. fuscum* DC. (= *sabinae*), with telia which become yellow (CMID545, EE150, PH43, WH119).

B62. *KICKXIA*

One smut (**Ustilaginales: Tilletiaceae**) galls the, probably native, round-leaved fluellen, *K. spuria* (L.) Dum.

Roots with cylindrical or bullet-shaped, hard swellings containing dark brown to black sticky masses of ustilospores; very rare
.... ***Melanotaenium hypogaeum*** (Tul. & C. Tul.) Schellenb.
EE375, MA30. May be extinct in Britain.

B63. *KNAUTIA*

A downy mildew (**Peronosporales: Peronosporaceae**) galls field scabious, *K. arvensis* (L.) Coulter.

Flowers enlarged, dull in colour and sterile .... ***Peronospora violacea*** Berk.
EE375
The anther smuts *Ustilago flosculorum* (DC) Fr. (MA52) and *U. scabiosae* (Sow.) Winter (MA55) (**Ustilaginales: Ustilaginaceae**) are not thought to cause galls.

B64. *LAMIUM*

A smut (**Ustilaginales: Tilletiaceae**) galls white dead-nettle, *L. album* L.

Buds swollen, they and underground stems with blister-like swellings, or tuberous growths, 0.5-2 cm across; swellings contain dark brown to black mass of ustilospores
.... ***Melanotaenium lamii*** Beer
MA30, EE376

B65. *LAPSANA*

One rust (**Uredinales: Pucciniaceae**) galls nipplewort, *L. communis* L.

Leaves and petioles grossly distorted, with reddish purple blisters which occur on both sides of the leaves, bearing orange aecia (I) with spermogonia (0), uredinia (II) and telia (III) present later; often on seedlings .... ***Puccinia lapsanae*** Fuckel
EE377, PH131, WH208

B66. *LARIX*

An ascomycete (**Helotiales: Hyaloscyphaceae**) galls introduced European larch, *L. decidua* Mill.

Branches with woody cankers, variable in size ***Lachnellula willkommii*** (Hartig) Dennis
EE155. An important disease of larch plantations.

LAVATERA see MALVACEAE

B67. *LEUCANTHEMUM*

One ascomycete (**Protomycetales: Protomycetaceae**) galls oxeye daisy, *Leucanthemum vulgare* Lam.

Leaves with small, raised, pale yellow spots; uncommon
.... ***Protomycopsis leucanthemi*** Magnus
EE382

B68. *LIMONIUM*

One rust (**Uredinales: Pucciniaceae**) galls common sea-lavender, *L. vulgare* Mill., and cultivated florist's sea-lavender, *L. latifolium* (Sm.) Kuntze and *L. tataricum* Mill.

Leaves and stems with small, thickened spots bearing aecia (I), later uredinia (II) and telia (III) .... ***Uromyces limonii*** (DC) Lév.
EE379, PH205, WH346

B69. *LOTUS*

One fungus (**Blastocladiales: Physodermataceae**) galls common bird's-foot-trefoil, *Lotus corniculatus* L.

Stems and petioles with conspicuous brownish swellings about 1 cm across
.... ***Urophlyctis potteri*** Bartlett

B70. *MAHONIA*

Two rusts (**Uredinales: Pucciniaceae**) gall introduced Oregon-grape, *M. aquifolium* (Pursh) Nutt.

1 Immature fruits and underside of leaves with raised, thick, rounded areas, whitish, later yellow; spermogonia (0) and aecia (I) very rare, uredinia (II) and telia (III) very common... ***Cumminsiella mirabilissima*** (Peck) Nannf.
CMID261, EE162, PH36, WH300. Aecia illustrated in colour by Lucas (1988) after being found for the first time in Britain in 1987.

2 Raised areas on underside of leaves, yellow, later orange and purple-red; contain aecia (I) .... ***Puccinia graminis*** Pers.
EE93, PH119, WH25. Also on *Berberis*.

B71. **MALVACEAE**

One rust (**Uredinales: Pucciniaceae**) galls the native tree-mallow, *Lavatera arborea* L. and the introduced hollyhock, *Alcea rosea* L., rough marsh-mallow, *Althea hirsuta* L., and other species in the genera *Brotex*, *Clinopodium*, *Malva* and *Sidalcea*.

Gall a hard, rounded, swelling on the underside of leaves and on petioles, reddish to reddish brown, later becoming powdery with spores; only telia (III) present
.... ***Puccinia malvacearum*** Mont.
CMID265, EE384, PH138 WH132

B72. *MEDICAGO*

One fungus (**Blastocladiales: Physodermataceae**) galls the introduced lucerne, *Medicago sativa* L.

Leaves, stipules, buds and stems with large, conspicuous warts
.... ***Physoderma alfalfae*** (Pat. & Lagerh.) Karling
crownwart

B73. *MELAMPYRUM*

One rust (**Uredinales: Pucciniaceae**) galls common cow-wheat, *Melampyrum pratense* L.

Upper surface of leaves with reddish purple swellings bearing conspicuous aecia (I) and spermogonia (0); plant often blackened, with few flowers; very rare
.... ***Puccinia nemoralis*** Juel
EE386

B74. *MENTHA*

Two fungi gall water mint, *M. aquatica* L. and other *Mentha* species.

1 Young shoots and leaves thickened and distorted, with purple patches bearing spermogonia (0) and aecia (I), followed by uredinia (II) and telia (III); on *Mentha* spp.: **Uredinales: Pucciniaceae** .... ***Puccinia menthae*** Pers.

CMID7, EE387, PH139, WH179. Also found rarely on common calamint, *Clinopodium ascendens* (Jordan) Samp., wild basil, *C. vulgare* L., wild marjoram, *Origanum vulgare* L. and the introduced summer savory, *Satureja hortensis* L.

2   Stems and leaves with thick pustules containing golden brown sporangia; on *M. aquatica*: **Blastocladiales: Physodermataceae** .... ***Physoderma menthae*** Schroet.

B75. *MENYANTHES*

One fungus (**Blastocladiales: Physodermataceae**) galls bogbean, *M. trifoliata* L.

Stems and leaves with small, gregarious, reddish then blackish brown swellings, 1-1.5 mm across; uncommon .... ***Physoderma menyanthis*** de Bary

B76. *MERCURIALIS*

Two fungi gall dog's mercury, *M. perennis* L., and, the possibly native, annual mercury, *M. annua* L.

1   Rough, pale yellow swellings with whitish edges, up to 2 cm across, on tips of leaves, on swollen, twisted and distorted petioles and, less often, on stems, bearing spermogonia (0) and orange aecia (I); usually on isolated plants: **Uredinales: Melampsoraceae** .... ***Melampsora populnea*** (Pers.) Karst.
EE387, PH56, WH76. See also *Pinus*.

2   Small, glassy, yellow raised blisters on leaves and stems, containing black spores; April - May: **Chytridiales: Synchytriaceae** ...... ***Synchytrium mercurialis*** (Lib.) Fuckel
EE388

MESPILUS see *CRATAEGUS*

B77. *MEUM*

One rust (**Uredinales: Sphaerophragmiaceae**) galls spignel, *Meum athamanticum* Jacq.

Leaves, petioles and stems swollen and distorted; teliospores present; Scotland; rare .... ***Nyssopsora echinata*** (Lév.) Arth.
EE388, WH114

MOEHRINGIA see *DIANTHUS*

B78. *MUSCARI*

One smut (**Ustilaginales: Ustilaginaceae**) galls grape-hyacinths, *Muscari* species, and is also found occasionally on squills, *Scilla*, glory-of-the-snows, *Chionodoxa* and hyacinths, *Bellevalia* species.

Anthers, less often ovaries, swollen, with olive-brown powdery mass of ustilospores when mature .... ***Ustilago vaillantii*** Tul. & C. Tul.
EE389, MA59

B79. *MYOSOTIS*

One fungus (**Chytridiales: Synchytriaceae**) galls forget-me-nots, *Myosotis* spp.

Leaves with numerous, small, gregarious pustules .... ***Synchytrium myosotidis*** Kühn

B80. *MYRIOPHYLLUM*

One fungus (**Blastocladiales: Physodermataceae**) galls whorled water-milfoil, *Myriophyllum verticillatum* L.

Leaves and stems with numerous tuberous swellings up to 1 cm across
.... ***Physoderma myriophylli*** (Rostrup) Vestergren

B81. *MYRRHIS*

A rust (**Uredinales: Pucciniaceae**) galls the introduced sweet cicely, *M. odorata* (L.) Scop.

Leaves and shoots swollen and distorted by spermogonia (0) and yellow aecia (I); later uredinia (II) and telia (III) may be found .... ***Puccinia chaerophylli*** Purton
EE389, PH103, WH148

B82. *OENANTHE*

Two fungi gall hemlock water-dropwort, *Oenanthe crocata* L., tubular water-dropwort, *O. fistulosa* L. and parsley water-dropwort, *O. lachenalii* C.C. Gmel.

1   Leaves, petioles and stems distorted and bearing large, irregular swellings; on *O. crocata*: **Protomycetales: Protomycetaceae** .... ***Protomyces macrosporus*** Unger

2   Underside of leaves and petioles with slightly thickened, yellowish spots bearing aecia (I); on *Oenanthe* spp.; scarce: **Uredinales: Pucciniaceae**
.... ***Uromyces lineolatus*** (Desm.) Schroet.
EE391, WH357

ORIGANUM see *MENTHA*

B83. *ORNITHOGALUM*

A rust (**Uredinales: Pucciniaceae**) galls spiked star-of-Bethlehem, *O. pyrenaicum* L. and star-of-Bethlehem, *O. angustifolium* Boreau.

Leaves with swollen, compact, hard, yellow areas on both surfaces, with telia (III) producing brown spores, often in rings around spermogonia (0); affected plants do not flower .... ***Puccinia liliacearum*** Duby
EE394, WH220.
The aecia (I) of *Puccinia hordei* Otth was, perhaps, found once in Britain on this genus.

B84. *OXYRIA*

One smut (**Ustilaginales: Ustilaginaceae**) galls mountain sorrel, *Oxyria digyna* (L.) Hill.

Flower parts swollen, with powdery, purplish spore masses when mature
.... ***Ustilago vinosa*** Tul. & C. Tul.
EE394, MA60

B85. *PARNASSIA*

A rust (**Uredinales: Pucciniaceae**) galls grass-of-Parnassus, *Parnassia palustris* L.

Leaves, petioles and stems swollen and distorted, bearing aecia (I); Scotland and
Ireland .... ***Puccinia uliginosa*** Juel
WH233 (as *P. caricina*)

B86. *PEDICULARIS*

A rust (**Uredinales: Pucciniaceae**) galls marsh lousewort, *Pedicularis palustris* L.

Leaves, petioles and stems swollen and distorted, bearing aecia (I)
.... ***Puccinia paludosa*** Plowr.
WH233 (as *P. caricina*)

PELARGONIUM see *GERANIUM*

PERICALLIS see *SENECIO*

B87. *PERSICARIA*

Three smuts (**Ustilaginales: Ustilaginaceae**) gall common bistort, *P. bistorta* (L.) Samp.,
alpine bistort, *P. vivipara* (L.) Ronse Decraene, amphibious bistort, *P. amphibia* (L.) Gray,
water-pepper, *P. hydropiper* (L.) Spach, pale persicaria, *P. lapathifolia* (L.) Gray and redshank,
P. maculosa Gray (= *Polygonum persicaria*).

1   Leaves with round swellings, 2-5 mm across, scattered over the surface or in a
    continuous band around the margin; burst to release purple ustilospores when
    mature; on *P. bistorta*, *P. vivipara*, *P. amphibia* .... ***Ustilago bistortarum*** (DC.) Körn
    MA51, EE404

2   Ovaries swollen, containing dark powdery mass of spores when mature; on *P.
    hydropiper*; *P. maculosa*; widespread
    .... ***Ustilago anomala*** Kunze or ***Ustilago utriculosa*** (Nees) Tul. & C. Tul.
    EE404, MA51, MA59. These two species are also found on black-bindweed *Fallopia convolvulus* (L.) A.
    Löve. They can only be distinguished by microscopic examination of their ustilospores: *U. anomola* has
    ustilospores with a delicate reticulate pattern, up to 2 x 1 μm, *U. utriculosa* has ustilospores with a coarser,
    deeper, reticulate pattern 2 - 4 x 1 - 2 μm. Also on *P. lapathifolia*.

B88. *PEUCEDANUM*

Two rusts (**Uredinales: Pucciniaceae**) gall hog's fennel, *P. officinale* L. or milk-parsley, *P. palustre* (L.) Moench.

Leaves and petioles swollen and distorted; all spore stages occur:

On *P. officinale*; aecia (I) cinnamon brown; teliospores with a network of ridges; very rare .... ***Puccinia rugulosa*** Tranz.
EE398, WH156. Recorded in Essex in 1990 for the first time in Britain since 1931.

On *P. palustre*; teliospores smooth .... ***Puccinia angelicae*** (Schum.) Fuckel
PH42, WH145. *P. angelicae* is also found on *Angelica*.

B89. *PHILLYREA*

A rust (**Uredinales: Pucciniaceae**) galls the cultivated *Phillyrea latifolia* L.

Leaves and stems with rounded, swollen pustules bearing aecidia (I); rare
.... ***Zaghouania phillyreae*** Pat.
WH13

B90. *PHRAGMITES*

Two fungi gall common reed, *Phragmites australis* (Cav.) Trin. ex Steudel.

1 Inflorescence with very small ergots in individual florets: **Hypocreales: Clavicipitaceae** .... ***Claviceps microcephala*** (Wallr.) Tul.
EE511. Not often found but probably more common than records suggest.

2 Culm with raised, brown, longitudinal streaks, which sometimes completely encircle it, extending from one node to the next; brown ustilospores burst through, leaving the culm bare: **Ustilaginales: Ustilaginaceae** .... ***Ustilago grandis*** Fries
EE509, MA52

B91. *PIMPINELLA*

A rust (**Uredinales: Pucciniaceae**) galls both greater burnet-saxifrage *P. major* (L.) Hudson and burnet-saxifrage *P. saxifraga* L.

Leaves with raised swollen areas on underside, especially along the veins, bearing spermogonia (0) and yellowish aecia (I); uredinia (II) and telia (III) present later
.... ***Puccinia pimpinellae*** (Str.) Röhl.
EE400, PH148, WH155

B92. *PINUS*

Four rusts (**Uredinales**) gall Scots pine, *P. sylvestris* L., and the introduced Austrian pine, *P. nigra* J. F. Arnold, Weymouth pine, *P. strobus* L., western white pine, *P. monticola* Dougl. ex D. Don and maritime pine, *P. pinaster* Aiton. In addition, a dense twiggy witches' broom is occasionally seen on *P. sylvestris* (it has been found in northern Scotland, Entwistle, personal communication 2002, and in southeast England). Its cause is unknown. It may be caused by a phytoplasma or a fungus, or be due to genetic mutation of a bud.

1   Both surfaces of needles with cylindrical projections of aecia (I), 1-5 mm long; spermogonia (0) present; on *P. sylvestris* and *P. nigra*: **Coleosporiaceae** .... ***Coleosporium tussilaginis*** (Pers.) Berk. EE169, PH33, WH3

-   On trunk or branches 2

2   Trunk with large blisters from which aecia (I) project up to 3mm; spermogonia (0) present; often with resin exuding and running down the trunk; usually on *P. strobus* and *P. monticola*: **Cronartiaceae** .... ***Cronartium ribicola*** J. C. Fischer CMID283, EE180, PH35, WH55. *P. monticola* is now rare because of deaths caused by this blister rust.

-   Branches swollen or with cankers 3

3   Branches with large cankers, with bladder-like orange aecia (I) projecting 2-7 mm; spermogonia (0) present; on *P. sylvestris*: **Cronartiaceae** .... ***Cronartium flaccidum*** (Alb. & Schw.) Wint. EE180, WH51. In Scotland, a race of this species causes serious disease of the host. Also in Thetford Chase where it is called 'resin top'.

-   Branches swollen and distorted with aecia (I) erupting through the bark; on *P. sylvestris* and *P. pinaster*: **Melampsoraceae** .... ***Melampsora populnea*** (Pers.) Karst. EE387, PH56, WH76. See also *Mercurialis*.

B93. *PLANTAGO*

A chytrid (**Chytridiales: Synchytriaceae**) galls ribwort plantain, *Plantago lanceolata* L.

Leaves with tiny, gregarious pustules, < 0.5 mm across ...... ***Synchytrium erieum*** Karling

B94. **POACEAE**

Fungal galls on grasses are fairly common. Some of these attack many host genera and hence are treated together here. See also separate entries for *Phragmites* and *Zea*. (Common names and authors of species of grasses are not included here; if required, see Stace 1997.)

1   Gall in inflorescence.. 2

-   Gall on leaf, stem or root hair 3

2   Curved, elongate, purplish ergots project from individual florets (Fig. 9) (up to 3 cm long in *Spartina* spp.); common on *Lolium perenne* and occurs on many other species: **Hypocreales: Clavicipitaceae** .... ***Claviceps purpurea*** (Fr.) Tul. & C. Tul. **ergot** EE460. On *Lolium* and *Spartina*, ergots are sometimes pink, due to the hyperparasite *Gibberella gordonia* Booth (= *Fusarium heterosporum*) (**Hypocreales: Hypocreaceae**); see Preece *et al.* (1994).

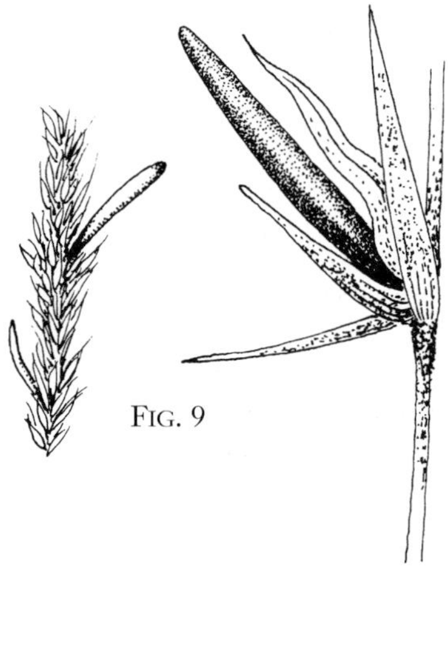

FIG. 9

- Inflorescence distorted and twisted; leaves often die back at tip but are not galled; black sori present: **Dothideales***

.... *Lidophia graminis* (Sacc.) Walker & B. Sutton

*Classification of this order uncertain.   (= *Dilophospora alopecuri*)

3 Root hairs with swollen cells containing spores; on *Catabrosa aquatica*, *Molinia caerulea* and *Glyceria fluitans*: **Plasmodiophorales: Plasmodiophoraceae**

.... *Sorosphaera radicalis* Cook

- On leaf or stem; smut gall: **Ustilaginales** **4**

4 Stem swollen, at first within leaf sheath, sometimes from one node to the next, often affecting successive internodes or the entire stem; opens early to release dark brown ustilospores; particularly striking on *Leymus arenarius* which often fails to produce flowers; also on *Bromopsis erecta*, *Elymus caninus*, *Elytrigia juncea*, *E. repens*, *Festuca gigantea*, *Trisetum flavescens*: **Ustilaginaceae**............ **Ustilago hypodytes** (Schlecht.) Fries
EE453, 495, MA53

- Not like this; leaf or stem with narrow blisters or streaks, sometimes extending whole length of blade **5**

5 Leaf with narrow, elongated blisters between veins; later burst to release powdery, dark brown to black ustilospores, splitting the leaves into ribbons; on *Agrostis capillaris*, *A. stolonifera*, *Alopecuris pratensis*, *Arrhenatherum elatius*, *Elytrigia atherica*, *E. repens*, *Festuca arenaria*, *F. arundinacea*, *Hordelymus europaeus*, *Lolium perenne*: **Tilletiaceae** .... **Urocystis agropyri** (Preuss) Schröter
CMID716, EE476, MA41

- Leaf with raised longitudinal streaks, which release dark brown ustilospores; stem sometimes distorted: **Ustilaginaceae** **6**

6 Leaves may split into ribbons; on *Arrhenatherum elatius*, *Dactylis glomerata*, *Deschampsia cespitosa*, *Festuca ovina*, *F. rubra*, *Holcus lanatus*, *H. mollis*, *Lolium perenne*, *Phalaris arundinacea*, *Phleum pratense*, *Poa annua*, *P. pratensis*, *P. trivialis*, *Sesleria caerulea* .... **Ustilago striiformis** (Westend.) Niessl.
EE453, MA58

- Leaves curled and wrinkled; culms often severely distorted; on *Bromopsis erecta*, *Calamagrostis canescens*, *Elytrigia juncea*, *E. repens*, *Phalaris arundinacea*
.... **Ustilago serpens** (Karsten) Lindeb.
EE453, MA57   To separate these species on the same host microscopic examination of the spores is necessary.

In addition, the scarce *Physoderma graminis* (Büsgen) de Wild. (Blastocladiales: Physodermataceae) may cause shortened internodes and more erect plants, with pale yellow streaks on leaves, in various grasses, but is perhaps not a true gall-causer.

B95. *POLEMONIUM*

One rust (**Uredinales: Pucciniaceae**) galls Jacob's ladder, *Polemonium caeruleum* L.

Petioles and leaf midrib slightly swollen, bearing small telia (III) which may merge; England; rare .... ***Puccinia polemonii*** Diet. & Holw.
WH171

B96. *POLYGONUM*

One smut (**Ustilaginales: Ustilaginaceae**) galls knotgrass, *Polygonum aviculare* L.

Stems and axis of inflorescence with marked swellings, spore masses not powdery when mature; very rare .... ***Melanopsichium nepalense*** (Liro) Zundel.
Recorded only once, see Spooner (1985).

B97. *POPULUS*

Three ascomycetes (**Taphrinales: Taphrinaceae**, see Mix 1949) gall black poplar, *P. nigra* L. and its hybrids, aspen, *P. tremula* L., or the introduced white poplar, *P. alba* L.

1   Leaves with bulges, concave surface bright yellow contrasting with the green of the unaffected leaf (Fig. 10); on *P. nigra* and hybrids
.... ***Taphrina populina*** Fr.
EE191

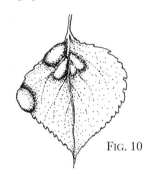
FIG. 10

2   Fruits distinctly swollen and golden yellow:

On *P. tremula* .... ***Taphrina johansonii*** Sadeb.
EE192

On *P. alba* .... ***Taphrina rhizophora*** Johanson

B98. *POTENTILLA*

Four fungi gall tormentil, *P. erecta* (L.) Raeusch., creeping cinquefoil, *P. reptans* L. or marsh cinquefoil, *P. palustris* (L.) Scop.

1   Leaves with raised spots on upper surface, with spermogonia (0) and orange aecia (I); later, yellow uredinia (II) and brown telia (III) appear on underside; on *P. erecta*, *P. reptans*; rare: **Uredinales: Phragmidiaceae**
.... ***Frommeella tormentillae*** (Fuckel) Cummins & Y. Hiratsuka
EE406, PH38, WH110.   (= *obtusa*)

2   Leaves with thickened yellow spots, stems thickened; on *P. erecta* in wet boggy places: **Taphrinales: Taphrinaceae** .... ***Taphrina potentillae*** (Farlow) Johanssen
EE407

3 Leaves with tiny, gregarious pustules <0.5 mm across; on *Potentilla* spp.: **Chytridiales: Synchytriaceae** .... ***Synchytrium cupulatum*** Thomas

4 Leaves with numerous thickened, dark violet spots about 1 mm across; on *P. palustris* **Blastocladiales: Physodermataceae** ...... ***Physoderma comari*** (Berk. & White) Lagerh.

B99. *PRUNELLA*

A chytrid (**Chytridiales: Synchytriaceae**) galls selfheal, *Prunella vulgaris* L.

Leaves with tiny, gregarious pustules <0.5 mm across ..... ***Synchytrium aureum*** Schroet.

B100. *PRUNUS*

Four fungi (**Taphrinales: Taphrinaceae**) gall blackthorn, *P. spinosa* L., bird cherry, *P. padus* L., and the introduced wild plum, *P. domestica* L., peach, *P. persica* (L.) Batsch, and almond, *P. dulcis* (Miller) D. Webb.

1 Fruits distorted and enlarged 2

- Leaves partly thickened and curled or witches' broom present 3

2 Fruits swollen on one side (Fig. 11), often remaining on tree all winter; shoots may be stunted, swollen, pale yellow tinged with red, with leaves reduced in size and strap-shaped; on *P. domestica, P. spinosa*
.... ***Taphrina pruni*** Tul.
EE196   **pocket plums**

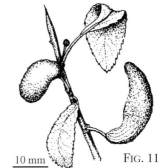
10 mm   FIG. 11

- Fruits elongated, styles persist; on *P. padus*
.... ***Taphrina padi*** (Jacz.) Mix
EE196

3 Thickening conspicuous (Fig. 12), bright red; on *P. persica, P. dulcis*, June – July
.... ***Taphrina deformans*** (Berk.) Tul.
EE196

- Thickening slight; also causes large witches' brooms; on *P. avium, P. cerasus*
.... ***Taphrina wiesneri*** (Rathay) Mix
EE196. See Mix (1949).   (= *cerasi*)

In addition, the powdery mildew *Sphaerotheca pannosa* (Wallr.) Lév. (**Erysiphales: Erysiphaceae**) (EE230) may cause distortion of shoots and young leaves; not thought to be a true gall causer

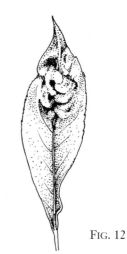
FIG. 12

B101. *PULICARIA*

A rust (**Uredinales: Pucciniaceae**) galls common fleabane, *Pulicaria dysenterica* (L.) Bernh.

Leaves with raised, yellow or purple-zoned spots, bearing aecia (I); mainly East Anglia; rare .... ***Uromyces junci*** (Desm.) Tul. & C. Tul.
EE409, PH203, WH355

B102. *PYROLA*

Two rusts (**Uredinales**) gall common wintergreen, *P. minor* L., and round-leaved wintergreen, *P. rotundifolia* L.

Petioles, petals and undersides of leaves with raised mounds 0.5 - 1 mm across; uredinia (II) present in winter, rarely followed by telia (III): **Coleosporiaceae**
.... ***Chrysomyxa pirolata*** Winter
EE409, WH61. *Pucciniastrum pyrolae* Diet. ex Arth. (**Pucciniastraceae**) is rare on these hosts.

B103. *PYRUS*

Two fungi gall pears, *Pyrus* spp. (see also *Juniperus*).

1   Leaves with orange spots and slight swellings on underside; acorn-shaped aecia (I), closed at the tips and with lacerated sides: **Uredinales: Pucciniaceae**
.... ***Gymnosporangium sabinae*** DC. (= *fuscum*)
CMID545, EE150, PH43, WH119   **European pear rust**

2   Leaves with blister-like swellings convex above, concave and lined with asci below:
Taphrinales: Taphrinaceae .... ***Taphrina bullata*** (Berk.) Tul. & C. Tul.
See Mix (1949).

B104. *RANUNCULUS*

Nine fungi gall meadow buttercup, *R. acris* L., bulbous buttercup, *R.. bulbosus* L., creeping buttercup, *R.repens* L., lesser celandine, *R. ficaria* L., greater spearwort, *R. lingua* L., and lesser spearwort, *R. flammula* L.

1   Leaf blades or petioles swollen, sometimes distorted, surface with swellings or blisters > 0.5 mm across which rupture to release dust-like spores **2**

-   Leaf blades or petioles with small pustules < 0.5 mm across; contain thick-walled resting spores; uncommon **4**

2   Swellings and spores chocolate brown or black when mature [there are three alternatives]:

Leaf blades swollen and distorted; telia (III) becoming chocolate brown with powdery masses of teliospores; on *R. ficaria*: **Uredinales: Pucciniaceae**
.... ***Uromyces ficariae*** (Alb. & Schw.) Lév.
EE410, PH201, WH310

Leaf blades and petioles with blister-like swellings, which rupture when mature to expose powdery ustilospores; on *R. acris*, *R. bulbosus*, *R. repens*: **Ustilaginales: Tilletiaceae**

.... ***Urocystis ranunculi*** (Lib.) Moesz
EE411, MA42

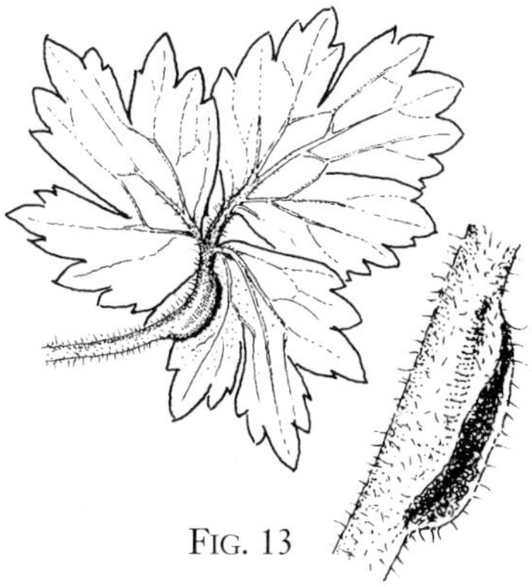

Leaves (usually underside), petioles (Fig. 13) and occasionally flowers with blister-like swellings 2 - 8 mm long, under the epidermis; these burst to release black ustilospores; on *R. repens*, *R. ficaria*: **Ustilaginales: Tilletiaceae**

.... ***Urocystis ficariae*** (Liro) Moesz
EE411, MA44

Fig. 13

5 mm

- Swellings and spores yellow or yellow brown **3**

3 Petioles swollen and distorted, with spermogonia (0) and yellow aecia (I); common in early spring on *R. ficaria*, less common on *R. acris*: **Uredinales: Pucciniaceae**
.... ***Uromyces dactylidis*** Otth
EE410, PH199, WH360. A very rare rust, *Puccinia recondita* f. sp. *perplexans* Plowr. produces spermogonia and yellow aecia on *R. acris* (see EE410, PH161, WH286); it has been recorded only a few times between 1884 and 1954.

- Small, round or oval swellings in leaves and stems:

Smut sori containing smooth, rather thick-walled, rounded spores 15 - 20 µm across; on *R. acris*, *R. repens*: **Ustilaginales: Tilletiaceae**
.... ***Entyloma microsporum*** (Unger) Schroet.
EE411, MA27

Rust aecia containing spores with finely roughened surfaces; on *R. bulbosus*, *R. flammula*, *R. lingua*, *R. repens*: **Uredinales: Pucciniaceae**
.... ***Puccinia magnusiana*** Körn
EE410, PH135, WH266

4 Scattered, irregular pustules on leaves or petioles; spores 20 - 35 µm across: **Blastocladiales: Physodermataceae** .... ***Physoderma vagans*** Schroet.

- Gregarious, hard pustules on leaves; spores 50 - 150 µm across; on *R. ficaria*: **Chytridiales: Synchytriaceae** .... ***Synchytrium anomalum*** Schroet.

B105. *RHAMNUS* and *FRANGULA*

A rust (**Uredinales: Pucciniaceae**) galls both buckthorn, *Rhamnus cathartica* L. and alder buckthorn, *Frangula alnus* Miller.

Leaves and petioles twisted and distorted, with yellowish swellings; orange aecia (I) on leaves .... ***Puccinia coronata*** Corda
EE136 (*Frangula*), 220 (*Rhamnus*), PH109, WH252

B106. *RHODODENDRON* (including *AZALEA*)

Two fungi (**Exobasidiales: Exobasidiaceae**) gall introduced *Rhododendron* species.

1   Leaves thickened and fleshy, with white covering on underside; on 'azaleas'
.... ***Exobasidium japonicum*** Shirai
CMID780, EE220

2   Leaves transformed into large, pink gall-apples; on garden rhododendrons
.... ***Exobasidium rhododendri*** (Fuckel) Cram.
EE220 (as *E. vaccinii*). For more information and coloured illustrations, see Ing (1998).

B107. *RIBES*

Two rusts (**Uredinales**) gall gooseberry, *R. uva-crispa* L., blackcurrant, *R. nigrum* L. and some other *Ribes* species.

1   Leaves and fruits bearing striking, yellow, raised areas, with orange aecia (I), preceded by spermogonia (0): **Pucciniaceae** .... ***Puccinia caricina*** (Kleb.) Henderson
EE225, PH100, WH236. This gall seems to be rarer now than it was in the 1950s.

2   Undersides of leaves with pale spots bearing yellowish uredinia (II) and telia (III); on *R. nigrum* and some other *Ribes* spp.; rare: **Cronartiaceae**
.... ***Cronartium ribicola*** J.C. Fisher
CMID283, EE180, PH35, WH55. See *PINUS*, its alternate host.

B108. *ROSA*

Three rusts (**Uredinales: Phragmidiaceae**) gall both cultivated and wild roses, *Rosa* species. They cannot easily be separated and, in any case, require further study. These notes are, therefore, provided for general guidance.

Two of the rusts appear on all species, with the exception of burnet rose *R. pimpinellifolia*. They have orange-yellow, swollen aecia (I) and can only be separated by detailed microscopic study of their aeciospores, urediniospores and teliospores:

    Phragmidium tuberculatum J. Müller (CMID208, EE228, PH75, WH106)

    Phragmidium mucronatum (Pers.) Schlecht. (CMID204, EE228, PH71, WH104).
    Most rusts on cultivated roses, except hybrids of burnet rose, seem to be the former.

    The aecia (I), and other stages, found on *R. pimpinellifolia* and its cultivated hybrids are ***Phragmidium rosae-pimpinellifoliae*** Diet. (CMID205, EE228, WH103).
    This is often confused with other rose rusts. Only more collecting and study will solve the problems associated with these rusts. Cecidologists should, perhaps, record '*Phragmidium* spp.' on all roses and keep herbarium specimens. When dealing with rusts found late in the season as uredinia (II) or, more strikingly, as black telia (III), attempts should be made to find the aecia (I) in the spring. See Graham & Primavesi (1993). In addition, the powdery mildew *Sphaerotheca pannosa* (Wallr.) Lév (EE230) may cause slight distortion of shoots and young leaves; not thought to be a true gall causer.

B109. *RUMEX*

Two fungi gall common sorrel, *R. acetosa* L., sheep's sorrel, *R. acetosella* L., curled dock, *R. crispus* L., clustered dock, *R. conglomeratus* Murray, water dock, *R. hydrolapathum* Huds., broad-leaved dock, *R. obtusifolius* L., and wood dock, *R. sanguineus* L.

1 Stems (and perhaps leaves) with blister-like swellings; ovaries swollen; purplish powdery spore mass when mature; on *R. acetosa*, *R. acetosella*, *R. crispus*: **Ustilaginales: Ustilaginaceae** .... ***Ustilago kuehneana*** Wolff
EE415, MA54

2 Leaves with red or purple blister–like swellings bearing aecia (I); on *R. acetosa*, *R. conglomeratus*, *R.crispus*, *R. hydrolapathum*, *R. obtusifolius*, *R. sanguineus*: **Uredinales: Pucciniaceae** .... ***Puccinia phragmitis*** (Schum.) Körn.
EE414, PH146, WH269

B110. *RUPPIA*

A fungus (**Plasmodiophorales: Plasmodiophoraceae**) galls beaked tasselweed, *Ruppia maritima* L.

Leaves and stems with conspicuous, irregular swellings .... ***Tetramyxa parasitica*** Goebel

B111. *SALIX*

Several rusts (**Uredinales**) gall *Salix* species but only one can be considered as cecidogenic, occurring on eared willow, *S. aurita* L., goat willow, *S. caprea* L., grey willow, *S. cinerea* L. and their hybrids.

Leaves and veins distorted and with irregular thickened spots, bearing orange-yellow uredinia (II): **Melampsoraceae** .... ***Melampsora caprearum*** Thuem.
EE244, PH48, WH77

B112. *SANGUISORBA*

Two rusts (**Uredinales**) gall salad burnet, *S. minor* Scop. or fodder great burnet, *S. officinalis* L.

1 Petioles and veins with elongated swellings which distort the leaves, bearing orange aecia (I); spermogonia (0) present on purple spots; uredinia (II) and telia (III) form later in summer; on *S. minor*; rare: **Phragmidiaceae**
.... ***Phragmidium sanguisorbae*** (DC.) Schroet.
EE407, PH74, WH102

2 Petioles and veins with purple, swollen spots, bearing aecia and telia; on *S. officinalis*: **Phragmidiaceae** .... ***Xenodochus carbonarius*** Schlecht.
EE417, PH218, WH109

B113. *SANICULA*

A rust (**Uredinales: Pucciniaceae**) galls sanicle, *Sanicula europaea* L.

Leaves with raised, brownish spots on the underside, bearing yellow aecia (I), or elongated swellings on petioles and veins; spermogonia (0) present; sometimes aecia, uredinia (II) and telia (III) found together early in the year ...... ***Puccinia saniculae*** Grev.
EE417, PH162, WH157

SATUREJA see *MENTHA*

SCILLA see *MUSCARI*

B114. *SCORZONERA*

An oomycete (**Peronosporales: Albuginaceae**) galls viper's-grass, *Scorzonera humilis* L.

Above ground plant parts covered with white blisters, sometimes crusty
.... ***Albugo tragopogonis*** (DC.) S.F.Gray
EE420

B115. *SCROPHULARIA*

A rust (**Uredinales: Pucciniaceae**) galls common figwort, *S. nodosa* L., water figwort, *S. auriculata* L., balm-leaved figwort, *S. scorodonia* L. and green figwort, *S. umbrosa* Dumort.

Leaves and stems distorted by scattered spermogonia (0) and plentiful aecia (I) and telia (III); distortions up to 10cms long, often found near the stem bases
.... ***Uromyces scrophulariae*** Fuckel
EE419, PH212, WH348

SELINUM see *ANGELICA*

B116. *SEMPERVIVUM*

One rust (**Uredinales: Pucciniaceae**) galls the introduced house-leek, *S. tectorum* L.

Leaves more upright and longer and narrower than usual, rosette less compact; with spermogonia (0) and yellowish brown telia (III) only; uncommon
.... ***Endophyllum sempervivi*** de Bary
EE420, PH38, WH309

B117. *SENECIO* and *PERICALLIS*

Three fungi gall groundsel, *S. vulgaris* L., the introduced Oxford ragwort, *S. squalidus* L. and garden cineraria, *P. hybrida* R. Nord.

1   Stems and leaves swollen and much distorted by vivid orange aecia (I); long, dark brown to black telia (III) may, rarely, be found at the same time; common, on *S. vulgaris*, *S. squalidus*: **Uredinales: Pucciniaceae** .... ***Puccinia lagenophorae*** Cooke
EE420, PH33, WH213. This rust was first recorded in Britain in 1961 and seems to have 'replaced' the following species.

2 Stems and leaves swollen and distorted, with powdery orange uredinia (II) and waxy reddish telia; on *S. vulgaris*, *S. squalidus*; now rare: **Uredinales: Coleosporiaceae** .... ***Coleosporium tussilaginis*** (Pers.) Berk.
EE420, 435, PH33, WH3. Other rusts occur on *Senecio* species but do not cause galls.

3 White blisters, sometimes crusty, on all above ground parts of plant; on *S. squalidus*, *P. hybrida*, recently spreading onto *S. vulgaris*: **Peronosporales: Albuginaceae** .... ***Albugo tragopogonis*** (DC.) S.F.Gray
EE420

SERRATULA see ASTERACEAE

B118. *SESELI*

A rust (**Uredinales: Pucciniaceae**) galls moon carrot, *Seseli libanotis* (L.) Koch.

Leaf veins enlarged, with large red-brown aecia (I); very rare ***Puccinia libanotidis*** Lindr

SIDALCEA see MALVACEAE

SILAUM see *ANGELICA*

B119. *SIUM*

Two fungi gall greater-water parsnip, *Sium latifolium* L.

1 Leaves with small yellow-white, often elongated swellings, sometimes causing distortion of leaf blade; uncommon on *Sium*: **Protomycetales: Protomycetaceae** .... ***Protomyces macrosporus*** Unger
See also *AEGOPODIUM*, *ANGELICA* and *ANTHRISCUS*. Also occurs on some other umbellifers, especially visible in early spring.

2 Leaves or petioles with small, scattered, irregular pustules, containing thick-walled sporangia 20–35 µm across; rare on this host: **Blastocladiales: Physodermataceae** .... ***Physoderma vagans*** Schroet.

B120. *SMYRNIUM*

A rust (**Uredinales: Pucciniaceae**) galls the introduced Alexanders, *Smyrnium olusatrum* L.

Both surfaces of leaves, and stems, thickened and blistered by spermogonia (0) and yellow aecia (I); followed by dark brown telia (III) on the undersides of leaves only .... ***Puccinia smyrnii*** Biv.-Bernh.
EE424, PH166, WH158

B121. *SOLANUM*

Three fungi gall cultivated potatoes, *Solanum tuberosum* L.

1   Tubers with protruding, large, dark brown growths, often like small cauliflowers (Fig. 14). packed with thick-walled sporangia: **Chytridiales: Synchytriaceae**
.... ***Synchytrium endobioticum*** (Schilb.) Perc.
wart disease

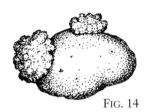

FIG. 14

EE427. Vigorous efforts have been made to control this extremely serious potato disease, and it is now very rare.

2   Tubers with brown, roughened, scabs (Fig. 15), often accompanied by small raised patches and bud-like outgrowths; scabs burst open to release masses of 'spore-balls': **Plasmodiophorales: Plasmodiophoraceae**
.... ***Spongospora subterranea*** (Wallr.) Lagerh.
EE427   **powdery or corky scab disease**

FIG. 15

3   Sprouts from tubers curved and swollen, sometimes developing side shoots below soil.. ***Verticillium nubilum*** Pethybr.
curled sprout disease

CMID258. This fungus belongs to the class Hyphomycetes; its order and family are unknown.

B122. *SORBUS*

Two rusts (**Uredinales**) gall rowan (mountain ash), *Sorbus aucuparia* L.

Undersides of leaves with rounded orange-yellow swellings bearing horn-shaped aecia (I) (Plate 8.7), up to 5 mm long, opening at the tip; black spermogonia (0) on the upperside; commoner in Scotland: **Pucciniaceae**
.... ***Gymnosporangium cornutum*** Kern

EE255, PH42, WH121. See also *JUNIPERUS* Key. Very rarely telia (III) of *Ochropsora ariae* (Fuckel) Ramsb. (**Chaconiaceae**) are found on *Sorbus* (EE255, PH29, WH11).

B123. *SPERGULARIA*

An oomycete (**Peronosporales: Albuginaceae**) galls sea-spurreys, *Spergularia* species.

Above ground plant parts covered with white blisters, sometimes crusty
.... ***Albugo lepigoni*** (de Bary) Kuntze
EE248

B124. *SUAEDA*

One rust (**Uredinales: Pucciniaceae**) galls annual sea-blite, *S. maritima* (L.) Dumort and shrubby sea-blite, *S. vera* Frosskaol ex Gmelin.

Leaves and sometimes stems with thickened areas bearing aecia (I), later with uredinia (II) and telia (III) .... ***Uromyces chenopodii*** (Duby) Schroet.
EE430, WH316

B125. *SUCCISA*

A fungus (**Chytridiales: Synchytriaceae**) galls devil's-bit scabious, *Succisa pratensis* Moench.

Leaves, petioles and stems with reddish orange or purplish red swellings, often large; contain resting spores .... ***Synchytrium succisae*** de Bary & Woronin
EE431

B126. *TARAXACUM*

Three fungi gall dandelions, *Taraxacum* species.

1   Upper surface of leaves with swollen reddish yellow spots, caused by aecia (I) with brown spores; spermogonia (0) and aecia in April - May, uredinia (II) and telia (III) later: **Uredinales: Pucciniaceae** .... ***Puccinia hieracii*** Mart.
EE369, 432, PH122, WH203. Another common rust, *Puccinia variabilis* Grev., (EE432, PH171, WH214), develops as very small orange spots (aecia) scattered over the whole leaf, with no spermogonia; uredinia follow, and masses of dark brown telia (the stage usually noted). It is not considered to be gall-causing but can be confused with *P. hieracii.*

2   Leaves swollen and distorted, with purplish red areas, often near veins, sometimes on flower stalks; very common: **Protomycetales: Protomycetaceae**
.... ***Protomyces pachydermus*** Thümen
EE433

3   Leaves peppered with numerous, very small, round pustules, yellow to orange or red, < 1mm across; also on petioles and flower stalks: **Chytridiales: Synchytriaceae**
.... ***Synchytrium taraxaci*** de Bary & Woron.
EE433. No studies have been carried out of the distribution of fungal galls on the 226 micro-species of dandelions. This would make an exciting project for cecidologists, particularly as the micro-species can now be identified (Dudman & Richards, 1997).

B127. *TEUCRIUM*

A very distinctive rust (**Uredinales: Pucciniaceae**) galls wood sage, *Teucrium scorodonia* L.

Undersides of leaves with dark brown lumps, of different sizes (Fig. 16), bearing telia (III)
.... ***Puccinia annularis*** (Str.) Röhl.
EE433, PH85, WH177

FIG. 16

B128. *THALICTRUM*

Five fungi gall common meadow-rue, *T. flavum* L., lesser meadow-rue, *T. minus* L. or alpine meadow-rue, *T. alpinum* L.

1   Leaflets entirely distorted by greatly swollen blisters, occasionally also on petioles and stems; blisters rupture to release black spores: **Ustilaginales: Tilletiaceae**
.... ***Urocystis sorosporioides*** Körn.
MA47, EE434

-   Leaves with swollen areas, caused by rusts; rare: **Uredinales** 2

2   Leaves much deformed, with dark brown telia (III); plant taller and paler than usual; on *T. minus*, *T. flavum*; very rare: **Uropyxidaceae**
.... ***Tranzschelia anemones*** (Pers.) Nannf.
EE433, PH182, WH303. Also found on *ANEMONE*.

-   Leaf swellings caused by aecia (I); other spore stages also present: **Pucciniaceae** 3

3   On *T. minus*, *T. flavum*; spermogonia (0) and aecia present
.... ***Puccinia recondita*** f. sp. ***persistens*** Plowr.
EE433, PH161, WH286

-   On *T. alpinum* (there are two alternatives):

Aecia cause extensive, violet swellings; uredinia (II) and telia present later
.... ***Puccinia septentrionalis*** Juel
EE433, WH167

Without marked discolouration; spermogonia and aecia present; very rare
.... ***Puccinia recondita*** f. sp. ***borealis*** Juel
EE433, PH161, WH281

B129. *THYMUS*

A fungus (**Chytridiales: Synchytriaceae**) galls Breckland thyme, *Thymus serpyllum* L.

Leaves with tiny, gregarious pustules <0.5 mm across ..... ***Synchytrium aureum*** Schroet.

B130. *TRAGOPOGON*

Two fungi gall goat's-beard, *Tragopogon pratensis* L.

1 All above ground parts of plant with white crusty blisters: **Peronosporales: Albuginaceae** .... *Albugo tragopogonis* (DC) S.F.Gray **white blister**
EE435

2 Stems and shoots distorted, covered with aecia (I): **Uredinales: Pucciniaceae**
.... *Puccinia hysterium* (Str.) Röhl.
EE435, PH128, WH207

B131. *TRIENTALIS*

A smut (**Ustilaginales: Tilletiaceae**) galls chickweed wintergreen, *Trientalis europaea* L.

Leaves and stems with blister-like swellings, which rupture to expose masses of black ustilospores .... *Urocystis trientalis* (Berk. & Broome)
MA48, EE435

B132. *TRIFOLIUM*

Four rusts (**Uredinales: Pucciniaceae**) gall white clover, *Trifolium repens* L, strawberry clover, *T. fragiferum*, red clover, *T. pratense* L., zigzag clover, *T. medium* L., crimson clover, *T. incarnatum* L., lesser yellow trefoil, *T. dubium* L., and the introduced alsike clover, *T. hybridum* L.

1 Leaf veins and petioles swollen and distorted by telia (III); swellings may be 2 mm long or more; on *T. repens*, *T. fragiferum* .... *Uromyces trifolii* (DC.) Fuckel
EE436, PH208, WH328   (= *U. nerviphilus*)

2 Leaves swollen and distorted with yellow areas, often affecting veins, in spring; spermogonia (0) and aecia (I) present, followed by masses of uredinia (II) and telia (III); on *T. repens*, *T. hybridum* .... *Uromyces trifolii-repentis* Liro
EE436, PH213, WH337.

3 Leaves and stems with swellings bearing aecia; on *T. pratense*, *T. medium*, *T. incarnatum*; rare .... *Uromyces fallens* (Arth.) Barth.
EE436, WH326

4 Leaves with swollen spots, bearing aecia; on *T. dubium*; rare .... *Uromyces minor* Schroet.
EE436, WH327
More collecting, detailed mycological work and correct naming of hosts is needed for rusts on *Trifolium*.

B133. *TROLLIUS*

One smut (**Ustilaginales: Ustilaginaceae**) galls globe flower, *Trollius europaeus* L.

Leaves and stems with blister-like swellings, rupture to expose black powdery spore mass when mature; very rare .... *Urocystis ficariae* (Liro) Moesz
EE410, MA44. See also *RANUNCULUS* Key.

B134. *TUSSILAGO*

A rust (**Uredinales: Pucciniaceae**) galls colt's-foot, *Tussilago farfara* L.

Leaves with thickened areas on undersides, bearing orange-red aecia (I) and spermogonia (0); locally common .... ***Puccinia poarum*** Niels.
EE440, PH149, WH274. The common uredinia (II) and telia (III) on *T. farfara* are of *Coleosporium tussilaginis* (Pers.) Berk., which is not a gall causer.

B135. *ULMUS*

One ascomycete (**Taphrinales: Taphrinaceae**) galls English elm, *Ulmus procera* Salisb.

Leaves with yellowish swellings, raised on the upperside, concave below and lined with asci .... ***Taphrina ulmi*** (Fuckel) Johanss.

B136. *URTICA*

One rust (**Uredinales: Pucciniaceae**) galls occurs on common (stinging) nettle, *Urtica dioica* L. and, rarely, small nettle, *U. urens* L.

Stems bearing large, discoloured, reddish swellings, up to 5 cm long (Fig. 17), also occurring on undersides of leaves (Plate 8.4) and petioles; stems may be bent back to form an inverted 'V'; spermogonia (0) and orange aecia (I) present
.... ***Puccinia urticata*** Kern
EE440, PH99, WH232   (= *P. caricina*)

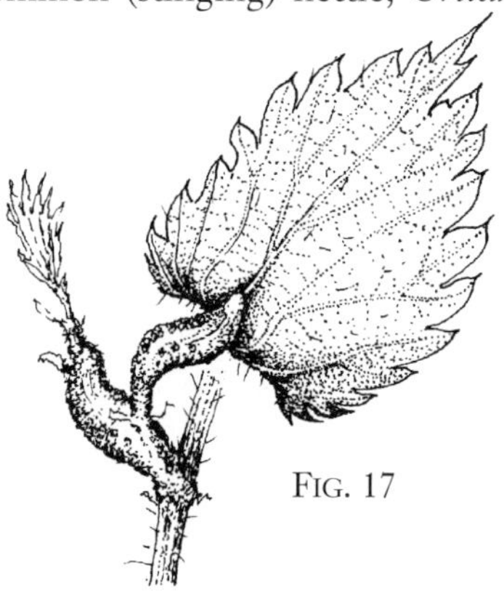

Fig. 17

B137. *VACCINIUM*

Six fungi gall small cranberry, *Vaccinium microcarpum* (Turcz. ex Rupr.) Schmalh., bilberry, *V. myrtillus* L., cranberry, *V. oxycoccus* L., bog bilberry, *V. uliginosum* L., cowberry, *V. vitis-idaea* L. and the introduced blueberry, *V. corymbosum* L. and American cranberry, *V. macrocarpon* Ait.

1   Stems swollen, bearing telia (III) which form a crust around the stems; on *V. corymbosum, V. vitis-idaea*: **Uredinales: Pucciniaceae**
.... ***Pucciniastrum goeppertianum*** (Kuhn) Kleb.
WH40

-   Leaves, often red or pink, swollen or with raised blisters or thickened spots; shoot often enlarged and distorted: **Exobasidiales: Exobasidiaceae** 2
EE220

2   Leaves enlarged, red or pink; shoots elongated, swollen and distorted:

On *V. myrtillus* (Plate 8.9); leaves red .... ***Exobasidium myrtilli*** Siegm.

On *V. vitis-idaea*; leaves red .... ***Exobasidium juelianum*** Nannf.

On *V. microcarpum, V. macrocarpon, V. oxycoccus*; leaves pink
.... ***Exobasidium rostrupii*** Nannf.

-    Leaves with reddened swellings or thickened spots **3**

3   Leaves with red, thickened spots; on *V. uliginosum* .... ***Exobasidium pachysporum*** Nannf.

-    Leaves with reddened raised blisters; on *V. vitis-idaea*
.... ***Exobasidium vaccinii*** (Fuckel) Woronin

For more information, and coloured illustrations, see Ing (1998).

B138. *VALERIANA*

Two rusts (**Uredinales: Pucciniaceae**) gall common valerian, *Valeriana officinalis* L. and marsh valerian, *V. dioica* L.

Leaf veins, petioles and stems with thickened spots bearing spermogonia (0) and yellow aecia (I); later uredinia (II) on the undersides of leaves and, very rarely, telia (III) may form:

Common; on *V. officinalis, V. dioica* .... ***Uromyces valerianae*** (DC.) Fuckel
E444, PH215, WH348.

Scotland; very rare; on *V. officinalis* .... ***Puccinia commutata*** P. & H. Sydow
EE444, WH189

B139. *VERONICA*

Five fungi gall wood speedwell, *V. montana* L., germander speedwell, *V. chamaedrys* L., alpine speedwell, *V. alpina* L., spiked speedwell, *V. spicata* L. and pink water-speedwell, *V. catenata* Pennell.

1   Seed capsules swollen, with granular spore mass .... ***Schroeteria delastrina*** (Tul.) Winter
MA31. This fungus belongs to the class Hyphomycetes; its order and family are unknown.

-    Stem, leaf veins, and sometimes roots, swollen or with thickened spots **2**

2   Swellings at base of stem and on leaf veins (Fig. 18), roots with large distinct nodules: **Plasmodiophorales: Plasmodiophoraceae** .... ***Sorosphaera veronicae*** (J. Schröt.) J. Schröt.

Not seen on *V. chamaedrys* for many years until 1999; in the same year, it was also found, as a new world record, on *V. catenata*, in London.

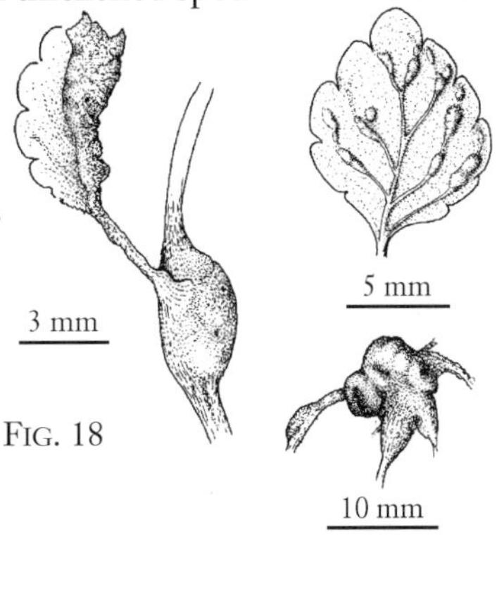

3 mm

5 mm

10 mm

FIG. 18

- Thickened spots on leaves, sometimes also on stems, with telia (III): **Uredinales: Pucciniaceae:**

On *V. montana*; widespread and frequent............................ ***Puccinia veronicae*** Schroet.
EE445, PH173, WH176.

On *V. alpina*; Scotland; rare .... ***Puccinia albulensis*** Magn.
EE445. PH172.

On *V. spicata*; England and Wales; rare .... ***Puccinia veronicae-longifoliae*** Savile
EE446.

B140. *VIOLA*

Three fungi gall sweet violet, *V. odorata* L., common dog-violet, *V. riviniana* Reichb., early dog-violet, *V. reichenbachiana* Jordan ex Boreau, hairy violet, *V. hirta* L., marsh violet, *V. palustris* L., wild pansy, *V. tricolor* L., mountain pansy, *V. lutea* Hudson, their garden cultivars and the introduced horned pansy, *V. cornuta* L.

1   Leaves with swollen areas, stems and petioles often with elongated swellings and curiously bent, bearing spermogonia (0) and aecia (I); uredinia (II) and telia (III) appear later but do not cause swellings; on *V. odorata*, *V. riviniana*, *V. reichenbachiana*, *V. tricolor*, *V. hirta*, *V. lutea* and garden cultivars: **Uredinales: Pucciniaceae**
    .... ***Puccinia violae*** DC.
   EE449, PH175, WH126

2   Leaves with rounded yellowish spots with chocolate brown telia; on *V. palustris*; very rare: **Uredinales: Pucciniaceae** .... ***Puccinia fergussonii*** Berk. & Br.
   EE449, WH126

3   Petioles distorted with elongated swellings (Plate 8.3), also on leaf veins and upper part of root stock; these burst to reveal a dark brown powdery mass of ustilospores, often in winter; on *V. odorata*, *V. riviniana*, *V. reichenbachiana* and garden cultivars: **Ustilaginales: Tilletiaceae** ....*Urocystis violae* (Sow.) A. Fischer v. Waldh.
   MA48, EE449

B141. *ZEA*

One smut (**Ustilaginales: Ustilaginaceae**) galls the introduced maize, *Zea mays* L.

Shoot, cob and sometimes other parts with large, rounded swellings, particularly causing grossly distended grains, becoming 1-10 cm across (Fig. 19); silvery white at first, later a dark brown or black mass of ustilospores inside; in south and east England, probably increasing
    .... ***Ustilago maydis*** (DC) Corda
CMID79, EE520, MA61   (= *U. zeae*) **maize smut**

The maize smut gall is fleshy and edible when young. The earliest known illustrations of galls, in the mid 16th century refer to this species (Preece 1993).

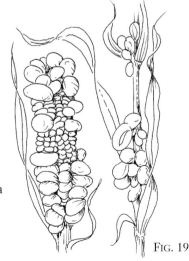

Fig. 19

B142. *ZOSTERA*

A fungus (**Plasmodiophorales: Plasmodiophoraceae**) galls dwarf eelgrass, *Zostera noltei* Hornem.

Stem with swelling .... ***Plasmodiophora bicaudata*** Feldm.

Section C.
Galls caused by Plants

Two genera of flowering plants are parasitic on other plants, attached to their hosts by haustoria. These cause distinct swellings in the host plant's branch or stem (they are, therefore, gall-causing) and serve to transfer nutrients from the host to the parasite.

Viscum album L. mistletoe, **Viscaceae**
A semi-parasitic evergreen shrub growing on branches of trees, e.g. apples, *Malus*, limes, *Tilia*, hawthorns, *Crataegus*, poplars, *Populus*; England and Wales north to Yorkshire, local, but common in the southwest midlands and southeast Wales.

Cuscuta spp. dodders, **Cuscutaceae**
Rootless parasites without visible chlorophyll, very thin pinkish stems twining around stems of host plants, attached by haustoria. There are three species in Britain:
C. epithymum (L.) L., dodder: native, mainly on gorse, *Ulex*, and heather, *Calluna*, on heathland; frequent in south Britain, scattered further north.
C. europaea L., greater dodder: native, on a range of hosts, especially nettle, *Urtica dioica*; England north to Northamptonshire, scattered and rare.
C. campestris Yunck, yellow dodder: introduced, on a range of cultivated plants, especially carrot, *Daucus carota*; scattered in England and Wales.

Section D.
Galls caused by Nematodes
By John Southey

Fig. 20
An eelworm

This is a large and varied group which includes animal and plant parasites, free-living forms and species which combine these modes of life. Plant parasites are often known as eelworms (Fig. 20). Animal parasites include, for example, roundworms, threadworms and hookworms.

Many are serious crop pests; some estimates put crop losses world-wide due to nematodes at 10% of all production. The losses are caused by malformation, rotting and gall formation. The plant-parasitic nematodes are generally too small (up to a few millimetres long) to be easily visible to the naked eye, especially as they are frequently almost transparent. Other small forms, parasitic in insects and slugs, have proved useful in biological pest control.

Six main groups of gall causers, on plants and on a lichen, may be distinguished. Only those species considered to cause true galls are included. Spooner (1999) includes a longer list.

1. Members of the genus *Anguina* and its near relatives (**Anguinidae**)

    These cause galls with distinct shapes according to the species of both causer and host. These galls are typically found in the flowers and on the leaves of Poaceae (grasses), on the leaves of Asteraceae (daisy family) or other plants, but only rarely on roots. The galls have an internal cavity and differentiation of tissues.

2. *Ditylenchus dipsaci* (stem nematode, **Anguinidae**)

    Commonly causes malformation in host plants, including swelling of tissues. The nematodes feed within these swellings but there is no cavity.

3. *Meloidogyne* spp. (root-knot nematodes, **Meloidogynidae**)

    Galls caused by this group appear on roots of many different plants throughout the world, especially in warmer climates. They are major crop pests. The galls, which may be multiple, vary in size from pinhead to grape. They are more or less solid, but around the head of the nematodes multinucleate 'giant-cells' form which concentrate nutrients. The females become pear-shaped and may burst through the gall surface. Their gelatinous egg-masses may be just visible.

4. *Naccobbus* spp. (false root-knot nematodes, **Pratylenchidae**)

    N. serendipiticus causes root galls similar to those of *Meloidogyne* on glasshouse tomatoes in England and the Netherlands. Otherwise a warm climate genus, mainly in N. America.

5. *Aphelenchoides* spp. (leaf and bud nematodes, **Aphelenchoididae**)

    An unusual group of gall causers as they combine with the bacterium *Corynebacterium* to produce 'cauliflower' galls on strawberry (*Fragaria)* which arise through fasciation of the growing point and suppression of the leaf blades. The microscopic nematodes mostly remain in water films between these structures.

6. Free-living soil nematodes

    A number of these – in particular *Xiphinema* (dagger nematodes), occasionally *Longidorus* (needle nematodes) (both **Longidoridae**), but also others – feed on growing roots from the outside, thus causing swelling of the root-tips. Examination of these reveals nothing of the causers because they are left in the soil; whether or not these are true galls is debatable. Species in the two genera mentioned are relatively large (5 mm or more in length) but, being transparent and very slender, are still difficult to see.

The key below provides examples of each of these types. Further information may be found in Goodey, 1933, Southey, 1969, 1978, Kir'yanova & Krall, 1971, Southey *et al.*, 1990, Krall, 1991, Gratwick, 1992, Evans *et al.*, 1993, and the listed Commonwealth Institute of Helminthology (C.I.H.) Descriptions of Plant-parasitic Nematodes.

The key is divided into galls on:

D1. *CLADONIA* (lichens)

D2. *POTTIA* (a moss)

D3. POACEAE (grasses)

D4. *ACHILLEA* (yarrow)

D5. *BRASSICA* (cabbages)

D6. *CLEMATIS, DAUCUS* (carrot) and other shrubs and vegetables (root galls)

D7. *FRAGARIA* (strawberry)

D8. *LIGUSTRUM* (privets)

D9. *LYCOPERSICON* (tomato)

D10. *NARCISSUS* (daffodils)

D11. *PLANTAGO* (plantains)

D12. *ROSA* (roses)

D1. *CLADONIA*

On *C. glauca* and possibly other spp.; irregular rounded swellings, 1.2 - 1.8 mm across, pinkish-white, on erect podetia (the upright branches of *Cladonia* spp.; Fig. 21)

.... *Nothanguina* sp.

Identification uncertain; for more information see Siddiqi & Hawksworth (1982).

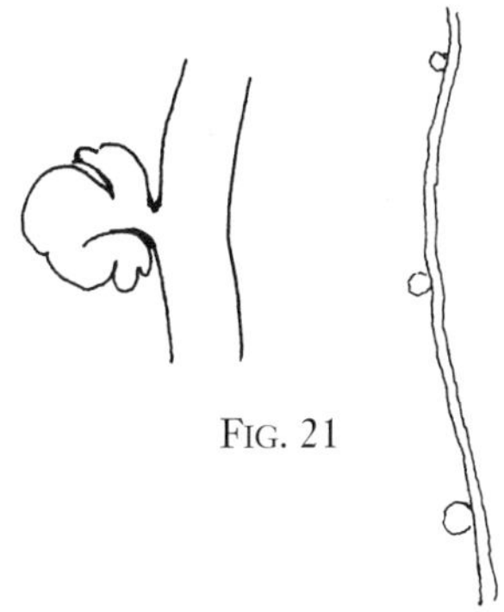

Fig. 21

D2. *POTTIA*

These are mosses in the family Pottiaceae. Only one gall-causer is known.

Pear-shaped gall at shoot tip (Fig. 22)

.... *Anguina brenani* (Goodey) Kir'yanova & Krall

Opening the galls under a microscope should reveal more or less coiled adult nematodes barely visible to the naked eye. Similar galls, apparently caused by other species of anguinid nematodes, are reported from several moss genera in mainland Europe.

ungalled shoot

gall

Fig. 22

D3. **POACEAE**

1 In roots **2**

- In leaves, florets or grains **3**

2 On *Poa annua* and other grasses and cereals; whitish galls, oval, kidney-shaped or spirally twisted (Fig. 23), usually on root-tips; internal cavity contains microscopic nematodes .... ***Subanguina radicicola*** (Greeff) Paramonov **grass root-gall nematode**

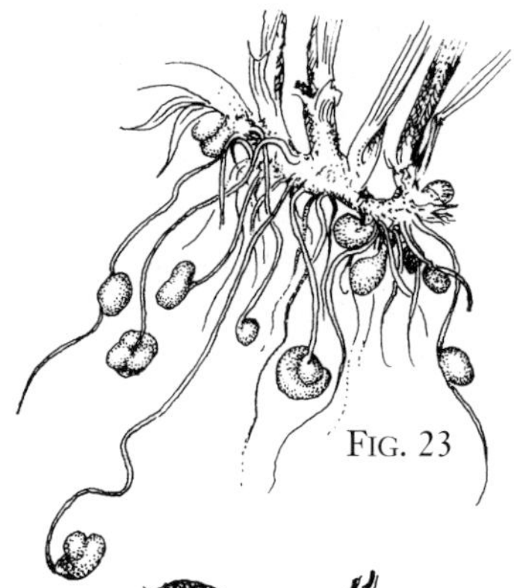

- On *Hordeum distichon*; small, spindle- or club-shaped swellings, may cause roots to form hooks or spirals (Fig. 24); contain glistening white, pear-shaped female nematodes which may be just visible to the naked eye .... ***Meloidogyne naasi*** Franklin **cereal root-knot nematode**

Also causes inconspicuous cylindrical galls on *Lolium perenne* perennial rye-grass and, rarely, galls sugar beet *Beta vulgaris* ssp. *vulgaris*.

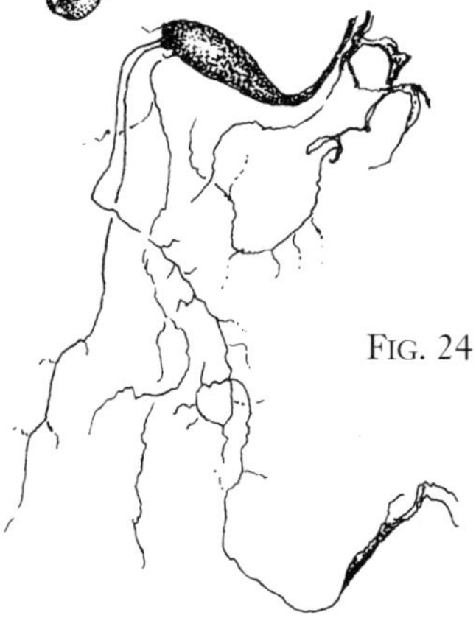

- On *Avena sativa* and possibly other cultivated cereals; small root galls with lateral root proliferation; under magnification, swollen female nematodes may be seen, usually only partially embedded in the plant tissue .... ***Meloidogyne artiella*** Franklin

3 In leaves **4**

- In florets, the galls replacing various floral parts **5**

4 On bents *Agrostis* spp.; elongate purplish galls, usually near the base of blade (Fig. 25) ...... ***Subanguina graminophila*** (T. Goodey) Chizhov **bent-grass leaf-gall nematode**

Two- or three-branched galls at the base of inflorescence branches have been reported from Russia; not known in Britain.

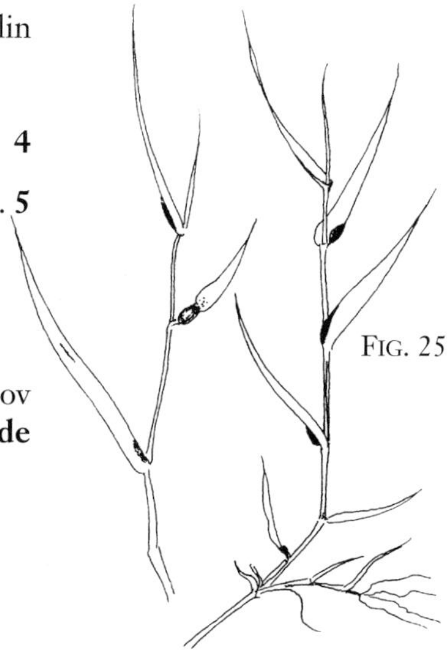

FIG. 23

FIG. 24

FIG. 25

- On fine-leaved fescues *Festuca* spp.; ± elongated purple swellings (Fig. 26); affected leaves often bent at site of gall, giving a characteristic 'knee-cap' appearance; contain one or more pairs of adult nematodes which may be just visible to the naked eye; adult worms, eggs or a mass of microscopic juveniles may be present; especially in coastal areas

.... ***Anguina graminis*** (Hardy) Filip'ev
fescue leaf-gall nematode

Fig. 26

5 On wheat, *Triticum aestivum*; rounded galls ('ear cockles') strikingly resembling seeds of corncockle *Agrostemma githago*, 2-3 mm in diameter, brown or black (Fig. 27); heavily infested ears small with abnormally spreading glumes; fresh galls may contain 40 or more pairs of adult nematodes, just visible to the naked eye, and up to 30,000 microscopic juveniles

.... ***Anguina tritici*** (Steinbuch) Chitwood
wheat gall nematode

May be confused with damage caused by *Tilletia* spp. (bunt) or *Claviceps purpurea* (ergot). Not recorded in Britain since 1956 – probably eliminated by modern seed cleaning.

- On grasses; cigar- or spindle-shaped........................... 6

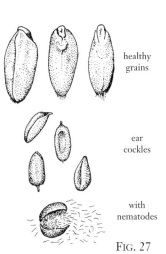

healthy grains

ear cockles

with nematodes

Fig. 27

6   Outer floral parts (glumes, lemma and palea) 3 - 5 times normal length; greenish to dark purple-brown cigar-shaped gall, 4 - 5 mm long; gall contains adult nematodes, with eggs, just visible to the naked eye and / or a mass of microscopic juveniles (the adults die soon after egg-laying):

On bents, *Agrostis* spp. (Figs 28 and 29)
.... ***Anguina agrostis*** (Steinbuch) Filip'ev
bent-grass seed-gall nematode

The effects of this nematode are so striking that affected plants have been mistakenly described as new forms or species, e.g. *Agrostis sylvatica*.

On saltmarsh grass *Puccinellia maritima*
.... ***Anguina*** sp.
saltmarsh grass seed-gall nematode

Believed to be an undescribed species (Southey *et al.*, 1990) though known since the 1930s when it was identified as *A. agrostis*.

\-   Outer floral parts of normal length **7**

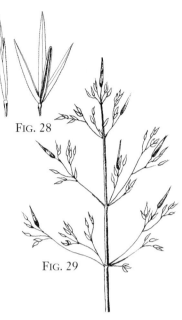

FIG. 28

FIG. 29

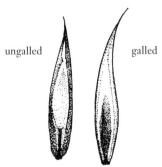

ungalled   galled

FIG. 30

7   On cock's-foot, *Dactylis glomerata*; purple or purplish, bottle-shaped gall (Fig. 30), difficult to detect in the field but found during seed testing; contains one or more adult nematodes, just visible to the naked eye, or a mass of microscopic juveniles .... ***Anguina*** sp.
cock's-foot seed-gall nematode

This species is apparently indistinguishable from *A. graminis*. Experimentally infested plants had gall-like swellings, purple pigmented, on lower parts of shoots (Fig. 31), also containing adult and juvenile nematodes.

\-   On soft-grass, *Holcus mollis*; elongate gall replacing some flower parts .... ***Anguina*** sp.
soft-grass seed-gall nematode

Probably an undescribed species; recorded near Sunningdale, Berkshire. What is probably the same species occurs in Australia on Yorkshire fog, *Holcus lanatus*, so this may be a host in Britain also.

FIG. 31

D4. *ACHILLEA*

Rounded, green gall on leaves (Fig. 32), 2-5 mm diameter, several may coalesce; each contains one or more pairs of adults or a mass of tiny juvenile worms
... **Subanguina millefolii** (Löw) Chizhov & Subbotin
yarrow leaf-gall nematode

On *A. millefolium* in Britain (also on other *Achillea* spp. and *Tanacetum* abroad).

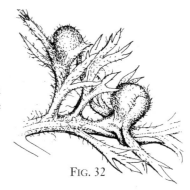

FIG. 32

D5. *BRASSICA*

Small rounded galls on roots, with lateral root proliferation; swollen female nematodes may be seen (magnification required) only partially embedded in galls; found especially on oil-seed rape *Brassica napus* ssp. *oleifera* in Britain
.... **Meloidogyne artiella** Franklin

D6. *CLEMATIS, DAUCUS* and **OTHERS**

Rounded galls in roots, 2-4 mm in diameter; associated with abnormal production of lateral roots, giving a knotted appearance to root systems; contain glistening white, pear-shaped females just visible to the naked eye............. **Meloidogyne hapla** Chitwood
northern root-knot nematode

This species occurs mainly in light soils. Its very wide host range includes vegetables, soft fruits and woody ornamentals.

D7. *FRAGARIA*

1   Small solid swellings, often curved or twisted, at the tips of lateral roots of strawberries; other parts of the roots sometimes thickened; the causers are external soil-dwelling nematodes.. **Longidorus** spp.
needle nematodes

Also found on *Rubus idaeus, Daucus carota* ssp. *sativus, Apium graveolens,* and other crop plants. *Longidorus* spp. are economically important vectors of plant viruses.

2   Bunching or fasciation on the crowns of plants ('cauliflower disease'); leaf and flower stalks stunted and thickened; leaf blades reduced or absent
.... **Aphelenchoides ritzemabosi** (Schwartz) Steiner & Buhrer
with **Corynebacterium fascians** (Tilford) Dowson

The typical 'cauliflower' effect is not produced unless both nematode and bacterium are present. It now appears to be rare.

D8. *LIGUSTRUM*

Rounded galls, 2-5 mm diameter, in roots of wild privet, *Ligustrum vulgare*
.... **Meloidogyne ardenensis** Santos
root-knot nematode

This species also recorded on *Vinca minor, Sambucus nigra, Fraxinus excelsior, Lonicera nitida, Astilbe* sp. and *Hepatica angulosa* (= *H. transsilvanica*).

D9. *LYCOPERSICON*

Rounded or irregular galls up to 20 mm or more diameter; on roots of tomato plants in heated glasshouses; mature galls contain many glistening white, pear-shaped females just visible to the naked eye .... *Meloidogyne* spp.
root-knot nematodes

Likely to be one of three tropical or sub-tropical species: *M. incognita* (Kofoid & White) Chitwood, *M. javanica* (Treub) Chitwood, *M. arenaria* (Neal) Chitwood. Recorded on many other cultivated plants in glasshouses. Note that a false root-knot nematode, *Naccobbus serendipiticus* Franklin, has been described from glasshouse tomatoes in England, causing similar root swellings.

D10. *NARCISSUS*

Small, pale yellowish swellings ('spickels') in leaves, often accompanied by growth distortion .... *Ditylenchus dipsaci* (Kühn) Filip'ev
stem nematode

On *Narcissus* spp. and daffodil cultivars. Occurs as a number of different biological races, and has been reported from more than 450 hosts. In most cases it causes generalised swellings and distortions, as in 'bloat' disease of onion, *Allium cepa*, or 'tulip root' of oats, *Avena sativa*, or rotting, for example in bulbs and tubers.

D11. *PLANTAGO*

Small, elongated, rounded or irregular swellings in plantain leaves (Fig. 33); similar to 'spickels' on *Narcissus* (above); usually cause distortion and stunting and swelling of flower stalks
.... *Ditylenchus dipsaci* (Kühn) Filip'ev
stem nematode

This description relates to galls on *P. lanceolata*. The nematode also occurs on *P. major*, *P. media* and *P. maritima*, but there is no information available about its effects on these hosts.

FIG. 33

D12. *ROSA*

Small solid swellings, often curved or twisted, at the tips of lateral roots; other parts of the roots sometimes thickened; the causers are external soil-dwelling nematodes
.... *Xiphinema diversicaudatum* (Micoletzky) Thorne
dagger nematode

On rose cultivars and other plants. This species is economically important as a vector of plant virus diseases.

Section E
Galls caused by Arthropods: Insects and Mites

E1. *ABIES*

No *Abies* species is native to Britain but several are commonly planted. Three insects, all aphids (**Hemiptera: Aphidoidea,** Fig. 34) cause gall-like distortions [these may not, however, be true galls] on silver fir, *A. alba* Mill., and other species. A rust fungus, *Melampsorella caryophyllacearum* Schroet. causes a twiggy 'witches' broom' on *A. alba* (see p. 221).

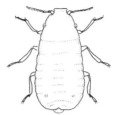

FIG. 34

The aphids affect the new shoots in May and June; they are widespread but uncommon, likely to occur wherever the host is planted.

1 Needles distorted, shortened and slightly thickened to form a 'bottle brush' (Fig. 35); contains many blackish aphids, each with a fringe of white wax, which produce copious honeydew: **Adelgidae**............*Adelges nordmannianae* (Eckstein)

2 Needles distorted, twisted and slightly swollen, attached to a stunted shoot; infested with dirty-grey aphids covered in copious fluffy white wax wool: **Adelgidae** ....*Adelges piceae* (Ratzeburg)

3 Internodes at shoot tip shortened to form a loose bunch of needles, each pale, shortened, twisted and slightly swollen (Fig. 36); small, pale yellowish-green aphids, covered in fluffy white wax, live between the needles: **Aphididae: Mindarinae**......................*Mindarus abietinus* Koch

FIG. 35

FIG. 36

E2. *ACER*

Includes galls on native field or hedge maple, *Acer campestre* L., and introduced and naturalised sycamore, *A. pseudoplatanus* L. Introduced Norway maple, *A. platanoides*, is quite common but rarely galled in Britain. Silver maple *A. saccharinum* L., introduced from N. America, is increasingly being planted.

1   Gall on twig, usually on one-year wood; a warty, irregular swelling up to 3 x 5 mm (Fig. 37); contains mites (Fig. 38); rare, on *A. campestre*, *A. platanoides*: **Acari: Eriophyoidea**
.... *Aceria heteronyx* (Nalepa)
(= Eriophyes)

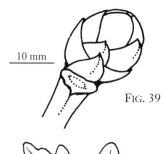

5 mm

Fig. 37

\-   Gall a big bud about 10 mm wide (Fig. 39); contains mites (Fig. 38); galled bud does not open but falls in early summer; on *A. pseudoplatanus*: **Acari: Eriophyoidea**
.... *Aceria vermicularis* (Nalepa)
Probably new to Britain – first recorded April 1997 in London.

\-   Gall in petiole or leaf blade 2

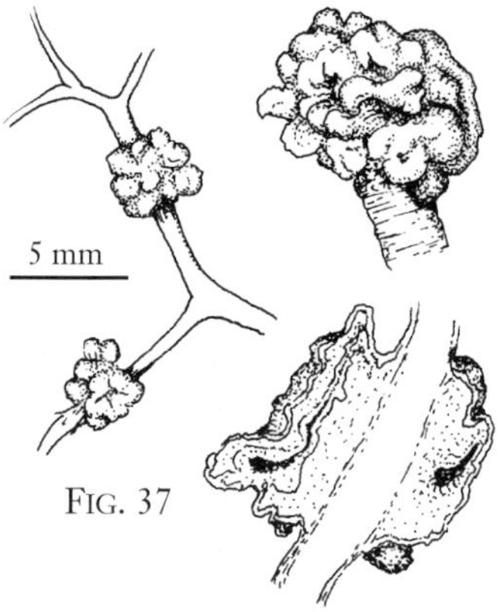

0.1 mm

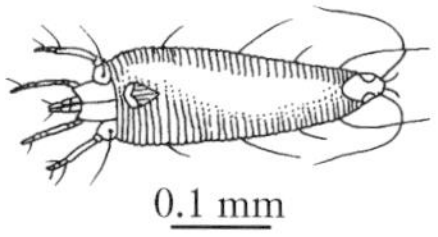

Fig. 38

2   Spindle-shaped, 5-10 x 2.5 mm, in petiole or main veins (Fig. 40); often purplish; single chamber with white larva in late spring and early summer; on *A. campestre*; uncommon: **Diptera: Cecidomyiidae**
.... *Atrichosema aceris* Kieffer

\-   In leaf blade or on veins 3

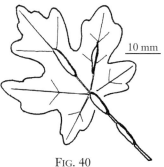

10 mm

Fig. 39

3   Leaf folded, wrinkled, buckled or pleated along vein or edge, or involving much of leaf; contains several larvae in late spring and early summer; on *A. campestre* and *A. pseudoplatanus*: **Diptera: Cecidomyiidae** 4

\-   A shallow depression, or blister, pustule or pouch, or erineum 5

10 mm

Fig. 40

4   Leaf wrinkled, usually folded upwards along the main veins which are thickened and wavy (Fig. 41) and without hairs; sometimes leaf margin rolled upwards and reddened; white, pink or reddish larvae within the folds on upper side; galled part often black after larvae leave
.... ***Dasineura irregularis*** (Bremi)
(= *acercrispans*)

The form on *A. campestre* may be a distinct species, *D. rubella* (Kieffer).

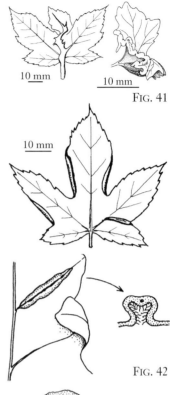

10 mm   10 mm

FIG. 41

10 mm

\-   Leaf margin folded downwards, or a narrow, slightly thickened pleat or groove alongside or between veins (Fig. 42); opening is a furrow on underside lined with white hairs; gall often blood-red; contains white larvae which can jump
.... ***Contarinia acerplicans*** (Kieffer)

A second generation may occur in July and August.

5   Gall a depression or hairless blister; larva present May - June: **Diptera: Cecidomyiidae** **6**

\-   An erineum, or pustule or pouch (Fig. 43) with hairs; contains mites (Fig. 38): **Acari: Eriophyoidea** **7**

FIG. 42

6   Depression on under side, 1 mm across and deep, often surrounded by a pale zone 5 - 7 mm in diameter; indistinct discoloured bulge on upper surface; contains a white to yellowish larva; normally on *A. pseudoplatanus*
.... ***Drisina glutinosa*** Giard
(= *Massalongia aceris*)

A similar species, *Harrisomyia vitrina* (Kieffer), may be present in Britain but has not been confirmed. For a detailed study of both species, see Skuhravá & Skuhravý 1986.

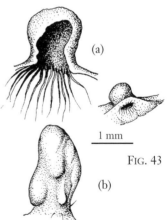

(a)

1 mm

FIG. 43

(b)

\-   Pale blister 4-8 mm across in leaf blade or over veins, visible on both sides of leaf, with central exit hole on underside (Fig. 44); gall turns brown when empty; on *A. campestre*
.... ***Dasineura tympani*** (Kieffer)

7   An erineum, usually on underside, with or without a bulge on opposite side **8**

\-   A pustule or pouch, usually on upperside with hairy opening below **9**

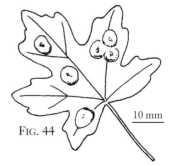

10 mm

FIG. 44

8 On *A. pseudoplatanus*; white or cream when fresh (pink on purple-leaved varities), later brown; upward bulge usually distinct and yellowish
.... ***Aceria pseudoplatani*** (Corti)

(= *Eriophyes*)

- On *A. campestre*; may cover all of the underside; first white, then red and finally brown; often without a discoloured upward bulge .... ***Aceria eriobius*** (Nalepa)

(= *Eriophyes*)

Other mites may cause erinea on *A. pseudoplatanus* and *A. campestre*. There are many probable synonyms and their taxonomy needs to be sorted out.

9 On *A. saccharinum*; gall round or elongate with a short, slender neck, 1.5-5 mm high, on veins or blade; surface wrinkled, glossy, yellowish green at first, becoming dark red and black; opening with single-celled hairs; galls may be very numerous
.... ***Vasates quadripedes*** Shimer

A new British record found in London (Wurzell, 2002); the mite and gall have been verified by Ostojá-Starzewski.

- On *A. campestre* or *A. pseudoplatanus* **10**

10 On *A. campestre*; gall rounded 2-4 mm across, with hard walls, often in angle between veins (Fig. 45); inner surface with many-celled hairs; not as numerous as the following species
.... ***Aceria macrochelus*** (Nalepa)

(= *Eriophyes*)

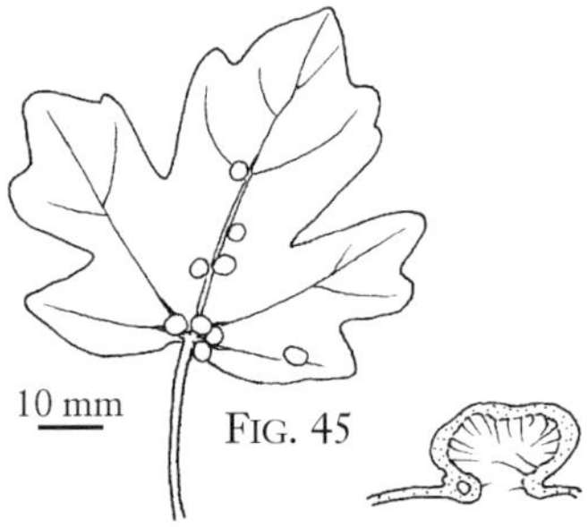

- On *A. pseudoplatanus* or *A. campestre*; gall rounded or elongated 0.5-6 mm high, with soft fleshy walls, usually on leaf blade; opening with single-celled hairs; galls often very numerous; bright red, especially in sunlight **11**

10 mm

Fig. 45

11 Less than 3 mm high with rounded apex (Fig. 46):

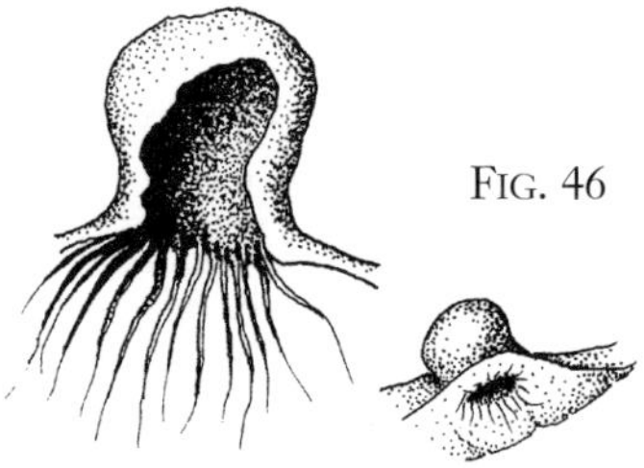

On *A. pseudoplatanus* ...... ***Aceria cephaloneus*** (Nalepa)

(= *Artacris* = *Aculodes*)

On *A. campestre* (Plate 1.9)
.... ***Aceria aceriscampestris*** (Nalepa)

(= *Artacris* = *Aculodes*)

- Up to 6 mm high, with pointed apex (Fig. 47); probably restricted to *A. pseudoplatanus*
.... ***Aceria macrorhynchus*** (Nalepa)

(= *Artacris* = *Aculodes*)

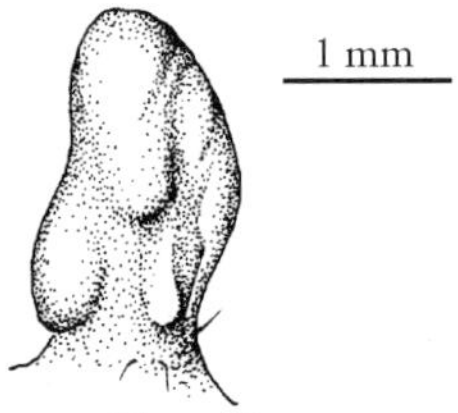

The size and shape of these galls varies and intermediates are common; there may be just one species on sycamore. Other mites have been recorded as causing pouch galls on *Acer*; it is uncertain whether or not they are distinct species.

Fig. 46

1 mm

Fig. 47

E3. *ACHILLEA*

There are two native species, yarrow, *A. millefolium* L. and sneezewort, *A. ptarmica* L.; some gall causers are restricted to one or the other (see below). Glossy nodules on the leaves, without distinct chambers, may be caused by nematodes (see p. 269).

1 Gall in stem, root or rhizome, of *A. millefolium* **2**

- Gall in bud, leaf or flower head **4**

2 Pit gall in stem, with ± thickened rim; often clustered, causing thickening and distortion of stem; contains a flat scale insect: **Hemiptera: Asterolecanidae**........ ***Planchonia arabidis*** (Signoret)
(= *Asterolecanium fimbriatum*)

Fɪɢ. 48

- Gall in base of stem, root or rhizome; contains one chamber with thick fleshy walls and one white larva (Fig. 48) in summer/winter, or puparium in spring/early summer: **Diptera: Tephritidae**
.... **3**

Ovoid galls of the cecid *Rhopalomyia millefolii* may occur in axillary buds at base of stem near the ground, see couplet 4.

3 Rounded gall, 5-8 mm across; S. England, rare
.... ***Oxyna flavipennis*** (Loew)

- Spindle-shaped gall, up to 12 x 2 mm; widespread
.... ***Dithryca guttularis*** (Meigen)
For certain identification, rear the adult and identify in White (1988).

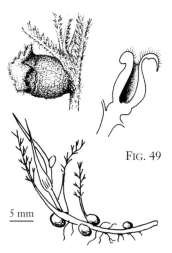

Fɪɢ. 49

5 mm

4 Ovoid gall 6-10 mm long; hairy lobes around opening when mature (Fig. 49); usually in bud in leaf axil, sometimes in florets, on leaf or in bud at base of stem; shiny, pale green at first, later tough and brown; contains one yellow larva (Fig. 50); usually on *A. millefolium*: **Diptera: Cecidomyiidae**
.... ***Rhopalomyia millefolii*** (Loew)

- Gall in leaf or flower head, not as above **5**

5 In leaf: petiole, midrib or blade; on *A. millefolium* only **6**

- In flower head: bract, receptacle or achene; or several heads may be affected; gall contains one larva (Fig. 50) or pupa **7**

Fɪɢ. 50

6 Slender spindle-shaped swelling in petiole or midrib, green or reddish; contains one red or yellow larva (Fig. 51); often several galls in a leaf: **Diptera: Cecidomyiidae**

.... ***Lasioptera francoisi*** (Kieffer)

(= *niveocincta*, *Dasineura francoisi*)

This synonymy may not be correct.

FIG. 51

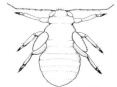

- Small depression on underside of leaf blade, containing a psyllid nymph (Fig. 52) in May and June, corresponding bulge above: **Hemiptera: Psylloidea** .... ***Craspedolepta nervosa*** (Förster)

FIG. 52

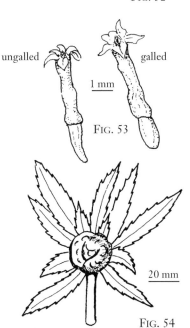

ungalled   galled

1 mm

FIG. 53

READ THREE ALTERNATIVES

7 Achene swollen to about twice normal size (Fig. 53), often several in a head; reddish-yellow larva in summer, or pupa later; usually on *A. millefolium*: **Diptera: Cecidomyiidae**

.... ***Ozirhincus millefolii*** (Wachtl)

(= *Clinorrhyncha*)

- Base of bract swollen, often several in a head; larva white when young, orange when full-grown; on *A. ptarmica* only: **Diptera: Cecidomyiidae**

.... ***Rhopalomyia palearum*** (Kieffer)

(= *Misospatha palearum*)

- Flower head enlarged, often several adjacent heads affected **8**

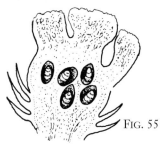

20 mm

FIG. 54

READ FOUR ALTERNATIVES

8 Flower head transformed into an irregular spongy multi-chambered gall (Fig. 54), very obvious if several adjacent heads affected; each chamber contains a white larva (Figs 51, 55); usually on *A. ptarmica*: **Diptera: Cecidomyiidae**

.... ***Rhopalomyia ptarmicae*** (Vallot)

- Head rounded or laterally compressed, may not open; often several affected heads bunched together; pedicels shortened and thickened; contains green and black aphids (Fig. 56) which exude wax; on both *Achillea* spp.: **Hemiptera: Aphididae** ...... ***Macrosiphoniella millefolii*** (De Geer)

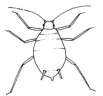

FIG. 55

FIG. 56

- Head deformed and discoloured, all flower parts thickened and misshapen; contains mites (Fig. 57); on *A. millefolium* only; rare (not recorded since 1928): **Acari: Eriophyoidea**....... *Aceria kiefferi* Nalepa
  (= *Eriophyes*)

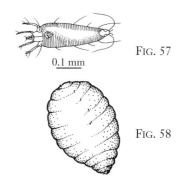

0.1 mm

FIG. 57

FIG. 58

- Receptacle enlarged and flower head deformed, with leaves bunched into a rosette beneath it; contains a chamber with one white larva (Fig. 58) or puparium; on *A. ptarmica* only; Scotland, rare: **Diptera: Tephritidae**
  .... *Campiglossa argyrocephala* (Loew)

AEGOPODIUM see APIACEAE

E4. *AESCULUS*

The introduced horse-chestnut, *A. hippocastanum* L., and red horse-chestnut, *A. carnea* J. Zeyh., are galled by one species of mite (**Acari: Eriophyoidea**).

Small tuft of hairs, white at first, later red-brown, in angle of veins on underside of leaflet, usually with distinct glossy bulge, above (Fig. 59); mites (Fig. 57) live amongst hairs; July - October, common .... *Aculus hippocastani* (Fockeu)
(= *Aceria* = *Vasates*)

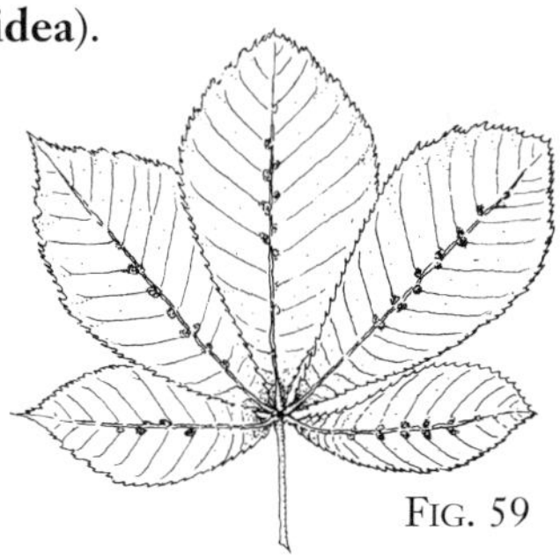

FIG. 59

AETHUSA see APIACEAE

E5. *AJUGA*

Two galls are found on bugle, *Ajuga reptans* L.

1 Terminal leaves, and the flowers in their axils, swollen and distorted, bunched together, densely covered with white hairs; leaves with rolled margins, often purplish or reddish; the whole structure variable in size; contains mites (Fig. 57); June - September, rare: **Acari: Eriophyoidea**
   .... *Aceria ajugae* (Nalepa)
   (= *Eriophyes*)

2 Leaf distorted, thickened, rolled upwards, not abnormally hairy (Fig. 60); usually lower leaves affected; contains dirty green aphids (Fig. 56), 1.4 - 2 mm long: **Hemiptera: Aphididae**
   .... *Myzus ajugae* Schouteden

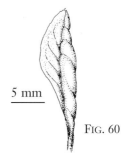

5 mm

FIG. 60

E6. *ALCHEMILLA*

A psyllid gall (**Hemiptera: Psylloidea**) is recorded on lady's-mantle, *Alchemilla vulgaris* L. (this is an aggregate name, which refers to 13 species, see Stace 1997). A gall caused by the rust fungus *Trachyspora intrusa* (Grev.) Arth., on leaves, was described on p. 222.

Leaf blade crumpled, coloured yellowish or reddish; several nymphs live on underside; uncommon: .... ***Trioza acutipennis*** (Zetterstedt)
This may not be a true gall.   (= *femoralis*)

ALLIARIA see BRASSICACEAE

E7. *ALNUS*

Includes galls on native alder, *Alnus glutinosa* (L.) Gaertn. Introduced species are probably rarely galled and are not included due to lack of knowledge. Root nodules caused by bacteria, *Frankia* sp., are mentioned on p. 219 whilst leaves and female catkins galled by fungi, *Taphrina* spp., are keyed on p. 223.

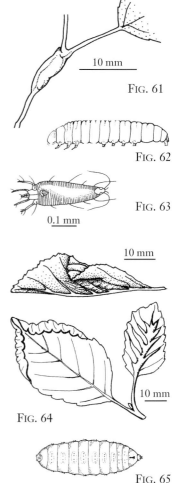

FIG. 61

FIG. 62

FIG. 63

FIG. 64

FIG. 65

1   Inconspicuous swelling up to 10 mm long in twig at base of petiole (Fig. 61); contains a caterpillar (Fig. 62) July - Aug.; common and widespread: **Lepidoptera: Tortricidae**
.... ***Epinotia tetraquetrana*** (Haworth)

-    Gall on leaf **2**

2.   Midrib or main veins thickened; gall without hairs; all or part of leaf may be folded upwards **3**

-    Gall a pouch or erineum with hairs and mites (Fig. 63), on leaf blade or in vein angles; common and widespread: **Acari: Eriophyoidea** **4**

3   Inconspicuous swelling of midrib and lateral vein(s) to about twice normal size, several cms. long, often associated with a blotch mine in blade; contains a caterpillar (Fig. 62) in summer: **Lepidoptera: Incurvariidae**
.... ***Heliozella resplendella*** (Stainton)

-    Leaf margins curled upwards, or whole young leaf puckered and folded upwards (Fig. 64); green at first, later red-brown; leaf often dies early; midrib and base of lateral veins thickened; contains several white or reddish larvae (Fig. 65) in late spring and early summer; uncommon: **Diptera: Cecidomyiidae**
.... ***Dasineura tortilis*** (Bremi)
(= *alni*)

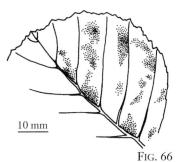

10 mm

FIG. 66

4 Erineum on lower surface (Fig. 66), slight pale-coloured bulge on upperside; hairs as in Fig. 67, white or yellowish at first, later rust-brown .... ***Acalitus brevitarsus*** (Fockeu) (= *Eriophyes*)

Erinea with hairs different from those in Fig. 67 are caused by other mite species.

FIG. 67

- Rounded pouch lined with hairs, on upper surface with opening below, 1-3 mm high and wide **5**

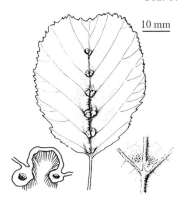

10 mm

5 In vein angles, with wide hairy opening below (Fig. 68); yellowish, later brown .... ***Eriophyes inangulis*** (Nalepa) (= *axillare*)

- Scattered over blade, often numerous, narrow opening below (Fig. 69); shiny, yellow-green, later red, purplish or brown .... ***Eriophyes laevis*** (Nalepa) (= *Phytopus*)

FIG. 68

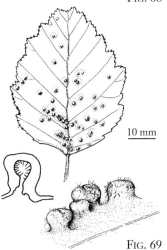

10 mm

FIG. 69

AMMOPHILA see POACEAE

E8. *ANDROMEDA*

One gall (**Acari: Eriophoyidea**) is recorded from bog-rosemary, *Andromeda polifolia* L.

Leaf margin thickened and rolled downwards; contains mites (Fig. 70)
.... *Cecidophyopsis rübsaameni* Nalepa
(= *Eriophyes*)

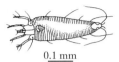

0.1 mm   FIG. 70

ANGELICA see APIACEAE

E9. *ANTHEMIS, MATRICARIA, TRIPLEUROSPERMUM*

These genera are grouped together because they share gall causers (although the complete host range is not known for certain). In Britain, the usual hosts are stinking chamomile (= stinking mayweed), *Anthemis cotula* L., and sea (or scentless) mayweed, *Tripleurospermum maritimum* (L.) Koch; other host species are recorded in mainland Europe.

Three gall causing species are known, all uncommon or rare. They are found in the flower heads and are not obvious from the outside. The white maggot of *Trupanea stellata* (Fuessly) (Diptera: Tephritidae) burrows through the flower head and may distort it, and aphids may deform the leaves, causing them to be bunched together and curled (e.g. the polyphagous *Brachycaudus helichrysi* (Kaltenbach)). These distortions are not regarded as true galls.

1   Achene swollen and base of corolla enlarged, often
    several affected in one flower head; each contains
    a yellow larva (Fig. 71): **Diptera: Cecidomyiidae**
    .... *Ozirhincus* sp.

    Host associations of *Ozirhincus* are poorly understood;
    identification to species requires specialist help.

FIG. 71

2   Floret transformed into a hard, barrel-shaped gall,
    3 mm tall and firmly attached to, or embedded in,
    the receptacle; often several in a flower head;
    contains a larva (Fig. 71): **Diptera: Cecidomyiidae**
    .... *Rhopalomyia syngenesiae* (Loew)

3   Base of flower head enlarged and hard, broader and
    flatter than normal; contains a white larva (Fig. 72);
    local: **Coleoptera: Brentidae: Apioninae**
    .... *Omphalapion sorbi* (F.)
    (= *laevigatum*)

    Omphalapion hookeri (Kirby), with larvae also in flower heads, is
    much commoner in Wales and S. England as far north as
    Yorkshire; whether it also causes gall tissue is unknown.

FIG. 72

ANTHRISCUS see APIACEAE

E10. **APIACEAE** (= UMBELLIFERAE)

This family is dealt with in one key both because some gall causers attack several genera, and others, although specific to a particular genus or species, cause similar types of galls on the different plants. Only members of the sub-family **Apioideae** are galled in Britain, the following species being affected (page numbers in brackets cross-refer to the fungus key):

Aegopodium podagraria L., ground-elder (p. 222)

Aethusa cynapium L., fool's parsley

Angelica sylvestris L., wild angelica (p. 224), *A. archangelica* L. garden angelica

Anthriscus sylvestris (L.) Hoffm., cow parsley (p. 224)

Carum spp., caraways

Crithmum maritimum L., rock samphire

Daucus carota L., wild carrot

Foeniculum vulgare Mill., fennel

Heracleum sphondylium L., hogweed (p. 238)

Oenanthe spp., water-dropworts (p. 243)

Pastinaca sativa L., parsnip

Peucedanum spp., hog's fennels

Petroselinum spp., parsleys

Pimpinella saxifraga L., burnet-saxifrage (p. 245)

P. major (L.) Huds., greater burnet-saxifrage (p. 245)

Silaum silaus (L.) Schinz & Thell., pepper-saxifrage (p. 224 under *Angelica*)

1   Gall in leaf or leaf sheaths; several adjacent leaves or a cluster at shoot tip may be affected **2**

-    Gall distorting whole inflorescence, or in an individual flower, fruit or flower stalk **6**

READ THREE ALTERNATIVES

2   Leaf sheaths enlarged and swollen, forming a pointed spindle-shaped gall (Fig. 73); upper surface hairless, reddened; leaf blades and flower buds remain undeveloped inside sheaths; contains orange-red larvae (Fig. 71); probably only on *Pimpinella saxifraga* in Britain; N. England and Scotland: **Diptera: Cecidomyiidae**
.... *Jaapiella hedickei* Rübsaamen

-    Upward bulge in leaf blade, up to 6 mm across, with corresponding depression beneath; often several, which may merge together, in a leaf **3**

-    Leaf folded, curled or crumpled, often blade or veins thickened, sometimes totally distorted; often several adjacent or cluster at shoot tip affected **4**

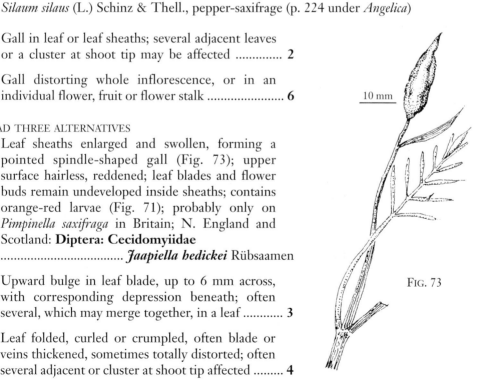

10 mm

FIG. 73

3   Depression contains egg or nymph: **Hemiptera: Psylloidea** (there are two alternatives):

On *Aegopodium podagraria* (Fig. 74); bulges same colour as leaf or purplish; rare
.... ***Trioza flavipennis*** Förster

FIG. 74

On *Crithmum maritimum*; coasts of S. England and Wales, uncommon
.... ***Trioza crithmi*** Löw

Trioza apicalis (couplet 4) may cause similar depressions on *Daucus carota* and, perhaps, other Apioideae.

FIG. 75

-   Depression contains a white, jumping larva (Fig. 75), or several larvae if bulges have merged; bulges yellowish; on *Heracleum sphondylium*: **Diptera: Cecidomyiidae**
.... ***Contarinia heraclei*** (Rübsaamen)

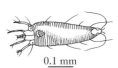

0.1 mm

FIG. 76

READ THREE ALTERNATIVES

4   Contains mites (Fig. 76); leaves often hairy and totally deformed (Fig. 77); on *Pimpinella*: **Acari: Eriophyoidea**
.... ***Aceria peucedani*** (Canestrini)
(= *Eriophyes*)

Also may gall inflorescence and flowers, couplet 6.

FIG. 77

-   Contains nymphs; leaves not hairy, may be yellowish; affects one leaf or several at shoot tip (Fig. 78); mainly on *Angelica, Anthriscus, Daucus* and *Pastinaca*; S. England, uncommon: **Hemiptera: Psylloidea**........................... ***Trioza apicalis*** Förster

-   Contains larvae; leaf, or several at shoot tip, folded upwards, with larvae in the folds: **Diptera: Cecidomyiidae** **5**

Aphids (Fig. 79) may distort, fold or roll leaves, particularly young leaves. Usually there is no associated thickening; these are not regarded as true galls.

FIG. 78

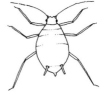

FIG. 79

5 On *Heracleum sphondylium* (Fig. 80), *Pastinaca sativa*; larvae white; leaf tissues blacken along folds
.... ***Macrolabis heraclei*** (Kaltenbach)
(= *corrugans*)

\- On *Silaum silaus*; larvae yellow, with reddened ends when full-grown
.... ***Jaapiella dittrichi*** (Rübsaamen)

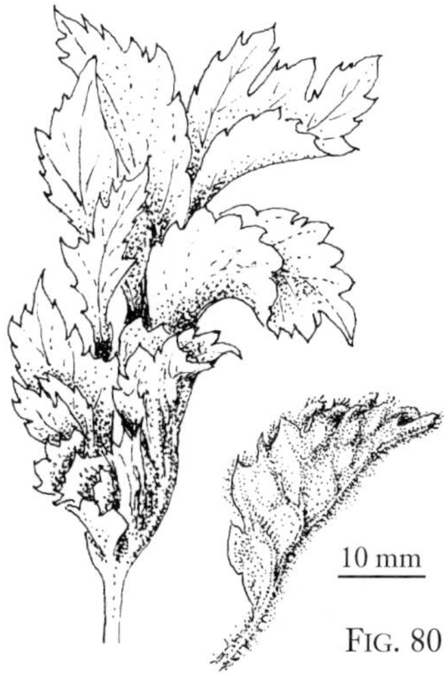

10 mm

FIG. 80

6 Inflorescence transformed; individual flowers elongated, thickened and greened (phyllanthy) (Fig. 81), with shortened stalks; contains mites (Fig. 76); on *Pimpinella*: **Acari: Eriophyoidea**
.... ***Aceria peucedani*** (Canestrini)
Also may gall leaves, couplet 4.   (= *Eriophyes*)

\- In individual flower, fruit or in flower stalk; contains one or more larvae or pupae: **Diptera: Cecidomyiidae** **7**

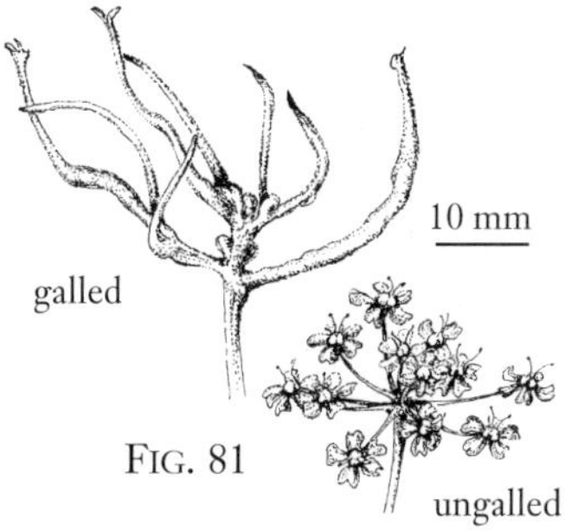

galled

10 mm

FIG. 81

ungalled

READ THREE ALTERNATIVES
7 Rounded swelling in flower stalk at base of primary or secondary umbel (Fig. 82), 2-4 mm across; chamber inside lined with fungal mycelium, larva (Fig. 83) orange-red; normally on *Daucus carota*, occasionally on *Pimpinella* and other species............................ ***Lasioptera carophila*** F. Löw

\- Flower ± swollen, remaining closed; often several affected in an umbel **8**

\- Fruit swollen, up to 5 mm across, may protrude above ungalled fruits; often several affected in an umbel; each contains one larva **11**

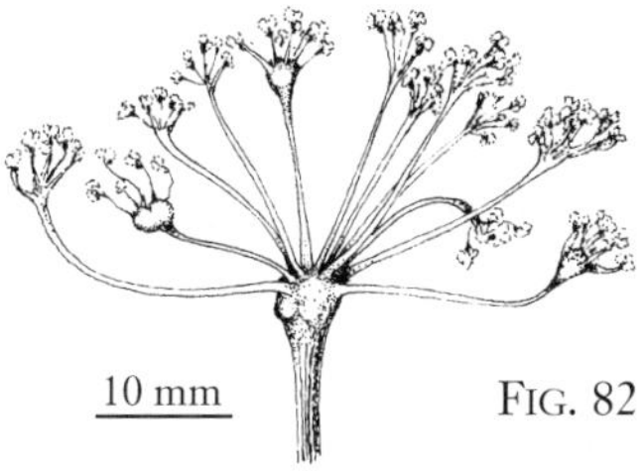

10 mm

FIG. 82

8 On *Angelica* or *Heracleum* **9**

\- On *Pimpinella*; larvae can jump **10**

FIG. 83

9 On *Angelica sylvestris* (Fig. 84); larva (Fig. 85) yellow-orange, non-jumping; N. England and Scotland .... ***Dasineura angelicae*** (Rübsaamen)

- On *Heracleum sphondylium* (Fig. 86); larvae (Fig. 87) white or pale yellow, can jump .... ***Contarinia nicolayi*** (Rübsaamen)

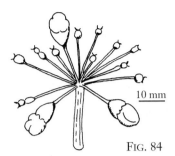

10 mm

FIG. 84

10 On *P. saxifraga*; larva lemon-yellow .... ***Diodaulus traili*** (Kieffer)

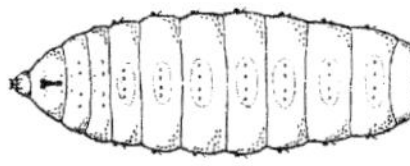

FIG. 85

- Normally on *P. major*; larva (Fig. 87) deep orange .... ***Contarinia umbellatarum*** Rübsaamen

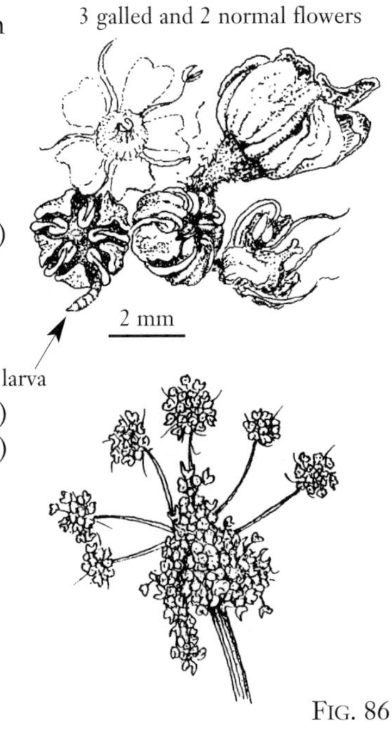

3 galled and 2 normal flowers

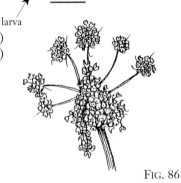

11 On *Pastinaca sativa*; larva (Fig. 87) yellow or orange-yellow, can jump .... ***Contarinia pastinaceae*** (Rübsaamen)

- Commonest on *Daucus* in Britain (Fig. 88, Plate 4.1), found occasionally on other Apioideae, non-jumping orange larva; late summer - autumn .... ***Kiefferia pericarpiicola*** (Bremi) (= *pimpinellae*)

larva

2 mm

FIG. 86

FIG. 87

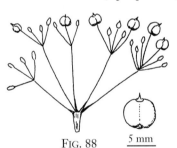

FIG. 88   5 mm

ARABIDOPSIS see BRASSICACEAE

ARABIS see BRASSICACEAE

E11. *ARCTIUM*

There are three native burdocks in Britain, greater burdock, *A. lappa* L., wood burdock, *A. nemorosum* Lej. and lesser burdock, *A. minus* (Hill) Bernh. Three species of gall causers are known: the first two are widespread and common especially in lesser burdock; the third is rare in burdocks but more common in thistles.

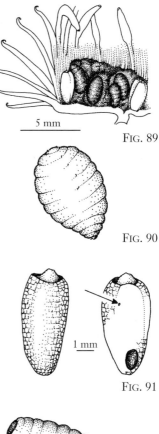

1   Receptacle hollowed out, florets and immature achenes eaten, replaced by blackened callous tissue and debris (Fig. 89); 1 - 6 larvae (Fig. 90) July - September, black puparia October - November: **Diptera: Tephritidae**
.... ***Tephritis bardanae*** (Schrank)

5 mm

Fig. 89

Fig. 90

2   Mature achene slightly swollen, with tiny larval entrance hole (arrowed) in upper third, and larger hole at base blocked with debris (Fig. 91); contains a larva (Fig. 92) August - May, or pale brown puparium May - June (in old head): **Diptera: Tephritidae**
.... ***Terellia   tussilaginis*** (F.)
(= *Cerajocera*)

Caterpillars are commonly found in flowerheads; they are not gall causers.

1 mm

Fig. 91

3   Gall in root or root collar; spindle-shaped, about 5 x 1 cm (Fig. 93), containing a larva (Fig. 94) or pupa (as in Fig. 93): **Coleoptera: Curculionidae**
.... ***Cleonis pigra*** (Scopoli)
(= *Cleonus*)

For change of genus, see Morris & Booth (1997). *C. pigra* is more usually found in *Cirsium arvense*.

Fig. 92

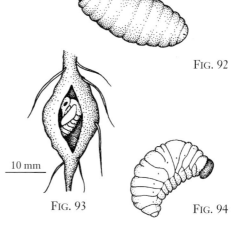

10 mm

Fig. 93

Fig. 94

E12. *ARCTOSTAPHYLOS*

One gall (**Acari: Eriophyoidea**) is recorded from bearberry, *A. uva-ursi* (L.) Sprengel.

Bud enlarged and deformed, contains mites (Fig. 95) .... *Aceria jaapi* (Nalepa)
(= *Eriophyes*)

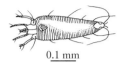

0.1 mm

FIG. 95

E13. *ARTEMISIA*

Most gall inducers on this genus are host specific. Mugwort, *A. vulgaris* L. is the species most commonly galled in Britain, with wormwood, *A. absinthium* L., and field wormwood, *A. campestris* L., occasionally recorded as hosts.

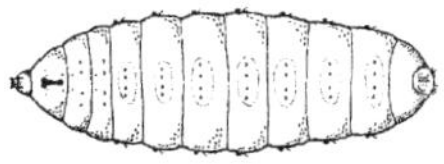

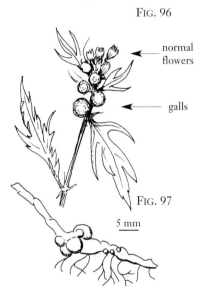

FIG. 96

normal flowers

galls

FIG. 97

5 mm

1   Flower head slightly enlarged and lengthened, reddened; between the florets inside is an ovoid translucent gall containing a larva (Fig. 96); on *A. vulgaris*, rare: **Diptera: Cecidomyiidae**
.... *Rhopalomyia florum* (Kieffer)

-   Gall in stem, leaf or leaf bud 2

2   In stem, or bud in leaf axil 3

-   In leaf blade or vein 4

3   Soft, globular gall, 2-6 mm across, in bud at base of stem or in leaf axil higher up, often several together (Fig. 97); light green to reddish; each contains an orange larva (Fig. 96); on *A. vulgaris*; local: **Diptera: Cecidomyiidae**
.... *Rhopalomyia baccarum* (Wachtl) (= *Misospatha*)

-   Swelling, open at top, in upper half of stem, which aborts above the gall (Fig. 98); contains a white larva (Fig. 99) or brown puparium; on *A. vulgaris* and *A. absinthium*; SE. England and E. Anglia: **Diptera: Tephritidae**
.... *Paroxyna misella* (Loew)

The first generation induces galls in stems in May - June; larvae of the second feed in flower heads without causing galls. A second tephritid *Oxyna parietina* (L.) bores down stems of *A. vulgaris*, causing a swelling about 15 mm long if several larvae are involved; this is probably an accumulation of callous tissue and not a true gall. To ensure correct identification, rear the adult and identify in White (1988).

FIG. 98

4 Part or all of blade thickened and curled loosely downwards, sometimes several leaves at tip of shoot affected and bunched together (Fig. 100); thickened parts often purple or reddish; aphids (Fig. 101) present on underside; on *A. vulgaris*: **Hemiptera: Aphididae**

.... ***Cryptosiphum artemisiae*** Buckton

- A pimple or pustule, usually several on a leaf **5**

Fig. 99

5 Ovoid or elongate pimples, without hairs, about 2 mm tall, on veins on upper surface; yellowish or reddish; opening at top when mature; each contains a larva (Fig. 96) or pupa; on *A. vulgaris*: **Diptera: Cecidomyiidae**

.... ***Rhopalomyia foliorum*** (Loew)

- Rounded pimples or pustules, up to 2 mm high, sometimes with hairs; contain mites (Fig. 95): **Acari: Eriophyoidea** **6**

Fig. 100

6 Pimples 1 - 2 mm high on upper surface (Fig. 102), often red, sometimes stalked and covered with white hairs; opening below ringed with hairs; usually on *A. vulgaris*

.... ***Aceria artemisiae*** (Canestrini)

Galls may occur on other plant parts also. (= *Eriophyes*)

- Pustules < 1mm high, usually on edge of leaf, not hairy; green, later brown; on *A. vulgaris, A. absinthium* .... ***Phyllocoptes tenuirostris*** (Nalepa)

(= *Eriophyes*)

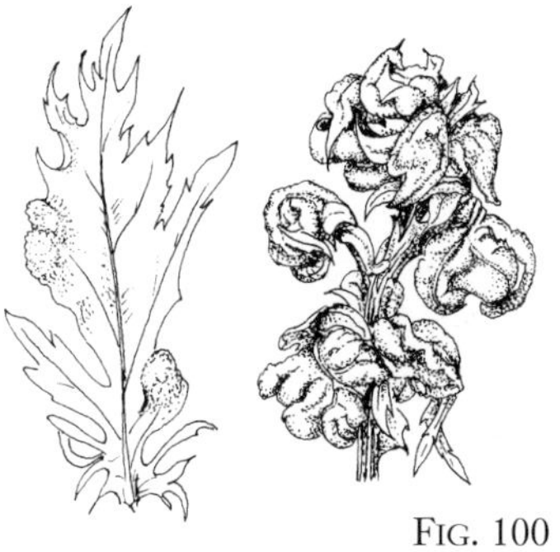

Fig. 101

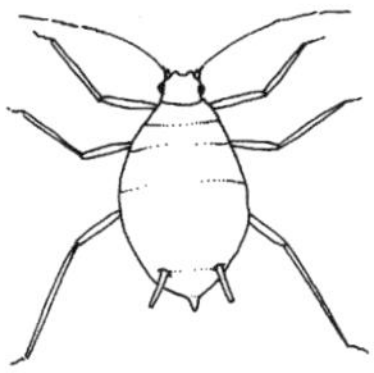

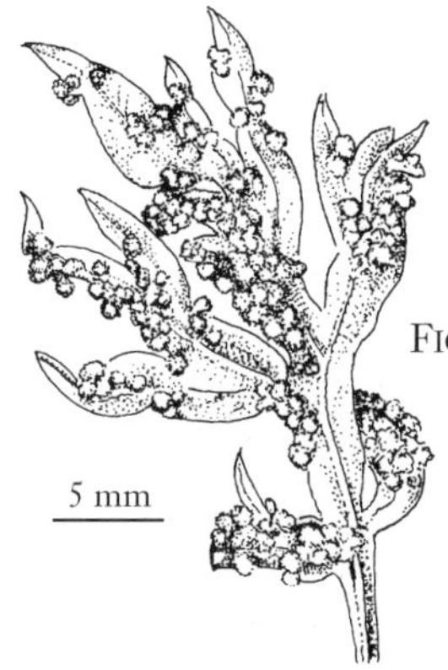

Fig. 102

5 mm

ASPERULA see *GALIUM*

E14. *ASTER*

There are two native species, sea aster, *A. tripolium* L., and goldilocks aster, *A. linosyris* (L.) Bernh. Two gall causers are known on these, one on each plant. The confused Michaelmas daisy, *A. novi-belgii* L. (a common garden plant) is often galled by a third species.

1 Flower head slightly swollen, lop-sided, producing a few ray florets or remaining closed; contains one or more white larvae (Fig. 99) or brown puparia; on *A. tripolium*; coasts of England, Wales and Ireland: **Diptera: Tephritidae**

.... ***Paroxyna plantaginis*** (Haliday)

2   Young leaves at shoot tip thickened, rolled and
    bunched together, sometimes forming a dense
    little bush; contain mites (Fig. 103); on *A. linosyris*;
    S. England, rare: **Acari: Eriophyoidea**
    .... *Aceria linosyrinus* (Nalepa)
                                           (= *Eriophyes*)

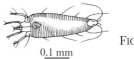

FIG. 103

0.1 mm

3   Florets forming a compact rosette of small green leaves (phyllanthy); contains mites
    with four pairs of legs; on *A. novi-belgii*: **Acari: Tasrsonemidae**
    .... *Phytonemus pallidas* (Banks)
    A polyphagous pest of many glasshouse plants and strawberries; present in Britain since the 1960s.

E15. *ASTRAGALUS*

Two cecid galls (**Diptera: Cecidomyiidae**) are known from this genus, one each on purple
milk-vetch, *A. danicus* Retz., and wild liquorice, *A. glycyphyllos* L.; each contains several
larvae (Fig. 104). Other galls remain unidentified; the cecids recorded from this genus are
in need of revision (Dauphin & Aniotsbehère 1993, 1997).

1   Leaflet swollen; larvae orange-yellow; on
    A. danicus .... *Dasineura rossi* Rübsaamen

2   Leaflet swollen and pod-like; larvae pink; on *A.
    glycyphyllos* .... *Dasineura glyciphylli* Rübsaamen

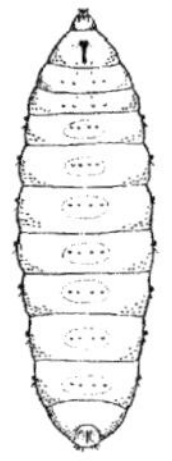

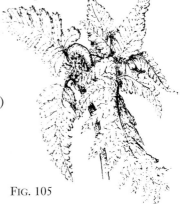

FIG. 104

E16. *ATHYRIUM* and *DRYOPTERIS*

These are the only fern genera with galls, apart from *Pteridium* (Key E.129, p. 396). Two galls
are recorded from lady-fern, *A. filix-femina* (L.) Roth, male-fern, *D. filix-mas* (L.) Schott,
broad buckler-fern, *D. dilatata* (Hoffm.) A.Gray and narrow buckler-fern, *D. carthusiana*
(Vill.) H. P. Fuchs. (See Glossary pp. 478, 480, Fig. 1022, for explanation of terms.)

1   Tip of frond rolled upwards into a loose,
    conspicuous mop-head involving many pinnae
    (Fig. 105); inside a white maggot mines along
    rachis causing it to coil; summer - autumn; on
    Athyrium and *Dryopteris* spp.; common: **Diptera:
    Anthomyiidae** .... *Chirosia betuleti* (Ringdahl)

2   Rounded swelling in rachis, about 2 mm long;
    contains a pale green caterpillar (Fig. 106) which
    bites a hole and ejects froth which covers the gall;
    July; on *A. filix-femina*; Staffs and SE. England,
    very rare: **Hymenoptera: Blasticotomidae**
    .... *Blasticotoma filiceti* Klug

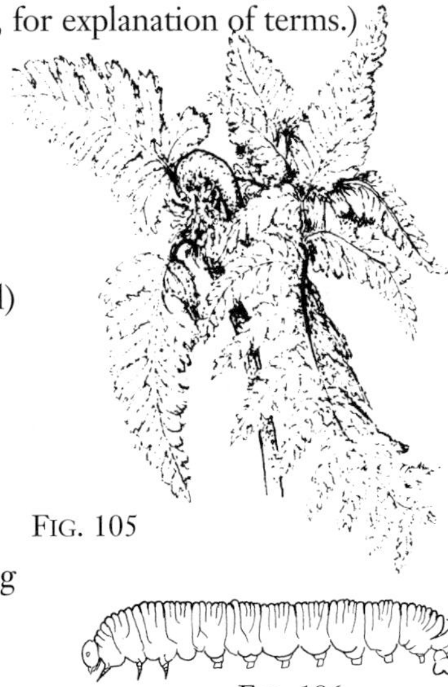

FIG. 105

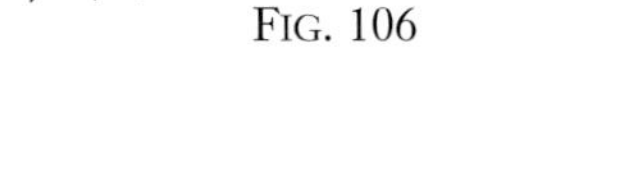

FIG. 106

E17. *ATRIPLEX* and *CHENOPODIUM*

Both genera are in the same family (Chenopodiaceae). Two galls are recorded on them. Hosts include common orache, *A. patula* L., sea-purslane, *A. portulacoides* L., fat-hen, *C. album* L., spear-leaved orache, *A. prostrata* Boucher ex DC., good-King-Henry, *C. bonus-henricus* L., and other species. A third gall, below, occurs on *Atriplex* only; it requires confirmation as a British species.

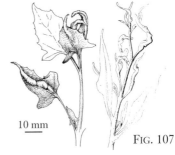

1 Margin of leaf thickened, rolled or folded upwards, or blade bulged upwards along midrib, petiole often twisted; often several leaves at shoot tip affected, the youngest inrolled to the midrib on both sides (Fig. 107); rolls often become yellowed; contain green waxy aphids (Fig. 108); common: **Hemiptera: Aphididae**
.... *Hayhurstia atriplicis* (L.)

10 mm

FIG. 107

1 mm   FIG. 108

2 Margins of leaf rolled upwards, only slightly thickened, often several leaves at shoot tip affected (Fig. 109); rolls contain psyllid nymphs, without wax; uncommon: **Hemiptera: Psylloidea**
.... *Trioza chenopodii* Reuter

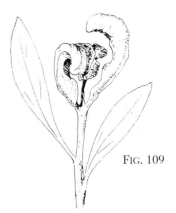

3 Slender spindle-shaped swelling in stem; contains several chambers, each with an orange-red larva; on *A. portulacoides*, probably also on *A. prostrata*: **Diptera: Cecidomyiidae**
.... *Stefaniella brevipalpis* Kieffer

FIG. 109

AVENA see POACEAE

E18. *BALLOTA*

One gall (**Diptera: Cecidomyiidae**) is recorded from black horehound, *Ballota nigra* L.

Leaves at shoot tip bunched, inrolled upwards, pale-coloured; or lateral bud enlarged, partly opened; contain white, jumping larvae (Fig. 110)
.... *Contarinia ballotae* Kieffer

FIG. 110

E19. *BERBERIS*

A cecid gall (**Diptera: Cecidomyiidae**) may be found on barberry, *Berberis vulgaris* L., a species probably introduced to, but long naturalised in, Britain. Young leaves at shoot tips may be incurled and bunched, infested by the aphid *Liosomaphis berberidis* (Kaltenbach) (**Hemiptera: Aphididae**); this is not thought to be a true gall. For rust galls on leaves of *B. vulgaris* and cultivated species see p. 227.

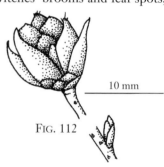

Young terminal leaves inrolled upwards, thickened, the rolls reddish or violet; affected leaves bunched due to shortening of internodes at shoot tip; buds in axils of these leaves often malformed; rolls contain larvae (Fig. 111), translucent at first, later white
.... *Dasineura berberidis* (Kieffer)

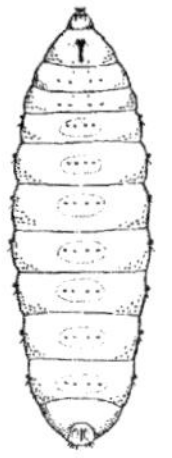

FIG. 111

E20. *BETULA*

Includes galls on downy birch, *B. pubescens* Ehrh. and silver birch, *B. pendula* Roth. Dwarf birch, *B. nana* L. is omitted due to lack of knowledge. For witches' brooms and leaf spots, see p. 227.

1   Gall causing 'big bud' (Fig. 112, Plate 1.6), contains mites (Fig. 113); leaves swollen and green, later brown and hard: **Acari: Eriophyoidea**
.... *Acalitus calycophthirus* (Nalepa)
(= *Aceria*)

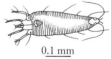

10 mm

FIG. 112

Formerly classified as a subspecies of *Aceria rudis* Nalepa (= *Phytoptus* = *Eriophyes*), see couplet 8.

-   Gall in stem or twig, often on young shoots of small and coppiced trees: **Lepidoptera** **2**

-   Gall in female catkin or fruit, with one larva (Fig. 114) which overwinters and pupates in the gall in spring; widespread: **Diptera: Cecidomyiidae**.......... **3**

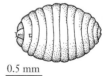

0.1 mm   FIG. 113

-   Gall in leaf **5**

2   Inconspicuous spindle-shaped swelling, 5-10 mm long, slightly thicker than normal twig; opening with neat tube of silk and frass extending 4-5 mm along twig; single caterpillar (Fig. 115) July - August, fairly common throughout Britain: **Tortricidae** .... *Epinotia tetraquetrana* (Haworth)

0.5 mm

FIG. 114

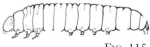

FIG. 115

- Conspicuous swelling usually at node, about twice as wide as normal twig (Fig. 116); opening sealed with silk and red-brown frass; one caterpillar (occasionally two, Fig. 115) July - April, pupates in gall in May - June; uncommon, S. & NW. England and Scotland: **Incurvariidae**
.... ***Lampronia fuscatella*** (Tengstrom)

This gall may have been overlooked. Slight swelling of twig tip (also in midrib of leaf) with associated leaf mine caused by *Heliozella hammoniella* Sorhagen (= *betulae*).

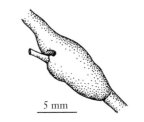

5 mm

FIG. 116

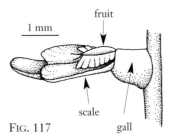

1 mm   fruit

scale

FIG. 117   gall

3 Gall fused to spindle of catkin, between it and scale (Fig. 117); scale and fruit easily detached; up to 2 mm long, without a window-pit
.... ***Semudobia skuhravae*** Roskam

- Gall in fruit, not fused to scale or spindle **4**

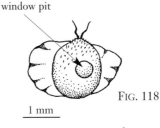

window pit

FIG. 118

1 mm

4 Window-pit distinct; gall oval, up to 2 mm, upper half hairy; wings of fruit present but reduced (Fig. 118) .... ***Semudobia betulae*** (Winnertz)

- Window-pit absent or indistinct; gall rounded, just over 2 mm diameter with a polished surface, hairs only at apex; wings of fruit quite or almost undeveloped (Fig. 119)
.... ***Semudobia tarda*** Roskam

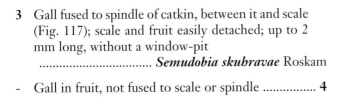

1 mm

FIG. 119

ungalled fruit

5 Gall with hairs inside or on rim of aperture, or an erineum (Fig. 120); contains mites (Fig. 113): **Acari: Eriophyoidea** **6**

- Inside and aperture of gall without hairs; contains larva(e) (Fig. 114): **Diptera: Cecidomyiidae** **10**

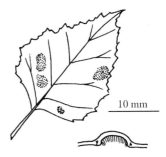

10 mm

FIG. 120

6 Gall hemispherical or wart-like on one side of leaf, conical on the other with opening (Figs 121, 122); pale or reddish-brown
.... ***Cecidophyopsis betulae*** (Nalepa)

- Gall an erineum on one side of leaf, with a bulge or hairy patch on the other **7**

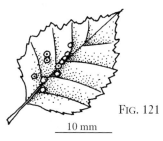

FIG. 121

10 mm

7 Erineum between or along veins, not hairy on other side; hairs of erineum blunt (Fig. 123), red, white or yellow when young **8**

- Erineum in angle of veins on underside, hairy bulge on upperside **9**

FIG. 122

8 Erineum usually on upperside; hairs short, bright red when young (Plate 1.2)
.... ***Acalitus longisetosus*** (Nalepa)
(= *Eriophyes* = *Aceria*)

- Erineum usually on underside, with or without a bulge on the other side (Fig. 124); hairs longer, white or yellowish when young, later a deep red-brown; the commonest mite gall on birch leaves
.... ***Acalitus rudis*** (Canestrini)
(= *Aceria* = *Phytoptus*)

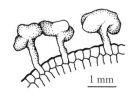

1 mm

FIG. 123

9 Hairs of erineum pointed, whitish when young; gall shown in Fig. 125
.... ***Eriophyes lissonotus*** Nalepa

- Hairs of erineum blunt, reddish-brown
.... ***Aculus leionotus*** (Nalepa)
(= *Phytoptus* = *Eriophyes lionotus*)

Fig. 126 may be the gall of *Aculus leionotus*. *Eriophyes lissonotus* is not listed in Amrine & Stasny (1994); it may not be distinct from *A. leionotus*. Birch mite taxonomy is complex and not fully sorted out.

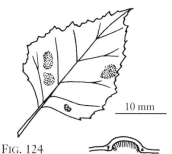

FIG. 124

10 mm

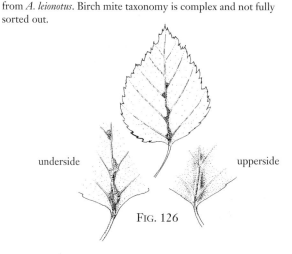

underside   upperside

FIG. 126

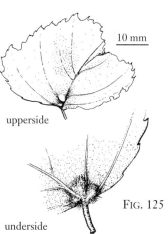

10 mm

upperside

underside

FIG. 125

10 Longitudinal swelling of midrib, often affecting main side veins; one or more larvae **11**

- Blister in leaf blade or side veins; usually with a single larva **12**

FIG. 127

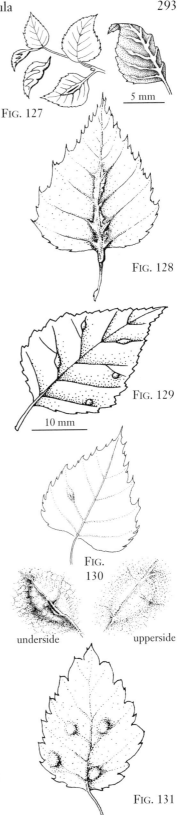

11 Young terminal leaf, or several bunched together, crinkled and folded upwards, main veins swollen (Fig. 127), equally visible on both sides; contain white or yellowish larvae with strong sternal spatula briefly in late spring and early summer; widespread but not common
.... ***Plemeliella betulicola*** (Kieffer)

- Fully expanded leaf with elongated (up to 10 mm) woody swelling of midrib (Fig. 128, which shows two galls running together) or petiole, sometimes extending into base of lateral veins; more prominent on underside; green, later red-purple and brown, sometimes surrounded by green patch on yellowing leaf; larvae white or yellowish when young, red when mature, with weak sternal spatula
.... ***Massalongia rubra*** (Kieffer)

FIG. 128

FIG. 129

12 Gall green, often more prominent on underside, often surrounded by a green patch on the yellowing leaf in autumn; larva whitish to yellow-orange, without sternal spatula; slit-shaped exit hole in underside; widespread:
.... ***Massalongia betulifolia*** Harris

(a) inconspicuous shallow circular blister 3 mm diameter in blade (Fig. 129); larva leaves gall in June, gall then turns yellow-brown
....**(generation 1)**

(b) diamond-shaped blister over veins (Fig. 130); larva leaves gall in Sept. - Oct.
.... **(generation 2)**

- Deeper circular blister 2.5 mm across, 1.5 mm deep, yellowish to red-purple, in blade or veins (Fig. 131), more prominent on upper surface; larva pale yellow with conspicuous sternal spatula, leaves gall July - Sept. by circular hole in underside; widespread and quite common
.... ***Anisostephus betulinus*** (Kieffer)

FIG. 130

underside   upperside

FIG. 131

E21. *BOLBOSCHOENUS* (= *SCIRPUS*)

One gall-causing fly (**Diptera: Chloropidae**) is known from Britain (Ismay, 1999) but its gall, on sea club-rush, *Bolboschoenus maritimus* (Asch.) Palla, has not yet been recorded. The gall has been described in Israel (Kaplan, 1977).

1   Swelling in stem, about 1.5 cm long, at junction of leaf blade and sheath (Fig. 132), probably on stunted shoots; contains a white larva (Fig. 133) or pupa; adults recorded from England, Wales and Scotland

    .... ***Eurina lurida*** Meigen

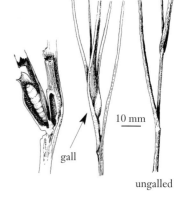

10 mm

gall

ungalled

Fig. 132

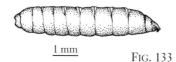

1 mm

Fig. 133

BRACHYPODIUM see POACEAE

BRASSICA see BRASSICACEAE

E22. **BRASSICACEAE** (= CRUCIFERAE)

This family is treated in one Key because many gall causers attack several genera. The genera most commonly galled in Britain are listed, though it is possible that others may occasionally be attacked. This is a complex family whose galls are poorly known; the Key should be regarded as preliminary only.

Tribe SISYMBRIEAE: *Sisymbrium*, rockets; *S. officinale* (L.) Scop., hedge mustard
                           Alliaria petiolata (M. Bieb.) Cavara & Grande, garlic mustard
                           Arabidopsis thaliana (L.) Heynh., thale cress

Tribe HESPERIDEAE: *Erysimum* (= *Cheiranthus*), wallflowers

Tribe ARABIDEAE: *Rorippa*, water-cresses
                           Cardamine, bitter-cresses; *C. amara* L., large bitter-cress
                           C. pratensis, cuckooflower
                           Arabis, rock-cresses; *A. caucasica* Willd. ex Schltdl., garden arabis

Tribe ALYSSEAE: *Erophila*, whitlowgrasses

Tribe LEPIDEAE: *Thlaspi*, penny-cresses
                           Capsella, shepherd's-purses

Tribe BRASSICEAE: *Brassica*, cabbages; *B. oleracea* L., wild cabbage, and cultivated
                           varieties: kale, cauliflower, brussels sprouts, kohl-rabi
                           B. napus L., rape, oilseed rape, swede
                           B. rapa L., turnip

Descurainia sophia (L.) Webb ex Prantl., flixweed
Sinapis, mustards; *S. arvensis* L., charlock
Raphanus, radishes

Fungal galls may be found on roots and shoots of crucifers (see p. 228).

1 Gall in root, root collar or stem; leaf petiole or midrib, or flower stalk **2**

- Gall in leaf blade, leaf- or flower-bud, or pod; or affecting whole inflorescence or young leaves at shoot tip **5**

2 Rounded swelling in root or root collar (Fig. 134), 5-15 mm long, sometimes several coalescing; each with a white larva (Fig. 135): **Coleoptera: Curculionidae** **3**

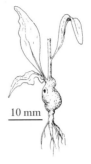

10 mm

FIG. 134

- Swelling in stem, sometimes near base; or in petiole, midrib or flower stalk **4**

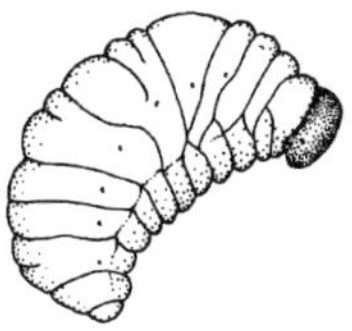

FIG. 135

3 On Brassiceae, especially crop plants, and on *Alliaria, Arabis* and other genera; common
.... ***Ceutorhynchus assimilis*** (Paykull)
(= *pleurostigma*) **cabbage and turnip gall weevil**

- On wild cabbage, *B. oleracea*; coastal, rare
.... ***Baris laticollis*** (Marsham)

Crucifer weevil galls are difficult to separate. For certain identification, rear adult and identify in Joy (1932), Dauphin & Aniotsbehère (1993, Appendix 3a), Hodge & Jones (1995).

FIG. 136

4 Swelling at base of petiole or flower stalk, sometimes involving adjacent stem; contains a bright red larva (Fig. 136); on *Cardamine*: **Diptera: Cecidomyiidae**
........................***Dasineura cardaminicola*** Rübsaamen

For a pale yellow spongy round mass in leaf axil of *Rorippa*, containing several orange-red larvae, see couplet 9.

- Smooth, fleshy swelling in stem, or petiole (or midrib of robust species), > 4 mm long (usually > 10 mm long); contains one chamber with a white larva (Fig. 135) or pupa; sometimes several galls coalesce: **Coleoptera: Curculionidae:** (there are five alternatives)

On *Cardamine* (Fig. 137); England, Wales, S. Scotland, not common
.... ***Ceutorhynchus pectoralis*** Weise

FIG. 137

On *Arabidopsis* (Fig. 138); England (one Scottish record); local
.... ***Ceutorhynchus atomus*** Boheman

On *Erophila*; swelling 5-7 x 2-4 mm at base of stem; throughout Britain; local on coastal sand-dunes .... ***Ceutorhynchus hirtulus*** Germar

On *Sisymbrium*, *Thlaspi*, *Capsella* (perhaps also on other genera); common
.... ***Ceutorhynchus chalybaeus*** Germar
(= *timidus*)

On Brassicaceae (e.g. *Descurainia sophia*); uncommon
.... ***Ceutorhynchus rapae*** Gyllenhal
See note beneath couplet 3. Identifications should be checked by an expert.

FIG. 138

5   In pod or individual flower or flower bud; contains larvae: **Diptera: Cecidomyiidae** **6**

-   In individual leaf, or several leaves crowded at shoot tip due to shortening of internodes; or in inflorescence, incorporating several flower buds and their stalks **9**

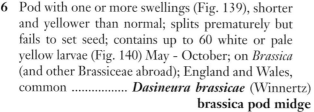

5 mm   FIG. 139

6   Pod with one or more swellings (Fig. 139), shorter and yellower than normal; splits prematurely but fails to set seed; contains up to 60 white or pale yellow larvae (Fig. 140) May - October; on *Brassica* (and other Brassiceae abroad); England and Wales, common .... ***Dasineura brassicae*** (Winnertz)
brassica pod midge
Usually lays eggs in pods already damaged by feeding and oviposition holes of the common non-galling weevil *Ceutorhynchus assimilis* (Paykull). Together, they are important pests of cultivated brassicas.

FIG. 140

-   Flower or flower bud swollen, remaining closed **7**

7   Calyx not enlarged, petals greened and thickened at base (Fig. 141); 4 to 8 red, non-jumping larvae (Fig. 140); on *Cardamine amara*, *pratensis*, local
.... ***Dasineura cardaminis*** (Winnertz)

-   Calyx enlarged, petals short, not greened **8**

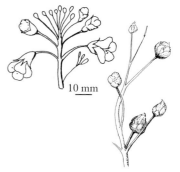

10 mm

FIG. 141

8 Larvae (Fig. 142) yellowish-white when young, later lemon-yellow, jumping; on *Brassica* (Fig. 143) (and other genera abroad); locally common
.... ***Contarinia nasturtii*** (Kieffer)
swede midge

See also couplets 10 and 11.

- Larvae whitish at all ages, non-jumping; on *Brassica*, *Raphanus* (Fig. 144) (and other genera abroad)
.... ***Gephyraulus raphanistri*** (Kieffer)

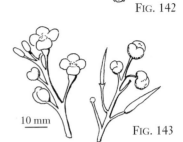

FIG. 142

10 mm

FIG. 143

READ THREE ALTERNATIVES

9 Pale yellow, spongy, rounded mass at tip of inflorescence, 5-10 mm across (Fig. 145); sometimes in axil of flower stalk or petiole (Fig. 146); contains orange-red larvae (Fig. 140): on *Rorippa* (and other genera abroad), local: **Diptera: Cecidomyiidae**
.... ***Dasineura sisymbrii*** (Schrank)

- Leaves crowded at shoot tip, their bases thickened; may form a rosette; contain larvae: **Diptera: Cecidomyiidae** **10**

- Gall in individual leaf, though several adjacent leaves may be affected **11**

Aphids (Fig. 147) may cause crumpling and incurling of leaves, distorting stem, shoot tip or inflorescence if numbers are high. The waxy green nymphs of *Brevicoryne brassicae* (L.) form dense colonies, wet with honeydew, on Brassiceae spp.; *Lipaphis erysimi* (Kaltenbach), also green and waxy, infests *Sisymbrium*. Other species may also be present, but none is considered to cause a true gall.

FIG. 144

10 mm

FIG. 145

FIG. 146

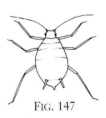

FIG. 147

10 Rosette of leaves, 2 x 1 cm or larger (Fig. 148); contains red, non-jumping larvae (Fig. 149) in summer and autumn; on *Arabis caucasica*
.... ***Dasineura alpestris*** (Kieffer)

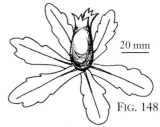

FIG. 148

\- Leaves small, forming a terminal bunch; jumping larvae (Fig. 150), yellowish-white when young, later lemon-yellow, live between leaf bases; on *Brassica*, locally common
.... ***Contarinia nasturtii*** (Kieffer)
See also couplets 7, 8 and 11.   **swede midge**

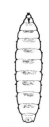

FIG. 149   FIG. 150

11 Leaf folded upwards or crumpled, with local thickenings, not unusually hairy; jumping larvae, yellowish-white when young, later lemon-yellow (Fig. 150), live in creases; on *Brassica*, locally common: **Diptera: Cecidomyiidae**
.... ***Contarinia nasturtii*** (Kieffer)
See also couplets 7, 8 and 10.

\- Leaf wrinkled, unusually hairy, often margin inrolled upwards or with irregular red-violet swellings on upper surface (Fig. 151); contains mites (Fig. 152); on many crucifers: **Acari: Eriophyoidea**

.... ***Aceria drabae*** (Nalepa)

This species causes varied effects on different hosts. In small host species, several leaves at shoot tip may be bunched together, reduced in size and very hairy. In species with large leaves, only part of leaf or its margin may be affected.

FIG. 151

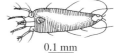

0.1 mm   FIG. 152

E23. *BRYONIA*

There is one British species, the native white bryony, *Bryonia dioica* Jacq. Two cecids (**Diptera: Cecidomyiidae**) cause galls; both contain gregarious white larvae (Fig. 149) in summer.

1 Young leaves and buds at shoot tip distorted, thickened and hairy, forming an irregular mass (Fig. 153); Durham southwards, locally common
.... ***Jaapiella bryoniae*** (Bouché)

2 Flower bud swollen, remaining closed, turning brown and falling early
.... ***Jaapiella parvula*** (Liebel)

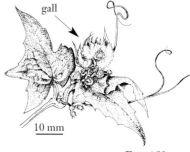

gall

10 mm

FIG. 153

E24. *BUXUS*

Includes galls on box, *Buxus sempervirens* L. For small thickened purplish-brown leaf patches, caused by a rust, see p. 229.

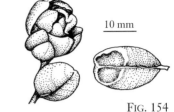

1 Gall distorts or enlarges flower or bud; contains mites (Fig. 152); uncommon or rare: **Acari: Eriophyoidea** **2**

- Gall on leaf or affecting several leaves at shoot tip ... **3**

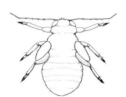

FIG. 154

2 Flower gall; flower green with thickened fleshy inner parts .... *Eriophyes canestrinii* (Nalepa)

- Bud enlarged and hairy, 4 mm across
   .... *Aceria unguiculatus* (Canestrini)
   (= *Eriophyes*)

FIG. 155

3 Leaves at shoot tip concave, slightly thickened and crowded, like a small cabbage (Fig. 154 left); single leaves may be affected (Fig. 154 right); greenish nymphs (Fig. 155) or their white waxy deposits present; common: **Hemiptera: Psylloidea**
   .... *Spanioneura buxi* (L.)
   (= *Psylla*)

galls opened by birds

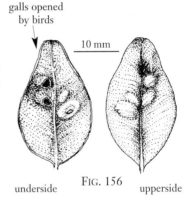

- Leaf with indistinct shallow irregular blisters, of variable size, apparent on both sides (Fig. 156); underside often yellowish; exit hole below, off-centre; larva white when young, later yellow-orange; locally common: **Diptera: Cecidomyiidae**
   .... *Monarthropalpus flavus* (Schrank)
   (= *buxi*)

underside FIG. 156 upperside

CALAMAGROSTIS see POACEAE

E25. *CALLUNA*

One mite gall (**Acari: Eriophyoidea**) is recorded on heather, *Calluna vulgaris* (L.) Hull.

Shoot transformed into a small witches' broom, stem and leaves distorted, thickened, abnormally hairy (Fig. 157); often yellowish-green or reddish; contains mites (Fig. 152)
   .... *Aceria exiguus* (Liro)

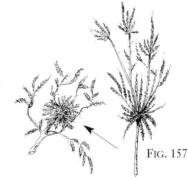

FIG. 157

CALYSTEGIA see *CONVOLVULUS*

E26. *CAMPANULA* and *PHYTEUMA*

Galls are found on harebell, *C. rotundifolia* L., creeping bellflower, *C. rapunculoides* L., clustered bellflower, *C. glomerata* L., peach-leaved bellflower, *C. persicifolia* L., Canterbury-bells, *C. medium* L. and nettle-leaved bellflower, *C. trachelium* L. The weevil gall, below, may also be found on rampions, *Phyteuma* spp.

1   Gall in leaf or leaf bud **2**

-   Flower bud or seed capsule swollen; or flower parts greened and leaflike (phyllanthy) **3**

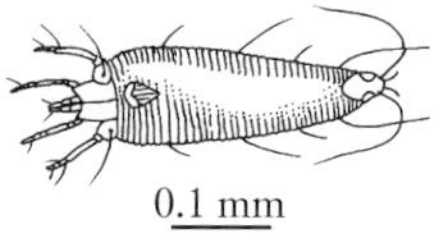

FIG. 158

0.1 mm

2   Felt-like erineum on blade or petiole; leaf margin may be inrolled, thickened, hairy; contains mites (Fig. 158): **Acari : Eriophyoidea**
    .... *Aceria campanulae* (Lindroth)
    (= *Eriophyes*)

-   Axillary leaf bud swollen, bulb-shaped, up to 5 mm across; may be several at shoot tip forming an irregular group up to 12mm across (Fig. 159); each contains one, or a few, red larvae (Fig. 160); July - September; on *C. rotundifolia*: **Diptera: Cecidomyiidae**
    .... *Geocrypta trachelii* (Wachtl)

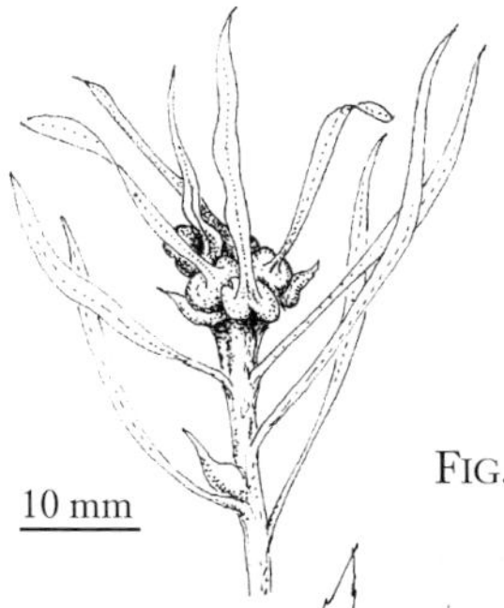

FIG. 159

10 mm

3   Flower parts greened and leaflike, covered with white hairs (Fig. 161): **Acari: Eriophyoidea**
    .... *Aculus schmardae* (Nalepa)
    (= *Eriophyes*)

-   Ovary within the seed capsule (gall not obvious from the outside), or flower bud, swollen **4**

FIG. 160

FIG. 161

4   Whole flower bud swollen, sometimes >1 cm across (Fig. 162), this or swollen ovary contains one, or a few, white larvae with dark head capsules (Fig. 163), or pupae; adults (see fig. in Morris, 1991) emerge in September; on *Campanula*, *Phyteuma* spp.: **Coleoptera: Curculionidae**
    .... *Miarus campanulae* (L.)

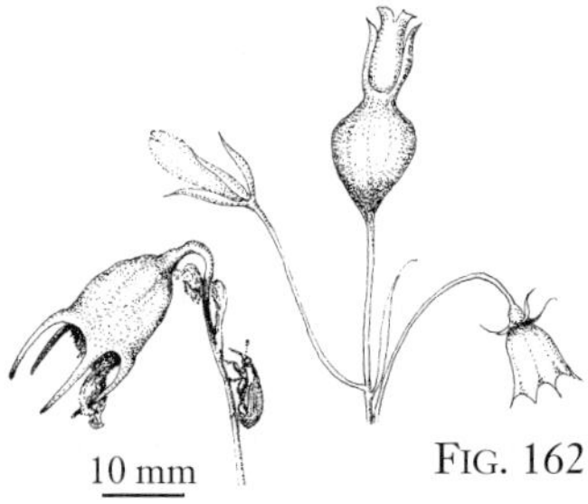

10 mm

FIG. 162

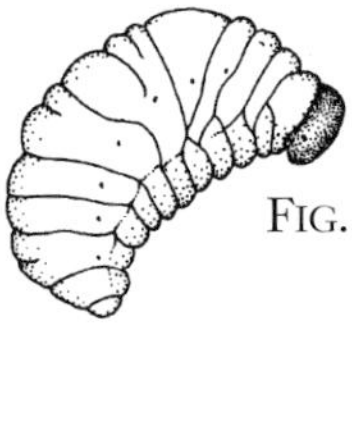

FIG. 163

- Base of flower bud swollen (Fig. 164); contains several white larvae with minute head capsules; pupate in soil: **Diptera: Cecidomyiidae**
.... **5**

10 mm

FIG. 164

5 Larvae (Fig. 165) can jump
.... ***Contarinia campanulae*** (Kieffer)

- Larvae (Fig. 160) cannot jump
.... ***Dasineura campanulae*** Rübsaamen

FIG. 165

CAPSELLA see BRASSICACEAE

CARDAMINE see BRASSICACEAE

E27. *CARDUUS*

Most galls are found in the large-headed nodding or musk thistle, *Carduus nutans* L. Other species have not been investigated thoroughly.

1 Gall in root or root collar; spindle-shaped, up to about 5 x 1cm (Fig. 166), containing a larva (Fig. 163) or pupa (as in Fig. 166); England and Scotland, uncommon: **Coleoptera: Curculionidae**
.... ***Cleonis pigra*** (Scopoli)
(= *Cleonus*)

For change of genus, see Morris & Booth (1997).

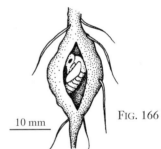

10 mm

FIG. 166

- Gall in flower head, not obvious from outside **2**

2 Part or all of receptacle and achenes transformed into a hard woody gall containing one or more chambers, each with a larva July - April or puparium May - June (Fig. 167) in old head; usually in *C. nutans*; midland and southern England: **Diptera: Tephritidae** .... ***Urophora solstitialis*** (L.)
(= *Euribia*)

This gall may have been overlooked or confused with the common *U. stylata*, usually found in *Cirsium vulgare* (Fig. 168); both species are occasionally found in each other's host plant. For certain identification, rear the adults and identify in White (1988).

[see p. 302 for the second part of this couplet]

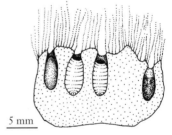

5 mm

FIG. 167

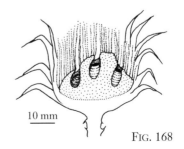

10 mm

FIG. 168

- Receptacle hollowed out, florets and achenes eaten, replaced with hardened callous tissue and frass; contains one or more white larvae (Fig. 169) July - August, or pupae in black cocoons (Fig. 170) August - September; southern England: **Coleoptera: Curculionidae**

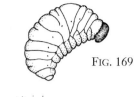

FIG. 169

.... *Rhinocyllus conicus* (Fröhlich)

Presence of larvae inside indicated by eggs, each covered by a yellow-brown cap of chewed plant tissue, on bracts on underside of flower head. Similar damage is caused by the weevil *Larinus planus* (L.); adults should be reared and identified: *R. conicus* (Fig. 171), *L. planus* (Fig. 172). Both species are generally rare, though locally common in the far south e.g. Dorset.

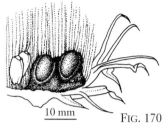

10 mm

FIG. 170

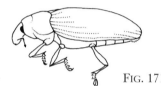

FIG. 171

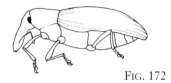

FIG. 172

E28. *CAREX*

This is a large genus on which galls are uncommon, difficult to find and probably under-recorded. Most galls on sedges are caused by Cecidomyiidae (the genus *Planetella* (= *Hormomyia*) specialises on sedges) and a smut (see p. 230). Thirteen species of *Planetella* have been recorded from Britain, either from galls on *Carex* or as adults. Taxonomic revision is necessary for the genus and host associations are poorly known. This key, therefore, should be regarded as preliminary only.

1   Gall in stem or leaf, or a bunch of modified leaves
   2

- Gall in inflorescence; utricle (which encloses the ovary) paler than normal, elongated and usually protruding from the spikelet, often many in one inflorescence; contains one larva (Fig. 173): **Diptera: Cecidomyiidae** **4**

Round dark-coloured galls protruding from spikelets are caused by smuts (see p. 230).

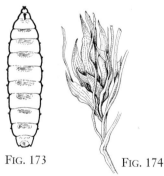

FIG. 173

FIG. 174

2   Leaves at tip of stem shorter and broader than normal, bunched together due to shortened internodes (Fig. 174); contains psyllid nymphs (Fig. 175); E. Anglia and NE England, rare: **Hemiptera: Psylloidea**

.... *Livia crefeldensis* (Mink)
                                (= *Diraphia*)

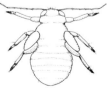

FIG. 175

- Ovoid swelling in leaf or stem, often near base or underground, sometimes several grouped together; contains one larva (Fig. 173): **Diptera: Cecidomyiidae** **3**

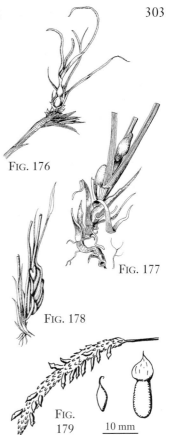

FIG. 176

3   On *C. arenaria*; often several galls together causing distortion of shoot (Fig. 176)
   ....***Planetella arenariae*** (Rübsaamen)

- Often on *C. pallescens*, but also on other species; swelling up to 4 x 1.5 mm, hard and brown, often just beneath soil surface
   .... ***Planetella granifex*** (Kieffer)

    Several other *Planetella* spp. are recorded, causing swellings in base of stems and leaves, e.g. *P. gallarum* (Rübsaamen) (Fig. 177), *P. fischeri* (Frauenfeld) (Fig. 178); knowledge of their galls and host plants is inadequate to separate them safely.

FIG. 177

FIG. 178

4   Gall 5-10 mm long (Fig. 179); larva orange; on *C. riparia*, *muricata* and other species
   .... ***Wachtliella caricis*** (Loew)
   (= *riparia*)

- Gall smaller, up to 5 mm long; larva pink; on *C. arenaria* .... ***Oligotrophus loewianus*** Kieffer

FIG. 179   10 mm

E29. *CARLINA*

One species only, carline thistle, *Carlina vulgaris* L. No species of gall causers are recorded in Britain, though Dauphin & Aniotsbehère (1993, 1997) include *Urophora solstitialis* (L.), **Diptera: Tephritidae**, and *Larinus planus* (F.), **Coleoptera: Curculionidae**. (For descriptions see *CARDUUS* and *CIRSIUM* keys.)

The caterpillar of *Metzneria aestivella* Zeller (= *carlinella* (Stainton)) **Lepidoptera: Gelechiidae** is common in the flower heads in summer. It over-winters, feeding on receptacle and achenes, causing some thickening and hardening of receptacle tissues. Whether this is true gall formation is not known.

E30. *CARPINUS*

There is one British species, hornbeam, *Carpinus betulus* L., native in SE England and planted elsewhere. In Britain, the arthropod gall causers attack the leaves.

A bushy witches' broom, composed of thickened branching stems with many leaves, may occur on branches or trunk; it is caused by *Taphrina carpini* Rostr. (see p. 230).

1　Smooth shiny upward bulge on upperside in angle between veins; hairy opening below (Fig. 180); contains mites (Fig 181.): **Acari: Eriophyoidea**
.... *Aceria tenellus* (Nalepa)
(= *Eriophyes*)

Erinea on the underside of leaves are caused by unidentified mites.

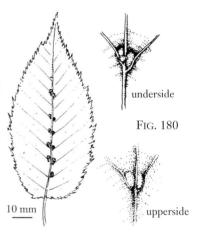

underside

FIG. 180

-　Midrib and / or side veins swollen 2

Dasineura ruebsaameni (Keiffer) **Diptera: Cecidomyiidae** causes a shallow pale-coloured blister in leaf blade, up to 5 mm across and slightly raised on both sides, with a central exit hole below; it contains a yellow larva (Fig. 182). It is a poorly known species, not certainly known to be British.

10 mm

upperside

2　Side of midrib with pale-coloured swelling on underside, about 4 mm across; often several coalesce to form a double row (Fig. 183) up to 30 mm long; sometimes in base of side vein; each contains a white larva (Fig. 182) July - October: **Diptera: Cecidomyiidae**
.... *Zygiobia carpini* (F. Löw)

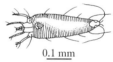

0.1 mm

FIG. 181

-　Underside of vein modified into a wavy ridge (Fig. 184), slit-like opening along vein on upperside (Fig. 185); often several on a leaf; contains mites (Fig. 181): **Acari: Eriophyoidea**
.... *Aceria macrotrichus* (Nalepa)
(= *Eriophyes*)

FIG. 182

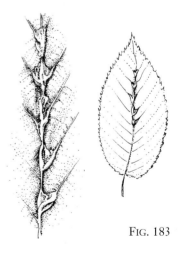

FIG. 183

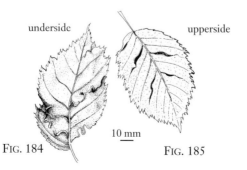

underside

upperside

10 mm

FIG. 184

FIG. 185

CARUM see APIACEAE

CATTLEYA see ORCHIDACEAE

E31. *CENTAUREA*

Two species are common in Britain, black knapweed or hardheads, *C. nigra* L., and greater knapweed, *C. scabiosa* L. They belong to different sub-genera and several gall causers favour one or the other. Other *Centaurea* species are uncommon or introduced; these may also be host plants but are less well known. For rust galls on leaves, see p. 230.

READ THREE ALTERNATIVES

1 Gall in stem or root collar (may not be obvious: split open the stem); contains one or more chambers each with a larva (Fig. 186): **Hymenoptera: Cynipidae** **2**

- Gall in leaf: petiole, vein or blade; visible on both sides **4**

- Gall in flower head, often not obvious from outside **6**

FIG. 186

2 Stem not, or only slightly, swollen, containing several separate hard-walled chambers < 5 x 1 mm (Fig. 187); in *C. nigra*, *C. scabiosa*, uncommon .... ***Phanacis centaureae*** Förster

- Stem or root collar clearly swollen, containing one or more chambers; in *C. scabiosa* only **3**

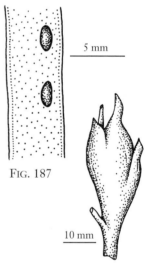

5 mm

FIG. 187

10 mm

FIG. 188

3 One chamber, hard-walled; swelling < 1 cm long; rare .... ***Isocolus fitchi*** (Kieffer)
Also in petiole and midrib of leaf, couplet 5.

- Several chambers, fleshy-walled; swelling 5 cm long or more (Fig. 188); uncommon .... ***Isocolus scabiosae*** (Giraud)

4 Swelling in blade, 1.5-2.5 mm across with round opening on upperside (Fig. 189), usually several in basal leaf; pale green, yellowish or violet; contains mites (Fig. 181); in several knapweeds: **Acari: Eriophyoidea** .... ***Aceria centaureae*** (Nalepa)
(= *Eriophyes* = *Phytoptus*)

- Swelling in petiole, midrib or side vein (rarely in blade), > 2.5 mm across; contains a larva; in *C. scabiosa* only **5**

upperside

10 mm

FIG. 189

5 Blister-like swelling < 5 mm across (Fig. 190), upperside with yellow or purple margin; larva (Fig. 191) yellow: **Diptera: Cecidomyiidae**
.... *Loewiola centaureae* (F. Löw)

- Fleshy or hard swelling up to 8 mm across in petiole or midrib; larva white (Fig. 192); rare: **Hymenoptera: Cynipidae**
.... *Isocolus fitchi* (Kieffer)

Also in stem, couplet 3.

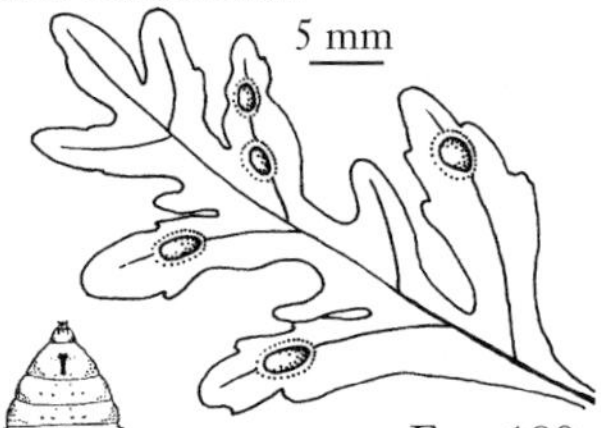

FIG. 190

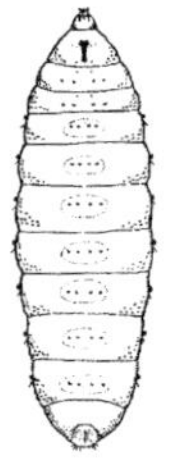

FIG. 191

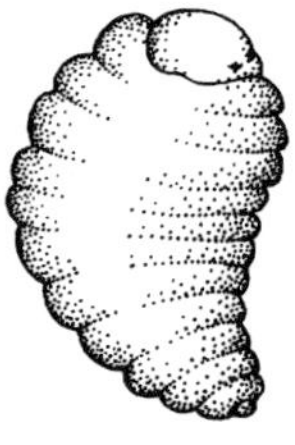

FIG. 192

6 Gall an enlarged achene or bract with woody or paper-thin walls; one or several per head, each with one larva **7**

- Gall incorporating receptacle and achenes, hard and woody, usually affecting most of head; usually with several chambers, each with one larva (Fig. 193) August - April or puparium May - June (in old head): **Diptera: Tephritidae** **9**

1 mm   FIG. 193

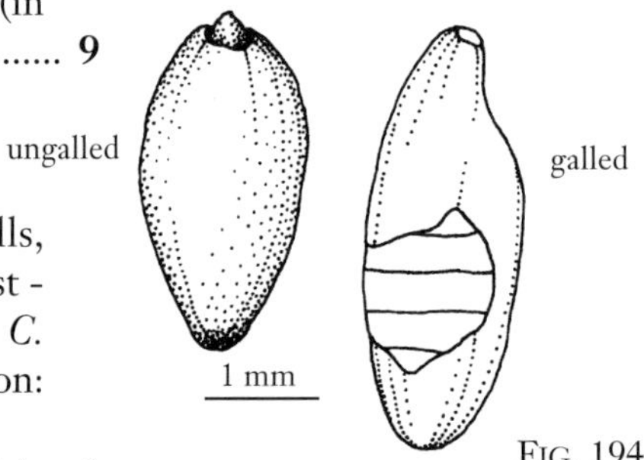

7 Galled achene with flimsy paper-thin walls, opening at top (Fig. 194); larva (Fig. 193) August - April, puparium May - June (in old head); in *C. nigra*; midland and southern England, uncommon: **Diptera: Tephritidae**
.... *Urophora quadrifasciata* (Meigen)
(= *Euribia*)

ungalled   galled

1 mm

FIG. 194

- Gall in achene or base of bract with hard woody walls, with round hole after adult emergence; contains a larva (Fig. 192) or pupa: **Hymenoptera: Cynipidae** **8**

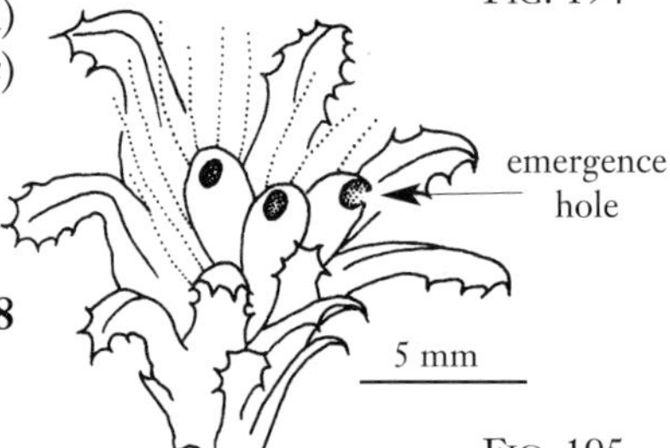

emergence hole

5 mm

FIG. 195

8 Galled achene 3-5 x 2.5 mm (Fig. 195); usually in *C. nigra* and related knapweeds; rare
.... *Isocolus jaceae* (Schenck)

- Gall in base of bract (Fig. 196) or in achene, swollen, up to 8 x 4.5 mm; in *C. scabiosa* only, locally common
.... *Isocolus rogenhoferi* Wachtl

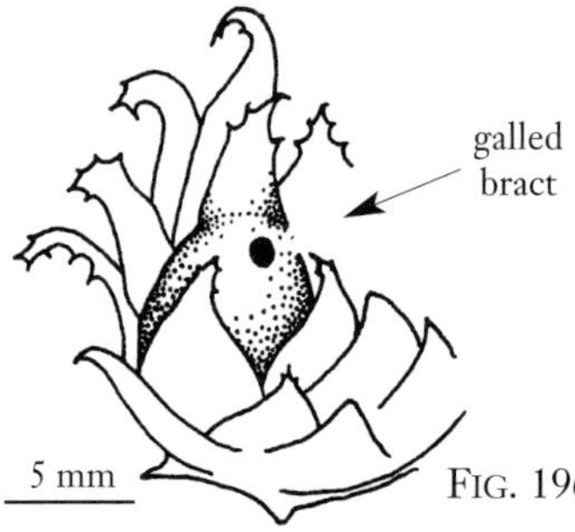

galled bract

5 mm   FIG. 196

9 Usually in *C. nigra* (Fig. 197); length of puparium
3.5-4.5 mm; throughout Britain, common
.... *Urophora jaceana* (Hering)

- Usually in *C. scabiosa*; length of puparium 4.6-5.4
mm; southern England, uncommon
.... *Urophora cuspidata* (Meigen)

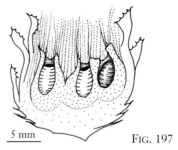

FIG. 197

For certain identification, rear adult and identify in White
(1988). Small, unopened, hairy flower heads may contain
orange-yellow larvae (Fig. 191) of *Dasineura miki* (Rübsaamen)
(**Diptera: Cecidomyiidae**). This is common in Scotland. Only
identified by the gall it needs confirming by rearing the adult.
Caterpillars of *Metzneria metzneriella* (Stainton) (**Lepidoptera:
Gelechiidae**) are common throughout Britain in heads of *C.
nigra*. They are not thought to be true gall causers.

CENTRANTHUS see *VALERIANELLA*

E32. *CERASTIUM*

Common mouse-ear, *Cerastium fontanum* Baumg. is the species most commonly galled,
though other species occasionally are hosts.

1 Seed capsule slightly swollen; contains orange larvae (Fig. 191): **Diptera:
Cecidomyiidae** .... *Dasineura fructum* (Rübsaamen)

- Gall formed from leaves at shoot tip; or flower bud swollen **2**

2 Terminal leaf pair thickened, meeting at margins to form a pouch; contains a red
larva (Fig. 191) or pupa: **Diptera: Cecidomyiidae**
.... *Dasineura lotharingiae* (Kieffer)
May also gall flower buds, which are swollen, remaining closed.

- Several pairs of leaves bunched at shoot tip, due to shortening of internodes **3**

3 Margins of leaves thickened and inrolled, usually
upwards, forming a rounded or ovoid bunch; rolls
contain yellow-green aphids (Fig. 198) powdered
with wax, in spring: **Hemiptera: Aphididae**
.... *Brachycolus cerastii* (Kaltenbach)

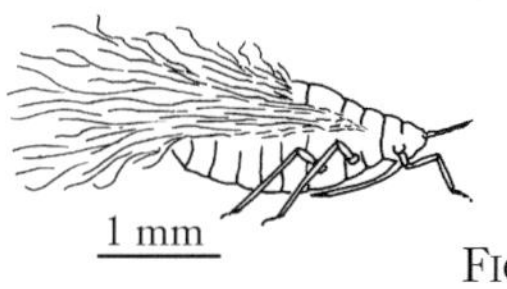

FIG. 198

- Gall leaves reddish, hairy; enclose a cavity
containing orange larvae (Fig. 191): **Diptera:
Cecidomyiidae**
.... *Dasineura cerastii* (Binnie)

- Gall a tuft or loose rosette, 0.5-1.5 cm high; leaves
very hairy; mites (Fig. 199) live amongst the hairs;
rare: **Acari: Eriophyoidea**
.... *Aceria cerastii* (Nalepa)
(= *Eriophyes*)

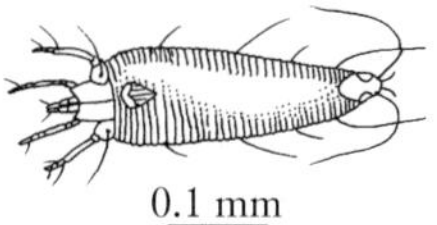

FIG. 199

E33. *CHAMAECYPARIS*

Cones of the introduced Lawson's cypress, *Chamaecyparis lawsoniana* (A. Murray) Parl. are affected by a North American cecid (**Diptera: Cecidomyiidae**) accidentally introduced into Europe more than 60 years ago (Harris, personal communication).

Developing cones are slightly discoloured and distorted (Fig. 200); inside, seeds are distorted and concave (Fig. 201); in each hollow lies a pale yellow, later orange larva, which pupates in a white cocoon in early spring; a cone may contain 20+ larvae; most records are from southern England, but this species is probably widespread in Britain .... *Janetiella siskiyou* Felt

This distortion may not be a true gall.

FIG. 200

ungalled seed

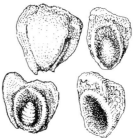

galled seeds

FIG. 201

E34. *CHAMERION* (= *CHAMAENERION*)

There is only one native species, rosebay willowherb, *C. angustifolium* (L.) Holub. Gall causers on this host are distinct from those on other willowherbs (see *Epilobium*, p. 323).

READ THREE ALTERNATIVES

1 Rounded or spindle-shaped swelling in stem or lower part of raceme, 10-30 mm long (Fig. 202, Plate 7.3), often reddened; contains reddish-brown caterpillar (Fig. 203) June - July (old galls obvious in dead stems): **Lepidoptera: Momphidae** .... *Mompha nodicolella* Fuchs

First generation galls are larger but less conspicuous in the thicker main stem; second generation galls smaller but more conspicuous in the thinner side stems.

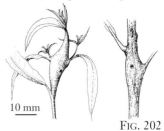

10 mm

FIG. 202

FIG. 203

- Flower bud swollen, remains closed (Fig. 204); contains yellowish-orange larvae (Fig. 205): **Diptera: Cecidomyiidae** .... *Dasineura epilobii* (F. Löw)

- Gall on leaf: margin inrolled, sometimes also folded and crumpled **2**

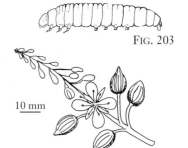

10 mm

FIG. 204

2 Margin roll or fold downward, narrow, tight and thickened, often flattened (Fig. 206); 7-10mm long, contains a pale yellow larva (Fig. 205) in summer, without wax; often several coalesce into a longer roll; common and widespread: **Diptera: Cecidomyiidae**

.... ***Dasineura kiefferiana*** (Rübsaamen)

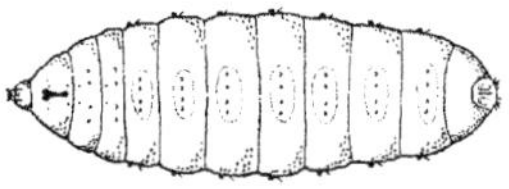

FIG. 205

- Margin rolled upward or downward, broad and loose, not or very slightly thickened, blade often crumpled; contains psyllid nymphs (Fig. 207) or their cast skins, and waxy deposits: **Hemiptera: Psylloidea** **3**

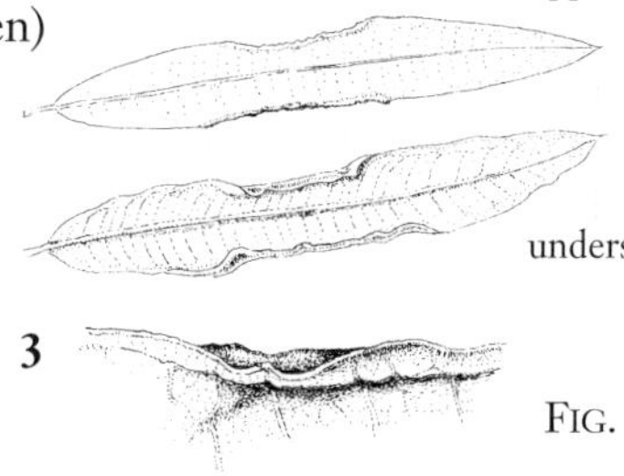

upperside

underside

FIG. 206

3 Final instar nymphs dark brown; common in southern Britain, scarce in north

.... ***Craspedolepta nebulosa*** (Zetterstedt)

- Final instar nymphs green or yellow; in southern England, uncommon

.... ***Craspedolepta subpunctata*** (Förster)

Separation is uncertain when psyllids are not present.

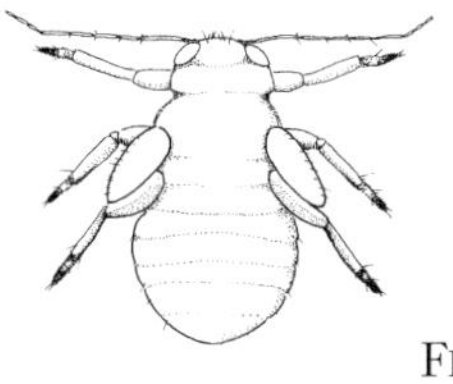

FIG. 207

CHENOPODIUM see *ATRIPLEX*

E35. *CHRYSANTHEMUM* and *LEUCANTHEMUM*

The usual host species are ox-eye daisy, *Leucanthemum vulgare* Lam. and florist's chrysanthemum, *Dendranthema* (DC.) Des Moul. hybrids.

1 Small, oval or conical gall, about 2 mm long, projecting obliquely from surface of leaf or leaf bud, stem, or bract of flower head, usually many together (Fig. 208); contains a white or reddish-orange larva (Fig. 205); severe infestation may stunt and distort the plant; on florist's chrysanthemums, larvae present any time of year in greenhouses: **Diptera: Cecidomyiidae**

.... ***Rhopalomyia chrysanthemi*** (Ahlberg)

First found in Britain in 1927 on imported plants, and became a pest in the 1940s; has not been reported since 1955 and may no longer be present in Britain.

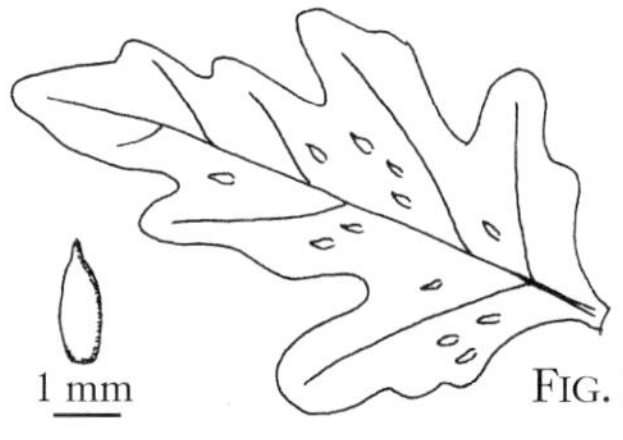

1 mm
FIG. 208

- Gall in root, stem, leaf bud or flower head; on *L. vulgare* (occasionally on cultivated varieties)

.... **2**

2 Pea-like swelling in root or root-collar; contains a white larva (Fig. 209) or brown puparium; south and central England and Wales, very rare: **Diptera: Tephritidae**
.... ***Oxyna nebulosa*** (Wiedemann)

- Swelling in stem, leaf bud, flower head or achene **3**

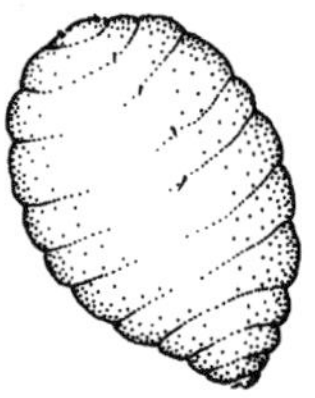

Fig. 209

3 Slight swelling of main stem below flower head, causing distortion of head, with lateral shoots growing past it (Fig. 210); larva (Fig. 211) tunnels inside stem and often into flower head from which frass may exude; larva May - June, pupa June - July in stem or head (or in ground); south and central England, uncommon: **Lepidoptera: Tortricidae**
.... ***Dichrorampha consortana*** Stephens

frass

Fig. 210

- Not like this; swelling contains one or more larvae: **Diptera: Cecidomyiidae** **4**

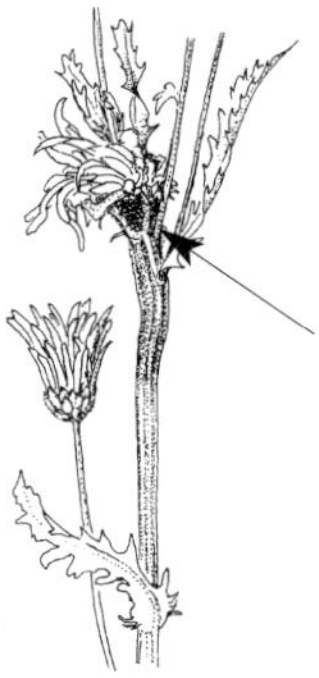

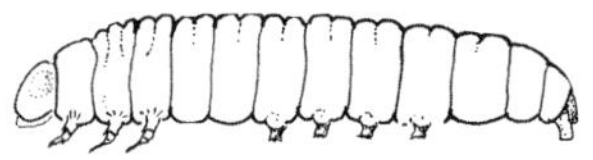

4 Stem swollen and contorted (Fig. 212); or enlarged bud in axil of leaf or on stem at ground level; larvae red (Fig. 219), pupate in the gall
.... ***Rhopalomyia hypogaea*** (F. Löw)

Fig. 211

- Flower head or achenes swollen **5**

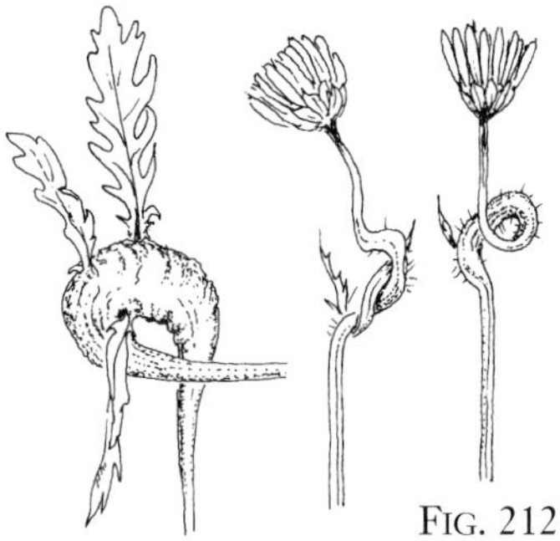

5 Flower head slightly swollen, remains closed; contains several yellow, jumping larvae (Fig. 213)
.... ***Contarinia chrysanthemi*** (Kieffer)

Fig. 212

- Achene swollen, often several in affected heads; each contains a yellow larva
.... ***Ozirhincus longicollis*** (Rondani)
(= *Clinorhyncha chrysanthemi* = *leucanthemi*)

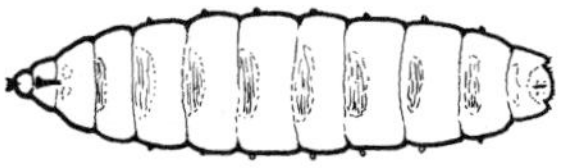

Fig. 213

E36. *CIRSIUM*

Of the many species of *Cirsium*, creeping thistle, *C. arvense* (L.) Scop., and spear thistle, *C. vulgare* (Savi) Ten., have been well studied. Other native species worthy of more attention are marsh thistle, *C. palustre* (L.) Scop., dwarf thistle, *C. acaule* (L.) Scop., woolly thistle, *C. eriophorum* (L.) Scop., meadow thistle, *C. dissectum* (L.) Hill and melancholy thistle, *C. heterophyllum* (L.) Hill (= *helenioides*).

A sweet-smelling rust fungus infests the leaves; see p. 231.

1   Gall in root or stem **2**

-   Gall in flower head, often not obvious from outside **3**

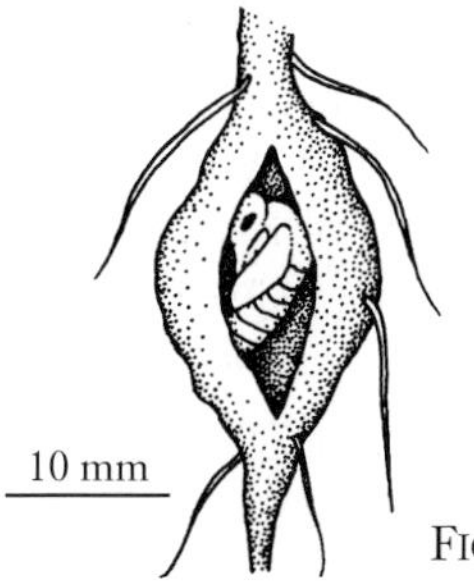

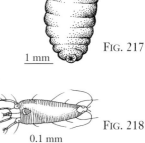

FIG. 214

FIG. 215

2   In several species; a spindle-shaped swelling in root or base of stem, about 5 x 1 cm (Fig. 214), containing a larva (Fig. 215) or pupa (as in Fig. 214); England and Scotland, uncommon: **Coleoptera: Curculionidae**
.... ***Cleonis pigra*** (Scopoli)
(= *Cleonus*)

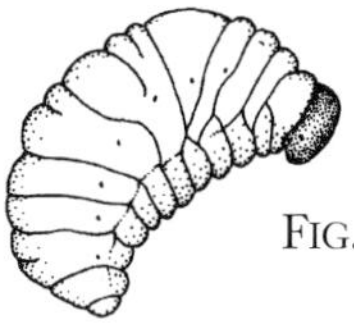

For change of genus, see Morris & Booth (1997).

-   In *C. arvense* only; swelling in stem, up to 10 x 3 cm, green and fleshy, later hard and woody (Fig. 216, Plate 4.3); contains one or more chambers, each with a larva (Fig. 217) July - April, or puparium May - June (in old head); English midlands southwards, locally common: **Diptera: Tephritidae** .... ***Urophora cardui*** (L.)
(= *Euribia*)

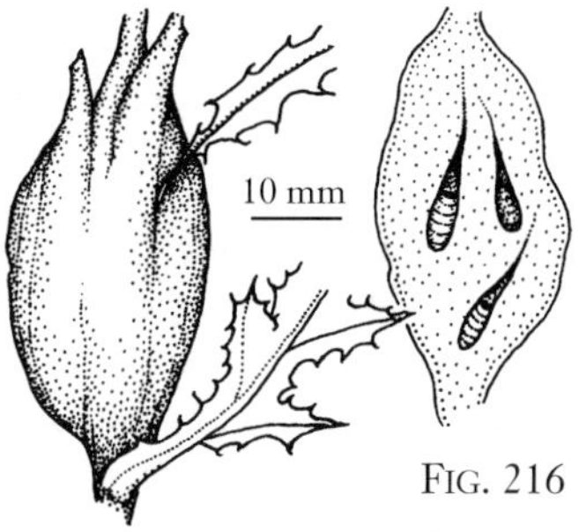

FIG. 216

3   Head distorted with florets greened and leafy (phyllanthy); contains mites (Fig. 218); in *C. arvense* and possibly other thistles; rare: **Acari: Eriophyoidea** .... ***Aceria anthocoptes*** (Nalepa)
(= *Eriophyes*)

-   Part or all of flower head twisted and distorted, with small thickened discoloured patches at base of bract, edge of receptacle or in young florets which remain unopened; each patch contains an orange-red larva (Fig. 219) in June - July; usually in *C. dissectum*: **Diptera: Cecidomyiidae**
.... ***Jaapiella cirsiicola*** Rübsaamen

FIG. 217

FIG. 218

-   Head not or only slightly distorted; receptacle enlarged and woody, or hollowed out and filled with hardened callous tissue, frass or debris **4**

FIG. 219

4   Part or all of receptacle and achenes transformed into a hard woody gall containing one or more chambers (Fig. 220), each with a larva (Fig. 221) July - April, or puparium May - June (in old head); usually in *C. vulgare*, occasionally in other large-headed thistle species and *C. arvense*; England from Yorkshire southwards and Wales, common: **Diptera: Tephritidae**

.... ***Urophora stylata*** (F.)
(= *Euribia*)

Urophora solstitiales (L.) occurs rarely in *Cirsium* species; it is usually found in *Carduus*. see p. 301

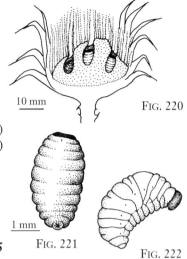

10 mm   FIG. 220

-    Receptacle hollowed out, florets and achenes eaten, replaced with hardened callous tissue, frass or debris; contains one or more larvae or black puparia or pupal cocoons 5

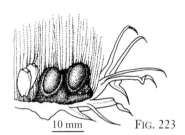

1 mm

FIG. 221   FIG. 222

5   Larvae white with brown head capsule (Fig. 222), July - August; black unsegmented pupal cocoons (Fig. 223), August - September; in *C. vulgare*; southern England, rare: **Coleoptera: Curculionidae**
.... ***Rhinocyllus conicus*** (Fröhlich)

More common in *Carduus nutans*. *Larinus planus* (F.) is similar and may also occur in *C. vulgare* (for more detail, see note on p. 302).

10 mm   FIG. 223

-    Larvae yellow-white without head capsule (Fig. 224), July - April; black segmented puparia May - June (Fig. 225) in old heads; in *C. palustre* and *C. heterophyllum*; Scotland and uplands in England and Wales, common in north: **Diptera: Tephritidae**
.... ***Tephritis conura*** (Loew)

FIG. 224   FIG. 225

E37. *CLEMATIS*

A mite gall (**Acari: Eriophyoidea**) is found on traveller's-joy, *Clematis vitalba* L., and a nematode causes root nodules on both this species and garden varieties (see p. 269).

Leaf margins curled upwards, usually several on same shoot affected; not noticeably thickened; contains mites (Fig. 226)
.... ***Aceria vitalbae*** (Canestrini)
(= *Eriophyes*)

This may not be a true gall.

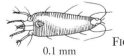

0.1 mm   FIG. 226

E38. *CONVALLARIA*

One gall (**Diptera: Cecidomyiidae**) is recorded on lily-of-the-valley, *Convallaria majalis* L. in Britain (also on the related Solomon's-seal, *Polygonatum* spp. abroad).

Flower bud swollen, remaining closed; contains white jumping larvae (Fig. 227)
.... ***Contarinia polygonati*** Rübsaamen

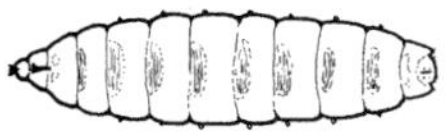

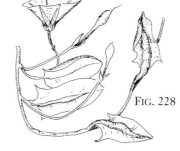

FIG. 227

E39. *CONVOLVULUS* and *CALYSTEGIA*

There is only one mite gall (**Acari: Eriophyoidea**) on bindweeds, recorded from *Convolvulus*, with no information on specific hosts. Whether it also occurs on the related genus *Calystegia* is unknown.

Leaves deformed, with swollen midrib and veins (Fig. 228); leaf margins are rolled upwards, covered with velvety hairs; contain mites (Fig. 226); rare .... ***Aceria convolvuli*** (Nalepa)
(= *Eriophyes*)

A second mite, *Vasates convolvuli* (Nalepa), may be found in deformed leaves but without the swelling and hairiness mentioned above. As this is not listed in Amrine & Stasny (1994), it is probably not a distinct species and, in any case, may not be a gall causer.

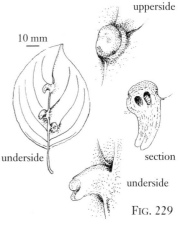

FIG. 228

E40. *CORNUS*

The native dogwood, *C. sanguinea* L. is galled by two species. Introduced *Cornus* species are unlikely to be hosts.

1 Hard flask-shaped gall obvious on both sides of leaf; domed above, 3-5 mm across; protruding below from midrib or side vein, 8-10 mm, often several on a leaf (Fig. 229, Plate 3.5); greenish-yellow, often tinged pink or purple; contains one or more thick-walled cavities opening below, each with an orange larva; appears in July, maturing August - September; locally common: **Diptera: Cecidomyiidae** .... ***Craneiobia corni*** (Giraud)
dogwood rivet gall

upperside

10 mm

underside

section

underside

FIG. 229

2 Leaf deformed, discoloured, margins thickened and inrolled, usually upwards (Fig. 230); often several leaves at tip of shoot affected; contains mites (Fig. 226): **Acari: Eriophyoidea**
.... ***Phyllocoptes depressus*** Nalepa
Other mite species may cause similar damage, see Dauphin & Aniotsbehère (1993, 1997).

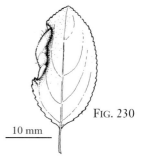

FIG. 230

10 mm

E41. *CORYLUS*

Includes galls on native hazel, *Corylus avellana* L.

READ THREE ALTERNATIVES

10 mm

1 Gall a big bud up to 10 mm across, sometimes opening slightly (Fig. 231); contains mites (Fig. 232): **Acari: Eriophyoidea**

FIG. 231

.... ***Phytoptus avellanae*** Nalepa
(= *Phytocoptella*)

This species has also been recorded on the introduced filbert, *C. maxima* Miller.

0.1 mm

FIG. 232

- Gall in leaf; contains mites (Fig. 232) or white larvae (Fig. 233) **2**

- Catkin wholly or partly enlarged **4**

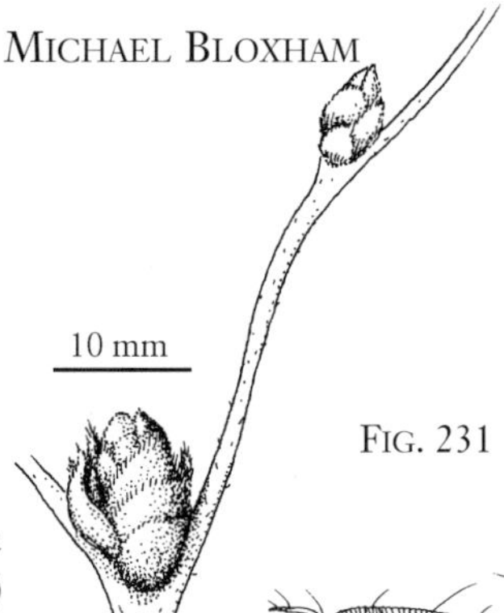

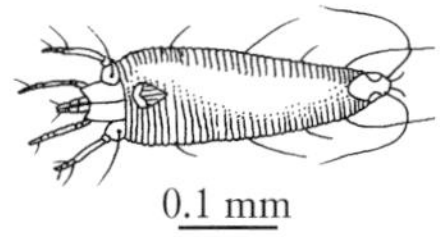

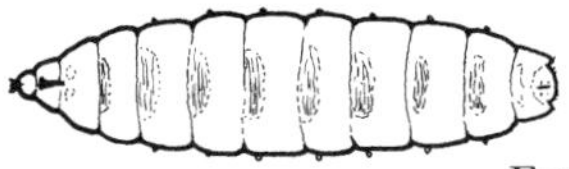

FIG. 233

2 Terminal leaves small, hairy, ± bunched together due to shortening of internodes; contains mites; SE England: **Acari: Eriophyoidea**

.... ***Cecidophyopsis vermiformis*** (Nalepa)

- Gall in leaf; contains one or more larvae (Fig. 233) May - June: **Diptera: Cecidomyiidae** **3**

3 Leaf folded and crumpled; contains jumping white larvae ...... ***Contarinia cybelae*** Gagné
(= *coryli*)

- Indistinct raised swelling on upperside 3-5 mm wide, with depression below containing a white larva, the depression encircled by a zone paler than the normal leaf; turns brown after larva has left .... ***Mikomya coryli*** (Kieffer)

This species is believed to occur in Britain, but this needs confirmation. It has been synonymised with *Oligotrophus tympanifex* Kieffer (which causes an indistinct blister in the leaf blade) by Skuhravá (1989). This synonymy requires confirmation.

4 Catkin rough-looking, distorted, with enlarged uneven scales when gall is full grown (Fig. 234); contains mites (Fig. 232): **Acari: Eriophyoidea**

10 mm

.... ***Phyllocoptes coryli*** Liro

- Catkin swollen, usually symetrical (Fig. 235); contains white jumping larvae (Fig. 233) from late spring to autumn: **Diptera: Cecidomyiidae**

.... ***Contarinia coryli*** (Kaltenbach)
(= *corylina*)

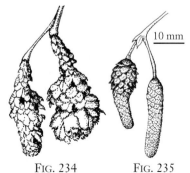

FIG. 234   FIG. 235

These two galls can only be safely distinguished if mites or cecid larvae are present.

E42. *COTINUS*

One psyllid gall (**Hemiptera: Psylloidea**) is recorded on the introduced smoke-tree, *Cotinus coggygria* Scop., grown in gardens. In other countries, this gall is also found on sumachs, *Rhus* species.

Leaf margin inrolled upwards, swollen (Fig. 236); usually affects young leaves; contains nymphs (Fig. 237); very rare .... *Calophya rhois* (Löw)
A single British record, from Hebrides (Hodkinson & White, 1979).

FIG. 237

FIG. 236

COTONEASTER see *MALUS*

E43. *CRATAEGUS*

Most species gall both native hawthorns, *C. monogyna* Jacq. and midland hawthorn, *C. laevigata* (Poir.) DC. (= *C. oxyacanthoides*) and their hybrids, but are more common on the former. For rust galls on leaves and fruit, see p. 232.

READ THREE ALTERNATIVES
1 Gall in bud or shoot tip **2**

- Gall in leaf **3**

- Gall in flower, which remains closed **9**

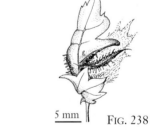

5 mm FIG. 238

READ THREE ALTERNATIVES
2 Terminal shoot stunted and distorted into an irregular rosette of many slightly thickened deformed leaves, with small red or green projections (Fig. 238); contains many orange-red larvae (Fig. 239) in June - July and Sept.; common, conspicuous in hedges: **Diptera: Cecidomyiidae** .... *Dasineura crataegi* (Winnertz) **hawthorn button-top gall**

FIG. 239

- Partly opened bud with outer leaves forming a 'cage' about 5 mm wide; encloses black decaying inner leaves and one larva (Fig. 240) in May and June, and a pupa later: **Coleoptera: Curculionidae** .... *Anthonomus bituberculatus* Thomson

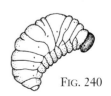

FIG. 240

- Swollen unopened bud, up to 6 x 3 mm, often abnormally hairy; contains mites (Fig. 241): **Acari: Eriophyoidea** .... *Eriophyes calicobius* Nalepa
(= *Phytoptus*)

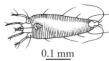

0.1 mm   FIG. 241

3 Gall a raised pock or erineum on blade; contains mites (Fig. 241): **Acari: Eriophyoidea** **4**

- Gall a tight or loose thickened downward roll or fold, affecting leaf margin, one lobe or most of blade **5**

   Small depression underneath with corresponding reddish bulge on upperside may be due to a psyllid, e.g. *Psylla melanoneura* Förster or *P. peregrina* Förster; the insect leaves in early summer.

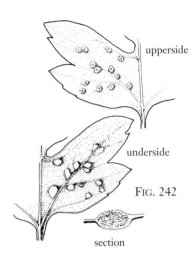

upperside

underside

FIG. 242

section

4 Small raised pocks on both surfaces, opening above or below; usually several on a leaf (Fig. 242); pale green at first, becoming brownish
.... *Aceria crataegi* (Canestrini)
(= *Eriophyes*)

   A slight bulge in vein angles on upperside, hairy below, may be caused by *Eriophyes albaespinae* Cotte.

- Erineum on underside with white, reddish or violet hairs with swollen tips
.... *Phyllocoptes goniothorax* (Nalepa)
(= *Eriophyes*)

   This mite more commonly causes a tight roll of the leaf margin, see couplet 5.

5 Tight margin roll, 3-15 mm long (Fig. 243 shows a small gall) often yellowish, sometimes red; hairy inside with mites (Fig. 241); often several on a leaf; very common: **Acari: Eriophyoidea**
.... *Phyllocoptes goniothorax* (Nalepa)
(= *Eriophyes*)

   This mite may also cause an erineum, see couplet 4.

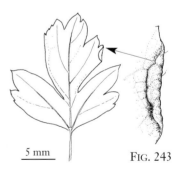

5 mm   FIG. 243

- A loose puckered bulge, roll or fold, affecting more than the leaf margin; contains aphids (Fig. 244) or their remains: **Hemiptera: Aphididae**
.... **6**

FIG. 244

6 Yellow, pink or red galls on individual leaves; contain waxy aphids **7**

- Gall same green as leaf; often affects tips of several adjacent leaves; contains non-waxy aphids **8**

7 Yellowed gall; leaf curled down, like an upturned boat; aphids deep grey beneath waxy bloom, present May - June
.... ***Dysaphis ranunculi*** (Kaltenbach)

- Crimson or purplish-red gall not affecting whole leaf (Plate 2.2); aphids pale green or pinkish, present April - May
.... ***Dysaphis crataegi***-group
The several species in this group need expert identification. Other aphids may also distort leaves.

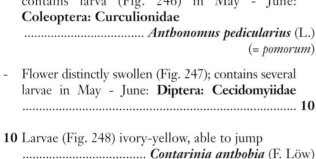

10 mm   FIG. 245

FIG. 246

8 Aphids yellow-green with green or brown siphons, leave gall by early June; one or more leaf lobes inrolled (Fig. 245)
.... ***Rhopalosiphum insertum*** (Walker)
(= *Aphis crataegella*)

- Aphids bright green with dark brown siphons; present in June and later, after other hawthorn gall aphids have left; leaf tips curled over all around
.... ***Aphis pomi*** De Geer
Other aphids may also distort leaves.

10 mm

FIG. 247

9 Flower slightly distorted by swollen ovary; turns brown early and becomes 'capped', failing to open; contains larva (Fig. 246) in May - June: **Coleoptera: Curculionidae**
.... ***Anthonomus pedicularius*** (L.)
(= *pomorum*)

- Flower distinctly swollen (Fig. 247); contains several larvae in May - June: **Diptera: Cecidomyiidae**
.... **10**

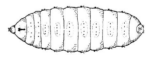

FIG. 248

10 Larvae (Fig. 248) ivory-yellow, able to jump
.... ***Contarinia anthobia*** (F. Löw)

- Larvae (Fig. 249) red, unable to jump
.... ***Dasineura oxyacanthae*** Rübsaamen
Orange-yellow larvae of *Dasineura fusca* (Rübsaamen) may occur in swollen flowers; these are probably inquilines.

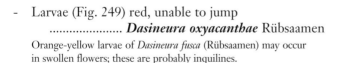

FIG. 249

E44. *CREPIS*

Galls are recorded in flower heads of rough hawk's-beard, *C. biennis* L., smooth hawk's-beard, *C. capillaris* (L.) Wallr., and marsh hawk's-beard, *C. paludosa* (L.) Moench.

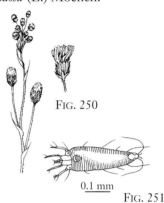

FIG. 250

1   Flower head greened and leafy, with a multiplication of flower stalks supporting small malformed flower heads (chloranthy) (Fig. 250); contains mites (Fig. 251): **Acari: Eriophyoidea** .... ***Aceria rechingeri*** (Nalepa) (= *Eriophyes*)

-   Flower head swollen, usually remaining closed **2**

0.1 mm

FIG. 251

2   Base of head slightly swollen; contains white larvae (Fig. 252) or brown puparia; in *C. capillaris*; southern England and E. Anglia: **Diptera: Tephritidae** .... ***Tephritis formosa*** (Loew)
Commoner in heads of *Sonchus*, see Fig. 253.

-   Swollen flower head contains mites (Fig. 251) or cecid larvae (Fig. 254) **3**

FIG. 252   FIG. 253

3   Flower head disfigured, containing distorted achenes; contains several yellow, jumping, larvae; in *C. biennis*: **Diptera: Cecidomyiidae** .... ***Contarinia hypochoeridis*** (Rübsaamen)
Commoner in heads of *Hypochaeris* (p. 349).

-   Flower head contains mites; in *C. paludosa*: **Acari: Eriophyoidea** .... ***Aceria anthocoptes*** (Nalepa)

FIG. 254

CRITHMUM see APIACEAE

CRUCIATA see *GALIUM*

E45. *CUSCUTA*

Galls are recorded on all three species found in Britain, dodder, *C. epithymum* (L.) L., greater dodder, *C. europaea* L., and yellow dodder, *C. campestris* Yunck.

1   Flower deformed, stunted; contains mites (Fig. 251); on *C. epithymum*: **Acari: Eriophyoidea** .... ***Eriophyes cuscutae*** Molliard

-   Fleshy, rounded or spindle-shaped swelling in stem, up to 8 x 5 mm (Fig. 255), often yellowish or reddish; one or two chambers, each with a larva (Fig. 256) or pupa; adult emerges July - August: **Coleoptera: Curculionidae** **2**

2 On *C. epithymum* .... ***Smicronyx coecus*** (Reich)

- On *Cuscuta* spp.
.... ***Smicronyx jungermanniae*** (Reich)
To separate, adults must be reared and identified (Fowler, 1891).

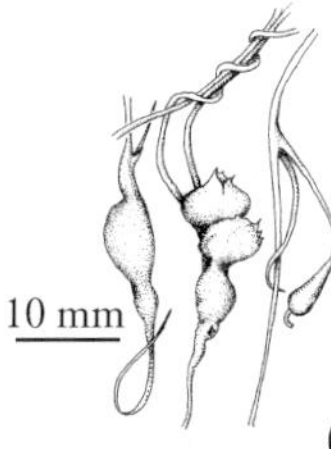

10 mm

FIG. 255

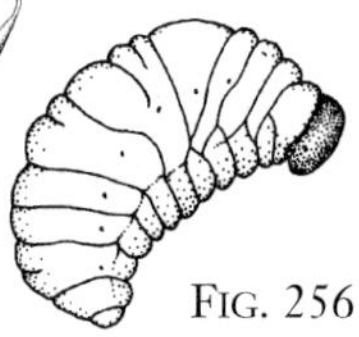

FIG. 256

E46. *CYTISUS* (= *SAROTHAMNUS*)

Galls occur on the native broom, *Cytisus scoparius* (L.) Link. Root nodules are caused by *Rhizobium* sp. (see p. 219).

READ THREE ALTERNATIVES
1 Gall in stem, flower stalks or leaves **2**

- Gall in bud **8**

- Gall in fruit (pod) **12**

2 Leaflets thickened, folded into a pod; contains red larvae (Fig. 257); rare: **Diptera: Cecidomyiidae**
.... ***Dasineura vallisumbrosae*** (Kieffer)
Only one British record, from Perthshire.

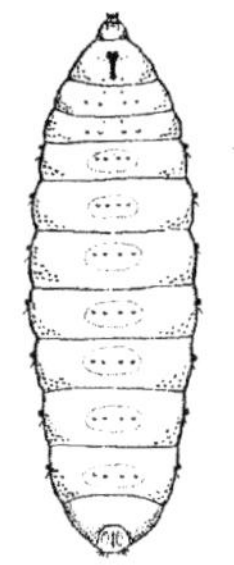

FIG. 257

- In stem, occasionally in petiole, leaf veins or flower stalk **3**

3 Rounded, depressed pit in young stem, usually several together; if numerous, may coalesce and distort the stem: **Hemiptera: Coccoidea: Diaspididae**
.... ***Chionaspis salicis*** (L.)

- Swelling in stem, petiole, vein or flower stalk **4**

4 Small swelling < 5 mm long, usually near tip of stem; contains a red or orange larva: **Diptera: Cecidomyiidae** **5**

- Larger swelling > 10 mm long **7**

5 Symmetrical swelling in stem, 1-3 mm long, sometimes in petiole, vein or flower stalk; larva (Fig. 258) orange ... ***Contarinia scoparii*** (Rübsaamen)
Also galls terminal buds, couplet 9.

FIG. 258

- Lateral swelling in stem, often several together **6**

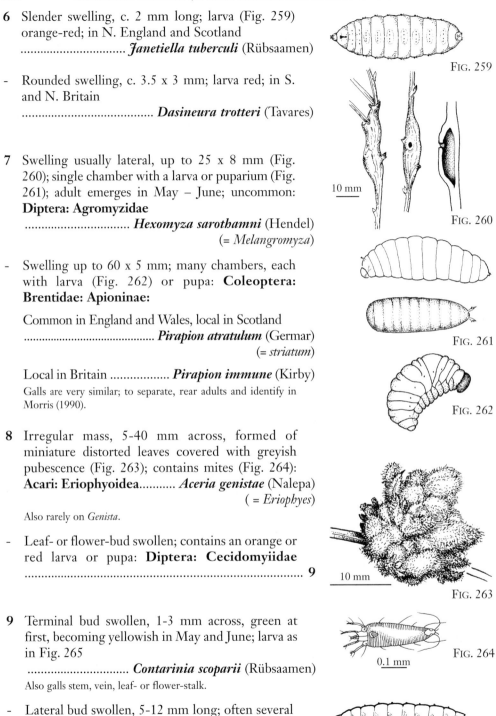

6   Slender swelling, c. 2 mm long; larva (Fig. 259) orange-red; in N. England and Scotland
.... ***Janetiella tuberculi*** (Rübsaamen)

FIG. 259

-    Rounded swelling, c. 3.5 x 3 mm; larva red; in S. and N. Britain
.... ***Dasineura trotteri*** (Tavares)

7   Swelling usually lateral, up to 25 x 8 mm (Fig. 260); single chamber with a larva or puparium (Fig. 261); adult emerges in May – June; uncommon: **Diptera: Agromyzidae**
.... ***Hexomyza sarothamni*** (Hendel)
(= *Melangromyza*)

10 mm

FIG. 260

-    Swelling up to 60 x 5 mm; many chambers, each with larva (Fig. 262) or pupa: **Coleoptera: Brentidae: Apioninae:**

Common in England and Wales, local in Scotland
.... ***Pirapion atratulum*** (Germar)
(= *striatum*)

FIG. 261

Local in Britain .... ***Pirapion immune*** (Kirby)
Galls are very similar; to separate, rear adults and identify in Morris (1990).

FIG. 262

8   Irregular mass, 5-40 mm across, formed of miniature distorted leaves covered with greyish pubescence (Fig. 263); contains mites (Fig. 264): **Acari: Eriophyoidea**........... ***Aceria genistae*** (Nalepa)
(= *Eriophyes*)

Also rarely on *Genista*.

-    Leaf- or flower-bud swollen; contains an orange or red larva or pupa: **Diptera: Cecidomyiidae**
.... **9**

10 mm

FIG. 263

9   Terminal bud swollen, 1-3 mm across, green at first, becoming yellowish in May and June; larva as in Fig. 265
.... ***Contarinia scoparii*** (Rübsaamen)
Also galls stem, vein, leaf- or flower-stalk.

FIG. 264

0.1 mm

-    Lateral bud swollen, 5-12 mm long; often several adjacent buds affected **10**

FIG. 265

10 Elongate, tubular, with 2 – 3 points at tip, pressed against stem (Fig. 266); without hairs or a stalk; larva (Fig. 259) in late summer and autumn; Surrey and S. Wales northwards, common in Scotland .... ***Dasineura tubicola*** (Kieffer)

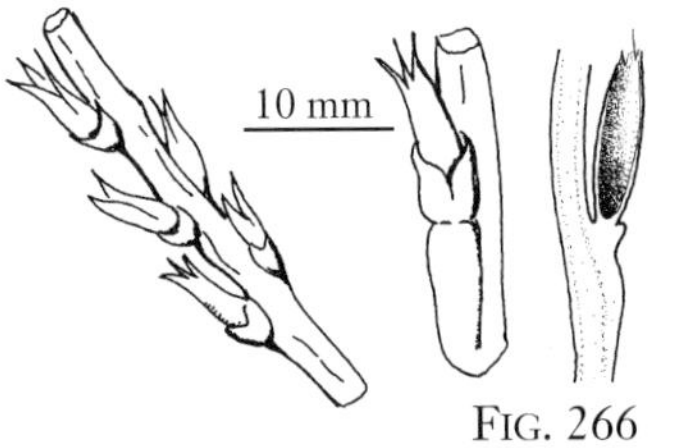

\- Ovoid with single point or projection at tip, with or without hairs and a stalk **11**

FIG. 266

11 With single point at tip, usually without a stalk (Fig. 267), with or without hairs; cavity lined with fungal mycelium; larva (Fig. 268) in spring; widespread.............. ***Asphondylia sarothamni*** (Loew) generation 1

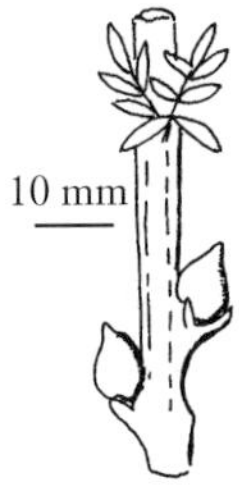

FIG. 267

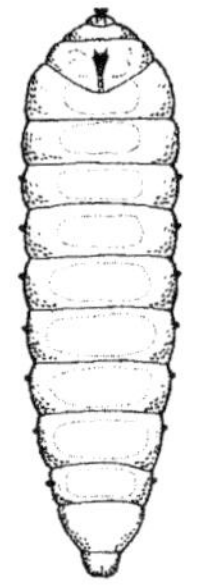

FIG. 268

A. pilosa Kieffer was synonymised with *A. sarathomni* by Skuhravá (1989), despite differences in size of adults and shape of the sternal spatula or larvae (Kieffer 1898, reference in Skuhravá, 1989). Recently, however, Harris (personal communication) has positively identified galls and larvae of *A. pilosa* from Dunsford, Surrey (collected 9.5.02). The gall, about 1 cm long, has conspicuous long hairs and a prominent projection forming more than half of its length. Thus, *A. pilosa* Kieffer should be reinstated as a good species.

\- With projection at tip, usually with a stalk (Fig. 269), without hairs; cavity without mycelium; N. England and Scotland .... ***Jaapiella sarothamni*** (Rübsaamen)

FIG. 269

12 Hard rounded growth in base of pod, containing a larva (Fig. 262) or pupa: **Coleoptera: Curculionidae** .... ***Tychius parallelus*** (Panzer) (= *venustus*)

\- Hard rounded or elongate swelling in wall of pod, often more than one, containing a larva or pupa: **Diptera: Cecidomyiidae** **13**

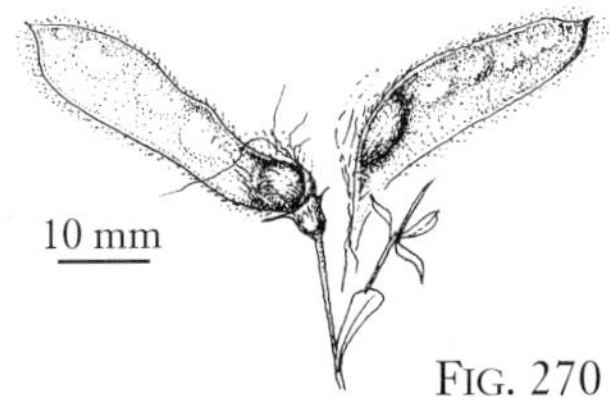

10 mm

FIG. 270

13 One or two galls in basal half of pod (Fig. 270); cavity inside lined with fungal mycelium; larva (Fig. 268) red or orange and cannot jump .... ***Asphondylia sarothamni*** (Loew) generation 2

See note, couplet 11. If several orange larvae are present, they may belong to the inquiline *Trotteria obtusa* (Loew).

\- Several swellings. c. 2 mm across, usually in distal half of pod (Fig. 271); cavity without mycelium; larva (Fig. 265) white and can jump .... ***Contarinia pulchripes*** (Kieffer)

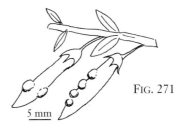

FIG. 271

5 mm

DACTYLIS see POACEAE

E47. *DAPHNE*

One gall (**Diptera: Cecidomyiidae**) is recorded on spurge-laurel, *Daphne laureola* L.

Leaves at shoot tip with margins thickened, inrolled, forming a tuft up to 3 cm long (Fig. 272); contains white larvae (Fig. 273); rare
.... ***Dasineura daphnes*** (Kieffer)

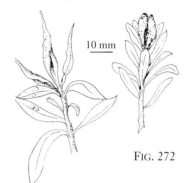

10 mm

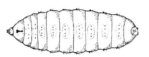

Fig. 273

Fig. 272

DAUCUS see APIACEAE

DENDRANTHEMA see *CHRYSANTHEMUM*

DESCHAMPSIA see POACEAE

DESCURAINIA see BRASSICACEAE

DRYOPTERIS see *ATHYRIUM*

E48. *ECHIUM*

Two galls are found on viper's-bugloss, *Echium vulgare* L.

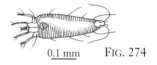

1   Flower parts deformed and leafy (phyllanthy), very hairy; contain mites (Fig. 274): **Acari: Eriophyoidea**
.... *Aceria echii* (Canestrini)
(= *Eriophyes*)

0.1 mm   Fig. 274

2   Swelling in lower part of stem or in leaf stalk, growth above gall aborted; contains a caterpillar August - June (pupates outside gall): **Lepidoptera: Pyralidae**
.... ***Cynaeda dentalis*** (D. & S.)

ELYTRIGIA see POACEAE

E49. *EMPETRUM*

One gall (**Acari: Eriophyoidea**) is found on crowberry, *Empetrum nigrum* L.

Gall at shoot tip; internodes shortened, leaves ± deformed, small, pale, often shiny; associated flowers malformed, greened; contains mites (Fig. 274)
.... ***Aceria empetri*** (Lindroth)

E50. *EPILOBIUM*

There are many species of native willowherbs and hybrids are common; thus identification can be difficult. Most galls, however, are found on great willowherb, *E. hirsutum* L. and broad-leaved willowherb, *E. montanum* L., and occasionally on marsh and spear-leaved willowherbs, *E. palustre* L. and *E. lanceolatum* Sebast. & Mauri. (For rose-bay willowherb, see *Chamerion* p. 308.)

Only three uncommon gall-causing insects are known, in S. England and Wales; all are *Mompha* spp. (**Lepidoptera: Momphidae**; larva Fig. 275).

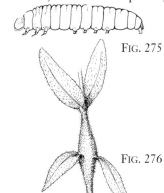

FIG. 275

FIG. 276

1   Rounded or spindle-shaped swelling in main stem, usually thickest (6-8 mm) at a node (Fig. 276), often reddened; elongate chamber contains a pale green caterpillar with dark head in June - July, or pupa in silken cocoon July - August; on *E. montanum, E. palustre* or *E. lanceolatum* .... ***Mompha divisella*** Herrich-Schäffer
(= *decorella*)

2   Small swelling in a side stem, 5-7 x 3 mm; chamber with caterpillar in July - August .... ***Mompha bradleyi*** Reidl

3   Seed pod slightly thickened and shortened, sometimes twisted, remaining closed; contains a red caterpillar with yellow-brown head in July - August; on *E. montanum* .... ***Mompha subbistrigella*** (Haworth)

In addition, several species of aphids (**Hemiptera: Aphididae**, Fig. 277) may be common, causing leaf-curl and sometimes distortion of inflorescence, seed pods and stems. They are not regarded as gall causers.

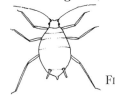

FIG. 277

E51. *ERICA*

Galls are found on cross-leaved heath, *E. tetralix* L., and the garden varieties of alpine or winter heath, *E. carnea* L. Two species, and possibly a third, are known.

1   Small witches' broom at tip of shoot; internodes shortened, stem distorted, leaves thickened and bunched; contains scale insects; on *E. tetralix*: **Hemiptera: Coccoidea**
.... ***Acanthococcus devoniensis*** (Green)
(= *Eriococcus*)

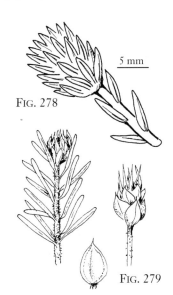

5 mm

FIG. 278

2   Artichoke gall at shoot tip (Fig. 278); leaves broader and shorter than normal (galled shoots are difficult to distinguish from ungalled shoots); contains a red larva (Fig. 273); on *E. carnea*: **Diptera: Cecidomyiidae**
.... ***Wachtliella ericina*** (F. Löw)
A smaller artichoke, up to 5 x 3 mm (Fig. 279), with an orange larva is caused by *Myricomyia mediterranea* (F. Löw) (**Diptera: Cecidomyiidae**) and found on tree heath, *Erica arborea* L. abroad. This may be British but Bagnall & Harrison's 1918 record on *E. tetralix* has not been verified (Harris, personal communication).

FIG. 279

E52. *ERIGERON*

Two gall-causing arthropods are recorded, both in the flower head of blue fleabane, *E. acer* L.

1   Base of flower head swollen, remaining closed; contains yellow, non-jumping larvae (Fig. 280): **Diptera: Cecidomyiidae**
.... ***Dasineura socialis*** (Kieffer)

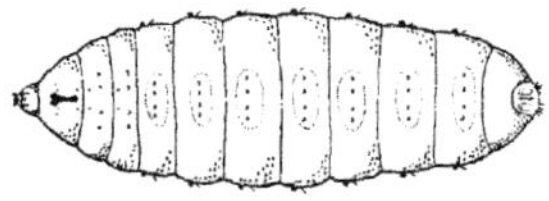

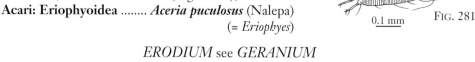

FIG. 280

2   Flower head swollen, florets reddened and deformed; contains mites (Fig. 281); rare: **Acari: Eriophyoidea** .... ***Aceria puculosus*** (Nalepa) (= *Eriophyes*)

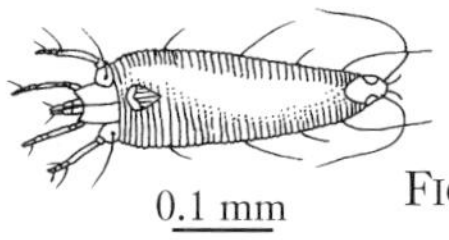

0.1 mm   FIG. 281

ERODIUM see *GERANIUM*

EROPHILA see BRASSICACEAE

ERYSIMUM see BRASSICACEAE

E53. *EUONYMUS*

Two mite galls (**Acari: Eriophyoidea**) are common on the leaves of the native spindle-tree, *Euonymus europaeus* L. In addition, young leaves at tips of shoots may be stunted, crumpled and distorted due to feeding by polyphagous aphids; these are not considered to be true galls. Introduced species are less likely to be galled.

1   Tight upward roll of leaf margin, affecting all or part of leaf (Fig. 282, Plate 1.3); occasionally in midrib; green or red; contains mites (Fig. 281)
.... ***Eriophyes convolvens*** (Nalepa)

10 mm

2   Erineum on underside of blade, with silver-white hairs; may affect most of leaf; mites (Fig. 281) live between the hairs
.... ***Cecidophyes psilonotus*** (Nalepa)

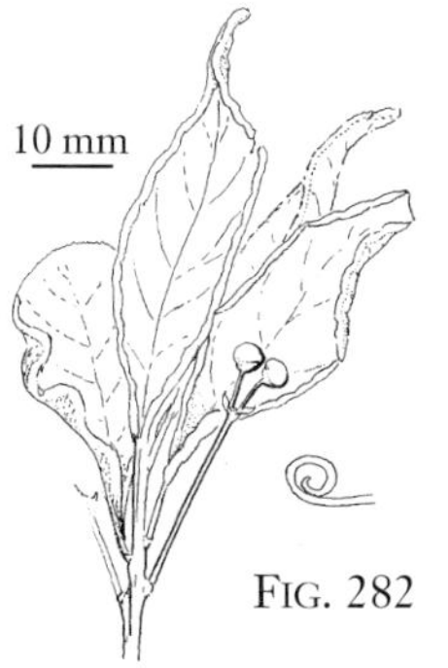

FIG. 282

E54. *EUPATORIUM*

The one species, hemp agrimony, *Eupatorium cannabinum* L., is galled by one insect (**Lepidoptera: Pterophoridae**).

Spindle-shaped or cylindrical swelling in main or side stem, near a node or in axils of flower stalks, about 10 mm long (Fig. 283); contains a pinkish-white caterpillar with a yellow-brown head (Fig. 284) in July and September - October, and frass
.... ***Adaina microdactyla*** Hübner

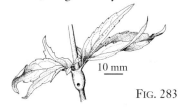

10 mm

FIG. 283

FIG. 284

E55. *EUPHORBIA*

Two, perhaps three, galls are found on cypress spurge, *E. cyparissias* L., and leafy spurge, *E. esula* L. The spurges interbreed to form fertile hybrids, with each other and with other species. Consequently, they are often difficult to distinguish (Stace 1997) and, unless determined by a specialist, should be referred to *E. esula* L. agg.

For rust galls on leaves, see p. 235.

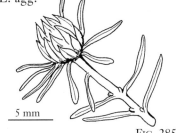

1   Fat artichoke gall at tip of shoot, up to 10 mm across (Fig. 285); outer leaves shorter and broader than normal; contains an orange-red larva (Fig. 280) or pupa; on *E. cyparissias*: **Diptera: Cecidomyiidae** .... *Spurgia capitigena* (Bremi)
    (= *Bayeriola capitigena* = *Bayeria capitigena* = *Dasineura subpatula*)

FIG. 285

For synonymy of *Dasineura subpatula* see Gagné (1990). A similar gall on *E. esula*, also with an orange-red larva, may be caused by *Spurgia esulae* Gagné. There seem to be no British records for either species supported by specimens (Harris, personal communication).The identity of cecid galls on *Euphorbia* is confused. Similar galls are caused by several gall midge species abroad, each narrowly restricted in its host range.

2   Leaf twisted, deformed, with narrow inrolling of margin; usually several adjacent leaves, or all at shoot tip, affected, sometimes forming a loose tuft; flowers may be deformed, remaining closed, sometimes becoming leafy (phyllanthy); contains mites (Fig. 281): **Acari: Eriophyoidea** .... *Eriophyes euphorbiae* (Nalepa)

E56. *EUPHRASIA*

A large and complex genus with about 20 species which frequently hybridise. All are eyebrights, with the aggregate *Euphrasia officinale* L. used for all but one (Stace 1997). One gall mite (**Acari: Eriophyoidea**) is recorded.

Whole plant may be stunted and distorted, with leaves curled, discoloured, with thick white hairy growths on underside (Fig. 286); flowers transformed into a mass of small hairy leaves; mites (Fig. 281) live amongst the hairs .... *Aceria euphrasiae* (Nalepa)

FIG. 286

E57. *FAGUS*

There is one native species, common beech *Fagus sylvatica* L.

1   Gall an enlarged partly-expanded bud 2

-   Gall on or in leaf 3

2   Young leaves of bud (usually a terminal bud)

deformed and slightly thickened; several whitish larvae (Fig. 287) between them in late spring - early summer: **Diptera: Cecidomyiidae**
.... *Contarinia fagi* Rübsaamen

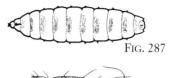

FIG. 287

- Young leaves thickly covered with silver-grey hairs, stunted, often folded with wavy veins; mites (Fig. 288) present in spring; gall withers in summer but may remain on tree over next winter: **Acari: Eriophyoidea** .... *Acalitus blastophthirus* (Nalepa)
(= *Aceria*)

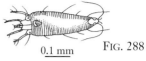

0.1 mm   FIG. 288

READ FOUR ALTERNATIVES

3 Tight upward marginal roll, short or long (may extend all round leaf edge) (Fig. 289); lined with hairs and containing mites (Fig. 288): **Acari: Eriophyoidea** .... *Acalitus stenaspis* (Nalepa)
(= *Eriophyes* = *Aceria*)

Tight downward marginal rolls have been found in Scotland (Entwistle, personal communication); these may be caused by the same species.

20 mm

FIG. 289

- Erineum between or along veins, or tuft of hairs in vein angles; contains mites (Fig. 288): **Acari: Eriophyoidea** **4**

- Rounded, conical, cylindrical or ovoid pouch or pustule, 0.5-10 mm high, with or without hairs; contains one larva or pupa: **Diptera: Cecidomyiidae** **5**

- Leaf folded along lateral veins, or inrolled and distorted with irregular bulges and depressions; may affect one or two veins, or part or all of leaf **6**

READ THREE ALTERNATIVES

4 Erineum along vein on upperside, usually several on leaf (Fig. 290); white, later pink or brown; common
.... *Aceria nervisequus* (Canestrini)
(= *Eriophyes*)

- Erineum between veins, normally on underside, usually many on a leaf (Fig. 291, Plate 1.8); white, later pink or brown; common
.... *Aceria fagineus* (Nalepa)
Fresh erinea are pink on copper beeches.   (= *Eriophyes*)

- Tuft of hairs in depression in angle of veins on underside, often extending along midrib; corresponding pale-coloured bulge above
.... *Monochetus sulcatus* (Nalepa)

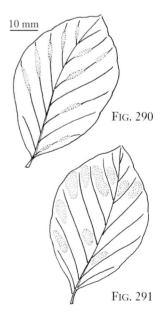

10 mm

FIG. 290

FIG. 291

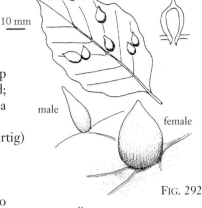

10 mm

5 Gall ovoid, hairless, 8 -10 x 3-6 mm, pointed at tip (Fig. 292, Plate 3.8), pale green or reddened; woody with large chamber, larva white, pupa bright orange-red; uncommon
.... ***Mikiola fagi*** (Hartig)
Rotund galls contain female larvae, slim galls male larvae.

male

female

FIG. 292

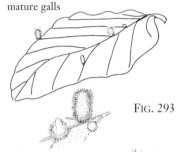

mature galls

- Mature gall cylindrical, hairy or smooth, up to 6mm high when mature in August-September rounded or ovoid when younger (Fig. 293) (galls fall to ground in autumn leaving circular holes in leaf); pale green, hairs pale or reddish brown; chamber large with woody walls; when young in June, the gall is a pustule raised on underside with a flat pale circle above (Fig. 294); larva white; common .... ***Hartigiola annulipes*** (Hartig)
(= *Oligotrophus fagineus* = *Phegobia tornatella*)

FIG. 293

Identification has been confused: the smooth galls were thought to be caused by *P. tornatella* (Bremi), and *O. fagineus* Kieffer has been used for the immature small rounded pustules; both now shown to be synonyms of *H. annulipes* (Skuhravá 1989). Development of the gall, which takes 5 months, is described in detail by Rohfritsch (1992). It has been suggested (Robbins, personal communication) that a small blister-like gall, similar to the early stage of *H. annulipes* but whose full-grown larva departs in summer through a small central hole, is caused by *O. fagineus* (*i.e.* that this is a good species). This has not yet been proven.

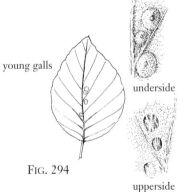

young galls

underside

FIG. 294

upperside

READ THREE ALTERNATIVES
6 Leaf folded along lateral vein, swollen below with a slit-like opening on upperside (Fig. 295), without hairs; contains 2 - 3 reddish larvae (Fig. 287): **Diptera: Cecidomyiidae**
.... ***Phegomyia fagicola*** (Kieffer)

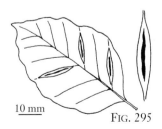

10 mm

FIG. 295

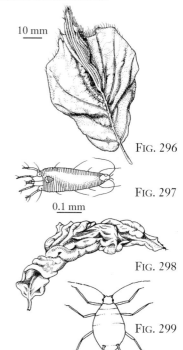

10 mm

Fig. 296

- Distal part, or most of leaf, with folds, covered with hairs and often reddish (Fig. 296); leaf stunted and small; contains mites (Fig. 297): **Acari: Eriophyoidea**

.... *Acalitus plicans* (Nalepa)

(= *Aceria*)

Fig. 297

0.1 mm

- Part or most of leaf with irregular upward bulges, often with incurled margins (Fig. 298); waxy aphids (Fig. 299) live in depressions on underside: **Homoptera: Aphididae**

....*Phyllaphis fagi* (L.)

Fig. 298

Fig. 299

FESTUCA see POACEAE

FILAGO see *GNAPHALIUM*

E58. *FILIPENDULA*

There are two native species, meadowsweet, *Filipendula ulmaria* (L.) Maxim. and dropwort, *F. vulgaris* Moensch. All the gall causers below attack meadowsweet, except for *Dasineura filipendulae* on dropwort. For rusts and smut galls, see p. 236.

READ THREE ALTERNATIVES

1 Irregular fleshy swelling in stem or petiole (Fig. 300), sometimes reddened; contains several chambers, each with a red larva (Fig. 301); N. England and Scotland, uncommon: **Diptera: Cecidomyiidae**

.... *Dasineura harrisoni* (Bagnall)

- Gall in leaf blade... 2

- Gall in flower bud; contains a larva (Fig. 301): **Diptera: Cecidomyiidae** 5

5 mm

Fig. 300

Fig. 301

2 Young leaflets reduced in size, thickened and rolled transversely into tight coils (Fig. 302), often several leaves affected at tip of stem; internodes may be shortened to form a coiled mass; contain aphids (Fig. 299), mottled green and yellow, 1.2 - 2.4 mm long, may be attended by ants; local: **Hemiptera: Aphididae**

.... *Aphis ulmariae* Schrank

Macrosiphum (= *Macrosiphoniella*) *cholodkovskyi* Mordvilko induces loose rolls which are not thickened; the aphids are 4 mm long, shiny green or reddish. These are probably not true galls.

FIG. 302

- Swelling or pustule in blade, usually several in a leaf; contains a larva (Fig. 301): **Diptera: Cecidomyiidae** **3**

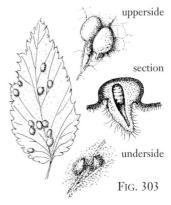

FIG. 303

3 Upper surface with smooth, reddish, rounded swellings, 1-2 mm across, with pale yellow, hairy, conical projections below, 2-4 mm long (Fig. 303); usually on veins; pale yellow larva June - July, pupa August; common

.... *Dasineura ulmaria* (Bremi)

- Swellings raised on upper surface, depression or hairy groove below **4**

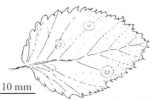

FIG. 304

4 Small swellings above, c. 1 mm across, with shallow dimple below, each surrounded by a yellow patch up to 5 mm across (Fig. 304); pale larva in dimple in early summer; common
.... *Dasineura pustulans* (Rübsaamen)

- Larger elongated, wrinkled, yellowish, pleat-like swellings above, with hairy indentations below (Fig. 305); white, later pink, larva present in spring or early summer, pupa later; uncommon
.... *Dasineura engstfeldi* (Rübsaamen)
generation 1

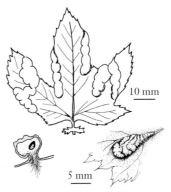

FIG. 305

5   Flower bud swollen, reddened and abnormally
     hairy; white, later pink, larva in summer;
     uncommon .... ***Dasineura engstfeldi*** (Rübsaamen)
     generation 2

-    Flower bud swollen, reddened, not hairy (Fig.
     306); red larva in summer, or pupa; uncommon or
     rare:

     On *F. ulmaria* .... ***Dasineura spiraeae*** (Loiselle)

     On *F. vulgaris* .... ***Dasineura filipendulae*** (Kieffer)

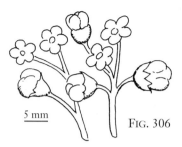

5 mm

FIG. 306

FOENICULUM see APIACEAE

E59. *FRANGULA*

There is one species, alder buckthorn, *Frangula alnus*
Miller. For a rust gall on leaves, see p. 251.

1   Leaf margin thickened, rolled upwards, 0.5-2 cm
     long (Fig. 307); often tinted red or purplish;
     contains nymphs (Fig. 308); locally common in S.
     England, scarcer north to Cumbria: **Hemiptera:
     Psylloidea** .... ***Trichochermes walkeri*** Förster
     (= *Trichopsylla*)

-    Flower bud slightly swollen, remaining closed;
     contains larvae: **Diptera: Cecidomyiidae** **2**

FIG. 307

No drawing is available of the gall of
T. walkeri on *Frangula*; this is the gall
on *Rhamnus cathartica*.

FIG. 308

2   Larvae (Fig. 309) white when young, sulphur-
     yellow later, jumping
     .... ***Contarinia rhamni*** (Rübsaamen)

-    Larvae (Fig. 310) reddish-yellow, non-jumping
     .... ***Dasineura frangulae*** (Rübsaamen)
     D. frangulae may occur only as an inquiline in galls of *C. rhamni*.

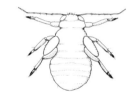

FIG. 309 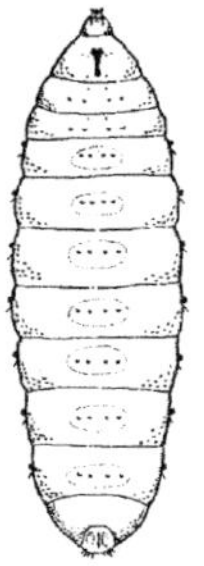   FIG. 310

E60. *FRAXINUS*

The one native species is common ash, *Fraxinus excelsior* L. Exotic species planted in parks, gardens and on roadsides are rarely galled. Most galls are on the compound leaves; each leaf has a petiole and rachis with 9 - 13 leaflets.

See p. 218 for a disfiguring growth caused by a *Pseudomonas* bacterium.

1 Gall in bud, inflorescence or fruit **2**

- Gall in petiole, rachis or leaflet, or affecting most or all of the compound leaf **3**

2 Leaf bud or inflorescence transformed into an irregular cauliflower-like growth, 0.5-2 cm across, often many in a cluster (Fig. 311, Plate 1.5); green at first, later brown or black and very conspicuous in canopy after leaf fall; contains mites (Fig. 312); widespread and common: **Acari: Eriophyoidea** .... *Aceria fraxinivorus* (Nalepa)
(= *Eriophyes*)

10 mm

Occasionally also found on twigs and petioles.

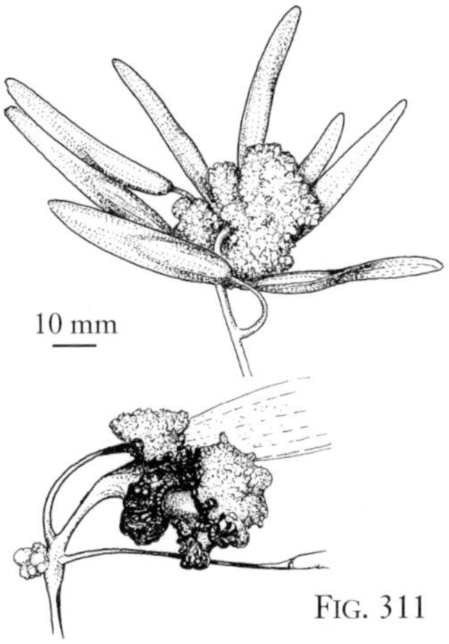

FIG. 311

- Fruit, and seed within, slightly swollen; contains several yellow larvae (Fig. 309) in June - July; N. England and Scotland, rare (no recent records): **Diptera: Cecidomyiidae** .... *Contarinia marchali* Kieffer

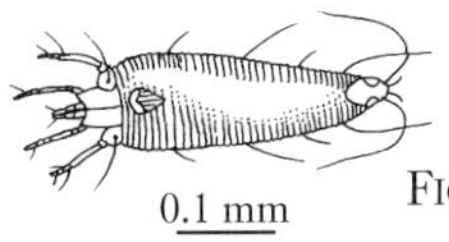

0.1 mm   FIG. 312

3 Petiole and leaflets distorted, bunched together to form a leaf nest; contains woolly aphids (Fig. 313) in May - June, and copious wax; rare: **Hemiptera: Aphididae: Pemphiginae** .... *Prociphilus fraxini* (Hartig)
or *P. bumeliae* (Schrank)

1 mm   FIG. 313

Leaf nests induced by these species are very similar; to separate, the aphids must be identified (Heie 1980, Blackman & Eastop 1994). It is not certain that these distortions should be included as galls.

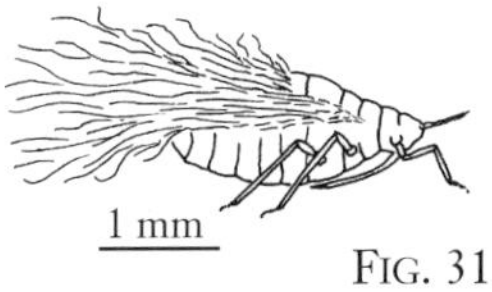

- Gall in individual leaflet; contains one or more larvae (Fig. 310), nymphs (Fig. 308) or mites (Fig. 312) **4**

READ FOUR ALTERNATIVES

4   Leaflet thickened and folded upwards to form a pod (Fig. 314); contains many white larvae in late spring and early summer; widespread and common: **Diptera: Cecidomyiidae**

..................................*Dasineura acrophila* (Winnertz)

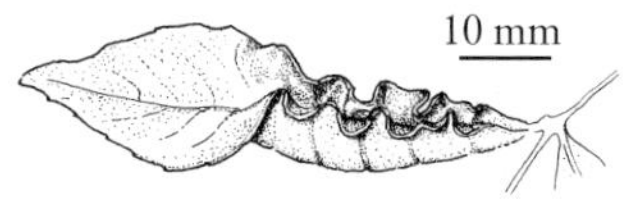

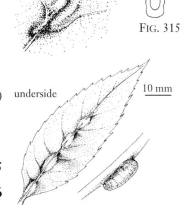

upperside

FIG. 314

-     Underside of main vein of leaflet swollen to form one or more pouches, with a slit-like opening on upperside (Fig. 315, Plate 3.2); 5-30mm long with one orange larva in each pouch (pouches may coalesce), June - October; sometimes in rachis or petiole (Fig. 316); widespread and common: **Diptera: Cecidomyiidae**

.... *Dasineura fraxini* (Bremi)

FIG. 315

If there are several cecid larvae in a pouch, some may be inquilines.

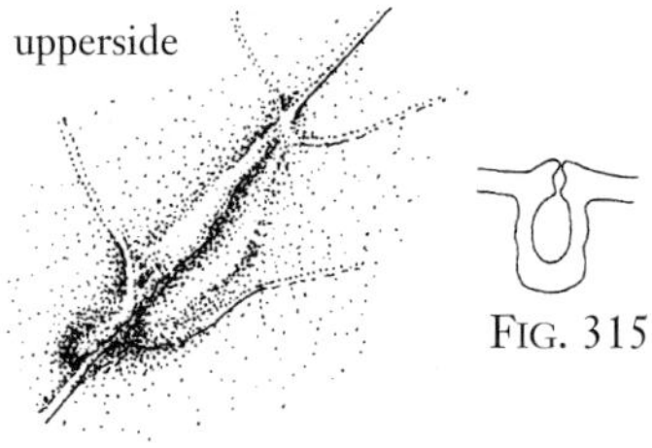

-     Margin of leaflet thickened and rolled or folded downwards **5**

-     Gall in blade of leaflet, not pod-like **6**

underside

on petiole

FIG. 316

5   Narrow tight roll; hairy inside with mites (Fig. 317): **Acari: Eriophyoidea**

.... *Aculus fraxini* (Nalepa)
(= *Phyllocoptes* = *Vasates*)

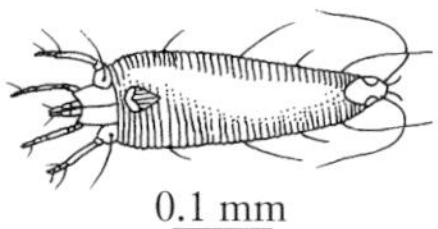

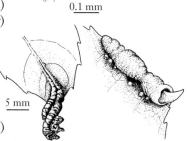

FIG. 317

0.1 mm

-     Broader loose roll or fold (Fig. 318); pale-coloured with reddish or violet markings (Plate 7.1); contains psyllid nymphs (Fig. 319) covered with white wax; widespread and common: **Hemiptera: Psylloidea**

.... *Psyllopsis fraxini* (L.)

The rare *Psyllopsis discrepans* (Flor) has similar galls; separation requires identification of the nymphs (White & Hodkinson 1982).

5 mm

FIG. 318

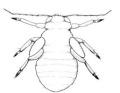

FIG. 319

6 Inconspicuous circular blister, 6-8 mm across, slightly raised on upper surface, with irregular rounded opening on underside (Fig. 320); green or yellowish at first, brown after larva has left; often several in a leaflet; contains one white larva (Fig. 321) in early summer: **Diptera: Cecidomyiidae**
.... ***Dasineura fraxinea*** Kieffer

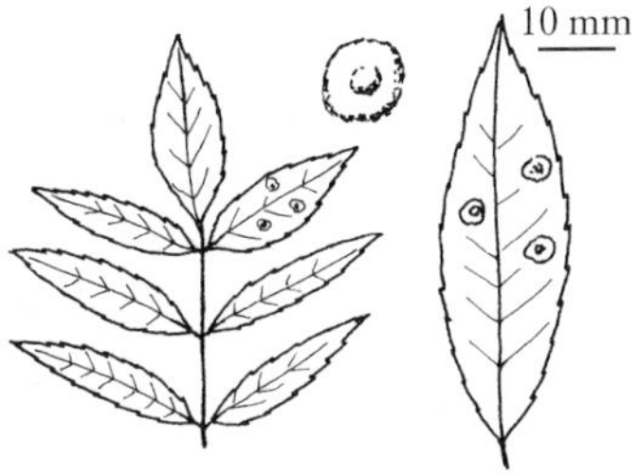

FIG. 320

\- Rounded or pointed tubercle, 2-3 mm across x 1.5 mm high, usually on upperside with opening below, usually several on a leaflet (Fig. 322); occasionally on rachis or petiole; contains mites (Fig. 317); rare: **Acari: Eriophyoidea**
.....................................*Aceria fraxinicola* (Nalepa)
(= *Eriophyes*)

FIG. 321

\- Shallow depression or erineum on underside, sometimes with a bulge above **7**

7 Erineum alongside the main vein, occasionally elsewhere on leaflet; hairs multicellular, reddish at first, later brown; contains mites (Fig. 317): **Acari: Eriophyoidea**
.... ***Aculus epiphyllus*** (Nalepa)
(= *Vasates*)

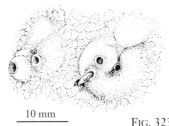

FIG. 322

\- Shallow depression without hairs, discoloured bulge above; several waxy nymphs (Fig. 319) in depression; common: **Hemiptera: Psylloidea**
.... *Psyllopsis fraxinicola* (Förster)

E61. **FUNGI**

Only three insect species are known to cause true galls on fungi, and all affect polypores. Notes are included on three further dipterous species, recorded as gall inducers by Docters van Leeuwen (1957) or Buhr (1964), probably in error.

1 On *Peniophora cinerea* (Fr.) Cooke; soft spongy swellings on upper surface of fruiting body, coalesce into irregular masses up to 3 cm across (Fig. 323); light brown to red colour contrasts with ash-grey of young fruiting body (nearly black when old); each gall contains several larvae (Fig. 324) or pupae, pupal skins protrude from gall aperture after adult emergence; south and central England, locally common: **Diptera: Cecidomyiidae**
.... ***Brachyneurina peniophorae*** Harris
For more information, see Harris & Evans (1979).

FIG. 323

2   On *Hypoxylon rubiginosum* Pers. ex Fr.; rounded, hard black structures on upper surface of fruiting body, up to about 2 mm across (these are canopies of hardened silk, secreted and constructed by the larvae, and are not galls); each contains and is surrounded by bright yellow fungal tissue (this is the gall, the larva stimulating its production and feeding on it); each canopy contains a white larva or pupa, pupal skin protrudes from gall aperture after adult emergence; south and central England: **Diptera: Cecidomyiidae** .... ***Mycocecis ovalis*** Edwards

For more information, see R.E. Evans (1970); L. Evans (1986, 1992).

3   On *Ganoderma applanatum* (Fr. ex Pers.) Patouillard; cylindrical or conical galls, with rounded ends, 5-10 mm long, protruding from underside of fruiting body (Fig. 324), occasionally on upperside; each contains a larva (Fig. 325); when full-grown, it emerges through a circular opening at tip, 1-3 mm wide, to pupate in soil; galls are engulfed by next year's growth of fungus; Kent, Surrey: **Diptera: Platypezidae** ....***Agathomyia wankowiczii*** (Schnabl)

10 mm

FIG. 324

FIG. 325

Known only from gall and larva, from four localities in England; probably a recent introduction and likely to extend its range (Chandler, personal communication).

Mycetophila blanda Winnertz (**Diptera: Mycetophilidae**)
Polyphagous, on *Lactarius, Russula, Panus, Hygrophoropsis* spp.; larvae feed in fruiting body and probably pupate there in tough cocoons; if several cocoons are present, fruiting body may be distorted (but are not true galls; Chandler, personal communication).

Megaselia lutescens (Wood) (**Diptera: Phoridae**)
On *Panaeolus* spp., *Russula foetens* (Pers. ex Fr.) Fr.; adult emerges from rounded galls on gill lamellae (*M. lutescens* is possibly a parasitoid or predator of the (unknown) gall causer; Disney, personal communication).

Drosophila phalerata Meigen (**Diptera: Drosophilidae**)
Reported from *Psathyra* sp., from swellings in gill lamellae; unlikely to be a true gall causer as this species is polyphagous, feeding in fruiting bodies which have started to decompose (Chandler, personal communication).

E62. *GALEOPSIS*

Two galls are found on hemp-nettles, neither of them well known.

1   Flower bud swollen; contains a white or pale reddish yellow larva (Fig. 326); on common hemp-nettle *G. tetrahit* L.; N. England and Scotland: **Diptera: Cecidomyiidae** .... ***Dasineura tetrahit*** (Kieffer)

FIG. 326

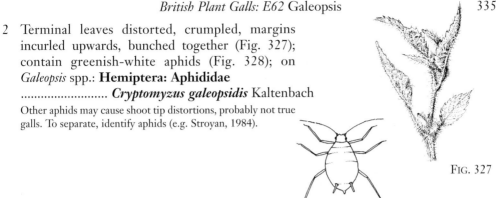

2   Terminal leaves distorted, crumpled, margins incurled upwards, bunched together (Fig. 327); contain greenish-white aphids (Fig. 328); on *Galeopsis* spp.: **Hemiptera: Aphididae**
.... ***Cryptomyzus galeopsidis*** Kaltenbach

Other aphids may cause shoot tip distortions, probably not true galls. To separate, identify aphids (e.g. Stroyan, 1984).

FIG. 327

FIG. 328

E63. *GALIUM, CRUCIATA* and *ASPERULA*

Galium (bedstraws) is a large genus; the other two genera included here each have only one native species, crosswort, *C. laevipes* Opiz and squinancywort, *A. cynanchica* L. On *Galium*, galls are known from woodruff, *G. odoratum* (L.) Scop., hedge bedstraw, *G. mollugo* L., lady's bedstraw, *G. verum* L., common marsh-bedstraw, *G. palustre* L., fen bedstraw, *G. uliginosum* L. and goosegrass or cleavers, *G. aparine* L. Some galls are recorded from several host plants (perhaps others in addition to those listed), while others are host specific. The host range of many of the gall-causing Cecidomyiidae is not clearly established; this key, therefore, should be regarded as preliminary only.

Rust and smut galls may be found on stems and leaves (see p. 236).

1   Smooth fleshy swelling in stem at node, often 4 or 5 together forming a complete ring around the stem or flower stalk, 3-10 mm across (Fig. 329); pale green, sometimes reddish, sometimes brown later; each swelling contains an orange larva (Fig. 326) in summer; usually on *G. mollugo, G. verum*; common: **Diptera: Cecidomyiidae**
.... ***Geocrypta galii*** (Loew)

A second cecidomyiid gall on *G. verum* is widespread in Scotland (Bland, personal communication). It is a more or less conical projection from the stem between nodes often ending in a downward point, about 3mm long. Although not in Chandler (1998) in 1873 Trail named it *"Dasineura galiicaulis"* from the gall only.

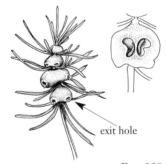

exit hole

FIG. 329

-   Not like this; gall in bud, leaf or fruit, sometimes affecting leaves at shoot tip, or whole inflorescence, or under soil surface **2**

READ THREE ALTERNATIVES

2 Bud at base of stem or under soil surface swollen, with a navel-like depression, brown; contains a larva; on *G. mollugo*: **Diptera: Cecidomyiidae**
.... *Ametrodiplosis auripes* (F. Löw)

- Not like this; in leaf or leaf bud, sometimes adjacent stem swollen **3**

- In flower bud or fruit, affecting whole inflorescence **10**

3 Single leaf swollen, buckled or abnormally hairy, often all leaves of a whorl affected; contains mites (Fig. 330): **Acari: Eriophyoidea** 4

0.1 mm   FIG. 330

- Terminal or axillary bud swollen, often several clustered together with adjacent stem swollen; may form an artichoke gall **5**

4 Whole or part of leaf with both margins thickened and inrolled, leaf often twisted and distorted (Fig. 331); green, often becoming reddish or brown; usually affecting younger leaves; roll hairy inside, usually on *G. aparine*; common
.... *Cecidophyes galii* (Karpeles)
(= *Eriophyes*)

20 mm   FIG. 331

- Leaf buckled, underside very hairy (often adjacent stem also affected)
.... *Coptophylla calvus* (Liro)
It is not certain that this species is found in Britain.

5 Leafy artichoke gall at tip of shoot **6**

- Terminal or lateral bud enlarged, may be hairy; sometimes adjacent stem thickened and fleshy forming a mass of galls due to shortening of internodes; contains one or more larvae or pupae: **Diptera: Cecidomyiidae** **8**

6 Leaves of artichoke gall short, broad and thickened (Fig. 332), pale green, sometimes reddish; contains flattened nymphs; on *C. laevipes* and many *Galium* spp.; locally common: **Hemiptera: Psylloidea** .... *Trioza galii* Förster

- Artichoke gall contains one or more larvae: **Diptera: Cecidomyiidae** **7**

10 mm   FIG. 332

7   Gall looser, leaves similar to normal leaves in length (Fig. 333); usually a single orange-yellow larva (Fig. 334); usually on *G. mollugo* and *G. verum* .... ***Dasineura galiicola*** (F. Löw)

-   Gall tighter, leaves shorter than normal leaves (Fig. 335); several yellowish-white larvae (Fig. 336); on *G. mollugo*, rare .... ***Contarinia molluginis*** (Rübsaamen)

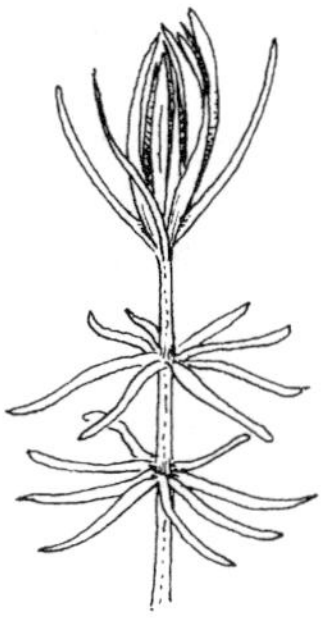

FIG. 334

FIG. 333

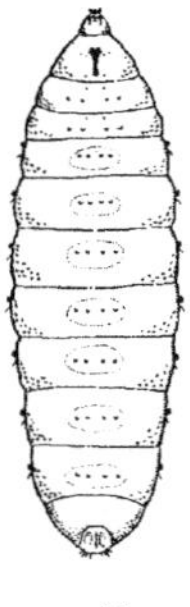

8   Buds and adjacent stem thickened, hairy and fleshy, sometimes clustered into a mass at tip of shoot (Fig. 337); one white or yellow-cream larva (Fig. 334) per galled bud; on *G. aparine* .... ***Dasineura aparines*** (Kieffer)

-   Terminal bud enlarged and rounded, may be partly enveloped in bract-like leaves **9**

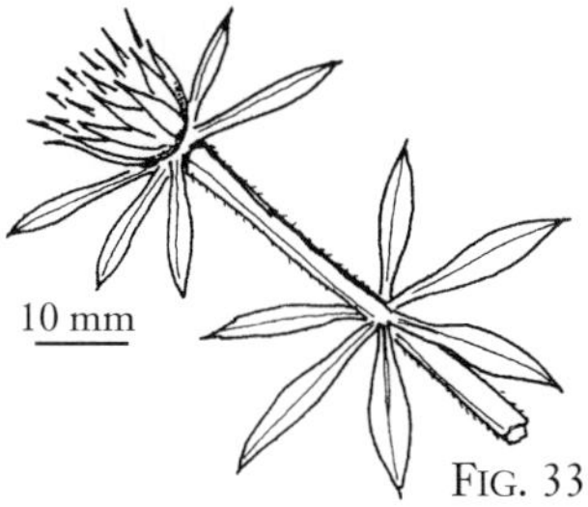

10 mm

FIG. 335

9   Bud firm, white, partly enclosed in the bract-like leaves of the last whorl; contains several yellow larvae (Fig. 334); on *G. palustre* .... ***Dasineura hygrophila*** (Mik)

FIG. 336

-   Bud spongy; contains several orange-red larvae (Fig. 336); on *G. odoratum* (in Britain, on *Asperula* abroad) .... ***Contarinia asperulae*** (Kieffer)

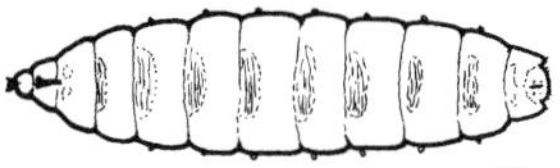

5 mm

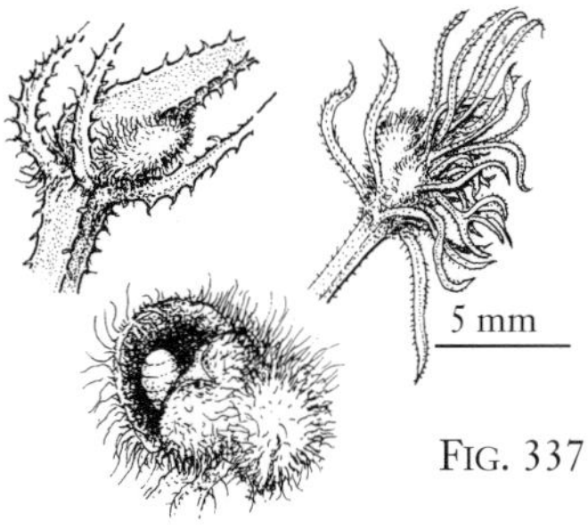

FIG. 337

10 Whole inflorescence deformed and compact, flowers green and leaf-like with shortened stalks (Fig. 338); contains mites (Fig. 330): **Acari: Eriophyoidea:**

On *G. verum*, *G. aparine*.. ***Aculus anthobius*** (Nalepa) (= *Vasates*)

On *A. cynanchica* .... ***Aculus minutus*** (Nalepa) (= *Vasates*)

-   One or more flowers or fruits swollen, ovoid **11**

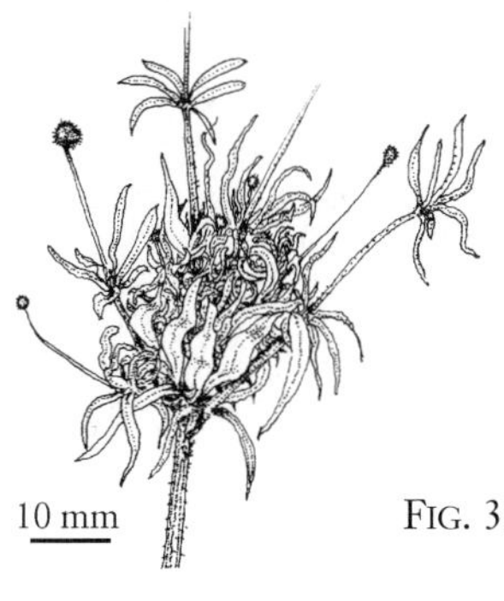

10 mm

FIG. 338

11 Flower swollen, 3 - 4 mm wide, remaining closed
(Fig. 339); green, sometimes dark violet; inside
lined with fungal mycelium, containing 1 - 3
yellow larvae or pupae; usually on *G. verum*:
Diptera: Cecidomyiidae
.... *Schizomyia galiorum* Kieffer

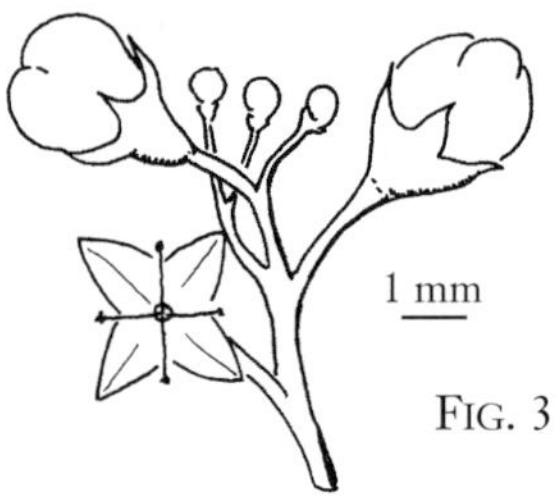

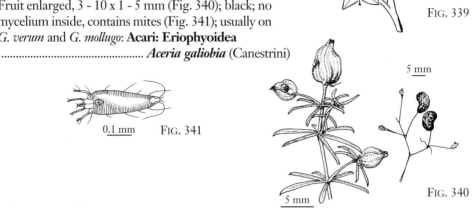

FIG. 339

- Fruit enlarged, 3 - 10 x 1 - 5 mm (Fig. 340); black; no
mycelium inside, contains mites (Fig. 341); usually on
G. verum and *G. mollugo*: **Acari: Eriophyoidea**
.... *Aceria galiobia* (Canestrini)

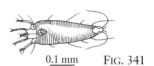

0.1 mm   FIG. 341

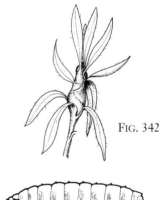

FIG. 340

E64. *GENISTA*

There are three native species, all of which are galled: dyer's greenweed, *G. tinctoria* L.,
petty whin, *G. anglica* L. and hairy greenweed, *G. pilosa* L.

1 Fleshy swelling at tip of stem on *G. tinctoria*, 8-10
mm diameter, surface often with irregular bumps
(Fig. 342); leaves arising from gall reduced in size;
contains several chambers (rarely one), each with a
yellowish white larva (Fig. 343) which can jump:
Diptera: Cecidomyiidae
.... *Contarinia melanocera* Kieffer

FIG. 342

- Gall in leaf- or flower-bud; may form an artichoke
gall, or a bunch of crowded leaves at tip of shoot,
or an irregular hairy mass of deformed leaves **2**

Weevil larvae (Fig. 344), *Exapion genistae* (Kirby) and *E. difficile*
(Herbst.) may cause swellings in pods; it is not known whether
these are galls.

FIG. 343

FIG. 344

2   Hairless ovoid gall in axil of leaf, c. 7 x 4mm;
    contains 1 or 2 larvae (Fig. 345); rare, on *Genista*
    spp.: **Diptera: Cecidomyiidae**
    .... *Asphondylia genistae* (Loew)

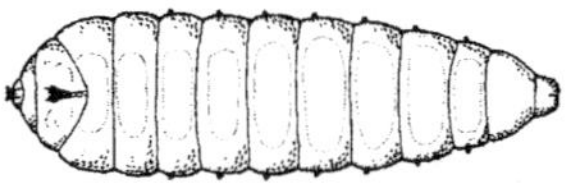

FIG. 345

-   Hairy leafy gall at tip of shoot or in axillary bud,
    forming an artichoke or an irregular mass of
    deformed leaves **3**

3   Irregular mass of miniature deformed leaves, may
    affect several adjacent buds (Fig. 346, see also E46
    CYTISUS Fig. 263 p. 320); large galls, bushy, up to 3
    cm across; contain mites (Fig. 341); rare (commoner
    on *Cytisus*): **Acari: Eriophyoidea**
    .... *Aceria genistae* (Nalepa)
                                              (= *Eriophyes*)

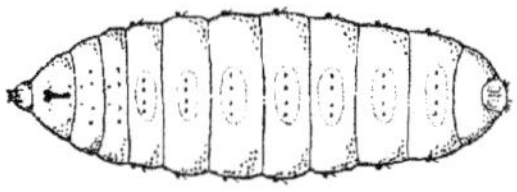

FIG. 346

-   Artichoke gall usually at shoot tip; contains larvae
    (Fig. 347): **Diptera: Cecidomyiidae** **4**

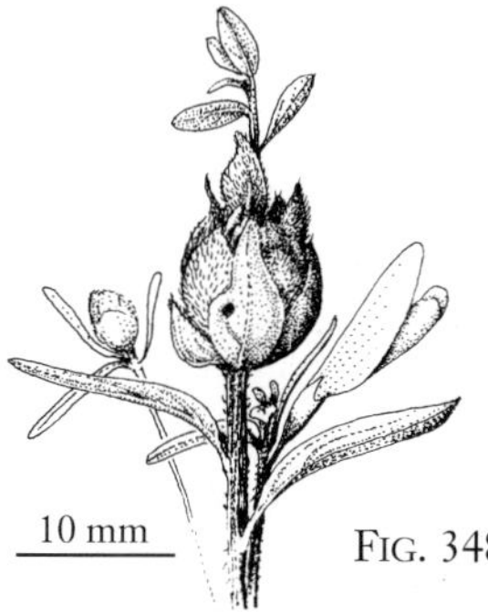

FIG. 347

4   Up to 15 mm across, leaves broadened, shell-
    shaped, covered with white hairs (Fig. 348, Plate
    3.3); larvae white when young, later pink, present
    in summer and early autumn; on *G. tinctoria* (also
    G. anglica abroad)
    .... *Jaapiella genisticola* (F. Löw)

-   Smaller, leaves with inrolled margins; larvae
    orange; on *G. tinctoria*, *G. pilosa*
    .... *Jaapiella genistamtorquens* (Kieffer)

10 mm   FIG. 348

E65. *GENTIANELLA* and *GENTIANA*

Three galls have been recorded on field gentian, *Gentianella campestris* (L.) Börner, autumn
gentian, *G. amarella* (L.) Börner, and Chiltern gentian, *G. germanica* (Willd.) Börner, and
one on spring gentian, *Gentiana verna* L.

1   Seed head scarcely swollen; contains a larva (Fig. 344) or pupa; S. England,
    uncommon or rare: **Coleoptera: Curculionidae** .... *Smicronyx reichi* (Gyllenhal)
    This may not be a true gall. In Britain it is found in the seed head (Morris, personal communication),
    although Buhr (1964) describes it as causing a gall, 4 mm long, in stem or root collar.

2   Flower bud swollen, deformed, remaining closed; contains yellowish larvae (Fig. 347);
    on *G. campestris*, *G. amarella*: **Diptera: Cecidomyiidae**
    .... *Dasineura gentianae* (Kieffer)

3   Flower parts transformed into a mass of small leaves
    (phyllanthy); contains mites (Fig. 349): **Acari:**
    Eriophyoidea .... *Eriophyes kerneri* (Nalepa)
                                        (= *Aceria*)

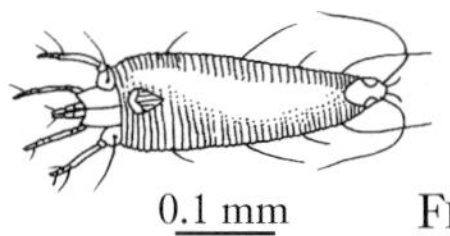

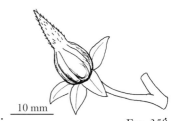

0.1 mm   FIG. 349

This species has been recorded on *G. verna* (Dauphin &
Aniotsbehère 1997), although it is not listed in Amrine &
Stasny (1994).

E66. *GERANIUM* and *ERODIUM*

Two out of the three galls found on these genera are common to both. Although both
genera contain many species, galls have been recorded mainly on two: bloody crane's-bill,
Geranium sanguineum L. and common stork's-bill, *Erodium cicutarium* (L.) L'Her. It is
probable that other species may also be galled.

For rust galls on leaves of *Geranium* spp., see p. 237.

1   Flower bud swollen, remaining closed (Fig. 350);
    fruit sometimes also deformed; contains white or
    yellow larvae (Fig. 351) or pupae; on *G. sanguineum*,
    E. cicutarium: **Diptera: Cecidomyiidae**
    .... *Dasineura geranii* (Kieffer)

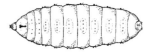

10 mm
FIG. 350

The identity of cecids in swollen flowers is confused;
identification is tentative. Orange larvae have also been
recorded from *E. cicutarium*, and white or yellow larvae occur
in seeds or flowers of other species (Bagnall & Harrison, 1918,
records from N. England and S. Scotland.). This suggests that
more than one unnamed species may be present. They may not
all cause galls.

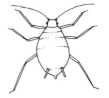

FIG. 351

2   Young leaves deformed, puckered, with down-
    curled margins; contain pale-green aphids (Fig.
    352) c. 2.5 mm long; on *Geranium* and *Erodium*
    spp.: **Hemiptera: Aphididae**
    .. *Acyrthosiphon pelargonii* ssp. *geranii* (Kaltenbach)

This may not be a true gall.

FIG. 352

3   Leaf blades thickened, inrolled, usually upwards
    and bunched into a loose mop head (Fig. 353);
    green or yellow-green at first, later reddish; stem
    below thickened; contain mites (Fig. 349); on
    Geranium spp.: **Acari: Eriophyoidea**
    .... *Aceria geranii* (Canestrini)

Similar deformations may be caused on *G. sanguineum* by *Aceria*
dolichosoma (Canestrini), the leaves being abnormally hairy and
with additional inrolled leaf divisions.

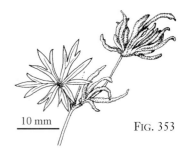

10 mm
FIG. 353

E67. *GEUM*

Two galls are found on the two native species, wood avens, *G. urbanum* L. and water avens, *G. rivale* L., and on their hybrid, *G.* x *intermedium* Ehrh., which is common wherever the two parents occur together.

1   Leaf veins swollen, with sections of blade between them folded upwards; white or reddish larvae (Fig. 354) live in creases on upperside; affected parts go brown after larvae have left: **Diptera: Cecidomyiidae** .... *Contarinia gei* Kieffer
(= *geicola*)

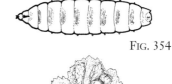

Fig. 354

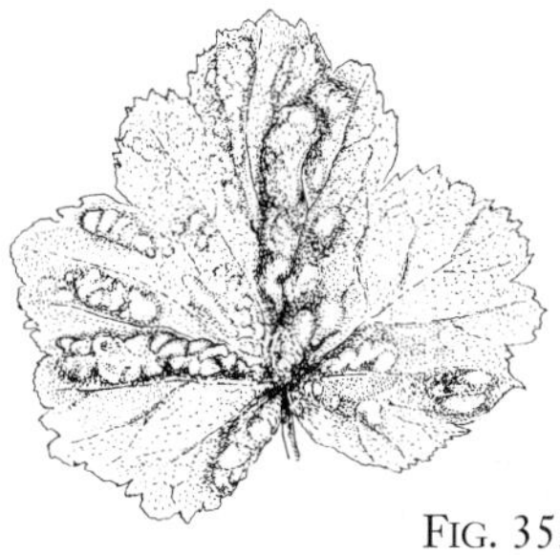

2   Erineum, usually on underside, often several on a leaf; white at first, becoming brownish red; corresponding bulges on the other side (Fig. 355), light green, yellowish or reddish; erinea may also occur on petiole, flower stalk or sepals; mites (Fig. 349) live between the hairs: **Acari: Eriophyoidea** .... *Cecidophyes nudus* Nalepa
(= *Eriophyes*)

Fig. 355

E68. *GLECHOMA*

Three insects cause galls on ground-ivy, *Glechoma hederacea* L. For a rust gall causing swollen yellow, brown or black stems, petioles or leaf veins, see p. 238.

1   Globular hairy swelling, 5-20 mm diameter, on underside of leaf or apparent on both sides, or on stem (Fig. 356, Plate 5.2); green, or reddish in sunlight; soft, becoming hard; contains a white larva (Fig. 357) or pupa: **Hymenoptera: Cynipidae** .... *Liposthenes glechomae* (Kieffer)
(= *latreillei*)

2   A hairy cylinder, up to 4 mm tall, often several on upper surface of leaf (Fig. 358, Plate 4.6); green, later light red or red-brown; contains a white larva (Fig. 351); galls fall off leaf in August - September, leaving neat circular holes; common: **Diptera: Cecidomyiidae** .... *Rondaniola bursaria* (Bremi)
lighthouse gall

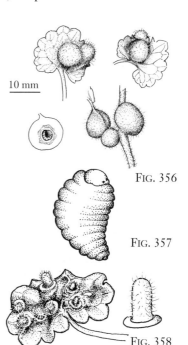

10 mm

Fig. 356

Fig. 357

Fig. 358

3   The two terminal leaves reduced in size, thickened and pressed together to form a pouch (Fig. 359); or flower bud swollen and remaining closed; contains several white larvae (Fig. 360); uncommon: **Diptera: Cecidomyiidae**......... *Dasineura glechomae* (Kieffer)

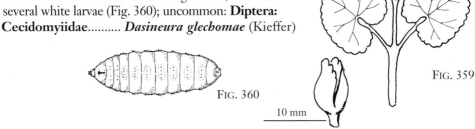

FIG. 360

FIG. 359

10 mm

E69. *GLEDITSIA*

One species only, the introduced honey locust, *Gleditsia triacanthos* L. One gall occurs in Britain caused by a gall midge (**Diptera: Cecidomyiidae**), accidentally introduced from N. America and now well established.

Leaflets thickened and folded to form pods, up to 10 mm long (Fig. 361); each contains several orange larvae (Fig. 360); southern England, spreading north (has reached Leics.)
.... *Dasineura gleditchiae* (Osten-Sacken)

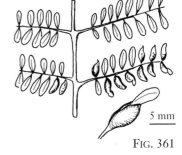

5 mm

FIG. 361

E70. *GNAPHALIUM* and *FILAGO*

Two insect galls are recorded from cudweeds. Both are found on several species within both genera.

1   Flower head distorted, often rosette and stem leaves twisted with inrolled margins, and stem shortened; infested with green or yellowish aphids (Fig. 362) covered with white wax: **Hemiptera: Aphididae: Pemphiginae**
.... *Pemphigus populinigrae* (Schrank)
<small>Cudweeds are the secondary host of this aphid; for gall on primary host, see Fig. 622, p. 393.</small>

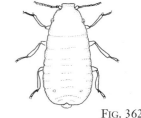

FIG. 362

2   Hard ovoid swelling in flower head or pedicel, young leaves thickened; contains a white larva (Fig. 363) or pupa; very rare, S. England: **Coleoptera: Brentidae: Apioninae**
.... *Taphrotopium brunnipes* (Boheman)

FIG. 363

E71. *HEDERA*

One gall causer (**Diptera: Cecidomyiidae**) is found on native ivy, *Hedera helix* L.

Flower bud slightly swollen, remaining closed; contains a larva (Fig. 360), white when young, later orange .... ***Dasineura kiefferi*** Marchal
Recorded from gall only (Chandler 1998); needs verifying by rearing and identifying adult.

E72. *HELIANTHEMUM*

Two arthropod galls are recorded from common rock rose, *H. nummularium* (L.) Miller; they are probably also found on other *Helianthemum* species.

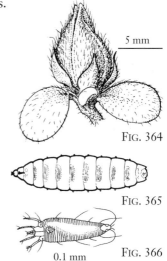

1   Leaves at tip of shoot thickened, concave and often very hairy, forming an artichoke gall (Fig. 364); contains orange larvae (Fig. 365): **Diptera: Cecidomyiidae**
    .... ***Contarinia helianthemi*** (Hardy)

FIG. 364

2   Tip of shoot including flowers transformed into a mass of small, very hairy leaves; contains mites (Fig. 366): **Acari: Eriophyoidea**
    .... ***Aceria rosalia*** (Nalepa)
                                                (= *Eriophyes*)

FIG. 365

FIG. 366

E73. *HEMEROCALLIS*

Orange day-lily, *Hemerocallis fulva* (L.) L. is one of several introduced species and varieties grown in gardens and sometimes appearing on waste ground. One gall is recorded, caused by an introduced gall midge (**Diptera: Cecidomyiidae**) and first seen in 1989 (Halstead, 1995).

Flower bud swollen, deformed, failing to open (Fig. 367); inside, many white larvae (Fig. 365) between abnormally thickened and twisted petals, June - July; can be a pest; SE. England
    .... ***Contarinia quinquenotata*** (F. Löw)

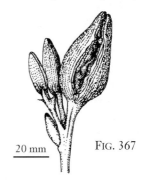

FIG. 367

HERACLEUM see APIACEAE

E74. *HIERACIUM* and *PILOSELLA*

Hawkweeds are a variable group, difficult to identify, with many microspecies. *Pilosella*, formerly a subgenus of *Hieracium*, was recently raised to generic status, but Stace (1997) notes that it is doubtfully distinct. Host relations of gall inducers are not well known; it seems that most are restricted to one or other genus, though a few can cause galls on both. The hosts specified in the key should be regarded as tentative only, awaiting more information. Most hosts are recorded as *Hieracium*, with no indication of species, apart from the mouse-ear-hawkweed, *Pilosella officinarum* F. Schultze & Schultze-Bip.

1   Globular or elongate swelling in stem, or in stolon beneath leaf rosette; contains several chambers each with a white larva (Fig. 368) or pupa: **Hymenoptera: Cynipidae** 2

-   Gall in leaf or flower head 3

FIG. 368

2   Hard globular swelling, about 1 cm across, in stolon beneath leaf rosette (Fig. 369); in *P. officinarum*, rare
.... ***Aulacidea subterminalis*** Niblett

-   Rounded, ovoid or elongate swelling in stem, up to 4 cm long (Fig. 370); green and succulent at first, often covered with short hairs, later brown and hard; in *Hieracium* spp., locally common
.... ***Aulacidea hieracii*** (Bouché)

FIG. 369

3   Gall in leaf, sometimes involving more than one leaf 4

-   Flower head swollen (sometimes only slightly), usually remaining closed 13

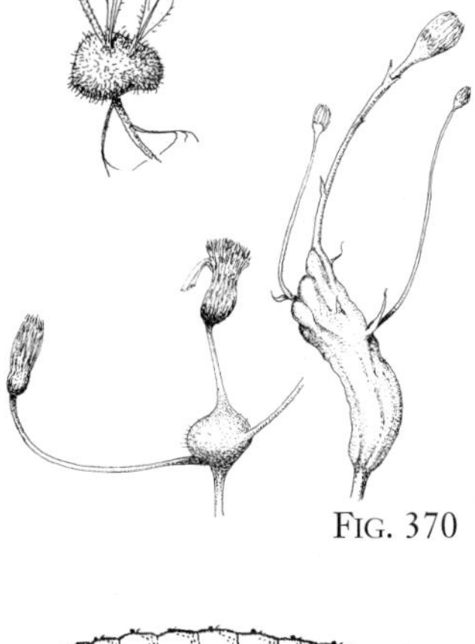

FIG. 370

4   Two or more young leaves at shoot tip thickened, forming a rosette or pouch; contains one or more larvae (Fig. 371): **Diptera: Cecidomyiidae** 5

-   Gall in blade, midrib or petiole of a leaf (several affected leaves may be clustered together) 6

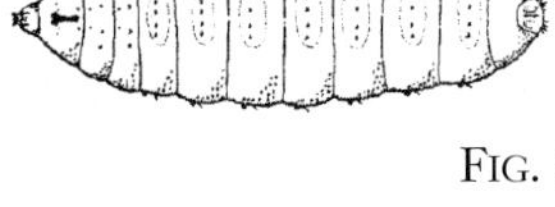

FIG. 371

5 Terminal pair of leaves concave, meeting at their margins to form a pouch; contains several white or pale yellow larvae; on *Hieracium* spp., rare .... ***Macrolabis hieracii*** Rübsaamen

- Several terminal leaves rolled, forming a tight or loose rosette (Fig. 372); contains white, later red, larvae; on *P. officinarum*, quite common .... ***Macrolabis pilosellae*** (Binnie)

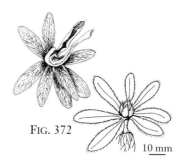

FIG. 372

10 mm

6 In petiole or midrib; on *P. officinarum*; NE. England, rare **7**

- In blade **8**

7 Hard swelling, 2 - 4 x 2 mm, on underside, often several in one midrib (Fig. 373), sometimes coalescing; each contains a white larva (Fig. 368) or pupa: **Hymenoptera: Cynipidae** .... ***Aulacidea pilosellae*** (Kieffer)

- Gall similar; contains an orange larva (Fig. 371): **Diptera: Cecidomyiidae** .... ***Dasineura nervicola*** (Kieffer)

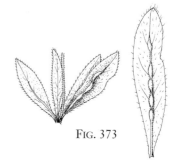

FIG. 373

8 Pustule or dimple, usually several in a leaf **9**

- Whole leaf, or margin only, rolled **10**

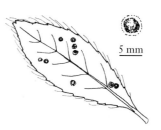

5 mm

FIG. 374

9 Circular pustule 4-6 mm across, yellow-green or red, surrounded by a red or purple zone (Fig. 374); contains an orange-red larva (Fig. 371); opening on underside when mature; on *Hieracium* or *Pilosella*: **Diptera: Cecidomyiidae** .... ***Cystiphora sanguinea*** (Bremi)
(= *C. hieracii* = *C. pilosellae*)

Until recently, the species on *Hieracium* spp. and *P. officinarum* were thought to be distinct; they were synonymised by Harris (1975).

- Small dimple opening on upper surface (Fig. 375); contains a flattened nymph; very rare: **Hemiptera: Psylloidea** ....***Trioza proxima*** Flor

One British record only, from *P. officinarum* in Durham (Hodkinson & White, 1979).

FIG. 375

10 Narrow upward inrolling of leaf margin(s); contains mites (Fig. 376): **Acari: Eriophyoidea**
.... **11**

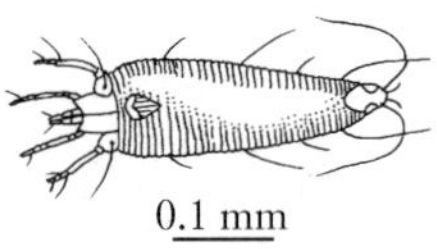

FIG. 376

0.1 mm

- Whole blade loosely rolled or curled upwards on both sides of midrib, exposing the white underside; contains aphids (Fig. 377), green with black markings: **Hemiptera: Aphididae** **12**

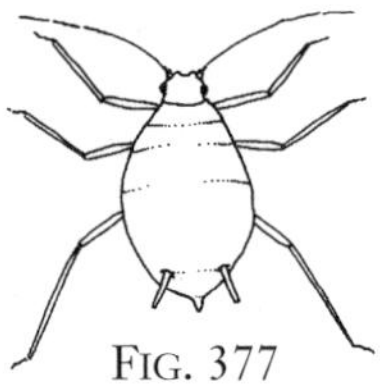

FIG. 377

11 Small brittle roll, 1 mm wide, covered with white hairs; on *P. officinarum*
.... *Aceria pilosellae* (Nalepa)
(= *Eriophyes*)

- Longer roll, involving most of leaf margin, sometimes on both sides (Fig. 378), not abnormally hairy; on *Hieracium* spp., rare
.... *Aceria longisetus* (Nalepa)
(= *Eriophyes*)

FIG. 378

This mite may also infest flower heads, see couplet 13.

12 On *P. officinarum* (Fig. 379)
.... *Nasonovia pilosellae* Börner

- On *Hieracium* spp.
.... *Nasonovia nigra* Hille Ris Lambers

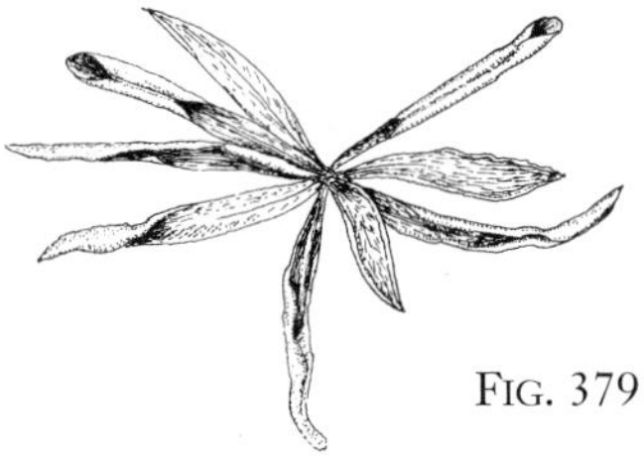

FIG. 379

13 Flower head hemispherical, containing stunted green florets and mites (Fig. 376); rare:
Acari: Eriophyoidea .... *Aceria longisetus* (Nalepa)
This mite may also induce leaf galls, see couplet 11   (= *Eriophyes*)

- Some or all florets stunted or aborted; head contains one or more larvae **14**

14 Contains several yellow larvae (Fig. 380); on *P. officinarum*: **Diptera: Cecidomyiidae**
....*Contarinia pilosellae* Kieffer

- Receptacle swollen; contains 1-4 white or grey larvae (not as in Fig. 380) or black puparia **15**

FIG. 380

15 Larvae as in Fig. 381; recorded from *H. vulgatum*;
Scotland, rare: **Hymenoptera: Cynipidae**
.... ***Aulacidea nibletti*** Quinlan & Askew

- Larvae as in Fig. 382, or black puparia: **Diptera:**
Tephritidae **16**

FIG. 381   FIG. 382

16 Larvae white, puparia ovoid; in *P. officinarum* .... ***Tephritis ruralis*** (Loew)

- Larvae grey, puparia pear-shaped; in *Hieracium* spp.; Yorkshire southwards
.... ***Noeeta pupillata*** (Fallén)

E75. *HIPPOCREPIS*

There is one cecid gall (**Diptera: Cecidomyiidae**) on the native horseshoe vetch, *Hippocrepis comosa* L. Nodules caused by *Rhizobium* sp. may form on the roots (see p. 219).

Leaflet folded into a fleshy pod, often several adjacent leaflets affected; contains
several larvae (Fig. 380) .... ***Macrolabis hippocrepidis*** Kieffer

Buhr (1964) attributes this gall to *Dasineura comosae* Rübsaamen, with *M. hippocrepidis* an inquiline within
it. *D. comosae* is not however confirmed as British (Chandler 1998); identification is still to be confirmed.

E76. *HIPPOPHAE*

One mite gall (**Acari: Eriophyoidea**) is recorded on sea buckthorn, *Hippophae rhamnoides* L. Root nodules are common (see p. 219).

Leaf deformed, up to five times normal width,
sometimes totally contorted, margins thickened,
folded or rolled down or upwards (Fig. 383); or
blade bulged upwards with depressions beneath
(Fig. 384); several leaves together may be affected;
contain mites (Fig. 376)
.... ***Aceria hippophaenus*** (Nalepa)
(= *Eriophyes*)

FIG. 383

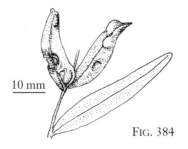

10 mm

FIG. 384

HOLCHUS see POACEAE

HORDEUM see POACEAE

E77. *HYPERICUM*

Galls are found on perforate St John's-wort, *H. perforatum* L., slender St John's-wort, *H. pulchrum* L., hairy St John's-wort, *H. hirsutum* L., and sometimes other native species. All known causers are gall midges (**Diptera: Cecidomyiidae**). Their galls are often similar; some species have been separated on the basis of larval colour, which may not be safe. To confirm identifications, adults should be reared and determined by an expert.

1 Leaf margin inrolled downwards (Fig. 385), ± hairy; contains several white larvae (Fig. 386); on *H. perforatum*, *H. hirsutum* .... ***Macrolabis marteli*** Kieffer

- Gall at shoot tip, or in flower bud, or in axillary bud on stem or underground; contains one or more larvae **2**

2 Underground axillary bud enlarged, with fleshy, yellowish, overlapping scale leaves (Fig. 387) .... ***Geocrypta braueri*** (Handlirsch)

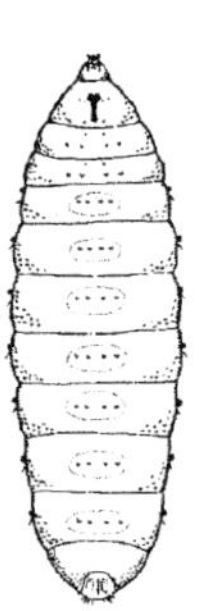

- Gall in leaf- or flower-bud, or at shoot tip **3**

3 Flower bud swollen, remaining closed; larvae (Fig. 388) white, jumping .... ***Contarinia hyperici*** Barnes

- Terminal or lateral leaf bud or shoot galled **4**

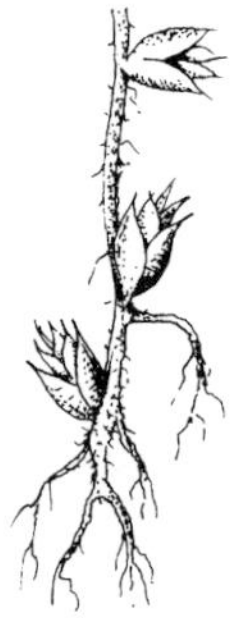

4 Two innermost leaves of bud thickened, meeting to form a spherical chamber (Fig. 389); contains one or more reddish yellow larvae or pupae .... ***Zeuxidiplosis giardi*** (Kieffer)

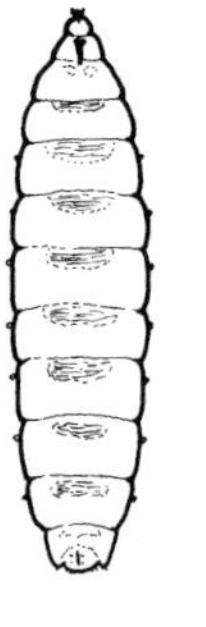

This is a central and southern European species at the northern limit of its range. It has been recorded from flower buds in Britain, but these records probably relate to *Contarinia hyperici* (Harris, personal communication).

- Two or more pairs of leaves at shoot tip opposed, forming a pouch or artichoke, with broad lower pair enclosing small upper pair(s); white or red larvae (Fig. 386) **5**

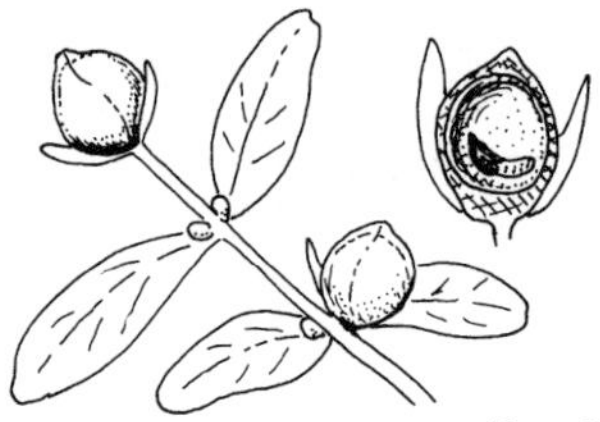

FIG. 385

FIG. 386

FIG. 387

FIG. 388

FIG. 389

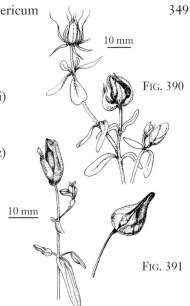

FIG. 390

FIG. 391

10 mm

10 mm

5 Lower (outer) leaves drawn together to enclose the pointed bud (Fig. 390); usually green, seldom red; contains several larvae, white when young, red when older, pupate in gall
.... ***Dasineura hyperici*** (Bremi)

- Lower leaves slightly swollen and keeled (Fig. 391); often reddened; larvae white, pupate in soil
.... ***Dasineura serotina*** (Winnertz)

Galls of these two species are very similar; mature larvae are necessary to confirm identification. Occasionally recorded also from unopened flowers when infestation is heavy, but may have been confused with *Contarinia hyperici* (Harris, personal communication).

E78. *HYPOCHAERIS*

Two galls are recorded from common cat's-ear, *Hypochaeris radicata* L., both of them rare. In addition, the white maggot of *Tephritis vespertina* (Loew) (**Diptera: Tephritidae**) is common in the flower heads; it is not a gall causer.

For a rust gall on leaves, see p. 226.

1 Elongate swelling in main stem, sometimes in flower stalk or petiole, 10-50 mm long (Fig. 392); succulent at first, later hard, surface often wrinkled; inside up to 50 chambers, each with a yellowish white larva (Fig. 393) or pupa: **Hymenoptera: Cynipidae**
.... ***Phanacis hypochoeridis*** (Kieffer)
(= *Aylax* = *Aulacidea*)

2 Flower head disfigured, with patch of florets and their achenes at side of receptacle stunted; contain yellow, jumping larvae (Fig. 388): **Diptera: Cecidomyiidae**
.... ***Contarinia hypochoeridis*** (Rübsaamen)

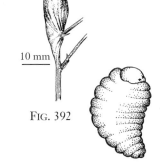

10 mm

FIG. 392

FIG. 393

E79. *INULA*

Two species are included here: golden samphire, *Inula crithmoides* L., and ploughman's spikenard, *I. conyzae* (Griess.) Meikle. Three galls are known in Britain.

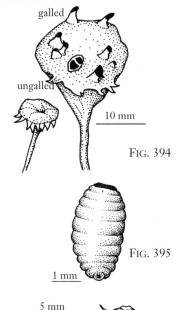

galled

ungalled

10 mm

FIG. 394

1 Base of flower head enlarged and hard, with elongate projections (Fig. 394), each the tip of a chamber containing one larva (Fig. 395); in *I. crithmoides*, southern England: **Diptera: Tephritidae**
.... *Myopites eximia* Séguy
(= *inulae*)

FIG. 395

1 mm

2 Smooth globular gall, c. 5 mm across; in bud at shoot tip, or in stem, or in flower head, sometimes several clustered together (Fig. 396); yellow-green to red; one chamber with one larva (Fig. 397); on *I. conyzae*, S. England, rare: **Diptera: Cecidomyiidae**
.... *Acodiplosis inulae* (H. Loew)

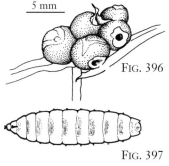

5 mm

FIG. 396

3 Partly-open bud or young leaves are densely hairy (Fig. 398); contain yellow-orange larvae (Fig. 397); in *I. conyzae*, often in rosette leaves, northern England: **Diptera: Cecidomyiidae**
.... *Neomikiella beckiana* (Mik)

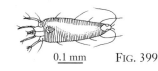

FIG. 397

FIG. 398

E80. *JASIONE*

One gall causer (**Acari: Eriophyoidea**) is found on sheep's-bit, *Jasione montana* L.

Whole plant ± deformed, with leaves bunched, rosette-like, covered with a thick felt of white hairs; flowers are sterile, greened, leafy (chloranthy) and hairy; contain mites (Fig. 399); rare: .... *Aceria enanthus* (Nalepa)
(= *Eriophyes*)

0.1 mm FIG. 399

E81. *JUGLANS*

Two galls caused by mites (Fig. 399) (**Acari: Eriophyoidea**) are found on leaves of walnut, *Juglans regia* L. Both may also infest the green fruits.

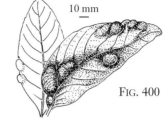

FIG. 400

1 Upper surface with a shiny yellowish-green bulge between two veins, often several on a leaflet (Fig. 400); depression on underside lined with a felt of white or buff coloured hairs
.... ***Aceria erineus*** (Nalepa)
(= *Eriophyes*)

2 Rounded pustule, 1-2 mm across, raised on both surfaces, usually several on a leaflet, mainly along veins (Fig. 401); green at first, later brown; local
.... ***Aceria tristriatus*** (Nalepa)
(= *Eriophyes*)

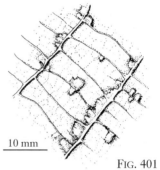

FIG. 401

E82. *JUNCUS*

There are 28 species of rush in Great Britain. Only one arthropod gall causer (**Hemiptera: Psylloidea**) is known; it attacks several species including jointed rush, *J. articulatus* L. and toad rush, *J. bufonius* L. Several smuts may gall the roots and stems (see p. 238).

Shoots shortened and thickened, bunched into a mass up to 8 cm long (Fig. 402, Plate 7.6); includes flowers whose parts become leafy and thickened; reddish at first, later brown; galled shoots often low down, obscured by ungalled shoots; contains nymphs (Fig. 403); June - October; locally common
.... ***Livia juncorum*** (Latreille)
tassel gall

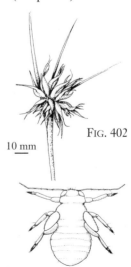

FIG. 402

FIG. 403

E83. *JUNIPERUS*

There is one native species, juniper, *Juniperus communis* L.
  For rust galls caused by *Gymnosporangium* spp., see p. 239.

1 Berry slightly swollen, with a three-rayed opening
    (Fig. 404); contains mites (Fig. 405): **Acari:**
    Eriophyoidea
    .... ***Trisetacus quadrisetus*** (Thomas)

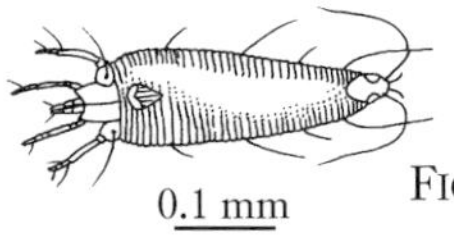

FIG. 404

- Bud-like gall formed of one or more whorls of
    needles, internodes between them shortened;
    terminal or axillary **2**

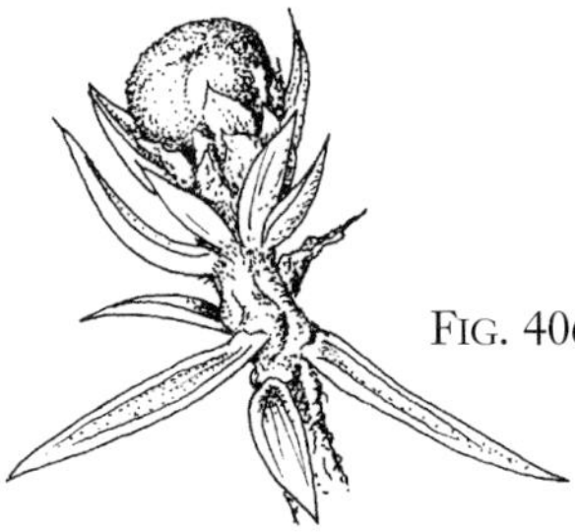

0.1 mm   FIG. 405

2 Crowded needles, each swollen at point of
    attachment (Fig. 406); contain mites (Fig. 405):
    Acari: Eriophyoidea
    .... ***Trisetacus juniperinus*** (Nalepa)

- Bud-like gall composed of one or two (rarely
    three) whorls of swollen needles; inner whorl
    encloses a chamber containing an orange or red
    larva or pupa: **Diptera: Cecidomyiidae** **3**

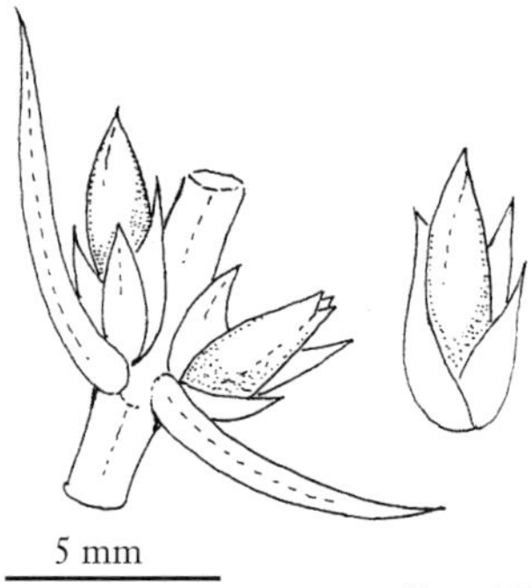

FIG. 406

3 One whorl of needles; sometimes with small
    needle-like scales at base **4**

- Two (rarely three) whorls of needles, the lower
    outer whorls concealing the inner whorl **5**

4 1-4 mm long, in leaf axils, with three short scale-
    like leaves at base (Fig. 407); larva pale orange;
    adult probably emerges April – May; galls
    inconspicuous, variable and easily overlooked;
    southern England, widespread but uncommon
    .... ***Schmidtiella gemmarum*** Rübsaamen

5 mm

FIG. 407

- 5-6 mm long, hard and tough, without scale-like needles at base; larva red; adult probably
    emerges mid-March; rare .... ***Oligotrophus schmidti*** Rübsaamen
    Recorded only from Durham and Northumberland by Bagnall & Harrison in 1922.

5 Pear-shaped with a blunt apex, 8-10 mm wide at
    base and 10-12 mm long (Fig. 408); inner whorl of
    leaves 4 mm long, brown; found on the exotic *J.*
    oxycedrus L.; rare
    .... ***Arceuthomyia valerii*** (Tavares)

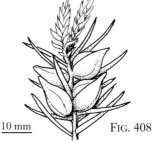

10 mm   FIG. 408

- More slender, 3-4 mm wide at base and 5-17 mm long; larva orange; adult May - June; N. England and Scotland **6**

FIG. 409

6 Gall with bulbous base and pointed apex (Fig. 409), 6-13.5 mm long; inner needles 3-6 mm long with pointed tips (Fig. 410)
.... ***Oligotrophus panteli*** Kieffer

larval chamber

FIG. 410

- Gall slender, with tips of outer needles recurved when mature (Fig. 411), 7-17 mm long; inner needles 5-10 mm long with blunt tips (Fig. 412); rarely a third, short, outer whorl of needles present
.... ***Oligotrophus juniperinus*** (L.)
Both species frequent in northern England and Scotland.

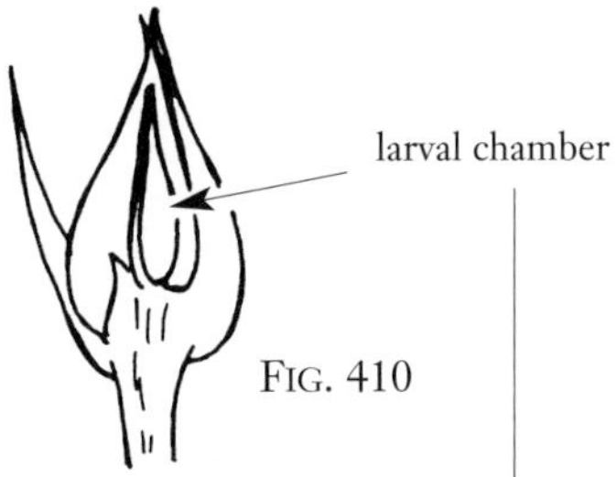

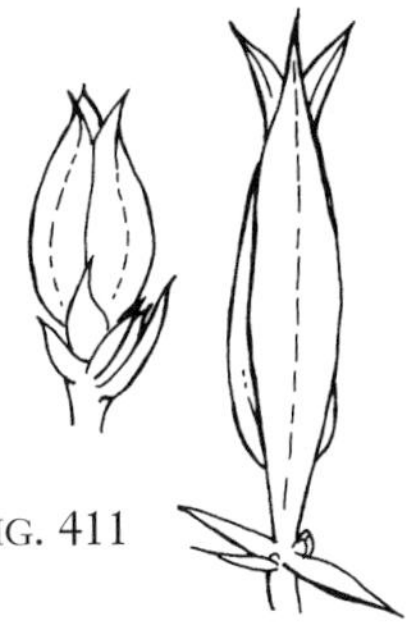

FIG. 411

FIG. 412

E84. *KNAUTIA*

There is one species, field scabious, *Knautia arvensis* (L.) Coult. Two rare galls are recorded.

1 Youngest leaves at tip of shoot deformed, forming an enlarged hairy bud; white or yellow-white larvae (Fig. 413) live between leaves: **Diptera: Cecidomyiidae**
.... ***Jaapiella knautiae*** Rübsaamen

2 Shallow depression in angle of veins on underside of leaf, contains a nymph; slight bulge above; often several in a leaf; N. England and Scotland: **Hemiptera: Psylloidea**
.... ***Trioza munda*** Förster

FIG. 413

LAELIA see ORCHIDACEAE

E85. *LAMIASTRUM*

The one species, yellow archangel, *Lamiastrum galeobdolon* (L.) Ehrend. & Polatschek (= *Lamium galeobdolon*), is galled by a cecid (**Diptera: Cecidomyiidae**). In addition, the pale greenish white aphid *Cryptomyzus galeopsidis* (Kaltenbach) causes downward incurling of the leaves in early summer; this is not thought to be a true gall.

Rounded or ovoid hairy gall, 3-5 mm across, formed from a pair of bud leaves pressed together in leaf axil; usually on stolons running along ground (Fig. 414), sometimes higher up; contains a white larva (Fig. 415); July - September; England, local .... ***Dasineura strumosa*** (Bremi) (= *galeobdolontis*)

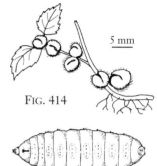

FIG. 414

FIG. 415

E86. *LAMIUM*

Three cecids (**Diptera: Cecidomyiidae**) gall white dead-nettle, *L. album* L. Hosts abroad include red dead-nettle, *L. purpureum* L. and the introduced spotted dead-nettle, *L. maculatum* (L.) L.

For a smut on the stem of *L. album*, see p. 239.

1 Flower swollen, up to 7 mm across, remaining closed; contains white larvae (Fig. 415); on *L. maculatum*, rare: **Diptera: Cecidomyiidae** .... ***Dasineura lamii*** (Kieffer)
One British record only, in a Durham garden.

- Gall covered with white hairs, in axillary bud on stolon, or formed from leaves at tip of shoot; contains white larvae (Fig. 415); on *L. album*: **Diptera: Cecidomyiidae** 2
Leaf curl, sometimes involving bunching of leaves, caused by aphids is common in young leaves in early summer; these are not true galls. Examples are *Aphis lamiorum* (Börner) and *Cryptomyzus* spp. (see Stroyan 1984).

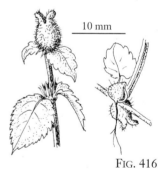

FIG. 416

2 Rounded pea-sized gall at shoot tip or on stolon (Fig. 416) .... ***Dasineura lamiicola*** (Mik)

- Elongate gall formed from terminal pair of thickened leaves, c. 4 mm long; may also fold or crinkle older leaves (Fig. 417) .... ***Macrolabis lamii*** Rübsaamen

FIG. 417

E87. *LAPSANA*

Only one insect gall (**Hymenoptera: Cynipidae**) is recorded on nipplewort, *Lapsana communis* L.

For a rust gall on leaves, see p. 240.

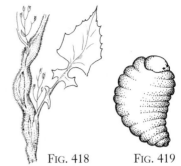

Irregular swelling in stem, up to 6 cm long by 10 mm wide (Fig. 418); contains several chambers each with a white larva (Fig. 419) or pupa; E. Midlands and E. Anglia, rare
.... ***Phanacis lampsanae*** (Perris)

FIG. 418   FIG. 419

E88. *LARIX*

All *Larix* species are introduced in Britain. European larch, *L. decidua* Mill. is widely planted and is the species most often galled. Japanese larch, *L. kaempferi* (Lindl.) Carrière and the hybrid between them are quite common and may be galled. The hybrid is *L.* x *marschlinsii* Coaz and is more widely planted for forestry than either parent.

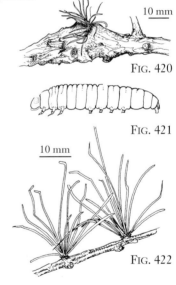

1   Gall in twig; an elongate resinous swelling about twice stem width at its widest (Fig. 420); soft and spongy, becoming hard and woody after emergence of adult May - June; contains a caterpillar (Fig. 421) for 22 months from June, pupa April - May second year; E. Anglia only, rare: **Lepidoptera: Tortricidae**
.... ***Cydia milleniana*** (Adamczewski)

10 mm

FIG. 420

FIG. 421

10 mm

-   Gall in bud or needles **2**

2   New needles slightly swollen, yellowed with an elbowed kink (Fig. 422); damage appears at feeding site of pale greenish aphids (Fig. 423) which produce little wax, April - May; uncommon: **Hemiptera: Adelgidae**
.... ***Adelges viridis*** (Ratzeburg)

FIG. 422

These distortions may not be true galls. A common adelgid on *Larix* is *Adelges laricis* Vallot, a blackish grey species infesting the needles and producing copious bluish white woolly wax and honeydew June - September. Attacked needles go brown and may be slightly distorted (not regarded as a gall).

-   Leaf or flower bud swollen, spherical or ovoid, up to 5 mm across **3**

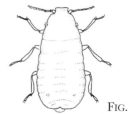

FIG. 423

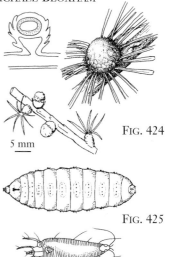

3 Lower half of bud covered with brown scales and capped with resin (Fig. 424); contains a yellowish red larva (Fig. 425) throughout summer, autumn and winter, pupa April - May: **Diptera: Cecidomyiidae** .... ***Dasineura kellneri*** (Henschel) (= *laricis*)

FIG. 424

5 mm

\- Not covered with scales or resin; contains mites (Fig. 426): **Acari: Eriophyoidea** .... ***Trisetacus laricis*** (Tubeuf)

FIG. 425

0.1 mm   FIG. 426

E89. *LATHYRUS*

Most galls are recorded from meadow vetchling, *L. pratensis* L., with some on narrow-leaved everlasting-pea, *L. sylvestris* L. and bitter vetch, *L. linifolius* (Reichard) Bässler. Most gall causers are cecids, and most are not well known. This key, therefore, should be regarded as preliminary only.

Bacterial root nodules are common (see p. 219).

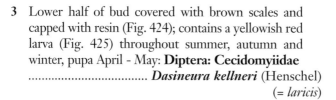

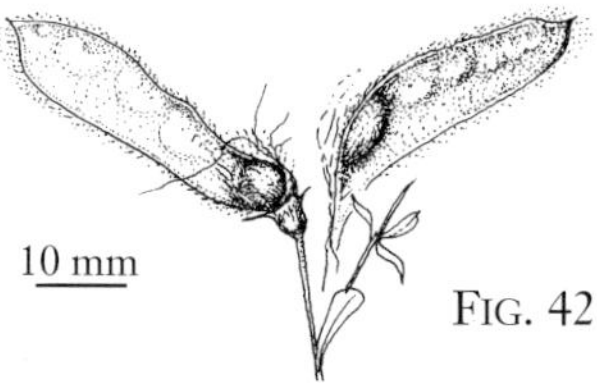

10 mm

READ THREE ALTERNATIVES

1 Small swelling in wall of pod, often several together (similar to galls of *A. sarothamni* on *Cytisus*: Fig. 427); each contains a yellow-orange larva (Fig. 428); on *L. pratensis*: **Diptera: Cecidomyiidae** .... ***Asphondylia lathyri*** Rübsaamen

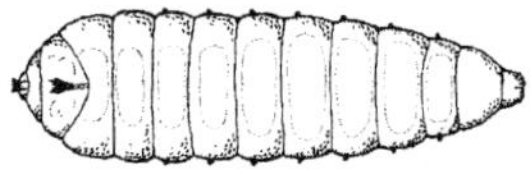

FIG. 427

FIG. 428

\- Gall in flower bud or inflorescence; contains one or more larvae: **Diptera: Cecidomyiidae** 2

\- Gall in leaflet or stipules, sometimes forming a swollen mass at shoot tip **4**

2 Inflorescence transformed into a round mass at tip of shoot; several white larvae (Fig. 425); on *L. pratensis*; rare .... ***Dasineura pratensis*** (Kieffer)

\- Flower bud swollen, remains closed; contains one larva **3**

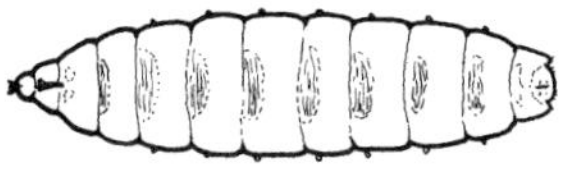

READ THREE ALTERNATIVES

3   Larva (Fig. 429) white or lemon-yellow, jumping;
    on *L. pratensis* .... **Contarinia lathyri** Kieffer

FIG. 429

-   Larva (Fig. 425) white, non-jumping; on *L. sylvestris, L. linifolius*. **Dasineura silvestris** (Kieffer)

-   Larva (Fig. 425) red, non-jumping; on *L. sylvestris* .... **Dasineura fairmairei** (Kieffer)

    It is possible that the last two species are the same; *D. silvestris* is probably a synonym of *D. fairmairei*.

4   Gall at shoot tip, formed from more than one leaflet or stipule; margins of adjacent
    leaflets may be rolled but not thickened; larvae present in shoot tip and marginal
    rolls: **Diptera: Cecidomyiidae** **5**

-   Single leaflet pod-like, or leaflet or stipule (usually away from the shoot tip) with
    rolled and ± thickened margin(s) **6**

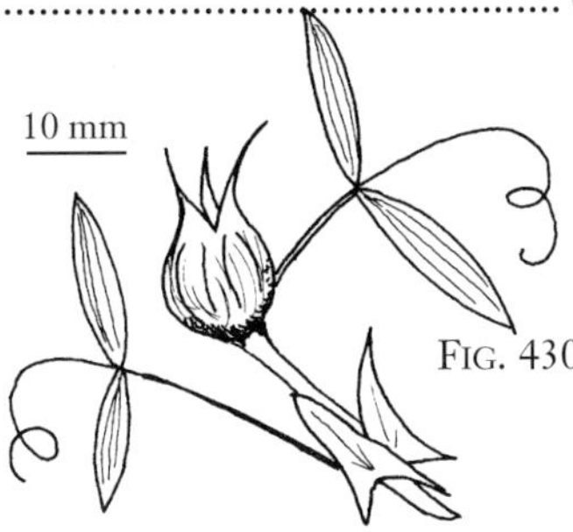

5   Terminal internodes shortened, forming a mass of
    thickened, overlapping leaflets and stipules; larvae
    (Fig. 429) yellowish white; on *L. pratensis*
    .... **Contarinia jaapi** Rübsaamen

10 mm

FIG. 430

-   Terminal stipules swollen at bases, discoloured (Fig.
    430), shoot beyond these dies; larvae (Fig. 425)
    yellowish white when young, later light orange or
    light red; on *L. pratensis* (and other species abroad)
    .... **Dasineura lathyricola** (Rübsaamen)
    (= *Jaapiella*)

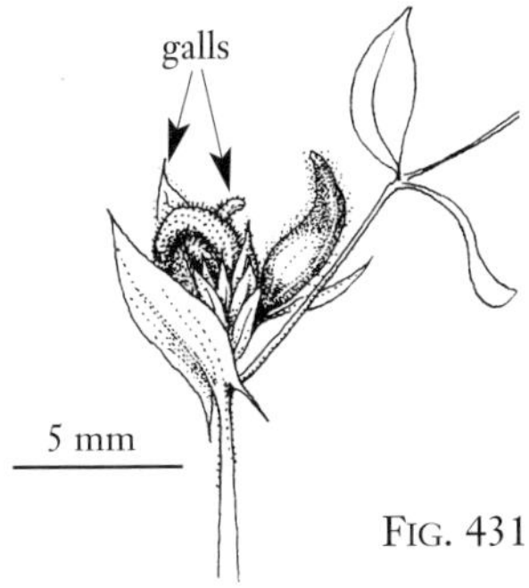

galls

5 mm

FIG. 431

6   Leaflet slightly swollen and folded forming a soft
    discoloured pod (Fig. 431); contains light orange
    larvae (Fig. 425); on *L. pratense*: **Diptera:**
    Cecidomyiidae .... **Dasineura lathyri** (Kieffer)

-   Margin(s) of leaflet or stipule rolled upwards **7**

7   Narrow roll (Fig. 432), discoloured red-brown or
    brown, ± hairy inside; contains mites (Fig. 426); on
    L. pratensis: **Acari: Eriophyoidea**
    .... **Aculus lathyri** (Nalepa)
    (= *Vasates*)

-   Roll not hairy inside; contains larvae: **Diptera:**
    Cecidomyiidae **8**

FIG. 432

8 Marginal rolls hardly thickened and not discoloured, often both margins inrolled (Fig. 433); larvae (Fig. 434) pale yellow or reddish; on *L. pratensis* (and others abroad):

......................................*Jaapiella volvens* Rübsaamen

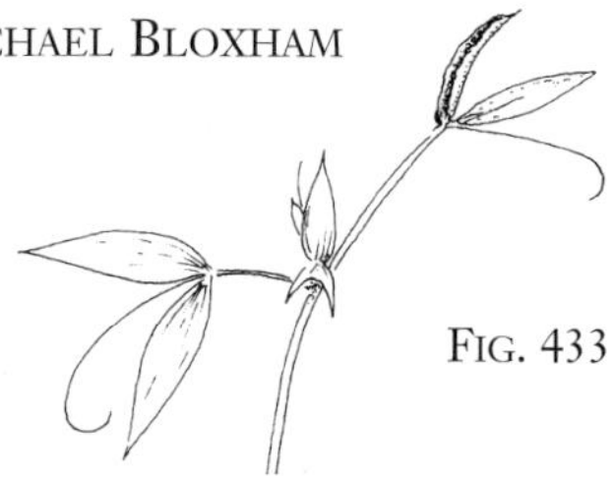

- Marginal roll thickened, ± discoloured purple or reddish **9**

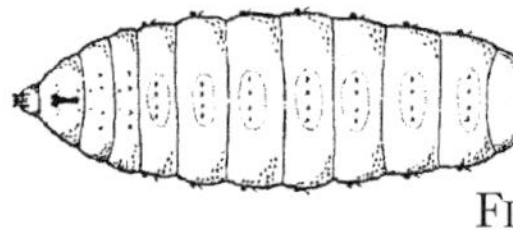

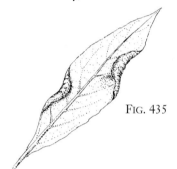

FIG. 433

FIG. 434

9 Larvae red; on *L. pratensis*, *L. sylvestris* .... ***Anabremia bellevoyei*** (Kieffer)
(= *Macrodiplosis*)

Anabremia spp. may be inquilines (Harris, personal communication); *A. bellevoyei* therefore may not be the gall causer.

- Larvae white, later pink; on *L. linifolius* .... ***Lathyromyza schlechtendali*** (Kieffer)

E90. *LAURUS*

One psyllid gall (**Hemiptera: Psylloidea**) is found on the introduced bay, *Laurus nobilis* L.

Leaf margin thickened and rolled downwards (Fig 435); often yellowish or reddish when fresh; contains flattened, yellowish green waxy nymphs and copious honeydew; introduced, common in gardens in southern England and Wales, spreading northwards .... ***Trioza alacris*** Flor

FIG. 435

E91. *LEONTODON*

Autumnal hawkbit, *L. autumnalis* L., lesser hawkbit, *L. saxatilis* Lam. and rough hawkbit, *L. hispidus* L. are galled by two insects and a rust (see under Asteraceae, p. 226).

1 Rounded pustule on upper side of leaf, about 4 mm across, purple-edged; usually several present; contains an orange larva (Fig. 434) which can be seen through the transparent lower epidermis; local: **Diptera: Cecidomyiidae**

.... ***Cystiphora leontodontis*** (Bremi)

2 Flower head slightly swollen and distorted, remaining closed; contains 1-3 white larvae (Fig. 436) or brown puparia; common: **Diptera: Tephritidae**

.... ***Tephritis leontodontis*** (De Geer)

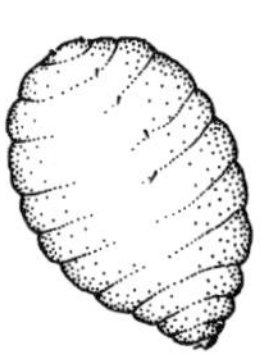

FIG. 436

LEUCANTHEMUM see *CHRYSANTHEMUM*

LEYMUS see POACEAE

E92. *LIGUSTRUM*

Two galls are found on wild privet, *Ligustrum vulgare* L.; the midge gall, below, may also occur on garden privet, *L. ovalifolium* Hassk.

1 Flower bud remaining closed, sometimes slightly swollen, often with several affected in an inflorescence (Fig. 437); contains a light orange, fairly active larva (Fig. 438): **Diptera: Cecidomyiidae** ....*Placochela ligustri* (Rübsaamen)

    There may be other causes of closed flowers; larvae needed to confirm the identification. *Trotteria ligustri* Barnes is an inquiline in these galls; it has a single larva, pale dirty yellow, with pink fat bodies when mature.

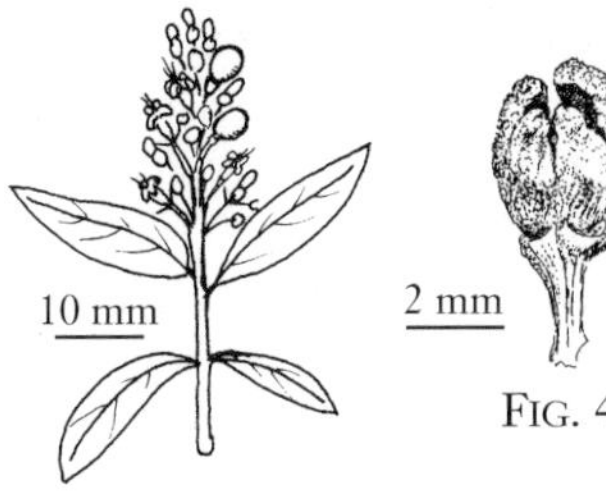

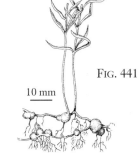

10 mm   2 mm

FIG. 437

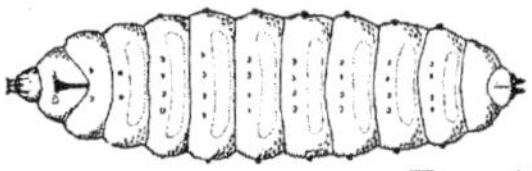

FIG. 438

2 Leaf distorted, slightly swollen, one or both margins curved downwards (Fig. 439) or rolled towards the midrib; shiny pale yellow or yellow-green aphids (Fig. 440) live on underside: **Hemiptera: Aphididae**
    .... *Myzus ligustri* (Mosley)

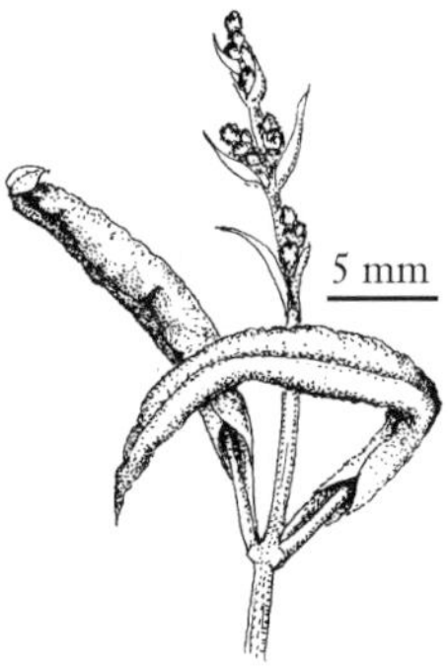

5 mm

FIG. 439

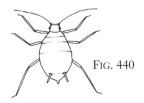

FIG. 440

E93. *LINARIA*

Most galls are recorded from the common toadflax, *Linaria vulgaris* Mill. The introduced purple toadflax, *L. purpurea* (L.) Mill. is occasionally galled.

1 Rounded nodule in root or root collar, up to 6 mm across (Fig. 441), sometimes several coalesce; each with one chamber, containing a larva (Fig. 442) or pupa: **Coleoptera: Curculionidae**:

    Larva with pale head
        .... *Gymnetron linariae* (Panzer)

    Larva with brown head
        .... *Gymnetron collinum* (Gyllenhal)

    For certain determination, rear the adult and identify in Dauphin & Aniotsbehère (1993, 1997, Appendix 3c).

- Gall in flower or fruit, or an artichoke gall at shoot
    tip **2**

FIG. 441

10 mm

FIG. 442

2 Tuft of short, broad leaves at shoot tip, forming an artichoke c. 5 mm across (Fig. 443); contains a white larva or pupa; on *L. vulgaris*, *L. purpurea*; England north to Lancs., local: **Diptera: Cecidomyiidae** .... ***Diodaulus linariae*** (Winnertz)

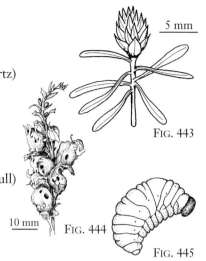

FIG. 443

- Flower closed, ± swollen (though often hardly at all), fruit becoming papery (Fig. 444, Plate 7.7); contains enlarged seeds each with a larva (Fig. 445) or pupa; adults emerge late August - September; locally common: **Coleoptera: Curculionidae** .... ***Gymnetron antirrhini*** (Paykull)

Other *Gymnetron* spp. may emerge from seed capsules. For firm determination, rear the adults and identify in Dauphin & Aniotsbehère (1993, 1997, Appendix 3c).

FIG. 444

FIG. 445

E94. *LINUM* and *RADIOLA*

One gall (**Diptera: Cecidomyiidae**) is found on both flaxes, *Linum* spp. and allseed, *Radiola linoides* Roth.

Artichoke gall at tip of shoot, formed from broadened leaves, about 8 x 4 mm; one chamber in centre with a white larva (Fig. 446) .... ***Dasineura sampaina*** (Tavares)

Recorded only by Bagnall & Harrison in Devon in 1921.

FIG. 446

E95. *LITHOSPERMUM*

One cecid gall (**Diptera: Cecidomyiidae**) is found on common gromwell, *Lithospermum officinale* L. Polyphagous aphids may distort and curl young terminal leaves, bunching them into a mass; this is not a true gall.

Hairy, thickened, deformed leaves form a tuft or rosette at tip of main or side shoot (Fig. 447); contains larvae (Fig. 446); rare .... ***Dasineura lithospermi*** (Loew)

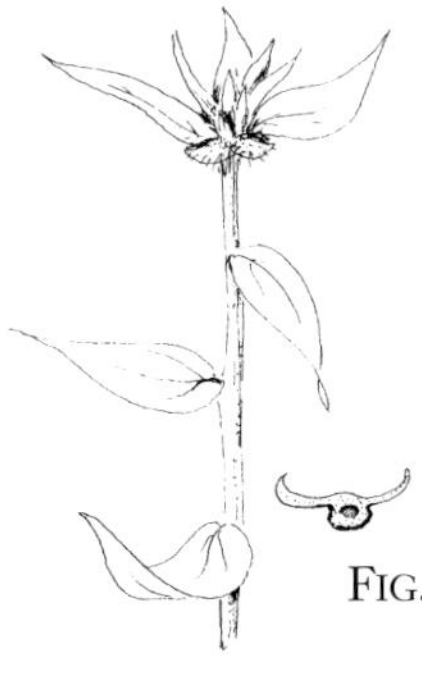

FIG. 447

E96. *LONICERA*

Galls are recorded from the common honeysuckle, *Lonicera periclymenum* L. and the rare fly honeysuckle, *L. xylosteum* L. Introduced cultivated species are not normally galled, although they may be attacked by aphids (see below). The moth caterpillar *Alucita hexadactyla* (L.) (**Lepidoptera: Alucitidae**) feeds in closed flower buds; it is not thought to be a true gall causer. True gall causers attack the leaves.

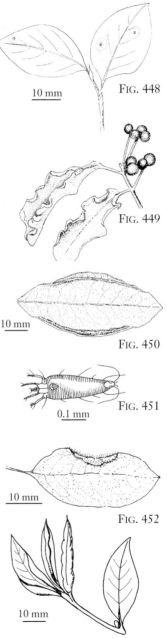

FIG. 448

10 mm

FIG. 449

FIG. 450

10 mm

FIG. 451

0.1 mm

FIG. 452

10 mm

FIG. 453

10 mm

1 Small dimple in leaf blade, c. 1 mm across, surrounded by a pale zone 4-7 mm across (Fig. 448); usually several in a leaf; a white larva (Fig. 446) in depression on underside in June; local: **Diptera: Cecidomyiidae**
.... ***Dasineura excavans*** (Kieffer)

Species described from gall only (Chandler 1998); it requires confirmation by rearing and identifying the adult.

- Margin of leaf ± thickened and pleated or rolled **2**

Curling, distortion, yellowing and bunching of young leaves at shoot tips is common in spring and early summer, caused by several species of aphids; sometimes flower buds may be affected. The damage of *Prociphilus xylostei* (De Geer) (**Hemiptera: Aphididae: Pemphiginae**) is particularly obvious due to the copious production of wax by the aphids. These are not considered to be true galls. (For more information, see Heie, 1980, Carter & Danielsson, 1993, Blackman & Eastop, 1994.)

2 Narrow tight roll, usually downwards, often reddish, clearly thickened and causing crinkling of the leaf margin (Fig. 449) or a pleat parallel to the leaf margin (Fig. 450); may be 2-3 mm long or affect most of both margins; roll lined with hairs, containing mites (Fig. 451): **Acari: Eriophyoidea**
.... ***Aculus xylostei*** (Canestrini)
(= *Eriophyes* = *Phyllocoptes*)

- Looser fleshy roll, usually upwards, yellowish or pale green, up to 10 x 3 mm, on one or both sides of leaf; leaf margin not crinkled; roll without hairs, containing several larvae (Fig. 446): **Diptera: Cecidomyiidae** **3**

3 Roll only slightly thickened (Fig. 452), larvae creamy-white .... ***Macrolabis lonicerae*** Rübsaamen

- Roll distinctly thickened (Fig. 453), larvae yellow, orange or red ... ***Dasineura periclymeni*** (Rübsaamen)

E97. *LOTUS*

Of the five British species, only two are common hosts: common bird's-foot-trefoil, *Lotus corniculatus* L. and greater bird's-foot-trefoil, *L. pedunculatus* Cav.
For root nodules, see p. 219

normal flower

1   Gall in flower or pod 2

-    Gall in stem or leaflet, or at tip of shoot 5

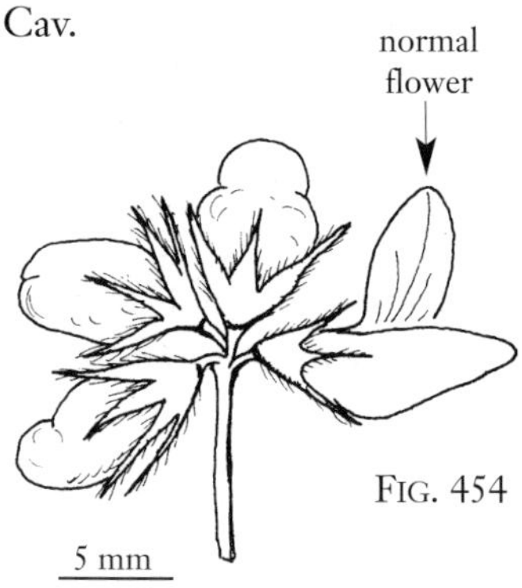

FIG. 454

2   Flower bud swollen, up to 12 mm long, remaining closed (Fig. 454); all flower parts inside are swollen; yellow green, becoming reddish or brown; contains several white or yellow jumping larvae (Fig. 455); June - September: **Diptera: Cecidomyiidae**

....*Contarinia loti* (De Geer)

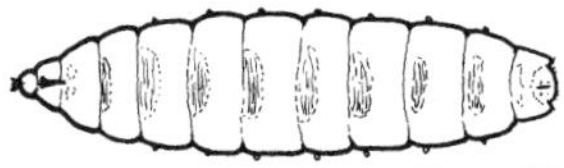

5 mm

FIG. 455

-    In pod 3

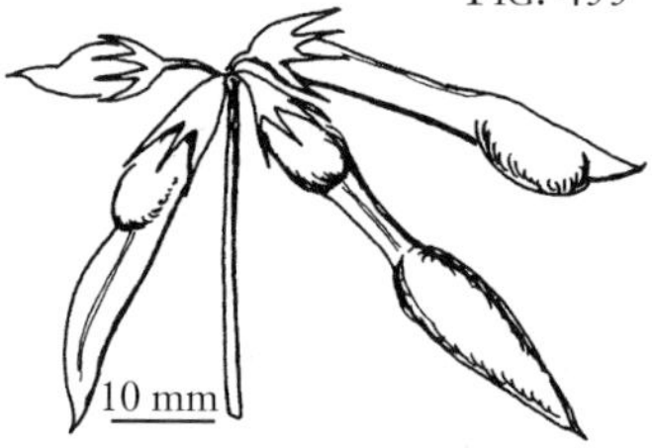

3   Pea-like swelling, 3-5 mm across, often several in wall of pod (Fig. 456); chamber inside lined with fungus, contains a yellow larva (Fig. 457) or pupa; on *L. corniculatus* (and *L. pedunculatus* abroad): **Diptera: Cecidomyiidae**

.... *Asphondylia melanopus* Kieffer

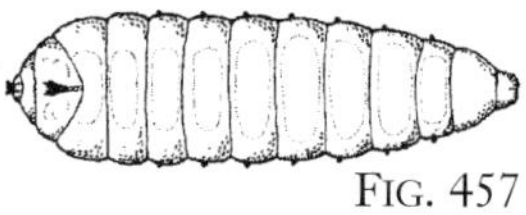

10 mm

FIG. 456

-    Pod slightly swollen; contains one or a few larvae (Fig. 458) or pupae, not lined with fungus: **Coleoptera: Brentidae: Apioninae** 4

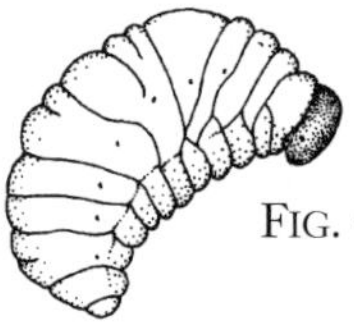

FIG. 457

4   On *L. corniculatus*; common

.... *Ischnopterapion loti* (Kirby)
(= *Eutrichapion*)

FIG. 458

-    On *L. pedunculatus*; S.E. England and S. Wales

...........................*Ischnopterapion modestum* (Germar)
(= *Eutrichapion*)

Discovered in 1970s; probably more widespread (Morris 1990). Common in Ireland.

READ THREE ALTERNATIVES

5 Slender elongate swelling in upper part of stem (Fig. 459); contains a larva or a puparium (Fig. 460); on *L. corniculatus*; S. England, uncommon: **Diptera: Agromyzidae**

............................*Melanagromyza cunctans* (Meigen)

- Margins of leaflet tightly rolled or folded upwards, thickened and hairy (Fig. 461), often yellow or reddish with white hairs; contains mites (Fig. 462); on *L. cornaculatus*, local: **Acari: Eriophyoidea**

.... *Aceria euaspis* (Nalepa)

(= *Eriophyes*)

- Ovoid gall at tip of shoot, formed from several thickened leaflets enclosing the meristem; usually contains several larvae: **Diptera: Cecidomyiidae 6**

6 Gall (Fig. 463) green, sometimes reddened; larvae (Fig. 464) orange or reddish, non-jumping, normally pupate in soil

.... *Jaapiella loticola* (Rübsaamen)

(= *Dasineura loti*)

- Gall (Fig. 465) green; white or yellowish jumping larvae (Fig. 455), pupate in gall

.... *Contarinia barbichi* (Kieffer)

(= *barbichei*)

These galls cannot be separated if larvae or pupae are not present. The synonymy of *D. loti* with *J. loticola* is uncertain and *D. loti*, therefore, may be a separate gall causer.

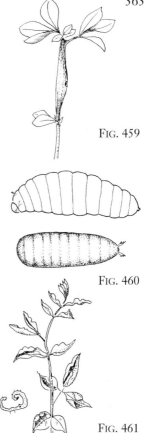

Fig. 459

Fig. 460

Fig. 461

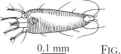

0.1 mm   Fig. 462

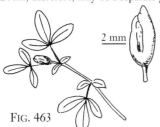

Fig. 463

2 mm

Fig. 464

2 mm

Fig. 465

E98. *LYCHNIS*

One cecid gall (**Diptera: Cecidomyiidae**) is found on ragged-robin, *Lychnis flos-cuculi* L.

Flower bud swollen, almost spherical, up to 6 mm across, remaining closed; petals thickened at base; contains a red larva (Fig. 464); rare .... *Dasineura praticola* (Kieffer)

(= *Jaapiella*)

LYCOPERSICON see *SOLANUM*

E99. *LYSIMACHIA*

One mite gall (**Acari: Eriophyoidea**) is recorded on yellow loosestrife, *Lysimachia vulgaris* L. and creeping-jenny, *L. nummularia* L. Aphids, sometimes covered with wax, are common on distorted crowded leaves at shoot tips; these distortions are not true galls.

Leaves at shoot tip inrolled, distorted, bunched together due to shortened internodes, ± hairy; adjacent inflorescence with malformed flower buds, or flowers greened and leafy (phyllanthy) (Fig. 466); contains mites (Fig. 467); rare
.... *Aceria laticinctus* (Nalepa)

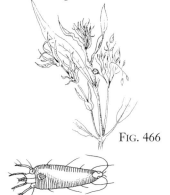

FIG. 466

0.1 mm   FIG. 467

E100. *LYTHRUM*

Two galls are recorded, one each on purple-loosestrife, *Lythrum salicaria* L. and water-purslane, *L. portula* (L.) D.Webb.

1   Gall at shoot tip or in lateral leaf- and flower-buds, often reddened; leaves are stunted, broadened and bunched together, or buds clustered, hard and swollen (Fig. 468); contains several orange-yellow larvae (Fig. 469); on *L. salicaria*; rare: **Diptera: Cecidomyiidae**
.... *Bayeriola salicariae* (Kieffer)
(= *Bayeria*)

2   Stem with spindle-shaped swelling, up to 5 mm long, usually in a side shoot; contains one chamber with a larva (Fig. 470) or pupa: on *L. portula*; S. England, local: **Coleoptera: Brentidae**
.... *Nanophyes gracilis* Redtenbacher

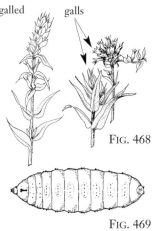

ungalled   galls

FIG. 468

FIG. 469

FIG. 470

E101. *MALUS*

Galls are found on crab apple, *Malus sylvestris* (L.) Mill. and cultivated apple, *M. domestica* Borkh. (Naturalised cultivated apple is commoner than both the native crab apple and their hybrid, and is difficult to distinguish from them, Stace 1997.)

1 Irregular lumpy swelling on root, trunk or branch (Fig. 471); variable in size (c. 1 cm across or much larger); soft at first, later woody; contains red, purple or brown woolly aphids (Fig. 472) covered with copious white wax; gall persists long after aphids have left; a pest: **Hemiptera: Aphididae: Pemphiginae** .... ***Eriosoma lanigerum*** (Hausmann) **woolly aphid**

Also recorded frequently from *Cotoneaster* and *Pyracantha*, and rarely on *Pyrus communis* and *Crateagus*.

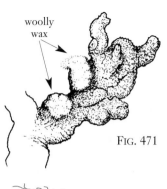

woolly wax

FIG. 471

- Gall in margin or blade of leaf, sometimes whole leaf distorted **2**

Larvae of *Anthonomus pomorum* (L.) and other *Anthonomus* species (**Coleoptera: Curculionidae**) feed in flower buds, causing 'capped' blossoms; these are not regarded as galls (Morris, personal communication).

1 mm   FIG. 472

2 Pustule or erineum in blade, often several on a leaf; contains mites (Fig. 467): **Acari: Eriophyoidea** **3**

- Margin inrolled; or whole leaf curled downwards or twisted and crumpled, yellow, green or red **4**

3 Pustules rounded, 2-4 mm across, light green to brown; raised on both sides with opening on underside ....***Phyllocoptes mali*** (Nalepa)

- Erineum usually on underside; whitish at first (pink on purple-leaved varieties of *M. sylvestris*), later rust-brown (Fig. 473) .... ***Phyllocoptes malinus*** (Nalepa)

FIG. 473

4 Leaf slightly thickened, curled downwards or crumpled and twisted; contains waxy aphids (Fig. 474) in spring and summer: **Hemiptera: Aphididae** **5**

- Margin thickened and rolled upwards, on one or both sides of leaf; contains larvae (Fig. 469) or mites (Fig. 467) **6**

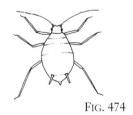

FIG. 474

5 Leaf crumpled, twisted, with margins incurled; yellowish, sometimes flecked with red; aphids red-brown, appearing greyish-white due to copious wax .... ***Dysaphis plantaginea*** (Passerini) **rosy apple aphid**

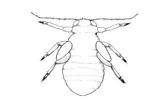

FIG. 475

- Leaf curled downwards and puckered, becoming bright red; aphids greyish white, dusted with wax .... ***Dysaphis devecta*** (Walker) **rosy leaf-curling aphid**

Other aphid species, with bright green apterae, are common on *Malus*, forming colonies on shoots and curling young leaves if abundant; these are not true galls. The fundatrix of *Dysaphis radicicola* (Mordvilko) does cause a gall, a small longitudinal fold near the midrib at tip of leaf; her offspring roll and redden the leaf margins (probably not true galls). This aphid is British but has not been found on *Malus* in Britain (Blackman & Eastop, 1994).

The psyllid *Psylla mali* (Schmidberger), a common pest of apples, twists and folds the leaves, causing small, light-brown specks where it has fed (not a true gall); the nymphs (Fig. 475) are yellow or pale green, later red or brown.

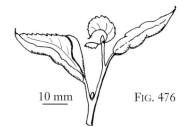

10 mm   FIG. 476

6 Roll > 3 mm broad, sometimes reaching midrib (Fig. 476); contains white or orange larvae (Fig. 477) for a few weeks in summer and early autumn; can be a pest: **Diptera: Cecidomyiidae** .... ***Dasineura mali*** (Kieffer) **apple leaf midge**

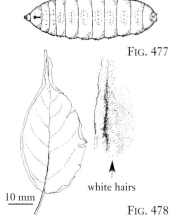

FIG. 477

- Roll, narrow, hard, c. 1 mm broad with white hairs alongside roll on upper surface (Fig. 478); contains mites: **Acari: Eriophyoidea** .... ***Eriophyes malimarginemtorquens*** (Nalepa) (= *Phytoptus*)

10 mm   white hairs

FIG. 478

MATRICARIA see *ANTHEMIS*

E102. *MEDICAGO*

Most galls are found on black medick *Medicago lupulina* L. and lucerne *M. sativa* L. (includes ssp. *falcata*), although abroad other species may be hosts.

For root nodules, see p. 219.

1 Gall in leaflet or side shoot 2

- Gall in bud, inflorescence or pod 6

A swelling in the stem may be caused by *Protapion filirostre* (Kirby) or *Catapion seniculus* (Kirby) (**Coleoptera: Brentidae: Apioninae**); contains a yellow-white larva (Fig. 479) or pupa. Biology not well known; swelling probably not a true gall (for more information, see Morris 1990, Gønget 1997).

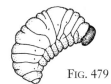

FIG. 479

2 Side shoot deformed and enveloped by two thickened stipules; contains a larva (Fig. 480) or pupa; on *M. lupulina*, N. England: **Diptera: Cecidomyiidae**.......... *Asphondylia lupulinae* Kieffer

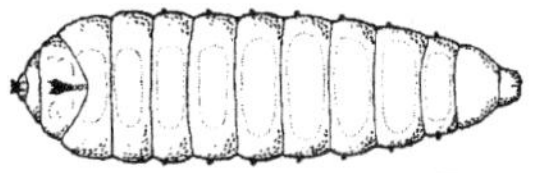

FIG. 480

- In leaflet **3**

3 Leaflet distorted, abnormally hairy, often violet in colour; contains mites (Fig. 481); on *M. lupulina*: **Acari: Eriophyoidea** .... *Aceria plicator* (Nalepa)
Also galls the inflorescence, couplet 6.   (= *Eriophyes*)

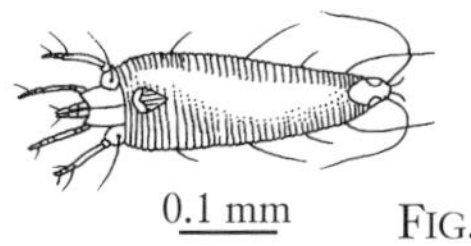

0.1 mm   FIG. 481

- Leaflet rolled, pod-like or with hard swellings **4**

4 Swelling in blade, sometimes affecting most of leaflet (Fig. 482); contains a white larva with dark head (Fig. 479); on *M. sativa*: **Coleoptera: Curculionidae** .... *Tychius crassirostris* (Kirsch)

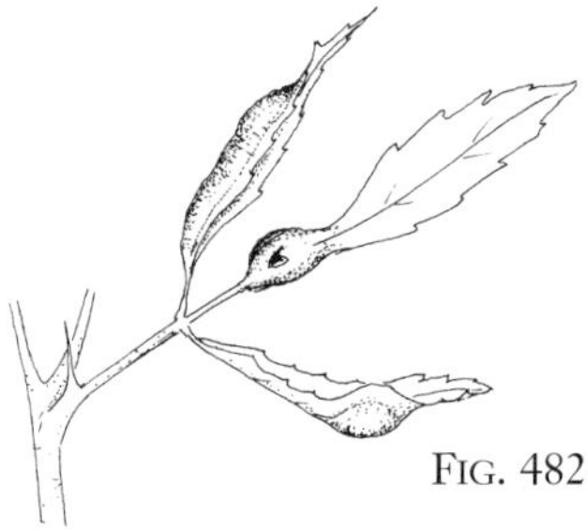

- Leaflet pod-like, or rolled into a pouch, often discoloured; contains larvae (Fig. 477) or pupae: **Diptera: Cecidomyiidae** **5**

FIG. 482

5 Whole leaflet folded upwards into a pod along mid-vein (Fig. 483); one or more white or pale orange larvae with rosy suffusions; on *M. sativa*, SE England
.... *Fabomyia medicaginis* (Rübsaamen)
(= *Jaapiella*) **lucerne leaf midge**

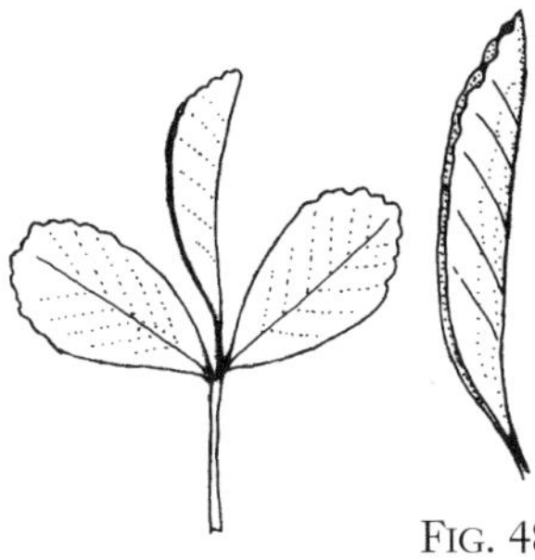

- Margins of leaflet folded upwards into a pod; larvae white or pale yellow; on *M. lupulina*
.................................*Jaapiella jaapiana* (Rübsaamen)

FIG. 483

6 Inflorescence transformed into a mass of leaflets (chloranthy); contains mites (Fig. 481); on *M. lupulina*: **Acari: Eriophyoidea**
.... *Aceria plicator* Nalepa
Also causes distorted hairy leaflets, couplet 3.   (= *Eriophyes*)

- In leaf- or flower-bud; contains larvae: **Diptera: Cecidomyiidae** **7**

The common weevil *Pseudotrichapion pisi* (F.) (**Coleoptera: Brentidae: Apioninae**) attacks buds, perhaps causing some swelling; each contains a larva (Fig. 479) or pupa. This probably is not a true gall.

7   Flower bud swollen, closed, up to 8 mm across
(Fig. 484); larvae white (Fig. 485), later yellow; on
M. sativa
.... ***Contarinia medicaginis*** Kieffer
lucerne flower gall midge

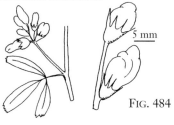

FIG. 484

-    Terminal or axillary leaf bud swollen and hairy,
often enveloped by stipules; with larvae (Fig. 486)
.... **8**

FIG. 485

8   Bud soft, onion-shaped (Fig. 487), with reddish-
yellow or orange-red larvae; on *M. sativa*
.... ***Dasineura medicaginis*** (Bremi)
(= *ignorata*)

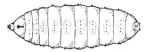

FIG. 486

-    Bud hard, with yellow to reddish yellow larvae; on
M. lupulina .... ***Dasineura lupulina*** (Kieffer)

FIG. 487

E103. *MELILOTUS*

Two weevils (**Coleoptera: Curculionidae**) cause galls in the leaflets of white melilot,
Melilotus albus Medik., ribbed melilot, *M. officinalis* (L.) Pall. and, occasionally, other species.
For nodules on the roots, see p. 219.

1   Leaflet thickened, folded upwards and fused, up to
6 mm wide (Fig. 488); chamber inside contains a
yellowish white larva (Fig. 489) or pupa; very rare
.... ***Tychius crassirostris*** (Kirsch)
Only one British record (Morris, personal communication).

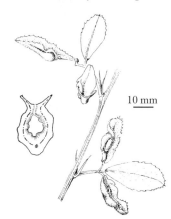

10 mm

2   Feeble swelling of main vein of leaflet, with leaflet
folded upwards, enclosing the larva (Fig. 489);
May – August; common
.... ***Tychius meliloti*** (Stephens)
Details from Buhr (1964) and Dauphin & Aniotsbehère (1993,
1997). In Britain these species are thought to feed in pods
without causing galls (Morris, personal communication).
Records should be confirmed by rearing and identifying adults.

FIG. 488

E104. *MENTHA*

Most records of galls are from water mint, *Mentha aquatica* L., corn mint, *M. arvensis* L. and pennyroyal, *M. pulegium* L., though other species may also be affected.

For fungal galls on stems and leaves, see p. 241.

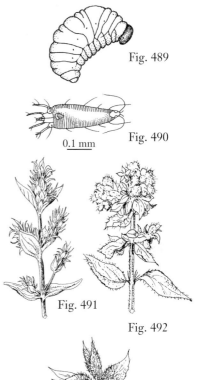

1 Swelling in stem, 4-6 x 2-3 mm, sometimes reddened, usually above a node; contains a white larva (Fig. 489); on *M. aquatica*; England north to Yorkshire, Wales, local: **Coleoptera: Brentidae: Apioninae** .... *Squamapion vicinum* (Kirby)
(= *Thymapion*)

Fig. 489

Fig. 490

0.1 mm

- Shoot tip or most of plant deformed, exhibiting chloranthy; contains mites (Fig. 490): **Acari: Eriophyoidea**... **2**

2 Whole plant modified (Fig. 491); flowers aborted, converted into bunches of crowded compact leaves of varying sizes with modified venation
.... *Eriophyes menthae* Molliard
This species may not be British.

Fig. 491

Fig. 492

- Leaves at shoot tip deformed and very hairy; degree of chloranthy varies, may incorporate the flowers:

On *M. aquatica* and other species (Fig. 492)
.... *Aceria megacerus* (Canestrini & Massalongo)
(= *Eriophyes*)

On *M. arvensis* (Fig. 493)
.... *Aceria mentharius* (Canestrini)
(= *Eriophyes*)

Fig. 493

MOLINIA see POACEAE

E105. *MYOSOTIS*

One cecid gall (**Diptera: Cecidomyiidae**) is recorded from field forget-me-not, *Myosotis arvensis* (L.) Hill and water forget-me-not, *M. scorpioides* L.

Calyx swollen, flower remaining closed; contains a yellowish white larva (Fig. 486)
.... *Dasineura myosotidis* (Kieffer)

E106. *MYOSOTON*

One cecid gall (**Diptera: Cecidomyiidae**) is recorded on water chickweed, *Myosoton aquaticum* (L.) Moench (= *Stellaria aquatica*).

Terminal pair of leaves thickened, with margins pressed together to form a small inconspicuous pouch (see Fig. 902, p. 451); contains white to lemon-yellow larvae (Fig. 486) .... *Macrolabis stellariae* (Liebel)

OENANTHE see APIACEAE

E107. *ONOBRYCHIS*

Three galls are found on sainfoin, *Onobrychis viciifolia* Scop.

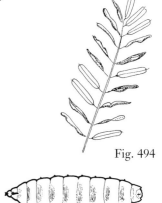

Fig. 494

1 Part or all of leaflet thickened, folded upwards to form a pod (Fig. 494), often several on adjacent leaflets; contains white or yellow non-jumping larvae; SE England: **Diptera: Cecidomyiidae**
.... ***Bremiola onobrychidis*** (Bremi)

2 Flower bud swollen, remaining closed; contains yellow jumping larvae (Fig. 495); south and east England: **Diptera: Cecidomyiidae**
.... ***Contarinia onobrychidis*** Kieffer

Fig. 495

3 Stalk of inflorescence swollen; contains a chamber with one larva (Fig. 496) or pupa; Yorkshire, Lancashire and Merioneth southwards: **Coleoptera: Brentidae: Apioninae**
.... ***Hemitrichapion reflexum*** (Gyllenhall)
(= *Eutrichapion*)

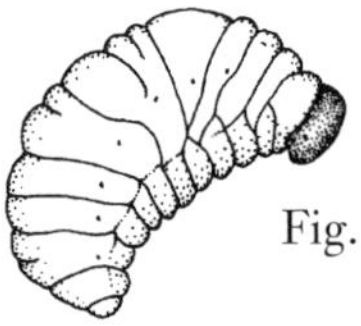

Fig. 496

E108. *ONONIS*

Two species may be galled, common restharrow, *Ononis repens* L., and spiny restharrow, *O. spinosa* L. Three galls are known.
For nodules on the roots, see p. 219.

1 Leaves at shoot tip deformed and irregular, bunched together due to shortening of internodes; contains yellow or orange-yellow larvae (Fig. 495); on *O. repens*; N. England and Scotland, local: **Diptera: Cecidomyiidae**
.... ***Contarinia ononidis*** Kieffer

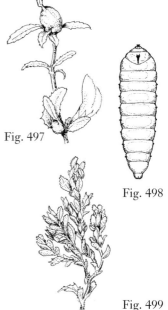

Fig. 497

2 Ovoid gall in leaf axil formed of thickened stipules (Fig. 497); single chamber lined with white fungal mycelium; contains a yellow larva (Fig. 498); on *O. repens* (and on *O. spinosa* abroad); N. England and S. Scotland: **Diptera: Cecidomyiidae**
.... ***Asphondylia ononidis*** F. Löw

Fig. 498

3 Tip of shoot transformed into a mass of abnormally hairy small leaves, flowers greened (Fig. 499); contains mites (Fig. 500); on *O. spinosa* and *O. repens*: **Acari: Eriophyoidea**
.... ***Aceria ononidis*** (Canestrini)
(= *Eriophyes*)

Fig. 499

E109. **ORCHIDACEAE**

One introduced cecid (**Diptera: Cecidomyiidae**) galls cultivated orchids (*Cattleya, Laelia*) in greenhouses.

Rounded swellings, up to 10 mm across, on aerial roots; with several chambers, each containing a bright orange larva .... ***Clinodiplosis cattleyae*** (Molliard)
(= *Parallelodiplosis*)

E110. *ORIGANUM*

Wild marjoram, *Origanum vulgare* L. may be galled by the three species below.
   For rust galls on shoots and leaves, see note under *Mentha*, p. 241.

1   Flowers and leaves at shoot tip thickened, distorted and matted with a felt of white hairs (Fig. 501); contain mites (Fig. 500): **Acari: Eriophyoidea**
.... ***Aceria origani*** (Nalepa)
(= *Phytoptus*)

Fig. 500

0.1 mm

2   Leaves at tip of shoot small, thickened, inrolled and bunched together (Fig. 502); contains aphids (Fig. 503); in early summer before the flowers develop; S. England: **Hemiptera: Aphididae**
.... ***Aphis origani*** Passerini

Fig. 501

5 mm

3   Tuft of hairy leaves at tip of main or side shoot, c. 15 x 10 mm; contains red larvae; July - October, S. England: **Diptera: Cecidomyiidae**
.... ***Blastomyia origani*** (Tavares)

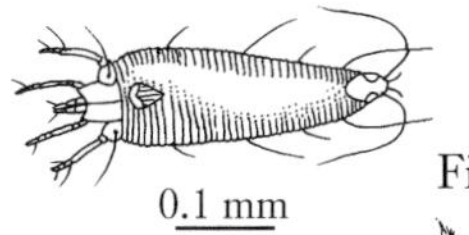

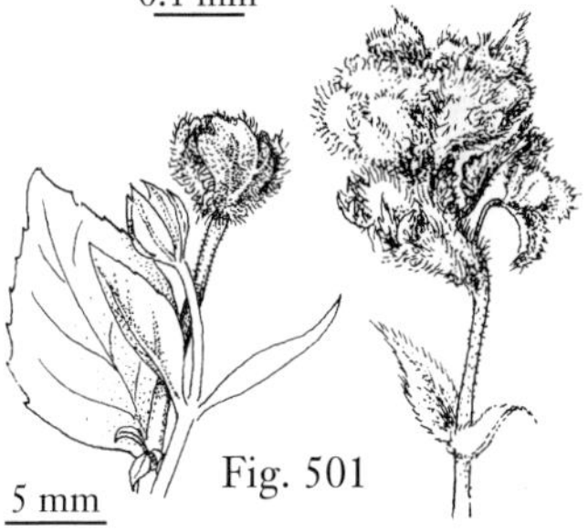

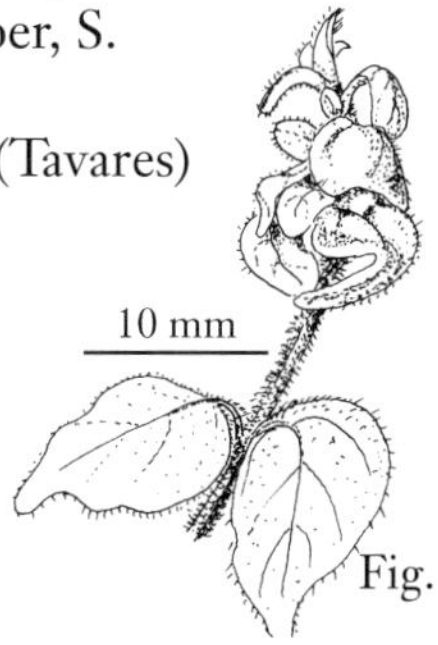

10 mm

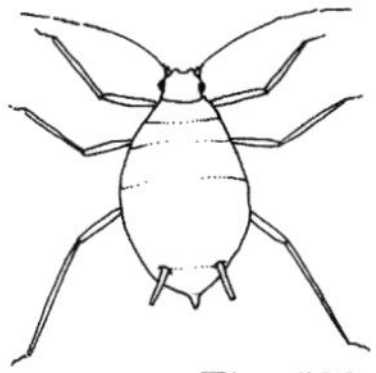

Fig. 503

Fig. 502

E111. *ORNITHOPUS*

A locally common genus, especially in south and east England. Bird's-foot, *Ornithopus perpusillus* L. is native, serradella, *O. sativa* Brot., and yellow serradella, *O. compressus* L., are rare introductions. One mite gall (**Acari: Eriophyoidea**) is recorded.
   For root nodules, see p. 219.

Inflorescence green and leafy (chloranthy), forming a bunch of leaflets with margins rolled upwards; abnormally hairy; contains mites (Fig. 500) ...... ***Aceria plicator*** (Nalepa)
(= *Eriophyes*)

E112. *PAPAVER*

Three galls may be found in the seed capsules of common or field poppy, *Papaver rhoeas* L. and long-headed poppy, *P. dubium* L. The galls may not be apparent from the outside.

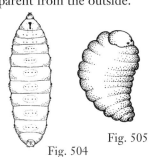

Fig. 505

Fig. 504

1   Capsule not distorted; septa inside are swollen, with many reddish yellow larvae (Fig. 504) between them; on *P. rhoeas*: **Diptera: Cecidomyiidae** .... ***Dasineura papaveris*** (Winnertz)

-   Capsule may be distorted or swollen; several galls inside, each with one chamber containing a white larva (Fig. 505) or pupa; on *P. rhoeas* and *P. dubium*; locally common: **Hymenoptera: Cynipidae** **2**

    Although not a gall, distortion of the capsule may be caused by fungal infection following penetration by orange larvae of *Clinodiplosis cilicrus* (Kieffer) (= *Carpodiplosis papaveris*) (**Diptera: Cecidomyiidae**).

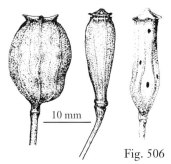

10 mm

Fig. 506

2   Capsule distorted, usually swollen (Fig. 506, Plate 5.4); inside, septa swollen and coalesced, many larval chambers (Fig. 507); septa fleshy in June - July, hard and dry when mature .... ***Aylax papaveris*** (Perris) (= *Aulax*)

-   Capsule usually not distorted and not swollen; inside, several ovoid galls attached to septa, which are not swollen (Fig. 508); galls develop from the ovules, fleshy in June - July, hard and dry when mature .... ***Aylax minor*** Hartig

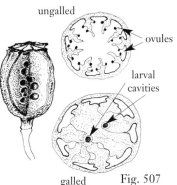

ungalled

ovules

larval cavities

galled   Fig. 507

Fig. 508

PASTINACA see APIACEAE

E113. *PEDICULARIS*

One mite gall (**Acari: Eriophyoidea**) is found on lousewort, *Pedicularis sylvatica* L., and marsh lousewort, *P. palustris* L.

Leaf margin inrolled downwards, often reddish, hairy inside and out, with mites (Fig. 509) .... ***Aculops pedicularis*** (Nalepa) (= *Vasates*)

0.1 mm   Fig. 509

E114. *PERSICARIA*

The knotweeds and bistorts are now in the genus *Persicaria*, separate from the knotgrasses, *Polygonum* (Stace 1997). Their insect galls are mostly different (see *Polygonum* p. 385); all on *Persicaria* are in the leaves. The species most commonly galled are amphibious bistort, *P. amphibia* (L.) Gray, redshank, *P. maculosa* Gray (= *Polygonum persicaria*), and common bistort, *P. bistorta* (L.) Samp. Galls have been found less often on water-pepper, *P. hydropiper* (L.) Spach, pale persicaria, *P. lapathifolia* (L.) Gray, and alpine bistort, *P. vivipara* (L.) Ronse Decr.

For a smut gall on leaves, see p. 244.

1   Small discoloured bump on upper surface of leaf, with flat nymph in corresponding depression below; often several in a leaf: **Hemiptera: Psylloidea**:

Common, throughout Britain.. ***Aphalara polygoni*** Förster

Rare, known only from Cumbria............................. ***Aphalara borealis*** Heslop-Harrison

To distinguish, the nymphs must be identified (Hodkinson & White, 1979, White & Hodkinson, 1982). The psyllids may also cause bunching and distortion of leaves and flowers, due to shortening of terminal internodes (Buhr, 1964, Dauphin & Aniotsbehère, 1993, 1997).

-   Leaf margin(s) rolled downwards, thickened, often yellow or reddened; contain larva(e) (Fig. 504): **Diptera: Cecidomyiidae** **2**

2   Marginal rolls usually on both sides of leaf, markedly thickened (Fig. 510), often spirally or otherwise contorted, cannot be unrolled without breaking the gall; often several leaves at shoot tip affected; several light red or orange-red larvae, or pupae; on *P. amphibia*, *P. maculosa*, July - September, common .... ***Wachtliella persicariae*** (L.)

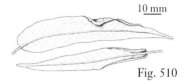

Fig. 510

-   Marginal roll(s) slightly thickened (Fig. 511), can be unrolled without breaking the gall; one white or pink larva, pupates in the soil; on *P. bistorta* .... ***Dasineura bistortae*** (Kieffer)
(= *polygoni*)

Fig. 511

D. bistortae has been identified in Britain from the gall only (Chandler, 1998); it should be confirmed by rearing and identifying the adult. *D. polygoni* was synonymised with *D. bistortae* by Skuhravá (1989).

PETROSELINUM see APIACEAE

PEUCEDANUM see APIACEAE

PHALARIS see POACEAE

PHLEUM see POACEAE

E115. *PHRAGMITES*

There is one native species, the common reed, *Phragmites australis* (Cav.) Trin. ex Steud. (= *P. communis*). For fungus galls, see p. 245.

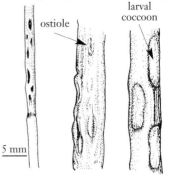

Fig. 512   Fig. 513   Fig. 514

1 Several galls, 3-10 mm long, resembling rice grains, attached to inner wall of stem (Fig. 512), which is not, or is only slightly thickened; each contains a white or pale yellow larva (Fig. 515) or pupa: **Diptera: Cecidomyiidae**
.... ***Giraudiella inclusa*** (Frauenfeld)

First generation galls are difficult to detect externally (Fig. 513); they occur low down on plant (internodes 1 to 8), adults emerge July. Second generation galls are open on surface of stem, covered by larval cocoon (Fig. 514); they occur higher up (internodes 8 to 15), adults emerge September.

- Gall at tip of shoot, internodes crowded **2**

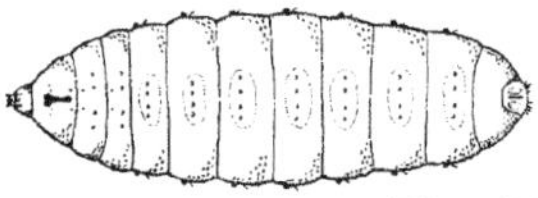

Fig. 515

2 Youngest leaves wrinkled, swollen, folded, twisted together, often breaking through the leaf sheaths (Fig. 516); hairy inside, containing mites (4 pairs of legs): **Acari: Tarsonemidae**
.... ***Steneotarsonemus phragmitidis*** (Schlechtendal)

- Tip of shoot with overlapping leaves, stem usually thickened (may be very slight); without hairs inside, containing one or more larvae or pupae **3**

Fig. 516

3 Side shoots shortened, slightly thickened; removing leaves reveals slits to galleries, each containing fungus (Fig. 517) and a reddish yellow larva (Fig. 518): **Diptera: Cecidomyiidae**
.... ***Lasioptera arundinis*** Schiner

- Main stem shortened, thickened (may be very slight), usually affecting shoots < 5 mm diameter; central chamber contains a yellow-white larva (Fig. 519) or brown puparium, without fungus: **Diptera: Chloropidae** **4**

Lipara similis Schiner causes telescoping of internodes at tip of shoot (Fig. 520) but without a chamber and no thickening of the stem. The larva lives between leaf sheaths growing from the two terminal nodes, its position marked by a dark brown rotting channel. This is not a true gall causer.

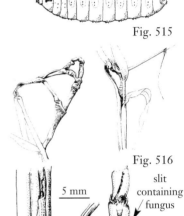

Fig. 517

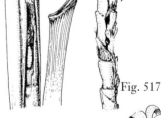

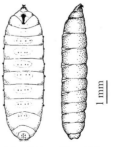

Fig. 518   Fig. 519

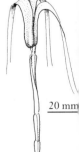

Fig. 520

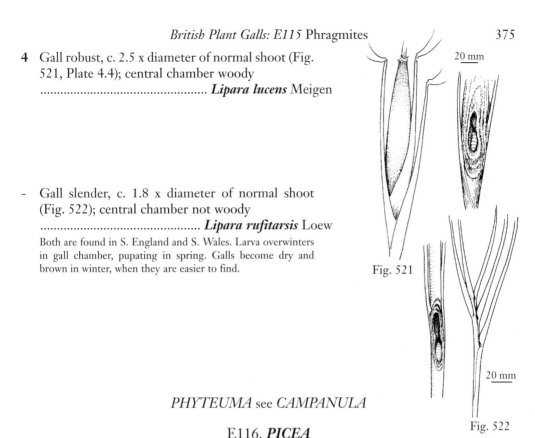

4   Gall robust, c. 2.5 x diameter of normal shoot (Fig. 521, Plate 4.4); central chamber woody
.... ***Lipara lucens*** Meigen

-   Gall slender, c. 1.8 x diameter of normal shoot (Fig. 522); central chamber not woody
.... ***Lipara rufitarsis*** Loew

Both are found in S. England and S. Wales. Larva overwinters in gall chamber, pupating in spring. Galls become dry and brown in winter, when they are easier to find.

Fig. 521

Fig. 522

PHYTEUMA see *CAMPANULA*

E116. *PICEA*

No spruce is native in Britain, although Norway spruce, *Picea abies* (L.) Karst. and Sitka spruce *P. sitchensis* (Bong.) Carr. are widely planted and are commonly galled. Other species are planted in arboreta and occasionally are galled. Most gall causers are aphids in the family **Adelgidae**, which feed exclusively on conifers.

READ THREE ALTERNATIVES

1   Small rounded swelling in bark of current year's shoot, usually several clustered together (Fig. 523); each contains an orange larva (Fig. 524) or pupa; on *P. abies*: **Diptera: Cecidomyiidae**
.... ***Dasineura abietiperda*** (Henschel)
(= *piceae*)

-   Scale in cone with slight swelling, sometimes warty, in base of inner face (Fig. 525), sometimes 2 or 3 together; each contains a red larva or pupa; on *P. abies*: **Diptera: Cecidomyiidae**
.... ***Kaltenbachiola strobi*** (Winnertz)

-   Bud and / or bases of needles swollen: **Hemiptera: Adelgidae** **2**

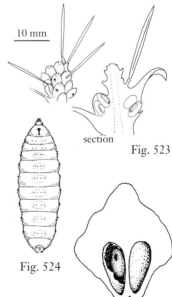

section

Fig. 523

Fig. 524

Fig. 525

2   Bases of adjacent needles swollen, not fused to axis
    of shoot, forming a loose structure 1-4 cm long;
    galled needles pale green or yellowish; adelgids
    only partially enclosed in gall (adult has 4 pairs of
    abdominal spiracles, Fig. 526); on *P. sitchensis*, N.
    England, rare .... ***Pineus similis*** (Gillette)
                                                    (= *orientalis*)

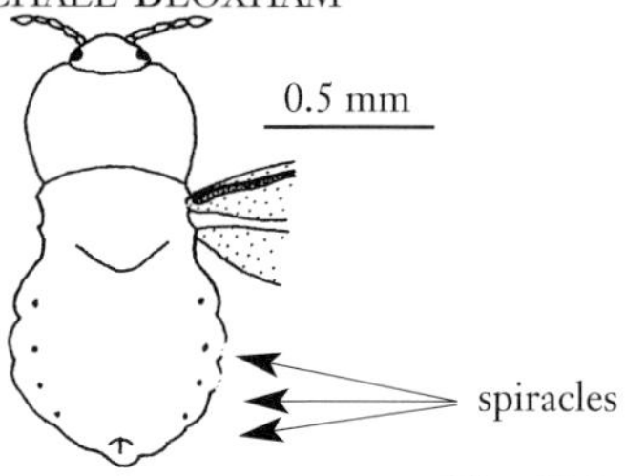

-   Bases of adjacent needles swollen, fused to axis of
    shoot to form a compact structure, completely
    enclosing adelgids (adult has 5 pairs of abdominal
    spiracles, Fig. 527) **3**

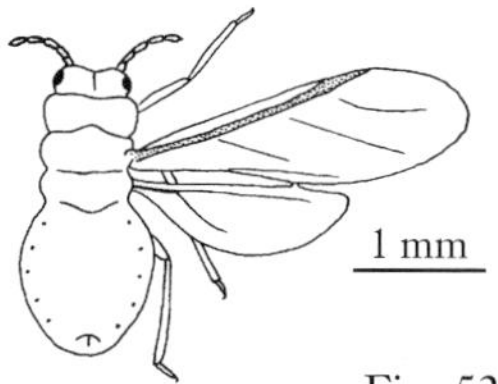

0.5 mm

spiracles

Fig. 526

1 mm

Fig. 527

3   Gall elongated, length > 1.5 x width, shoot often
    curved with needles slightly shorter than normal
    (Fig. 528); pale or yellow-green, with slits of gall
    chambers often pink or purple-red before opening
    in late summer; usually on *P. sitchensis*, common
    .... ***Adelges cooleyi*** (Gillette)

-   Gall globular or ellipsoidal, length < 1.5 x width;
    needles much shorter than normal; **pineapple
    gall**, on *P. abies* and *P. sitchensis*; widespread and
    common **4**

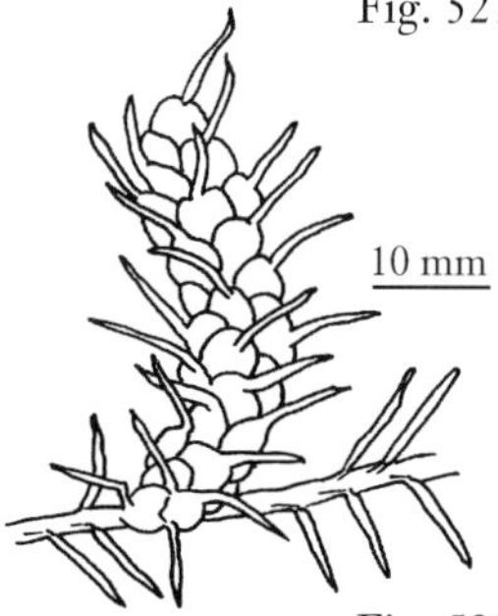

10 mm

Fig. 528

4   Gall globular, waxy, pale yellow or greenish white,
    usually at tip of shoot (Fig. 529); slits to gall
    chambers usually not red or pink, opening in June
    .... ***Adelges laricis*** Vallot

-   Gall ellipsoidal, only slightly paler green than
    normal shoot; slits to gall chambers often red or
    deep pink before opening **5**

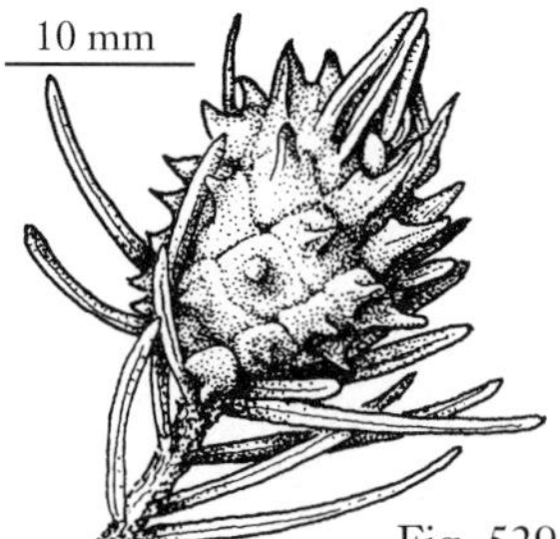

10 mm

Fig. 529

5   Gall chambers open June - July; gall single at tip of
    shoot, usually no growth beyond it in future years
    .... ***Adelges viridis*** (Ratzeburg)

-   Gall chambers open August - September; often 2
    or 3 galls together at base of adjacent shoots,
    growth often continuing beyond gall (Fig. 530,
    Plate 2.1) .... ***Adelges abietis*** (L.)

    Adelges nordmannianae (Eckstein) causes small cone-like galls, 1
    cm long, on *Picea orientalis* (L.) Link; rare, recorded in Kent
    (Carter 1971).

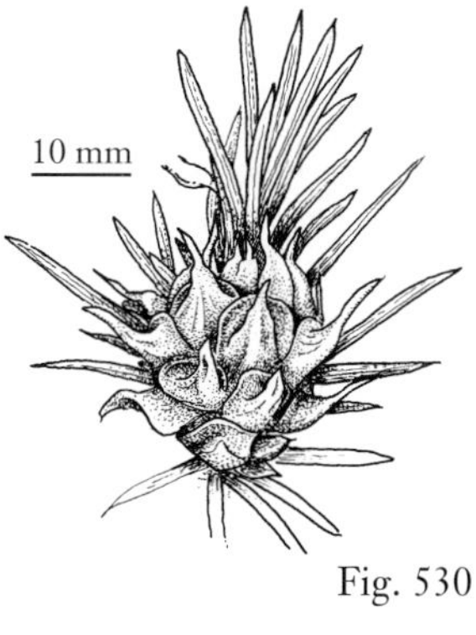

10 mm

Fig. 530

E117. *PICRIS*

One cynipid gall (**Hymenoptera: Cynipidae**) is found on bristly ox-tongue, *Picris echioides* L. For a rust gall on leaves, see p. 226 under Asteraceae.

Stem scarcely thickened (Fig. 531); inside are several chambers, 2.5-3 mm long, each with a white larva (Fig. 532) or pupa; SE England and E. Anglia .... ***Phanacis caulicola*** (Hedicke)

Gall easily missed until emergence holes of adults appear.

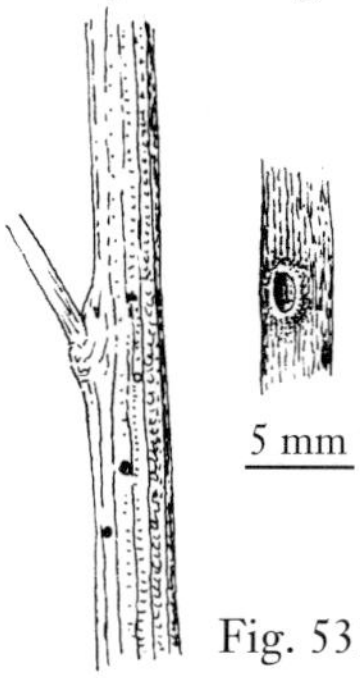

5 mm

Fig. 531 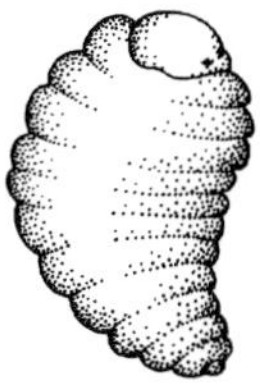   Fig. 532

PILOSELLA see *HIERACIUM*

PIMPINELLA see APIACEAE

E118. *PINUS*

Scots pine, *Pinus sylvestris* L., is native to Scotland and naturalised in the rest of Britain. It is more likely to be galled than non-native pines. For fungus galls on trunk, branches and needles, see p. 245.

1 Gall formed by two or more needles 2

- Gall in twig or bud, involving part or all of young shoot, may be resinous 3

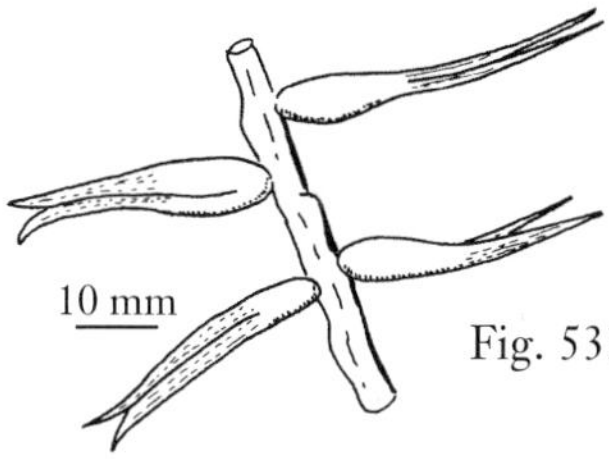

10 mm

Fig. 533

2 Pair of needles shortened, yellowed, thickened and coalesced (Fig. 533); chamber in base contains an orange-red larva (Fig. 534); commoner in N. Britain: **Diptera: Cecidomyiidae** .... ***Thecodiplosis brachyntera*** (Schwägrichen)

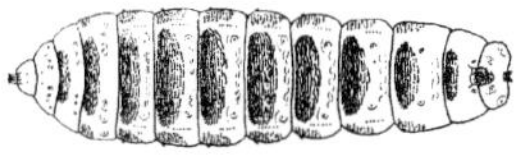

Fig. 534

- Several needles shortened, joined to form a bundle containing a larva (Fig. 535): **Coleoptera: Curculionidae** .... ***Brachonyx pineti*** (Paykull)

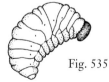

Fig. 535

3   A nodule in twig, usually rounded, 1-2 cm across, sometimes more elongate (Fig. 536), woody when mature; surface smooth at first, later roughened; contains mites (Fig. 537): **Acari: Eriophyoidea** .... *Trisetacus pini* (Nalepa)

\-   Resinous mass on stem, shoot or bud, often incorporating needles; contains silk and a caterpillar (Fig. 538) or pupa: **Lepidoptera: Tortricidae** **4**

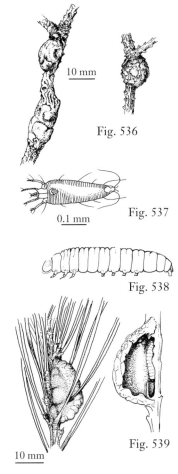

Fig. 536

Fig. 537

Fig. 538

10 mm

0.1 mm

4   Mass of resin 1-3 cm across, envelopes base of needles (Fig. 539); usually on stem below a whorl of shoots; caterpillar July to April of second year, pupa April - May, adult June; often on young trees about 3 m high; locally common in E. Britain, particularly E. Scotland .... *Retinia resinella* (L.) **pine resin-gall moth**
(= *Petrova* = *Evetria*)

\-   Resin and silk tent incorporating bud or young shoot (Fig. 540), later contorting most of shoot (Fig. 541); may leave a permanent bend in older stem; caterpillar September to May or June, pupa May - July, adult July - August; widespread, commoner in S. Britain
.... *Rhyacionia buoliana* (Denis & Schiffermüller)

It is not certain that these resin masses are true galls; it has not been shown that the plant stem inside is swollen. Other *Rhyacionia* species distort the stems involving exudations of resin, see Bradley *et al.* (1979).

Fig. 539

10 mm

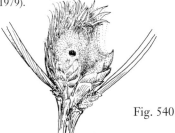

Fig. 540

Fig. 541

E119. *PISUM*

The only species is the introduced and cultivated garden pea, *Pisum sativum* L. There is one true gall, a cecid (**Diptera: Cecidomyiidae**), though aphids may distort the shoot tips and flower stems, and thrips cause 'silvering' of the pods. For a note on root nodules, see p. 219.

Shoot tip bushy, with flower buds closed and distorted, and young pods misshapen (Fig. 542); many white jumping larvae (Fig. 543) present for a short period in summer; England, Wales and S. Scotland .... ***Contarinia pisi*** (Winnertz) (= *pisicola*) **pea midge**

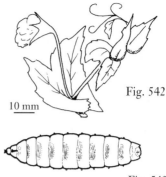

Fig. 542

There are two generations, the first in the shoot tips, the second in the pods (Robbins, personal communication). Orange and red non-jumping larvae are inquilines and predators.

10 mm

Fig. 543

E120. *PITTOSPORUM*

One psyllid gall (**Hemiptera: Triozidae**) is found on the introduced shrubs kohuhu, *Pittosporum tenuifolium* Gaertn., karo, *P. crassifolium* Banks & Sol. and related species.

Leaves at tip of shoot distorted and yellowish, with upward swellings on blade; depression below contains a flat, pale green nymph or yellow-green to black adult psyllid, which produces honeydew; SW. England .... ***Trioza vitreoradiata*** (Maskell)

First detected on *P. tenuifolium* in Cornwall in 1993 and since found on other *Pittosporum* spp. Well established in SW England and likely to spread (Halstead, personal communication).

E121. *PLANTAGO*

The four native species may be galled: ribwort plantain, *Plantago lanceolata* L., greater plantain, *P. major* L., hoary plantain, *P. media* L. and sea plantain, *P. maritima* L.
    Leaves may also be galled by *Ditylenchus dipsaci* (see p. 270).

1 Fruit slightly swollen, pointed apically and shorter than normal (Fig. 544, with larva); an affected head usually contains several galls (easily overlooked), and may be slightly shorter and stouter than normal; larva bright orange-red, between swollen fruits, July - Sept.; on *P. lanceolata* (also *P. major*, *P. media* abroad); England, locally common: **Diptera: Cecidomyiidae** .... ***Jaapiella schmidti*** (Rübsaamen)

-   Gall in stem, axis of inflorescence, or leaf **2**

Fig. 544

Seed heads of *P. lanceolata* may be distorted by the larva of *Falseuncaria degreyana* (McLachlan) (**Lepidoptera: Tortricidae**), E. Anglia, rare; this is probably not a true gall.

2   Leaf blade thickened, wrinkled, folded along vein;
        fold contains mites (Fig. 545); on *P. lanceolata*; rare:
        Acari: Eriophyoidea ... *Epitrimerus coactus* (Nalepa)

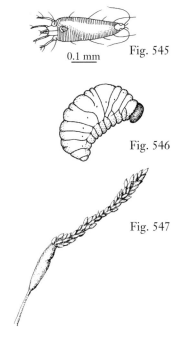

0.1 mm   Fig. 545

-       Spindle-shaped swelling in stem, or stalk within
        inflorescence, 1-2 cm long and up to 4 mm thick;
        contains a hard-walled chamber with a yellow-white
        larva (Fig. 546): **Coleoptera: Curculionidae** **3**

Fig. 546

3   On *P. maritima*; swelling, usually in upper part of
        stem (Fig. 547); larvae present June - autumn,
        pupa overwinters in gall; coastal, E. and W.
        England, Ireland, one record in S. Scotland; local
        .... ***Mecinus collaris*** Germar

Fig. 547

-       On *P. lanceolata*; swelling in stem, root collar or
        stalk of inflorescence; larva present June, pupates
        in gall, adult emerges July; widespread, common
        .... ***Mecinus pyraster*** (Herbst)

POA see POACEAE

E122. **POACEAE** (= GRAMINAE)

This key is to galls on all grasses, except for those on common reed *Phragmites australis* (see
p. 374). Galls on grasses are not well known; they are difficult to find and their host
associations are often unknown. The majority of species causing galls belongs to the
Cecidomyiidae (Diptera) or Eurytomidae (Hymenoptera: Chalcidoidea). The galls can be
rather similar, though most are specific to a particular grass genus. To name the gall causers,
therefore, the grasses must be accurately identified. Even so, this key is preliminary only
and should be used with caution. Authors of grass species are not included; if these are
required, see Stace (1997).

     For fungal and nematode galls see pages 246 and 266.

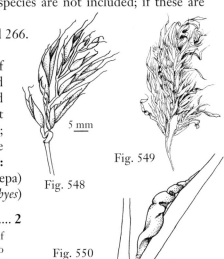

1   Gall in inflorescence; stalks of panicle and of
        individual spikelets shortened, spikelets broad and
        bunched together, their parts thickened, green and
        leaflike (phyllanthy) (Figs 548, 549); may affect
        young panicle still inside distorted sheath (Fig. 550);
        contains mites (Fig. 545) with 2 pairs of legs; cause
        variable damage on many grasses, common: **Acari:
        Eriophyoidea** .... ***Aceria tenuis*** (Nalepa)
                                          (= *Eriophyes*)

5 mm

Fig. 549

Fig. 548

-       Gall in stem, leaf sheath or blade, or tip of shoot **2**
        Several aphids roll, curl, crumple and otherwise distort leaf
        blades and sheaths; some are polyphagous, others specific to
        particular genera, but none are thought to be true gall causers.

Fig. 550

5 mm

READ THREE ALTERNATIVES

2 Surface of leaf sheath or blade ridged and wrinkled, sometimes covered with small tubercles; caused by mites with 4 pairs of legs: **Acari: Tarsonemidae**:

On *Festuca, Avena*
.... *Steneotarsonemus graminis* (Krämer)

On *Elytrigia*
.... *Steneotarsonemus canestrini* (Massalongo)

Fig. 551

- Shoot stunted, its tip with overlapping leaves due to shortening of internodes, sometimes several affected shoots bunched together; flowering stem usually aborted **3**

mandible

Fig. 552

- Gall in stem, often incorporating leaf sheath or hidden by it **4**

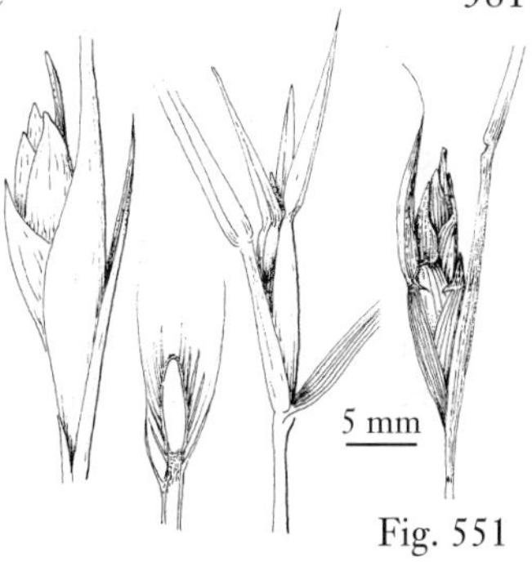

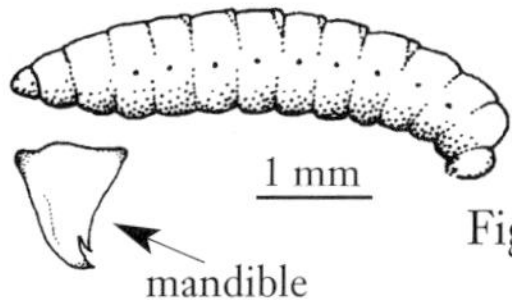

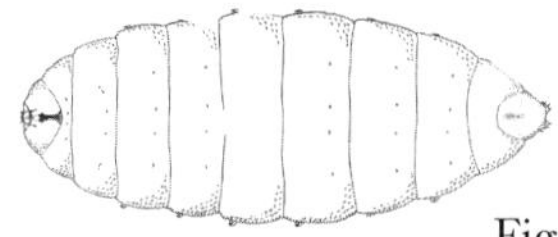

Fig. 553

READ THREE ALTERNATIVES

3 Overlapping leaves broad (looks like a miniature cigar gall of *Lipara lucens* on *Phragmites*, p. 375) enclosing a single chamber with woody walls (Fig. 551, Plate 5.1) and a yellowish white larva (Fig. 552) or pupa; on *Elytrigia*, more robust on *E. juncea* than *E. repens*; common: **Hymenoptera: Eurytomidae**
.... *Tetramesa hyalipennis* (Walker)

Fig. 554

- Tuft of leaves at shoot tip, c. 3 cm long; contains one or more white larvae (Fig. 553); on *Calamagrostis*: **Diptera: Cecidomyiidae**
.... *Mayetiola lanceolatae* (Rübsaamen)

- Overlapping leaves small and broad, enclosing chamber, with elongated twisted leaves extending beyond gall; often several affected shoots bunched together (Fig. 554); contains a yellowish white larva (Fig. 555) or brown puparium (Fig. 556); on several grasses (eg. *Elytrigia, Hordeum, Secale, Triticum, Avena*): **Diptera: Chloropidae**
.... *Chlorops pumilionis* (Bjerkander)
(= *taeniopus*)

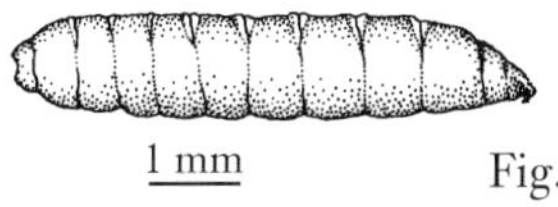

Fig. 555

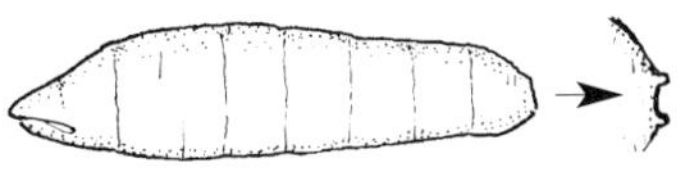

Fig. 556

4 Stem inside leaf sheath coiled for 2-3 cm (Fig. 557); contains mites with 4 pairs of legs; on *Avena* and other grasses: **Acari: Tarsonemidae**
.... *Steneotarsonemus spirifex* (Marchal)

- Not like this **5**

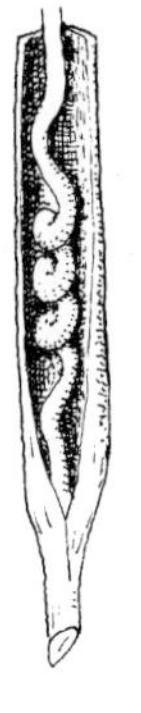

Fig. 557

READ THREE ALTERNATIVES

5 Several hard ovoid galls, 2-3 mm long, on inside wall of sheath or stem; each contains a yellowish white larva (Fig. 558) or pupa; flowering stem beyond galls stunted and panicle reduced or absent: **Hymenoptera: Eurytomidae:**
On *Elytrigia* (Fig. 559)
.... ***Tetramesa linearis*** (Walker)

On *Festuca ovina*, *F. rubra*
.... ***Tetramesa brevicornis*** (Walker)

- Stem ± swollen with shallow, thickened depression, often with raised rim, often low down near soil; contains a larva or pupa, sometimes covered with thin blackened epidermis; concealed by leaf sheath (so difficult to detect) or position marked by a dense tuft of hairs: **Diptera: Cecidomyiidae** **6**

- Slight or distinct swelling in flowering stem, or in stem beneath leaf sheath; contains one or more enclosed chambers **10**

6 Dense tuft of hair-like rootlets on stem above a node, on middle or upper part of plant; white larva (Fig. 560) in depression in stem on opposite side to rootlets, covered by leaf sheath (Fig. 561); on *Poa nemoralis* **7**

- Without hair-like rootlets; depression often saddle-shaped, up to 5 mm long; often several in one stem **8**

Cecid galls in grasses are not well known; in some there is obvious swelling. The list under couplet 8 is tentative only and all identifications based upon it should be confirmed by an expert (ideally the adults should be reared).

7 Rootlets emerge from gall either side of longitudinal furrow (Fig. 562); gall up to 8 mm long, green turning brown later; common but easily overlooked .... ***Mayetiola poae*** (Bosc)
(= *Poomyia*)

- Rootlets in a tangled mass, without longitudinal furrow (Fig. 563); N. England and Scotland, rare
.... ***Mayetiola radicifica*** (Rübsaamen)
(= *Caulomyia*)

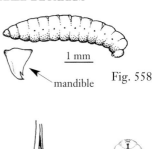
1 mm
mandible
Fig. 558

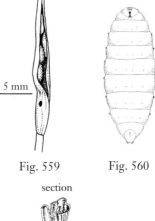
5 mm
Fig. 559   Fig. 560
section

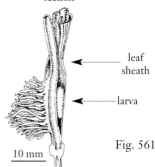
leaf sheath
larva
10 mm
Fig. 561

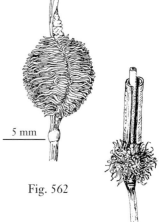
5 mm
Fig. 562

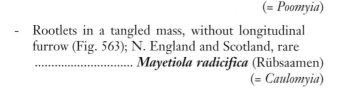
Fig. 563

8 Depression not covered by blackened epidermis, often associated with a swelling (*Mayetiola* larvae as in Fig. 560):

On *Avena fatua*, *A. sativa*; larva pale greenish white
.... ***Mayetiola avenae*** (Marchal)

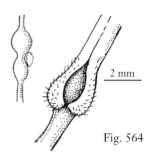

2 mm

Fig. 564

On *Brachypodium sylvaticum* (Fig. 564); larva white
.... ***Mayetiola hellwigi*** (Rübsaamen)

On *Calamagrostis* species, *Phalaris arundinacea*; larva(e) (Fig. 565) orange or red
.... ***Lasioptera calamagrostidis*** Rübsaamen
(= *Thomasiella*)

On *Dactylis glomerata*; larva white
.... ***Mayetiola dactylidis*** Kieffer

On Triticeae and others (Fig. 566); larva reddish, later yellow-white .... ***Mayetiola destructor*** (Say)

On Triticeae and others (Fig. 567); larva blood red
.... ***Haplodiplosis marginata*** (von Roser)
(= *equestris*)

Fig. 565

On Triticeae (no information on larva)
.... ***Mayetiola hordei*** Kieffer

On *Holcus lanatus*, *H. mollis*; larva white
.... ***Mayetiola holci*** Kieffer

On *Molinia caerulea*; larva white
.... ***Mayetiola moliniae*** (Rübsaamen)

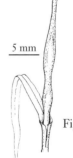

5 mm

Fig. 566

On *Phalaris arundinacea*; larva yellowish white
.... ***Mayetiola phalaris*** Barnes

On *Poa nemoralis*; larva(e) white
.... ***Mayetiola joannisi*** Kieffer

- Depression 3-4 mm long, covered by blackened epidermis **9**

9 On *Calamagrostis canescens*; larva (Fig. 560) orange
.... ***Mayetiola bimaculata*** (Rübsaamen)
(= *calamagrostidis*)

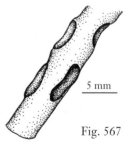

5 mm

Fig. 567

- On many grass species (including *C. canescens*); larva (Fig. 565) orange or red
.... ***Hybolasioptera cerealis*** (Lindemann)
(= *Lasioptera*)

10 Distinct swelling of base of stem, up to 10 x 6mm
(Fig. 568); contains a single chamber with many
white larvae (Fig. 569) or pupae; on *Molinia caerulea*;
on moorland, common: **Diptera: Cecidomyiidae**
.... ***Pemphigocecis ventricola*** (Rübsaamen)
(= *Mayetiola*)

- Swelling (often very slight) contains one or more
chambers, each with one larva (Fig. 570) or pupa:
Hymenoptera: Eurytomidae **11**

5 mm   Fig. 568

Fig. 569

1 mm
mandible   Fig. 570

11 Swelling very slight; several chambers one above
the other:
On *Calamagrostis* (Fig. 571)
.... ***Tetramesa calamagrostidis*** (von Schlechtendal)

On *Calamagrostis, Ammophila arenaria* (Fig. 572)
.... ***Tetramesa eximia*** (Giraud)

- Swelling more distinct; with one chamber:
On *Deschampsia cespitosa*
.... ***Tetramesa airae*** (von Schlechtendal)

On *Leymus arenarius*
.... ***Tetramesa brischkei*** (von Schlechtendal)

On *Festuca ovina, F. rubra* (Fig. 573)
.... ***Tetramesa brevicollis*** (Walker)

On *Festuca* species
.... ***Tetramesa giraudi*** (Hedicke)

On *Festuca ovina*
....................................***Tetramesa ruschkai*** (Hedicke)

On *Phleum* .... ***Tetramesa phleicola*** (Hedicke)

On *Poa nemoralis* (Fig. 574)
.... ***Tetramesa poicola*** (Hedicke)

Tetramesa spp. are highly host-specific, usually restricted to one
genus or species of grass. The group is not well known and this
list may not be complete. To separate those on the same grass
species the adult must be reared and identified. For more
information, see Claridge & Dawah (1994).

Fig. 571   Fig. 572

Fig. 573   Fig. 574

E123. *POLYGALA*

Two galls are recorded on common milkwort, *Polygala vulgaris* L.

1   Flower bud swollen, remaining closed; contains a
    lemon yellow larva (Fig. 575): **Diptera: Cecidomyiidae**
    .... ***Dasineura polygalae*** (Kieffer)
    <small>Identified from gall and larva only (Chandler, 1998); requires
    confirmation by rearing and identifying adult.</small>

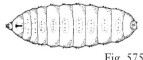

Fig. 575

2   Rounded mass of small leaves at shoot tip or in
    axil, covered with white hairs; flowers may be
    greened and leafy (phyllanthy); contains mites
    (Fig. 576); rare: **Acari: Eriophyoidea**
    .... ***Aceria brevirostris*** (Nalepa)
                                            (= *Eriophyes*)

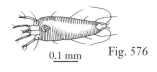

0.1 mm   Fig. 576

POLYGONATUM see *CONVALLARIA*

E124. *POLYGONUM*

Two galls are recorded from knotgrass, *Polygonum aviculare* L. (For knotweeds and bistorts
see *Persicaria*, p. 373, originally included in the genus *Polygonum*, Stace 1997.)

1   Conical or spindle-shaped swelling in leaf- or
    flower-bud (Fig. 577), up to 15 x 4 mm; often
    reddened; contains a caterpillar; S. England, very
    rare: **Lepidoptera: Coleophoridae**
    ....***Augasma aeratella*** (Zetterstedt)
    <small>Most recent records 1934 in South Essex, 1956 in Devon.</small>

10 mm

Fig. 577

2   Leaf deformed, margins curled downwards,
    wrinkled and puckered, often mottled yellow or
    red; not noticeably thickened; several affected
    leaves at shoot tip may be bunched together; yellow
    or brownish aphids (Fig. 578) on underside:
    Hemiptera: Aphididae
    .... ***Aspidaphis polygoni*** (Walker)
                                            (= *adjuvans*)
    <small>Other aphids also cause curling and distortion of young leaves;
    probably none of them causes a true gall. Identification should
    be verified by determining the aphids.</small>

Fig. 578

E125. *POPULUS*

Two species, aspen, *P. tremula* L. and black poplar, *P. nigra* L., are native in Britain. Black
poplar is now quite rare in most counties and the 'black poplars' which have been widely

planted are mostly hybrids; some of these hybrids are galled but others are not. Lombardy poplar is a form of *P. nigra* (var. *italica* Muenchh.); it and white poplar, *P. alba* L. and grey poplar, *P. x canescens* (Aiton) Smith are widely planted and are often galled in Britain. Other introduced species and hybrids are not included here. Sorting out the various hybrids is difficult, but Mitchell (1974) and Meikle (1984) will help.

These poplars form two distinct taxonomic groups: (i) *P. tremula*, *P. alba* and *P. x canescens* and (ii) *P. nigra* and its hybrids. Many of their galls are distinct also. Thus, three keys are provided:

A. IN A TWIG OR BUD OF A *POPULUS* SPECIES below
B. IN A LEAF BLADE OR PETIOLE OF *P. TREMULUS*, *P. ALBA* OR *P. X CANESCENS* page 388
C. IN A LEAF BLADE OR PETIOLE OF *P. NIGRA* OR ITS HYBRIDS page 392

For a fungal gall on leaves, see p. 248. Mistletoe *Viscum album* L. also may cause swellings in branches, see p. 263.

A. IN A TWIG OR BUD OF A *POPULUS* SPECIES

Two species are restricted to one or other group of poplars, see couplets 3 and 4; the rest may occur on both groups.

1   Gall in apical or lateral bud, often causing swelling of adjacent stem **2**

-   Gall in stem, not involving a bud **4**

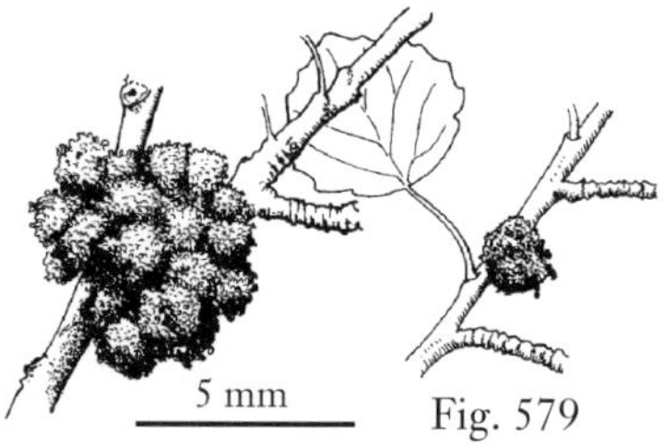

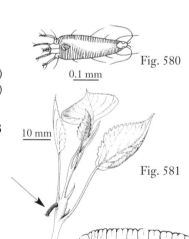

5 mm   Fig. 579

2   Irregular, warty, cauliflower-like growth, usually > 10 mm across (Fig. 579); soft and downy at first, grey, yellow or reddish, later woody; no internal chamber; contains mites (Fig. 580); locally common especially in Scotland: **Acari: Eriophyoidea**
.... *Aceria populi* (Nalepa)
(= *Eriophyes*)

Fig. 580
0.1 mm

-   Smooth elongate swelling, 10-20 mm long; internal chamber with a caterpillar or aphids **3**

10 mm

Fig. 581

3   Swelling 10-15 x 3-5 mm, often at tip of stem; internal elongate chamber opens by a circular hole into a projecting, frass-covered, silken tube (Fig. 581); caterpillar inside (Fig. 582) May - June; locally common in S. England and Wales, rare in north: **Lepidoptera: Tortricidae**
.... *Gypsonoma aceriana* (Duponchel)

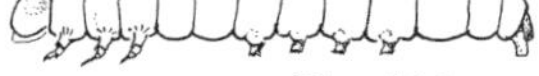

Fig. 582

-   Elongated pouch-shaped gall in lateral bud, 10-20 mm long with a slit-like opening (Fig. 583); green and soft at first, later woody; contains aphids; on *P. nigra* and hybrids only, rare: **Hemiptera: Aphididae: Pemphiginae**
.... ***Pemphigus borealis*** Tullgren

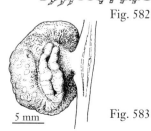

5 mm   Fig. 583

4 Indistinct elongate swelling, containing many orange larvae (Fig. 584) or pupae, each in a separate chamber just beneath the bark (Fig. 585); 'shot holes' appear in bark when adults emerge in spring; in *P. tremula* or *alba*; rare: **Diptera: Cecidomyiidae** .... ***Rabdophaga giraudiana*** Kieffer

(= *Dasineura*)

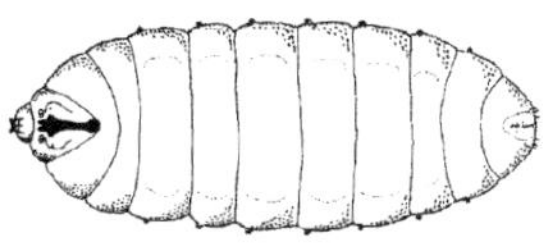

- Swelling (may be indistinct) with one chamber deep inside; contains one larva or pupa **5**

Fig. 584

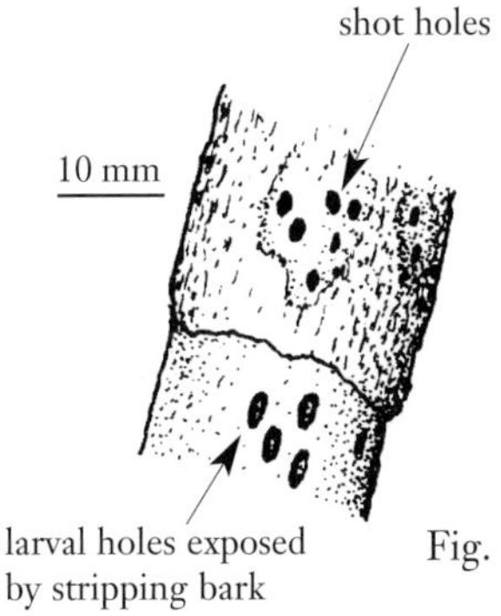

shot holes

10 mm

larval holes exposed by stripping bark   Fig. 585

5 Stem swollen all around, at least 20 mm long; contains an elongate gallery with frass (Fig. 586) and a beetle larva (Fig. 587) or pupa; exit hole left in spring; common especially in young twigs of *P. tremula*: **Coleoptera: Cerambycidae** .... ***Saperda populnea*** (L.)

- Smaller swelling, usually on one side of twig; with one or several rounded chambers **6**

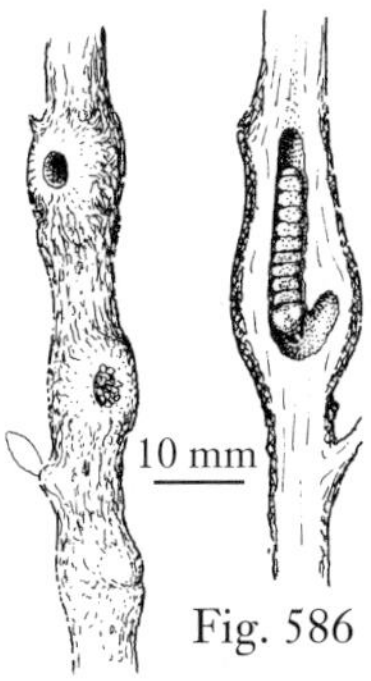

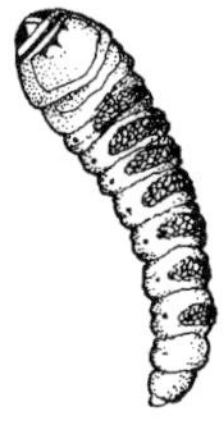

10 mm   Fig. 587

Fig. 586

6 Swelling up to 10 mm long (Fig. 588), sometimes several arranged spirally around twig; contains one white larva or brown puparium (Fig. 589), fly emerges May - June; rare, S. England: **Diptera: Agromyzidae**................ ***Hexomyza schineri*** (Giraud)

- Swelling > 10 mm long, containing one or more sawfly larvae (Fig. 590) or pupae; rare in *Populus* (more common in *Salix*): **Hymenoptera: Tenthredinidae** **7**

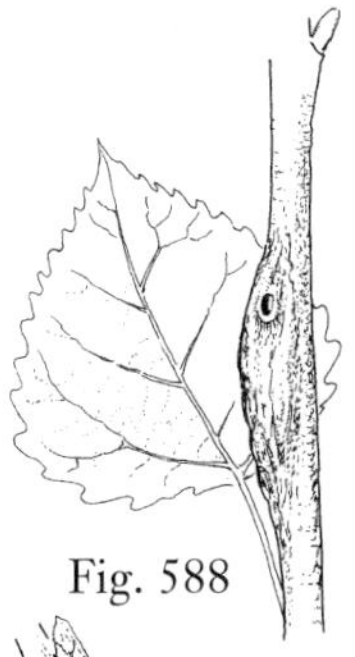

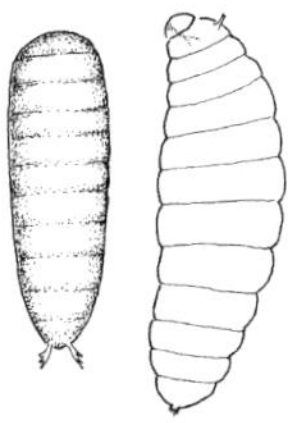

Fig. 589

Fig. 588

7 Swelling inconspicuous, 10-15 mm long, with one chamber; rare .... ***Euura atra*** (Jurine)

- Swelling distinct, 10-30 mm long with several chambers in larger galls (Fig. 591); N. England and Scotland .... ***Euura amerinae*** (L.)

Rare on *Populus* in Britain, more often on *Salix*.

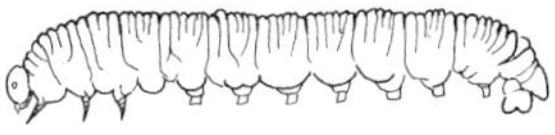

Fig. 590

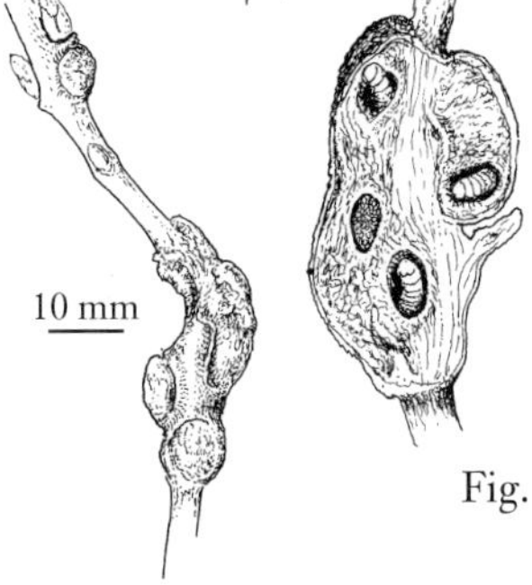

10 mm

Fig. 591

B. IN A LEAF BLADE OR PETIOLE OF *POPULUS TREMULUS*, *P. ALBA* OR *P.* X *CANESCENS*

1   In petiole **2**

-   In or on leaf blade **3**

    Waxy aphids *Pachypappa* spp. (**Hemiptera: Aphididae: Pemphiginae**) may distort petioles and leaves causing 'leaf nests' if numerous (Fig. 592); *Pachypappa tremulae* (L.) infests *P. tremula* and *Pachypappa warshavensis* (Nasonov) infests *P. alba* and *P.* x *canescens*. These are probably not true galls.

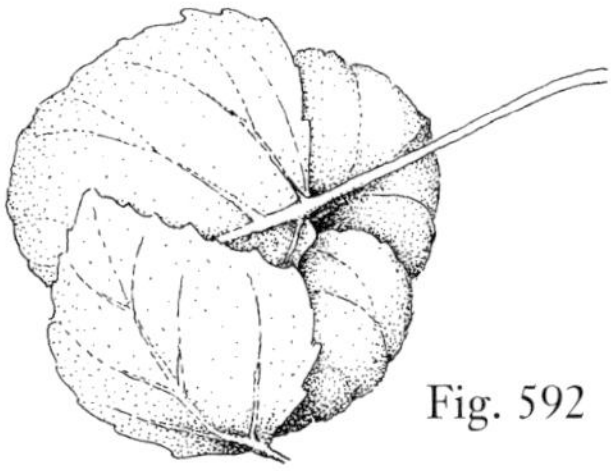

Fig. 592

2   Gall globular or pear-shaped, hard, 3-8 mm across (Fig. 593), sometimes reddened; contains one or a few chambers each with one orange larva (Fig. 594); a circular opening develops in mature gall through which larva leaves: **Diptera: Cecidomyiidae** ....***Contarinia petioli*** (Kieffer) (= *Syndiplosis*)

Galls may coalesce, and occasionally occur in stem at junction with a petiole (Fig. 595) or in midrib.

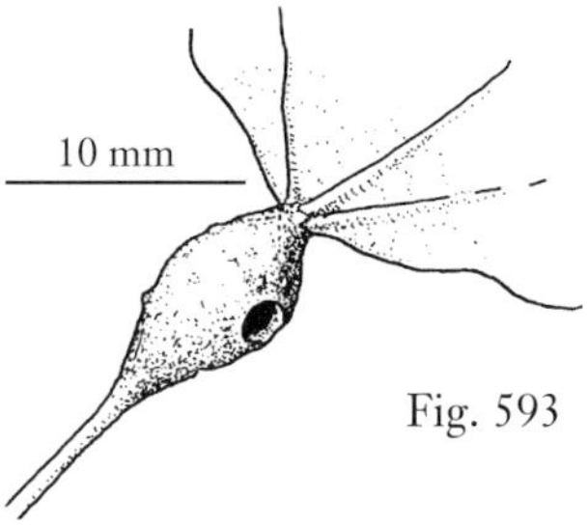

10 mm
Fig. 593

Fig. 594

-   Elongate swelling 10-15 mm long, petiole about twice normal thickness; contains larva (Fig. 596) briefly in spring; larva later mines blade causing a 'green island' when leaf yellows in autumn: **Lepidoptera: Nepticulidae**:
    In *P. tremula*; throughout Britain, locally common in England
    .... *Ectoedemia argyropeza* (Zeller)

    In *P.* x *canescens*; England, uncommon
    .... *Ectoedemia turbidella* (Herrich-Schaeffer)

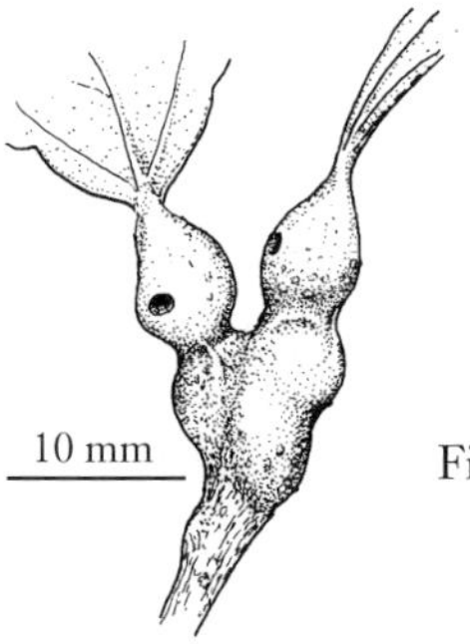

10 mm
Fig. 595

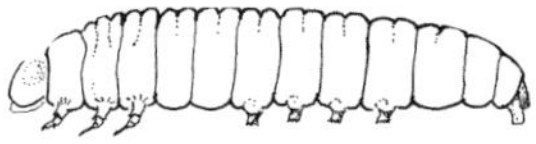

3   Most or all of leaf folded, blistered or with bag-like distortions, often yellowish or orange; contains waxy winged aphids in May - June, often spilling out of gall which is not closed; uncommon: **Hemiptera: Aphididae: Pemphiginae** **4**

-   Not like this; an erineum, or gall encloses causer(s) which are not aphids **5**

Fig. 596

4   On *P. alba*, *P.* x *canescens*
    .... ***Pachypappa vesicalis*** Koch

-   On *P. tremula* (Fig. 597)
    .... ***Pachypappella lactea*** (Tullgren)

    Non gall-causing aphids have been found on roots of the alternate host, *Picea sitchensis*, in S. Wales; the gall on *P. tremula* has not yet been recorded in Britain (Carter & Danielsson, 1993).

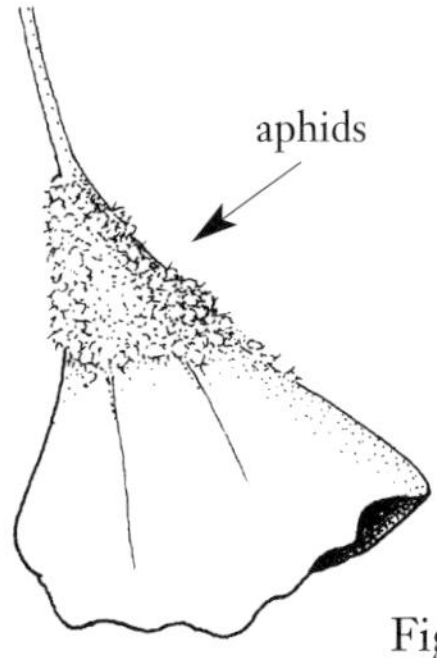

aphids
Fig. 597

READ THREE ALTERNATIVES

5 Rounded pustule or pouch on or beside a vein **6**

- Erineum; hairy patch usually on underside, with or without a discoloured bulge on other side; with mites (Fig. 598): **Acari: Eriophyoidea** **11**

- Leaf margin rolled and thickened (may involve most of young leaf) **12**

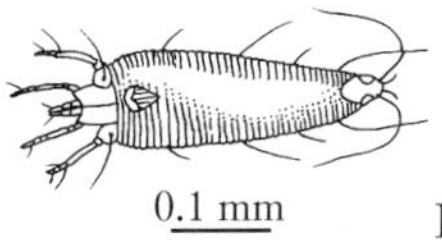

0.1 mm

Fig. 598

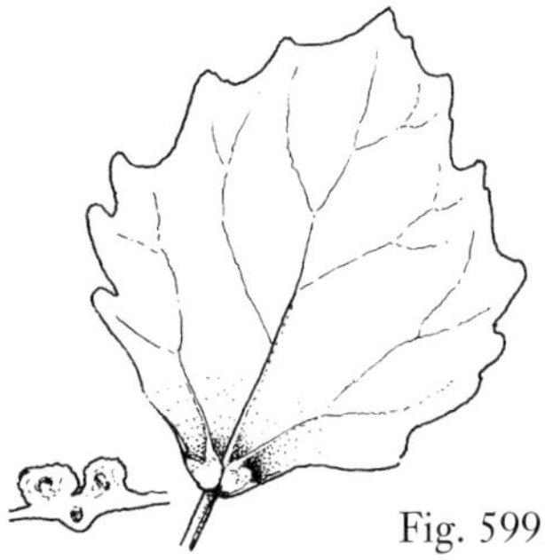

Fig. 599

6 Irregular, rounded reddened swelling at base of leaf, 1 - 4 mm across, on upperside without an obvious opening below, usually one either side of midrib (Fig. 599); contains mites (Fig. 598); on *P. tremula*, rare: **Acari: Eriophyoidea**
.... ***Eriophyes diversipunctatus*** (Nalepa)

- Rounded pouch or pustule, often reddened, on or beside a vein with an opening on other side; with one yellow, yellowish red or red larva: **Diptera: Cecidomyiidae** **7**

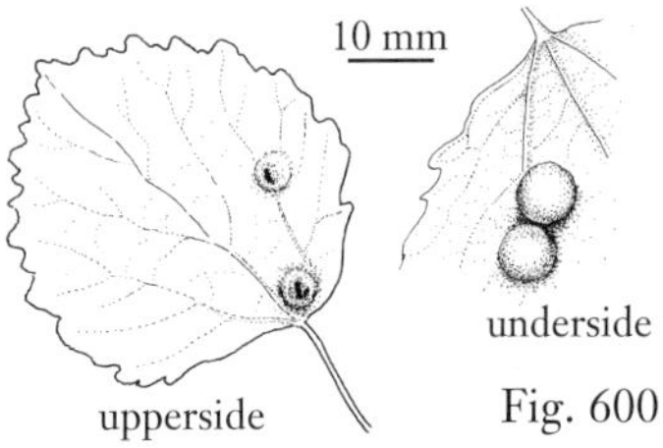

10 mm

underside

upperside

Fig. 600

7 Spherical pouch 4 - 5 mm across on underside, with raised thick-lipped slit-like opening above (Fig. 600); green or reddish with thick walls; on *P. tremula*, rare ....***Harmandiola cavernosa*** (Rübsaamen)
(= *Harmandia*)

The rare *Harmandiola populi* (Rübsaamen) is similar, 3 - 4 mm across with thin walls and protruding only slightly above.

- Pouch or pustule on upperside with opening below; on *P. tremula* or *P. alba* **8**

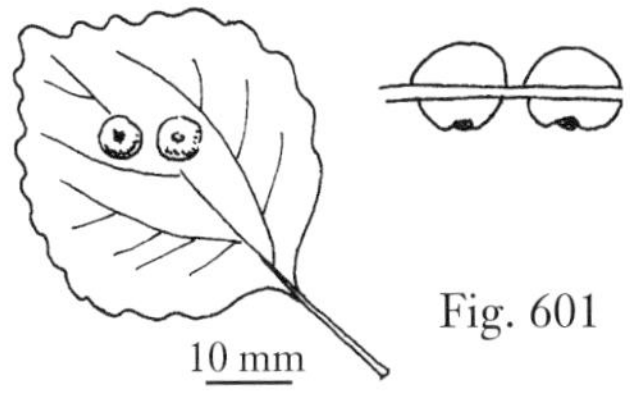

10 mm

Fig. 601

8 Pustule protruding distinctly on underside (Fig. 601) **9**

- Opening surrounded by lips which protrude only slightly on underside (Fig. 602) **10**

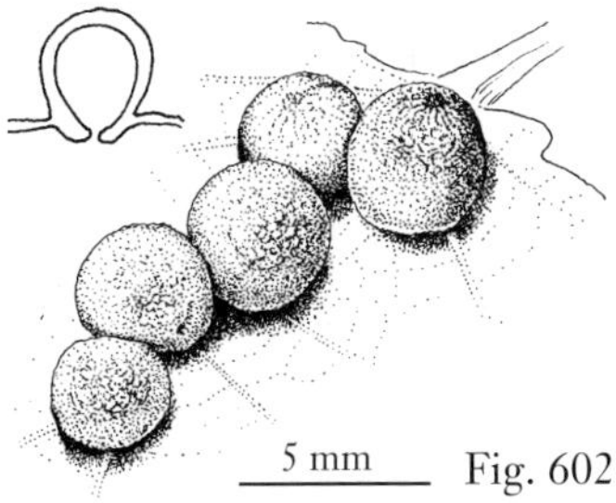

5 mm

Fig. 602

9 Gall thick-walled, 3-5 mm across, slightly conical above and hemispherical below (Fig. 603); larva (Fig. 604) orange; on *P. tremula* or   *P. alba*, widespread

.... ***Lasioptera populnea*** Wachtl

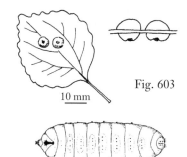

Fig. 603

10 mm

- Gall thin-walled, up to 3 mm across on upperside, narrow below (Fig. 605); larva yellow, later red; on *P. tremula*, Yorkshire, southwards, local

.... ***Harmandiola pustulans*** Kieffer
(= *Harmandia*)

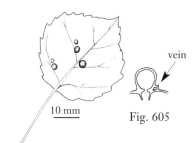

Fig. 604

Occasionally gall is reversed, with opening on upperside.

10 Ball-shaped, 3-4 mm across, with thick walls (Fig. 606), glossy red when mature; larva orange-red; on *P. tremula*, widespread

.... ***Harmandiola tremulae*** (Winnertz)
(= *Harmandia loewii*)

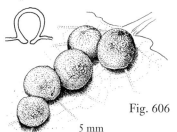

vein

10 mm

Fig. 605

- Rounded with a wide base surrounded by a collar-like ring (Fig. 607), often several on a leaf; 2.5 mm across with thin walls; dull red or yellowish; larva reddish yellow; on *P. tremula* or *P. alba*, widespread

.... ***Harmandiola globuli*** (Rübsaamen)
(= *Harmandia*)

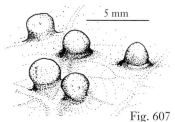

Fig. 606

5 mm

11 Erineum with a distinct yellowish bulge on upperside (Fig. 608); hairs below pale at first, reddish or brown later, each broadened at tip; usually on *P. tremula*, rarely on other poplars, widespread

.... ***Phyllocoptes populi*** Nalepa

5 mm

- Erineum without or with a slight bulge above; hairs red at first, later brown, each a short branched tuft; on *P. tremula*, uncommon

.... ***Aceria varius*** (Nalepa)
(= *Phytoptus*)

Fig. 607

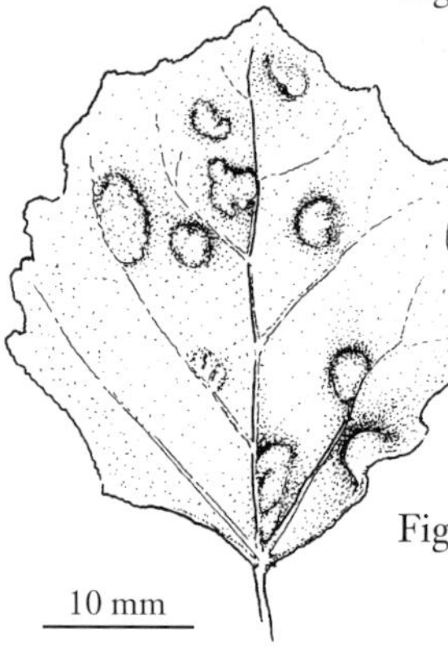

Fig. 608

10 mm

12 Usually both sides of young leaf rolled upwards towards midrib (Fig. 609); often involving many leaves which are small, distorted and remain bunched together (Fig. 610); rolls contain mites (Fig. 611); on *P. tremula*, rare: **Acari: Eriophyoidea** .... ***Aceria dispar*** (Nalepa)

See also couplet 13.   (= *Phytoptus* = *Eriophyes*)

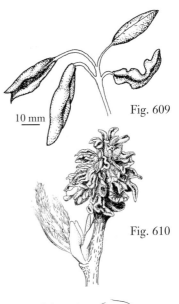

Fig. 609

Fig. 610

- Upward roll affecting just the margin of a mature leaf, usually on one side only **13**

13 Roll tight and narrow 0.5-1 mm wide (Fig. 612); contains mites (Fig. 611); on *P. tremula*: **Acari: Eriophyoide**a .... ***Aceria dispar*** (Nalepa)

See also couplet 12.   (= *Phytoptus* = *Eriophyes*).

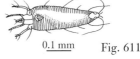

0.1 mm   Fig. 611

- Roll 3 mm wide or more, and less tight; contains white larvae; uncommon: **Diptera: Cecidomyiidae** **14**

14 Roll without hairs (Fig. 613); larvae (Fig. 614) can jump, mature in August; on *P. tremula*; rare .... ***Contarinia tremulae*** Kieffer

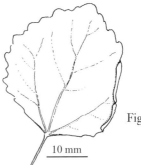

Fig. 612

- Loose roll covered with white hairs (Fig. 615); larvae (Fig. 616) cannot jump, mature in July and September (2 generations): on *P. tremula* or *P. alba* .... ***Dasineura populeti*** (Rübsaamen)

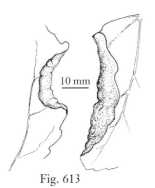

Fig. 613

Fig. 614

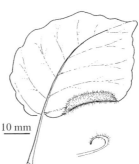

Fig. 615

Fig. 616

C. IN A LEAF BLADE OR PETIOLE OF *POPULUS NIGRA* OR ITS HYBRIDS

All galls are caused by woolly aphids, **Hemiptera: Aphididae: Pemphiginae**, and contain wax.

1 In petiole; a spiral or pouch gall, often reddened **2**

- In or on leaf blade **4**

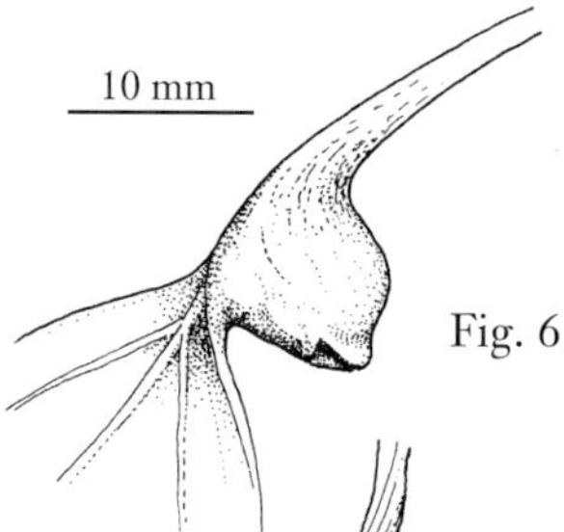

Fig. 617

2 Pouch gall, 8 - 15 x 6 - 8 mm, on one side of petiole (Fig. 617, Plate 2.3), opening in June to release aphids (all female: emergence continues until September); common
.... ***Pemphigus bursarius*** (L.)

- Petiole thickened, lengthened and spirally coiled; aphids released when coils loosen **3**

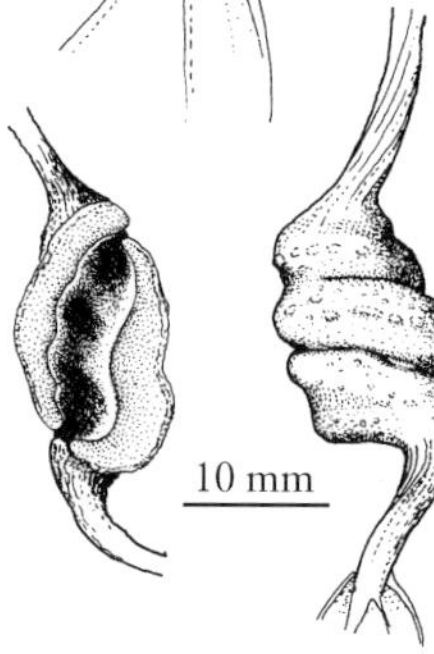

Fig. 618

3 Spiral with 2-3 twists (Fig. 618, Plate 2.4); matures and releases aphids in August - November, when 15-30 mm long; common
.... ***Pemphigus spyrothecae*** Passerini

- Spiral with > 3 twists, thickening of petiole only slight; matures and releases aphids in June and July; rare
.... ***Pemphigus protospirae*** Lichtenstein

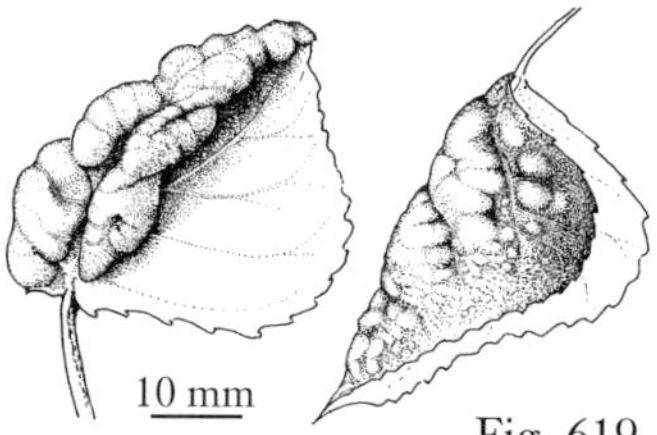

Fig. 619

4 Leaf blade thickened, pouched or folded downwards on one or both sides of midrib (Fig. 619), thickenings yellow or reddish on upperside; contain greenish aphids May - July
....................................***Thecabius affinis*** (Kaltenbach)

Leaf folds < 1 cm wide are induced by the fundatrix on young leaves (Fig 620).

- Upperside of midrib thickened and swollen, or bears a rounded gall; opening on underside **5**

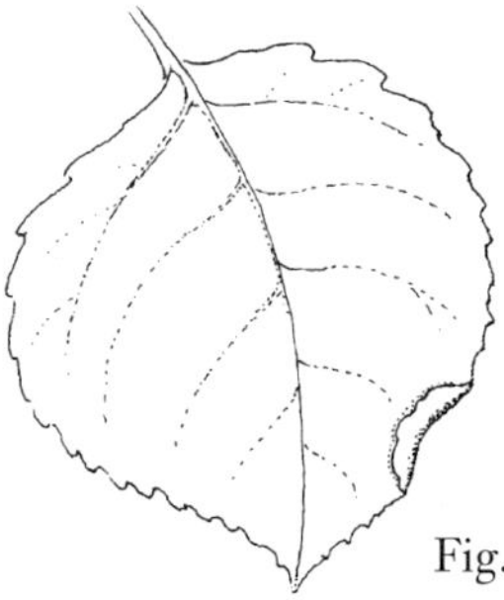

Fig. 620

5 Globular, sometimes cylindrical, spongy gall 10 - 15 mm across, attached to midrib by a short stalk (Fig. 621), same colour as the leaf; rounded opening below; opens to release aphids June – July; rare
.... ***Pemphigus populi*** Courchet

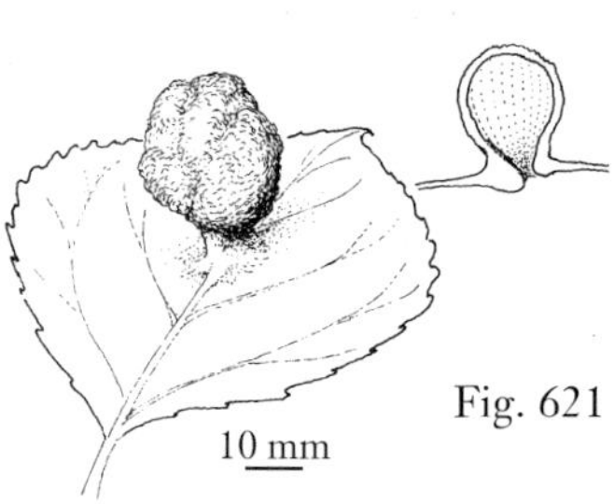

Fig. 621

- Upperside of midrib swollen into an elongate pouch, 10-25 x 5-8 mm (Fig. 622, Plate 2.5), often bright red; long slit-shaped opening below; opens to release aphids June - August:
Alatae dark green, nymphs grey
.... ***Pemphigus populinigrae*** (Schrank)
(= *filaginis*)

Alatae pale green, nymphs bluish green
.... ***Pemphigus phenax*** Börner & Blunck

Alatae pale green, nymphs yellow green
.... ***Pemphigus gairi*** Stroyan

Galls of the three species cannot be distinguished safely. Identify adults in Blackman & Eastop (1994).

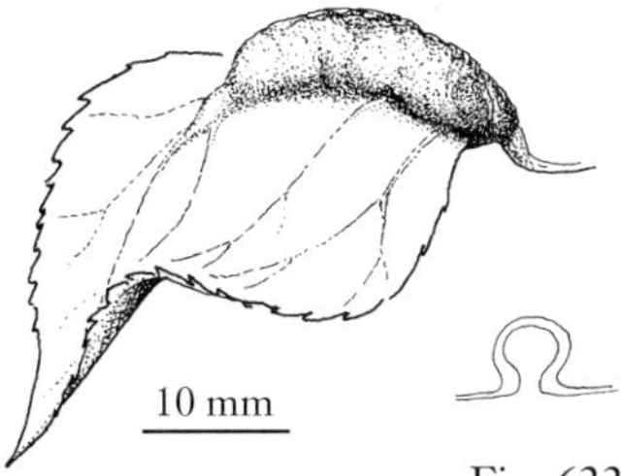

10 mm

Fig. 622

E126. *POTENTILLA*

Most gall causers are specific to a particular species: tormentil, *Potentilla erecta* (L.) Raeusch., creeping cinquefoil, *P. reptans* L., silverweed, *P. anserina* L. and hoary cinquefoil, *P. argentea* L. For fungal galls on stems and leaves see p. 248.

1 Flower bud swollen, abnormally hairy, remaining closed (Fig. 623); contains many orange-yellow or red larvae (Fig. 624), June - September; on *P. argentea*, rare: **Diptera: Cecidomyiidae**
.... ***Dasineura potentillae*** (Wachtl)

Fig. 623

- Gall in stem, petiole or leaf blade, occasionally on sepal **2**

2 A dense felt-like erineum, white or pale yellow; when on leaf it is on underside and may cause distortion; contains mites (Fig. 625); on *P. reptans*; rare **Acari: Eriophyoidea**
.... ***Phyllocoptes parvulus*** (Nalepa)
(= *Eriophyes*)

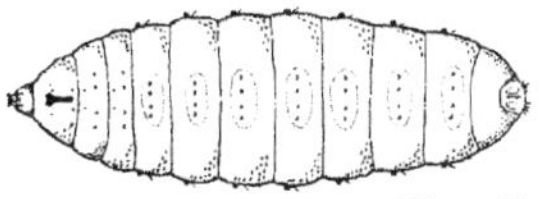

Large numbers of the eriophyid *Coptophylla potentillae* (Liro) may cause folding and rolling of leaf margin of *P. anserina*; this is not regarded as a true gall.

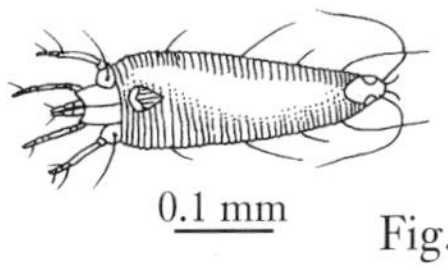

Fig. 624

0.1 mm

Fig. 625

- Rounded swelling 2-3 mm across, often several in a group or coalesced; in aerial or underground stem, or petiole; green or pink at first, later brown and hard; single chamber with a white larva (Fig. 626) summer and autumn, or pupa overwinter: **Hymenoptera: Cynipidae** **3**

Fig. 626

3   On *P. erecta*; usually in aerial stem (Fig. 627)
.... ***Xestophanes brevitarsis*** (Thomson)

-    On *P. reptans*; usually in stem close to or beneath
soil surface (Fig. 628); gall appears in July, matures
October................... ***Xestophanes potentillae*** (Retzius)

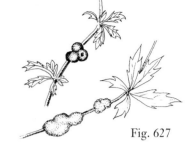

Fig. 627

Fig. 628

E127. *PRUNELLA*

One cecid gall (**Diptera: Cecidomyiidae**) is recorded on selfheal, *Prunella vulgaris* L.

Flower deformed, remaining closed; contains white larvae; recorded from Durham
.... ***Macrolabis brunellae*** Tavares

Dasineura brunellae (Kieffer) (**Diptera: Cecidomyiidae**) galls the shoot tip. Bagnall & Harrison's 1918
record is now thought to be erroneous (Chandler 1998). *Aphis brunellae* Schouteden (**Hemiptera:**
Aphididae) lives in colonies on stems or hidden among bracts of the inflorescence, sometimes causing
distortion. This is not thought to be a true gall.

E128. *PRUNUS*

There are three native *Prunus* species, sloe or blackthorn, *P. spinosa* L., gean or wild cherry,
P. avium (L.) L. and bird cherry, *P. padus* L. These, and the introduced wild plum, *P.
domestica* L., are commonly galled. Many other *Prunus* species have been introduced (peach,
almond, cherries etc.); these are not galled except by *Taphrina* species (see p. 249) and some
aphids affecting the leaves and fruits; crown gall (p. 218) may occur on the roots.

READ THREE ALTERNATIVES
1   Axillary bud enlarged, globular 4-5 mm across
with a brown tip (Fig. 629); green when young,
later yellow or reddish, then brown; large cavity,
lined with fungus, with one reddish yellow larva
(Fig. 630) in June - July: **Diptera: Cecidomyiidae**
.... ***Asphondylia pruniperda*** Rondani
(= *Ischnonyx prunorum*)

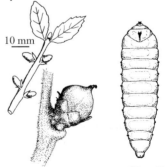

10 mm

-    Hard flat rounded cushion in bark of stem, c. 2 mm
high, usually on a leaf scar, often several clustered
together; irregular galleries inside, containing mites
(Fig. 631): **Acari: Eriophyoidea**
.... ***Acalitus phloeocoptes*** (Nalepa)
(= *Eriophyes*)

Fig. 629   Fig. 630

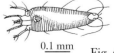

0.1 mm
Fig. 631

- In leaf blade or vein, or leaf rolled, sometimes shrivelled and crumpled with several bunched together **2**

READ THREE ALTERNATIVES
2   Pustule, tubercle or swelling in leaf blade or vein, often many on a leaf **3**

-   Margin of leaf or whole blade rolled; or an erineum **5**

-   Young leaves bunched together, shrivelled, swollen and rolled **7**

READ THREE ALTERNATIVES
3   Thick swelling on underside of midrib, up to 40 mm long with slit-like opening above (Fig. 632); contains orange larvae in May - June; usually on *P. spinosa*: **Diptera: Cecidomyiidae**
.... ***Putoniella pruni*** (Kaltenbach)
(= *marsupialis*)

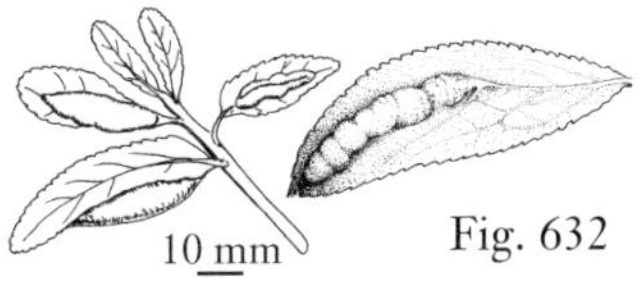

10 mm   Fig. 632

-   Small domed swelling on upper surface of blade with depression beneath, containing a psyllid nymph (Fig. 633); on *P. padus*, uncommon: **Hemiptera: Psylloidea**.......... ***Psylla pruni*** (Scopoli)

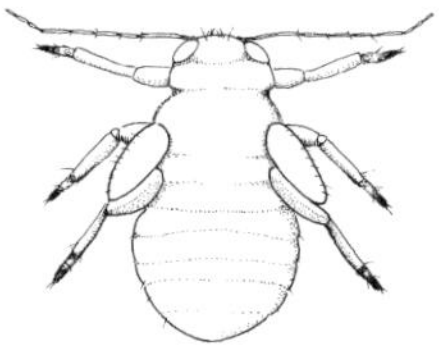

Fig. 633

-   Pustule or tubercle on leaf blade; green, often reddened, usually several on a leaf; hairy inside with mites (Fig. 631); common: **Acari: Eriophyoidea** **4**

4   Pustules raised on both surfaces, usually with opening above, commonest along leaf margin (Fig. 634)
On *P. domestica* .... ***Eriophyes similis*** (Nalepa)
(= *Phytoptus*)

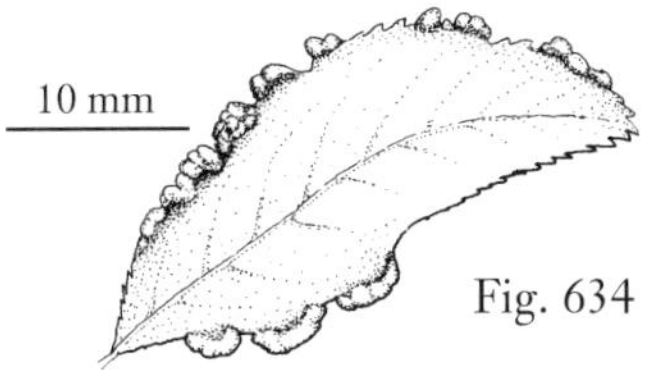

On *P. spinosa* (Plate 1.4)
.... ***Eriophyes prunispinosae*** Nalepa
(= *Phytoptus*)

10 mm
Fig. 634

-   Pustules raised on upper surface with opening below, often clustering along midrib (Fig. 635); on *Prunus* spp. .... ***Eriophyes padi*** (Nalepa)
(= *Phytoptus*)

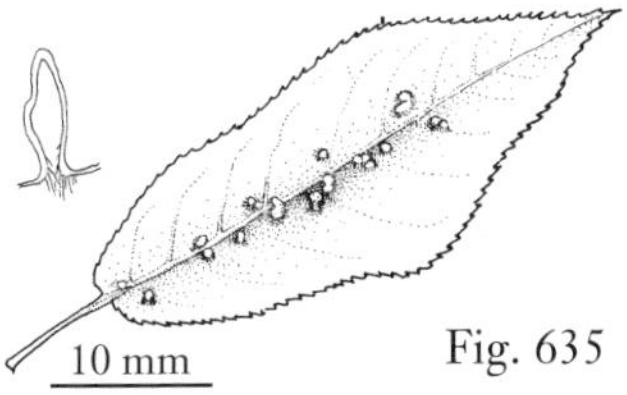

10 mm   Fig. 635

5   Margin of leaf rolled downwards along most of one side, sickle-shaped (Fig. 636); green becoming yellowish; contains a sawfly larva (Fig. 637): **Hymenoptera: Tenthredinidae**
.... ***Micronematus monogyniae*** (Hartig)

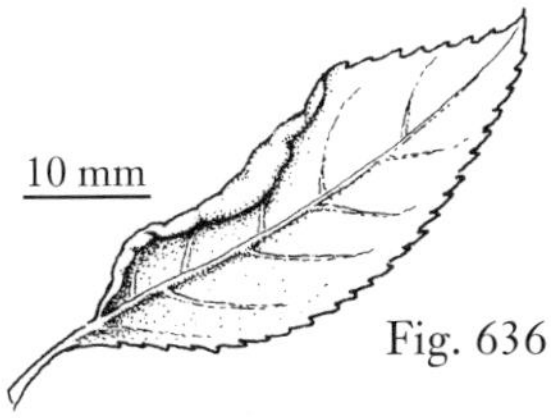

10 mm
Fig. 636

-   Margin of one or both sides rolled upwards; or an erineum; contains mites (Fig. 631): **Acari: Eriophyoidea** **6**

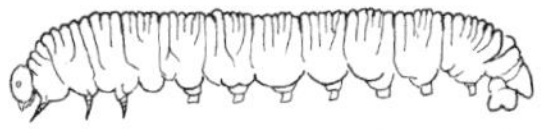

Fig. 637

6 Leaf stunted with both margins rolled to form a boat-shaped gall; green flecked with yellow, later brown .... *Aculus fockeui* (Nalepa & Trouessart)
(= *Vasates* = *Phyllocoptes*)

\- Erineum on underside between veins (Fig. 638), hairs green, later brown; leaf margin may be loosely rolled; on *P. padus*
.... *Eriophyes paderineus* Nalepa

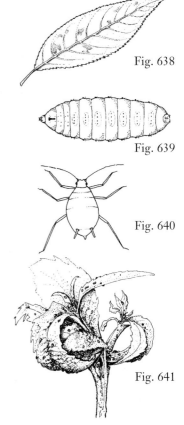

Fig. 638

Fig. 639

Fig. 640

7 Terminal leaves bunched together, rolled within one another, with leaf margins loosely rolled upwards; contain many white larvae (Fig. 639) in May - June: **Diptera: Cecidomyiidae**
.... *Dasineura tortrix* (F. Löw)

\- Leaves of young shoot irregularly curled, rolled or folded; aphids (Fig. 640) present, leaves may be shiny with honeydew
.... **Hemiptera: Aphidoidea**

Aphids may cause gall-like swellings and blistering if their density is high, e.g. distortion (Fig. 641) caused by *Myzus cerasi* (F.) on *Prunus cerasus* and *P. avium*, *Brachycaudus helichrysi* (Kaltenbach) on native and cultivated plums, *Prunus domestica*, and *Rhopalosiphum padi* (L.) and *Myzus padellus* Rog. & Hille on *Prunus padus* (Leather & Bland, 1999). These are probably not true galls. For identification, see Blackman & Eastop (1994).

Fig. 641

E129. *PTERIDIUM*

The one species is bracken, *Pteridium aquilinum* (L.) Kuhn. (See Fig. 1026, in the glossary p. 478, for explanation of morphological terms for ferns, after Merryweather & Hill, 1992.)

1 Slight swelling usually in main rachis, up to 15 mm (rarely to 25 mm) long; green, later brown; shoot beyond gall dies or is poorly developed; elongated chamber contains a red larva (Fig. 642) June - July, pupa July - August: **Lepidoptera: Gelechiidae**
.... *Paltodora cytisella* (Curtis)

\- Gall in pinna, involving several pinnules or a single pinnulet **2**

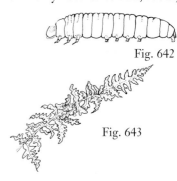

Fig. 642

Fig. 643

2 Much of pinna deformed, with pinnules twisted, often entangled (Fig. 643); margins of pinnulets curved downwards; contains mites (Fig. 644): **Acari: Eriophyoidea** ...... *Eriophyes pteridis* Molliard

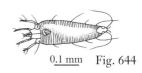

0.1 mm   Fig. 644

- Gall a roll at tip of pinnule, or margin of pinnulet rolled **3**

Fig. 645

3 Tip of pinnule rolled downwards, involving a few pinnulets (Fig. 645, Plate 3.6); inside, a white larva mines along main vein; common: **Diptera: Anthomyiidae**
.... ***Chirosia grossicauda*** (Strobl)
(= *parvicornis*)

- One or both margins of pinnulet rolled downwards, ± thickened; contains 1 - 4 larvae (Fig. 639) or pupae: **Diptera: Cecidomyiidae** **4**

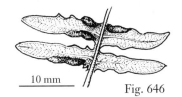

Fig. 646

4 Roll distinctly thickened, up to 5 mm long; pale green at first, later glossy dark brown or black (Fig. 646, Plate 3.4); single larva yellow-orange; June to autumn (2 generations); widespread and common
.... ***Dasineura filicina*** (Kieffer)
little black pudding

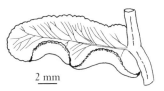

Fig. 647

- Roll slightly thickened, inconspicuous, usually > 5 mm long; pale green becoming yellowish to deep brown (Fig. 647); 1 - 4 white larvae; widespread but uncommon .... ***Dasineura pteridicola*** (Kieffer)

E130. *PULICARIA*

One tephritid gall (**Diptera: Tephritidae**) is found on common fleabane, *Pulicaria dysenterica* (L.) Bernh.

Base of flower head swollen, hard, containing one or more chambers (Fig. 648); each contains a white larva (Fig. 649) or brown puparium; SE. England, uncommon
................................***Myopites inulaedyssentericae*** Blot
(= *blotii*)

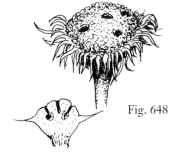

Fig. 648

This species may be extending northwards. The gall of *Neomikiella beckiana* (Mik) (see *INULA*, p. 350) has been recorded on *P. dysenterica*.

Fig. 649

PYRACANTHA see *MALUS*

E131. *PYRUS*

Galls are found on the naturalised and cultivated pear, *Pyrus communis* L. Fungal galls may be found on the leaves, see p. 250.

1   Young fruit swollen, misshapen, up to 20mm across (Fig. 650); contains many yellowish white, jumping larvae (Fig. 651) June - July; galled fruit turns black and falls prematurely; common in England and Wales, a pest: **Diptera: Cecidomyiidae**
....*Contarinia pyrivora* (Riley)
pear midge

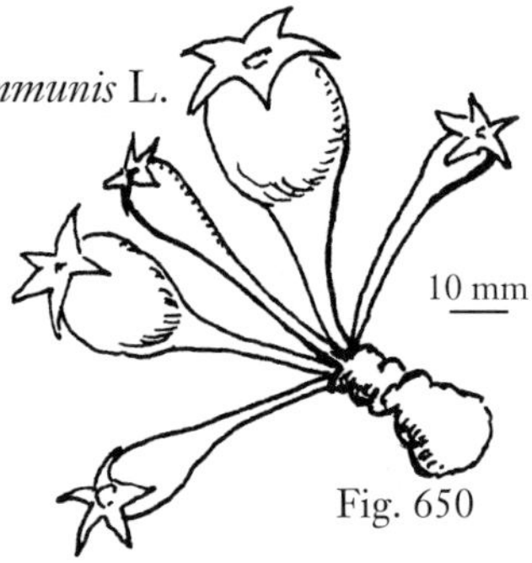

-   Gall in margin or blade of leaf, sometimes whole leaf distorted **2**

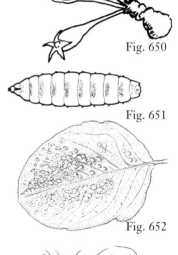

10 mm

Fig. 650

Fig. 651

2   Smooth pustules in blade, raised on both sides of leaf, 1-5 mm across (Fig. 652), with opening below; yellowish green in May, later red, purple or black, maturing in August; pustule ± solid with mites (Fig. 653) between the cells; locally common, can be a pest: **Acari: Eriophyoidea**
.... *Eriophyes pyri* (Pagenstecher)
(= *Phytoptus*) **pear leaf blister mite**

Fig. 652

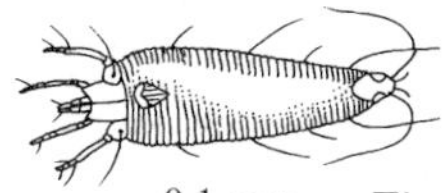

0.1 mm   Fig. 653

-   Marginal roll > 3 mm wide, thickened, often one on both sides of leaf (Fig. 654); usually affects new growth in late spring or early summer; contains white or reddish larvae (Fig. 655), can be a pest: **Diptera: Cecidomyiidae**
....*Dasineura pyri* (Bouché)
pear leaf midge

Several aphid species (Fig. 656), such as *Dysaphis pyri* (Boyer de Fonscolombe), *Anuraphis farfarae* (Koch) and *A. subterranea* (Walker), form colonies on shoots; if abundant, they curl and distort young leaves, which may become yellowed or reddened. Psyllids (Fig. 657) can cause similar distortions; also the mite *Epitrimerus pyrifoliae* Keifer (= *pyri*), which can be a pest. None of these are true gall causers.

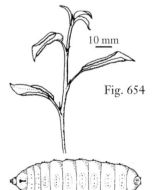

10 mm

Fig. 654

Fig. 655

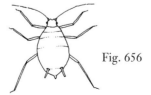

Fig. 656

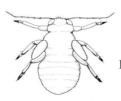

Fig. 657

E132. *QUERCUS*

There are two native species: pedunculate (also known as common or English) oak, *Quercus robur* L. and sessile oak, *Q. petraea* (Mattuschka) Liebl. Their hybrid, *Q. x rosacea* Bechst., is common and can be more abundant than either of its parents. Turkey oak, *Q. cerris* L., is widespread but introduced. Having been widely planted, it is now naturalised in the southern half of Britain; its presence has a significant impact on the presence, distribution and abundance of a number of species of gall wasps which have arrived in Britain during the last one hundred years. A hybrid of *Q. robur* and *Q. cerris* now occurs in southern England (Stace 1997), but there is no information about associated gall causers.

Apart from Turkey oak, many other species of oak have been introduced and may be found growing apparently wild in places which were once parkland or large gardens. Evergreen, or holm, oak, *Q. ilex* L., is frequently encountered in the southern half of England and in Wales. Galls of British gall causers occasionally appear on some of these trees but, with the exception of Turkey oak and a mite, *Aceria ilicis* on evergreen oak, there is no evidence of frequent or widespread galling. (See Welch, 1993, for a full review of this subject.)

All of the following galls are found on the two native species of oak, their hybrid and, except where noted, on Turkey oak. Most gall causers are gall wasps (Hymenoptera: Cynipidae) and nearly all of these have alternating sexual (♀♂) and asexual (♀♀) generations. The two generations cause very different galls, at different times of the year, and often on different parts of the trees. (For example the wasp, *Biorhiza pallida*, has a sexual generation which causes oak apple galls on buds in spring and early summer, and an asexual generation which causes galls on roots in autumn.) In addition, some species in the genus *Andricus* alternate between *Q. robur / petraea / x rosacea* and *Q. cerris*.

Several species of gall wasps appear to be extending their ranges westwards across Europe. Together with deliberate and accidental introductions, this means that new species frequently appear in Britain.

As for all other keys in this work, the descriptions of oak galls refer to mature, fully formed galls. The galls do vary, and we recommend the examination of several specimens if possible (see page 215). Oak galls are particularly likely to be invaded by inquilines of the genus *Synergus* (Hymenoptera: Cynipidae) which distort and may enlarge the gall, often considerably changing its shape. Another complication is the occurrence of *chimaeras*, where galls caused by different species merge as a result of their eggs being laid in the same bud (Stone, personal communication). These often involve *Andricus aries* (see couplet C10, p. 405) and one of the other woody bud galls, especially in years when the species concerned are unusually abundant. Distorted galls may also be found where several galls of the same species arise from adjacent buds.

The Key is divided as follows:

QUERCUS KEY A: GALLS ON ROOTS, TRUNKS OF MATURE TREES OR STEMS OF SAPLINGS

All gall causers are **Hymenoptera: Cynipidae**, with larvae as in Fig. 658.

Fig. 658

10 mm

1   Exposed or underground; globular or irregularly shaped, 7 mm or more across **2**

-   Always exposed; < 7 mm across; usually in clusters, embedded in bark or conical and ridged **4**

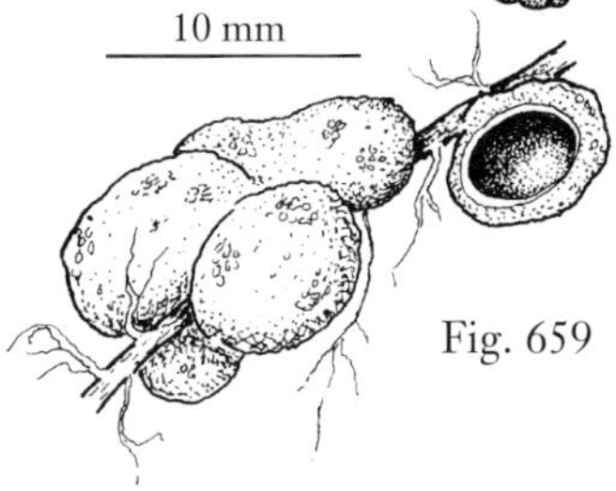

Fig. 659

2   On underground roots; globular, up to 8 mm across, coalesce into clusters 30 mm or more across; each gall has one large chamber (Fig. 659, Plate 6.9) containing a single larva (several chambers if invaded by inquilines, Fig. 660); common

.... ***Biorhiza pallida*** (Olivier)
♀♀ (= *aptera*)

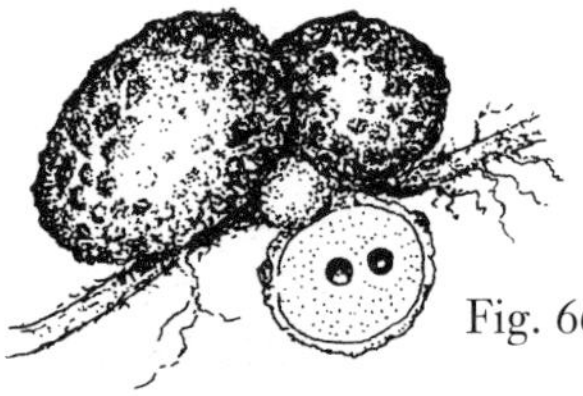

Fig. 660

-   Exposed or underground; irregularly shaped, up to 60mm across, or spherical, 10-15 mm across **3**

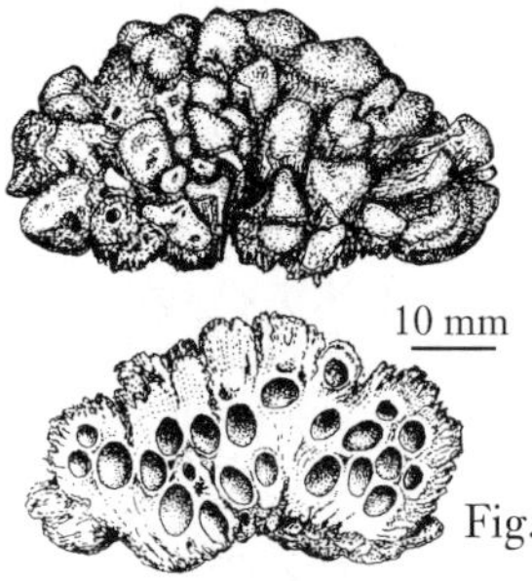

3   Irregularly shaped, soft at first, later hard and woody (Fig. 661); many small chambers each with a single larva

.... ***Andricus quercusradicis*** (F.)
♀♀ **truffle gall**

This gall has also been found in the canopy of trees in the Channel Islands.

10 mm

Fig. 661

-   In dormant buds low on trunk or stem; spherical (Fig. 662), waxy, white or pink at first, later red-brown; often on saplings up to 12 cm high; contains one larva; May-June; locally common in the north and west

.... ***Trigonapsis megaptera*** (Panzer)
See also couplet C7.   ♀ ♂

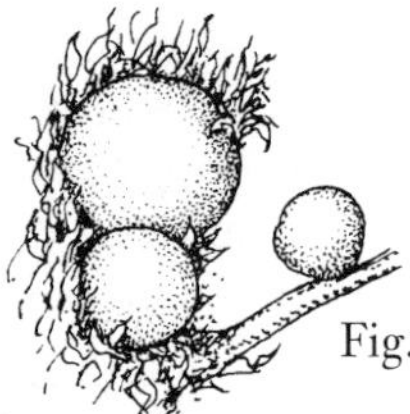

Fig. 662

4   Clusters embedded in bark, usually in callus; only the apex, 3 mm across, showing (Fig. 663); white at first, later brown; empty sockets persist; May; locally common

.... ***Andricus quercuscorticis*** (L.)
♀♀

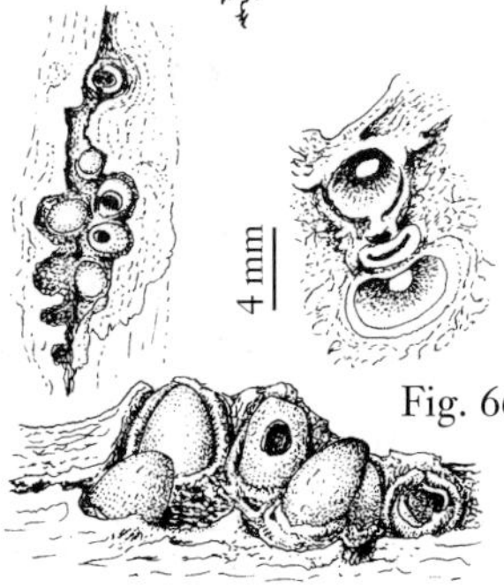

4 mm

Fig. 663

-   Conical or nearly so, may be ridged **5**

5 Wholly conical, tip frequently pointed, ridged (Fig. 664); stem may be swollen; often exudes sticky secretion attractive to ants; locally common .... ***Andricus testaceipes*** Hartig
♀♀ (= *sieboldi*) **barnacle gall**

- Rounded or flattened tip (Fig. 665); flat-topped cone remains after adult emerges; rare ....***Andricus rhizomae*** (Hartig)
♀♀

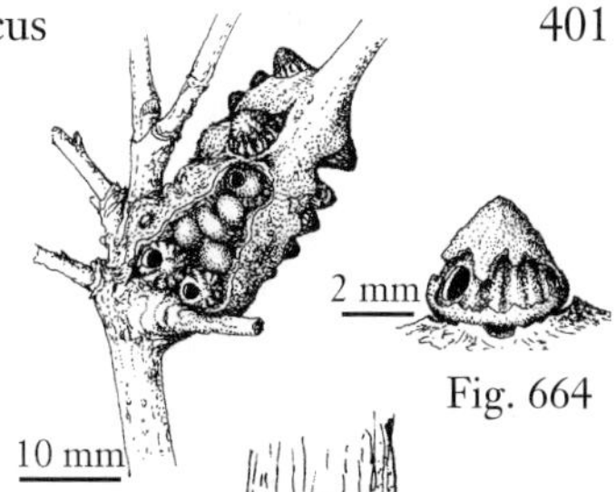

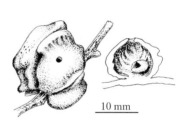

Fig. 664

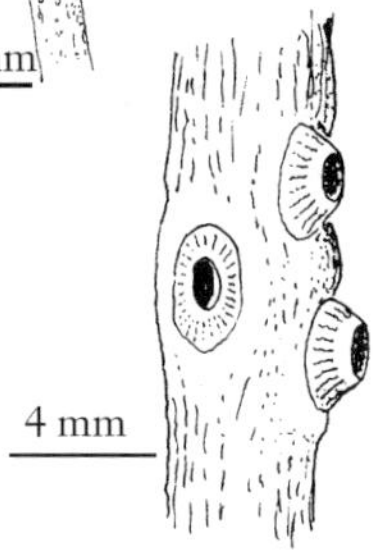

Fig. 665

QUERCUS Key B: Galls on Branches or Twigs

1 On *Q. cerris*; hard, 10-25 mm diameter; gall wrapped around twig, usually several coalesce (Fig. 666); large chamber with small inner gall; pale green when young, later brown; eastern England; rare: **Hymenoptera: Cynipidae**
.... ***Aphelonyx cerricola*** Giraud
♀♀

First recorded in Berkshire in 1997; its range is expanding slowly. The sexual generation is unknown.

- On *Q. robur, Q. petraea*, or their hybrid **2**

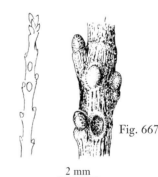

Fig. 666

READ THREE ALTERNATIVES
2 Rimmed pit in surface, 2 mm across (Fig. 667); contains grey-green scale insect in summer; common: **Hemiptera: Coccoidea: Asterolecaniidae**
.... ***Asterodiaspis*** sp.
(= *Asterolecanium*)
The three species of this genus cannot be separated in the field. Boratynski (1961) provides a key to nymphs and adult females.

- Conical and ridged galls
.... *QUERCUS* **Key A couplet 5**

- Twig swollen, distorted or with a knobbly appearance **3**

Fig. 667

3 Distinct swelling up to 15 mm across, twig may be bent through 180°; large interior cavity with small spherical inner gall: **Hymenoptera: Cynipidae** **4**

- Slight swelling or knobbly appearance; no inner gall **5**

4 Swelling at tip of twig; interior cavity long and narrow (Fig. 668); old galls persist and may have new shoots growing from them; common
.... *Andricus inflator* Hartig
♀♂

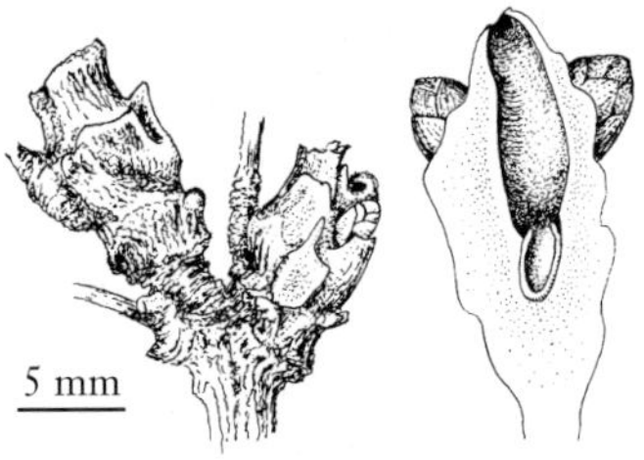

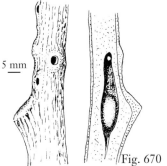

Fig. 668

- Swelling in twig (where it causes bending) or at tip (Fig. 669); interior cavity spherical or oval; common
.... *Andricus curvator* Hartig
♀♂

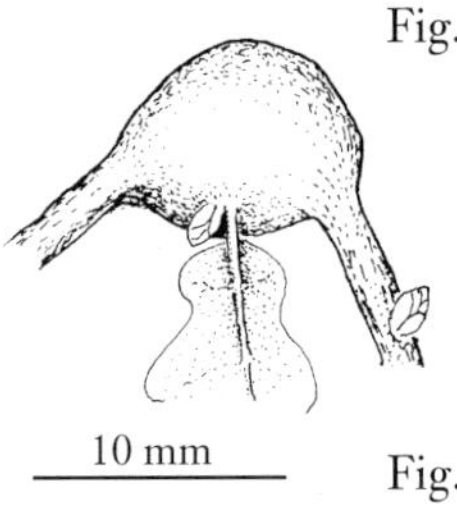

Fig. 669

5 Swelling < 60 mm long; contains frass; caterpillar present in June: **Lepidoptera: Gelechiidae**
.... *Stenolechia gemmella* (L.)

- Spindle-shaped swelling < 5 mm long; usually clustered and so giving a knobbly appearance; chambers inside twig have flat, circular rims, best seen if bark removed (Fig. 670); common: **Hymenoptera: Cynipidae**
.... *Andricus quercusradicis* (F.)
♀♂

Fig. 670

QUERCUS KEY C: GALLS ON TERMINAL AND LATERAL BUDS

All gall causers are **Hymenoptera: Cynipidae** (larva Fig. 671). All galls derive from buds although, when full grown, some appear to sit directly on a stem.

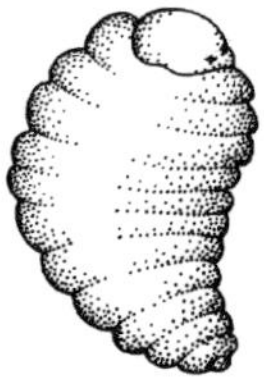

1 On *Q. cerris*; gall small, up to 3 x 2 mm **2**

- On *Q. robur*, *Q. petraea*, or *Q.* x *rosacea* **4**

Fig. 671

2 Thumb-shaped, apex usually the same colour as the rest of the gall (Fig. 672); often two or more galls in a bud, although single galls may be found; deep purple at first, later mid to light brown
.... *Andricus lignicola* (Hartig)
♀♂

Fig. 672

- More conical with a blunt and/or curved, often dark, tip **3**

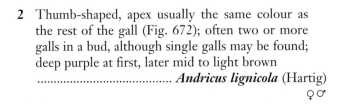

3 Wider (Fig. 673), almost always one gall in a bud (occasionally two are found together and extremely rarely three or more); mid to light brown or orangey

.... ***Andricus corruptrix*** (Schlechtendal)

♀♂

It is possible that this species, and its agamic form (see couplet C11), in Britain is *A. ambiguus* (Trotter) (Stone, 2001); Wehrmaker & Kwast (2002), however, consider the two species to be synonymous. Work continues on this species-complex.

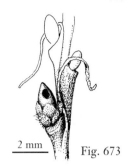

2 mm   Fig. 673

- Narrower (Fig. 674), sometimes distinctly banana-shaped; often two or more galls in a bud although single galls may be found; yellowish or light brown; may have a few hairs

....*Andricus kollari* (Hartig)

♀♂

These galls are very difficult to separate in the field; they pass through various colour stages (they may be suffused with pink, green, grey, orange or yellow) and they may be slightly hairy or have black, red or purple flecks. Where more than one gall is in a bud they are frequently deformed. Care is then needed to be sure whether or not a gall is pointed: *A. lignicola* galls may appear to be so, but close inspection reveals that the apparent point is where galls grow against each other, and is not the true apex. For certain identification adults must be reared and identified.

2 mm

Fig. 674

READ THREE ALTERNATIVES

4 Spiny ball 5-20 mm across, each spine 4-8 mm long, tipped with a small knob (Fig. 675); developing gall reddish, later pale green and sticky before drying and becoming brown and woody; old galls persist but lose spines; contains several chambers each with a larva; July onwards; rare, all modern records from the Ascot area, Regent's Park and Hampstead Heath, London

.... ***Andricus lucidus*** (Hartig)

♀♀ **hedgehog gall**

Walker (2002) has confirmed that the sexual generation of this species causes galls on the catkins of *Q. cerris* (see couplet E2, p. 415). Eady & Quinlan (1963) removed this species from the British list, but Stone & Sunnucks (1992) re-instated it. This gall also occurs on acorns (see couplet F4, p. 419).

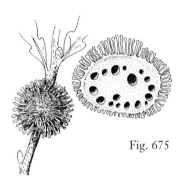

Fig. 675

- Globular swelling, 8-45 mm across, completely obscuring any traces of bud, smooth or papery, without spines **5**

- Bud swollen or distorted, sometimes only very slightly; usually <8 mm wide (but see couplet C13), without spines; gall wholly, partly or not at all enclosed in bud scales ... **8**

5   Large, up to 45 mm diameter; contains many chambers (Fig. 676, Plate 6.6); in spring smooth and spongy, cream suffused with pink and red, later light brown and papery; old galls persist; hard, dirty brown, often split open to reveal empty cells; wasps emerge July - September; common .... ***Biorhiza pallida*** (Olivier)

♀♂ **oak apple**

\-   Smaller, up to 20 mm diameter **6**

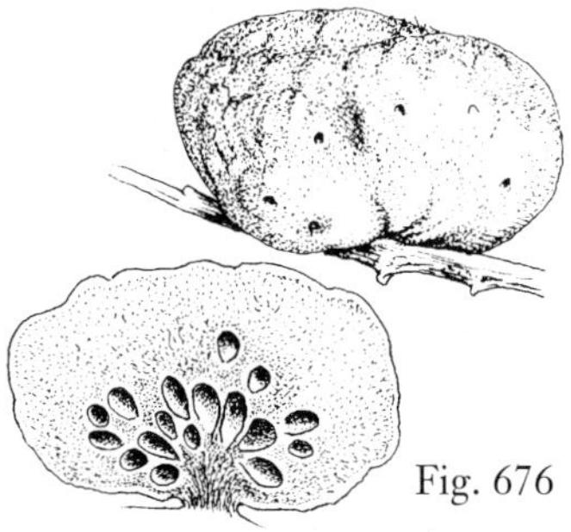

Fig. 676

6   Smooth and spherical, perhaps with surface bumps (Fig. 677); bright green in spring, later brown; very hard; old galls persist for years; can be very numerous especially on young trees; central chamber (Fig. 678) may be occupied by single larva of gall causer or several inquiline larvae, surrounding tissue usually contains cells with inquiline larvae; very common .... ***Andricus kollari*** (Hartig)

♀♀ **marble gall**

Stunted and/or fused marble galls can be confused with *A. lignicola* (couplet 7 below). Galls frequently distorted and enlarged by inquiline larvae, *Synergus* spp. (Cynipidae).

10 mm   Fig. 677

Fig. 678   10 mm

\-   Spherical, < 15 mm diameter, with waxy or scaly surface **7**

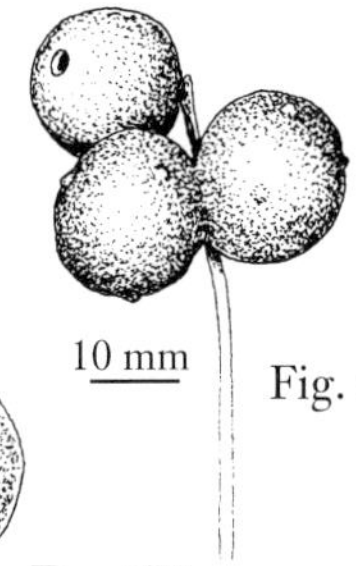

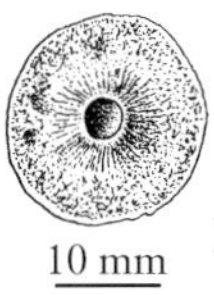

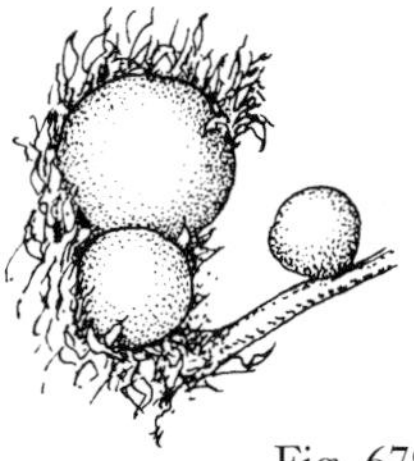

Fig. 679

7   Waxy and succulent; white or pink at first, later red-brown; often in buds on first or second year twigs and stems (Fig. 679); locally common in the north and west .... ***Trigonaspis megaptera*** (Panzer)

See also couplet A3   ♀♂

\-   Scaly, grey at first, later brown; very hard; old galls persist for years; often in clusters of two to five (Fig. 680); single chamber off-centre, exit hole always close to point of attachment; very common .... ***Andricus lignicola*** (Hartig)

Rarely occurs on acorn stalks.   ♀♀ **cola-nut gall**

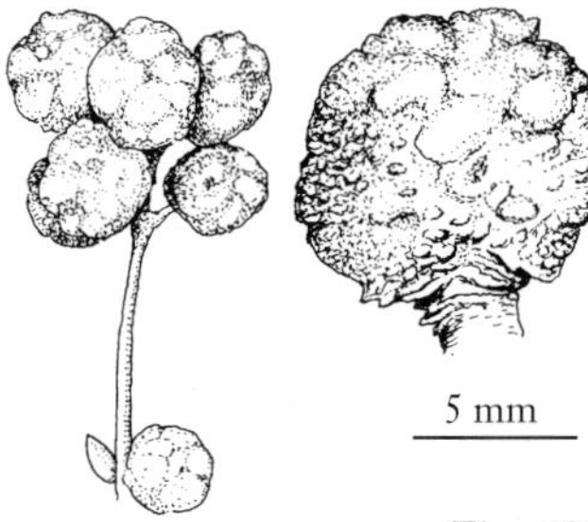

5 mm

Fig. 680

8   Gall not enclosed in bud, without bud scales; with or without a stalk **9**

\-   Gall partly or wholly enclosed in bud scales, or remnants of bud scales persist at base of gall (old galls may lose all traces of scales); or gall buried in expanding leaves; without a stalk **13**

This is sometimes a difficult separation to make; if your first choice seems incorrect try the alternative.

9 Gall rounded, or a slender cylinder, sometimes with long projections; in terminal or axillary bud, without a stalk **10**

- Gall spindle-shaped, tapering to point of attachment, or with a distinct stalk; in axillary bud.. **12**

10 Globular base with two tapering projections (these may be long, slender horns, fused into a single strap, or reduced to two points, Fig. 681); > 5 mm long; green at first, becoming brown, hard and woody .... *Andricus aries* Mayr

♀♀

This gall was first recorded in Britain in Maidenhead Thicket, Berkshire, in 1997 (Walker, personal communication). It is now (2001) common around London and in other parts of SE England, and it is rapidly extending its range. Its shape is very variable, especially when attacked by inquilines (*Synergus* spp), which cause enlargement of the bulbous base. No sexual generation is known.

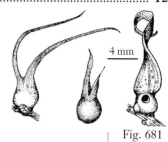

Fig. 681

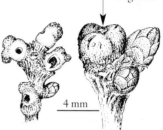

4 mm

Fig. 682

- Not like this, without projections; < 5 mm long **11**

11 Bud rounded, forming 1-5 smooth lobes, tiny 'rosettes' may be present (Fig. 682, arrowed); brown, hard and woody
.... *Andricus corruptrix* (Schlechtendal)
See note under couplet C3.   ♀♀

Fig. 683

- Slender, elongated, with a rounded tip (Fig. 683); surface appears granular, covered with tiny pustules containing liquid:
Common ....*Cynips divisa* Hartig
♀♂(= *verrucosa*)

Rare .... *Cynips disticha* Hartig
♀♂ (= *indistincta*)
These galls can form in a bud or on leaves, see couplet D14. The two species cannot be separated in the field. Eady & Quinlan (1963) provide a key to the adult wasps.

apical view

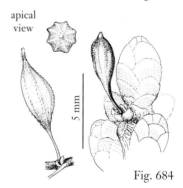

5 mm

Fig. 684

12 Stalk distinct from the rest of gall; gall spindle-shaped, longitudinally ridged and with an elongated tip (Fig. 684); May - September; uncommon
.... *Andricus callidoma* (Hartig)
♀♀

- Stalk short, merging into the gall; gall with a short, shiny tip and sparse white hairs (Plate 6.2; Fig. 685 shows a specimen on a withered catkin, an unusual position); September; rare .... *Andricus nudus* Adler
♀♀

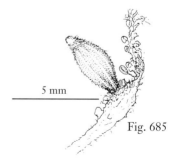

5 mm

Fig. 685

13 Artichoke-like, up to 30 x 20 mm, completely covered in bud scales (Fig. 686); large cavity contains small inner gall which is expelled when mature in August; old galls persist, often with scales opened outwards; common
.... *Andricus fecundator* (Hartig)
artichoke or hop gall ♀♀

- Not like this, no more than 10 mm long **14**

10 mm   Fig. 686

14 Almost or entirely concealed in bud (with only tip protruding), or buried in expanding leaves (Fig. 687; caution: bud scales may fall off old galls, see couplet C18 and Figs. 690, 691); exit hole often draws attention to these concealed galls **15**

- One third or more of mature gall protruding from bud **19**

15 Up to 10 mm long; mature April – June **16**

- Up to 5 mm long with a blunt tip; mature September – October **18**

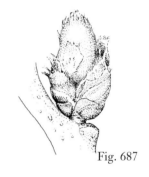

Fig. 687

16 Longer, up to 10 mm; greenish and succulent; tip of mature gall always visible among deformed expanding leaves (Fig. 687); common
.... *Neuroterus aprilinus* (Giraud)
♀♂

- Shorter, 2-4 mm; pale brown, not succulent; buried in expanding leaves or bud scales, but tip of mature gall may be visible **17**

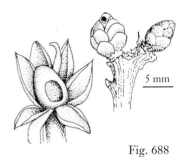

5 mm

Fig. 688

17 In terminal or axillary bud; length 3-4mm; buried in expanding leaves, often with distorted leaves attached to sides or tip (Fig. 688); usually gregarious; common
.... *Neuroterus anthracinus* (Curtis)
(= *Andricus ostreus* = *furunculus* = *anthracina*) ♀♂
Removed from *Andricus* and placed in *Neuroterus* by Pujade Villar *et al.* (1998).

- In axillary bud; length 2 mm; tip projects from bud (Fig. 689); uncommon... *Andricus quercuscorticis* (L.)
(= *gemmatus*) ♀♂

Fig. 689

18 Gall 3 x 2 mm; smooth, brown, not succulent; tip often encircled by a pale ring (Fig. 690, arrowed); common .... ***Andricus curvator*** Hartig
(= *collaris*) ♀♀

- Gall 5 x 4 mm; greenish, succulent; never with a pale ring around tip (Fig. 691); uncommon
.... ***Andricus quercusramuli*** (L.)
(= *autumnalis*) ♀♀

Bud scales may fall off old galls, see Figs 690, 691

19 Gall matures August – October; up to two thirds of mature gall enclosed in bud scales **20**

- Gall matures April – June; base of mature gall only contained in bud scales **22**

20 Almost spherical, 8-10 mm diameter (Fig. 692), often with a distinct point; green and succulent with netlike surface pattern when young; often on small twigs sprouting from trunk; local
.... ***Andricus inflator*** Hartig
(= *globuli*) ♀♀

- Elongate or conical, with pointed or elongate tip, < 7 mm long; woody when mature **21**

21 Gall elongate; tip 2-3 mm long and slightly curved; whole gall covered in red or golden hairs when young, later smooth (Fig. 693, Plate 6.3); no inner gall; common
.... ***Andricus solitarius*** (Fonscolombe)
♀♀

- Gall of variable shape but generally conical or bell-shaped, covered in silky white hairs (Fig. 694, Plate 6.8); tip short, light green, hairless; with inner gall; rare .... ***Andricus glandulae*** (Schenck)
♀♀

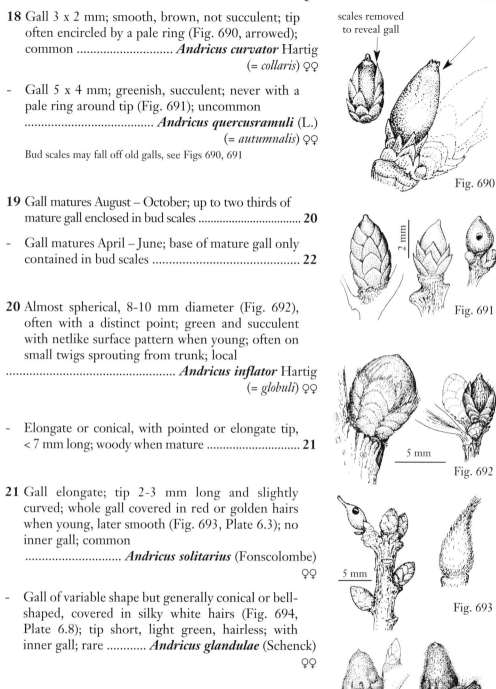

scales removed to reveal gall

Fig. 690

2 mm

Fig. 691

5 mm

Fig. 692

5 mm

Fig. 693

5 mm

Fig. 694

22 Gall up to 8 mm long, more than twice as long as broad; with longitudinal ridges, small blunt tip (Fig. 695); green and smooth at first, later brown with white or brown streaks or spots; uncommon .... ***Andricus albopunctatus*** (Schlechtendal)
♀♀

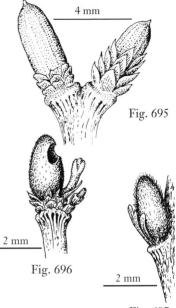

4 mm

Fig. 695

- Length 5 mm or less, about, or less than, twice as long as broad; velvety surface with short hairs; in buds in bark and on twigs near the base of trunk **23**

23 Dark purple to violet; minute hairs (Fig. 696); common ....***Cynips quercusfolii*** L.
♀ ♂ (= *taschenbergi*)

- Yellow or greenish grey; hairs slightly longer (Fig. 697); uncommon ....***Cynips longiventris*** Hartig
See also note to couplet D25.   ♀ ♂ (= *substituta*)

2 mm

Fig. 696

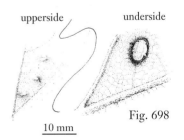

2 mm

Fig. 697

There are other bud galls which are obscure and difficult to find unless there is an exit hole. If any are found intact, rear the inhabitants and identify using Eady & Quinlan (1963). The causers concerned are: *Andricus gemmicola* Kieffer ♀ ♂, *Neuroterus albipes* (Schenck) ♀ ♂ and *Callirhytis bella* Dettmer ♀ ♂. Larvae of *Arnoldiola quercus* (Binnie) (**Diptera: Cecidomyiidae**) feed gregariously in buds and amongst young leaves and may cause severe malformations of developing shoots, especially Lammas shoots. Sometimes rosette-like deformations of the growing tips result, followed by excessive side branching, but larvae can also develop without causing such malformations (Harris, personal communication). *A. quercus* is included as a pest species by Alford (1984, 1995); it is not thought to be a true gall causer.

QUERCUS KEY D: GALLS ON LEAF BLADES AND PETIOLES

A rusty brown erineum on the underside of leaf blades is found occasionally on *Quercus ilex*. This is caused by *Aceria ilicis* (Canestrini) (= *Eriophyes*) (**Acari: Eriophyoidea**).

READ THREE ALTERNATIVES

1 Raised pimple 1-2 mm across on upperside of blade with depression below (Fig. 698), usually several on a leaf; depression contains a flat nymph; May - October; common: **Hemiptera: Psylloidea** .... ***Trioza remota*** Förster

upperside   underside

Fig. 698

10 mm

- Swelling of leaf stalk, midrib or blade, apparent on both sides of blade; leaf edge may be folded or rolled **2**

- Gall on leaf edge or attached to vein or blade; apparent on one side only or, at most, a scar showing on the other side: **Hymenoptera: Cynipidae** **11**

2   Swelling of leaf stalk or midrib **3**

-   Swelling of leaf blade (may also distort midrib); may be folded or rolled **4**

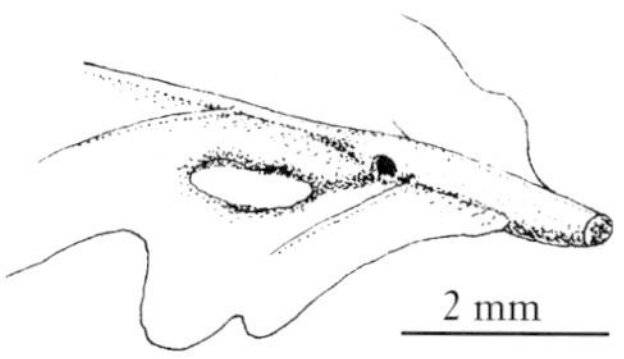

2 mm

Fig. 699

3   Slight swelling (Fig. 699) with a long chamber; contains a caterpillar June - July and frass: **Lepidoptera: Heliozelidae**
.... ***Heliozela sericiella*** (Haworth)
(= *steneella*)

-   Distinct swelling with a round chamber, often several coalesce (Fig. 700); contains a cynipid larva (Fig. 701) but no frass: **Hymenoptera: Cynipidae**
.... ***Andricus quercusradicis*** (F.) ♀♂
or ***A. testaceipes*** Hartig ♀♂

2 mm

Fig. 700

The gall of *A. quercusradicis* is common June - August; that of *A. testaceipes* is uncommon July - September. To confirm, identify male wasps using Eady & Quinlan (1963).

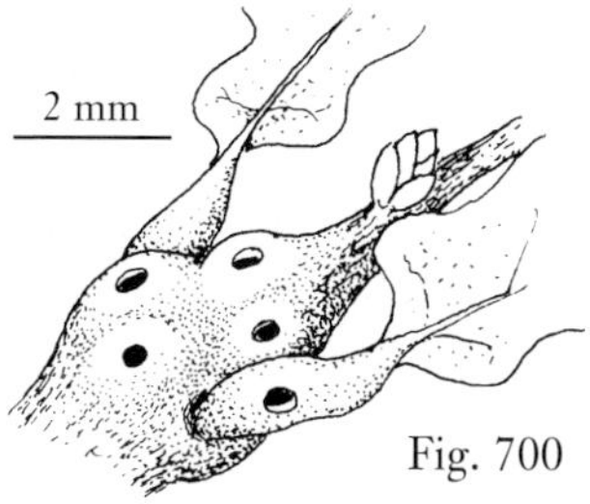

Fig. 701

4   Globular swelling or blister in blade **5**

-   Leaf margin thickened and rolled or folded **8**

5   Roughly globular swelling about 8 mm across, often distorts leaf and midrib (Fig. 702, Plate 6.7) and sometimes several galls coalesce; thin-walled cavity with small inner gall;   July; common: **Hymenoptera: Cynipidae**
.... ***Andricus curvator*** Hartig
♀♂

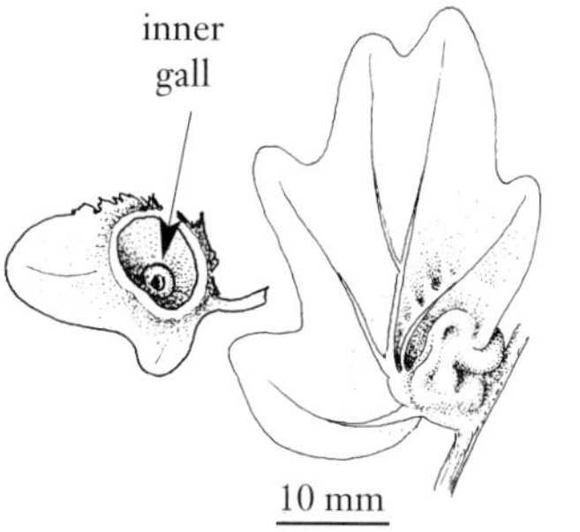

-   Blister apparent on both sides of blade, or upper surface raised with depression below; circular, 2-4 mm diameter; no inner gall; green May - June when larva present, later a combination of black, brown and green **6**

inner gall

10 mm

Fig. 702

6   Upper surface very slightly raised, with depression below (Fig. 703); containing a larva; rare: **Diptera: Cecidomyiidae** .... ***Arnoldiola libera*** (Kieffer)
(= *Arnoldia* = *Dasineura*)

-   Gall a blister which encloses the larva **7**

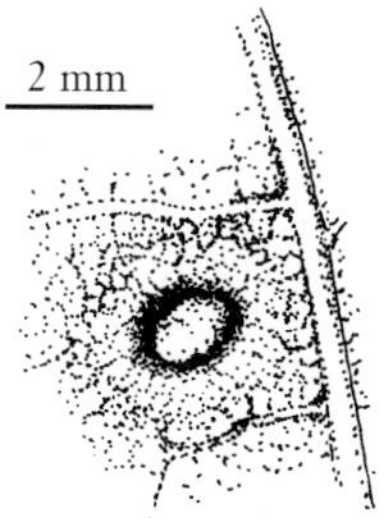

2 mm

Fig. 703

7   Blister with radiating lines (Fig. 704); contains a
    cynipid larva (Fig. 705); common: **Hymenoptera:
    Cynipidae**
    .... *Neuroterus numismalis* (Fourcroy)
    ♀♂ (= *vesicator*)

-   Blister more distinct on upper surface (central
    depression may appear in old gall, Fig. 706); larva
    (Fig. 707) escapes via a hole in lower surface; rare:
    Diptera: Cecidomyiidae
    .... *Polystepha malpighii* (Kieffer)
    (= *Dasineura*)

    A. *libera* and *P. malpighii* have been identified from the galls
    only and await confirmation by rearing adults; for more
    information on *P. malpighii*, see Entwistle (2001).

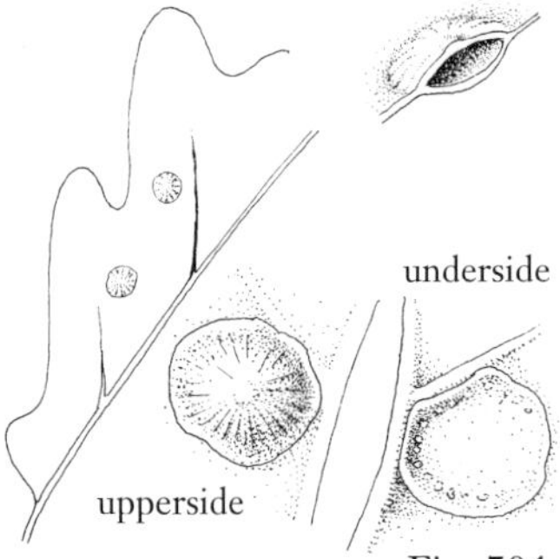

Fig. 704

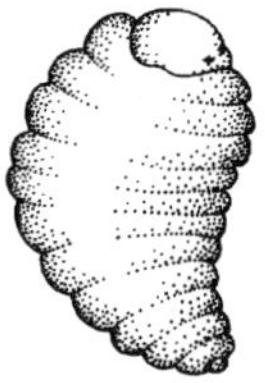

underside

upperside

Fig. 705

8   Margin folded or rolled upwards **9**

-   Margin folded or rolled downwards **10**

9   Margin of roll or fold crinkled;   contains mites:
    Acari: Eriophyoidea
    .... *Epitrimerus cristatus* Nalepa

-   Margin of roll or fold ± smooth; roll or fold usually
    between lobes (Fig. 708); contains one or more
    orange larvae (Fig. 707); June - September; common:
    Diptera: Cecidomyiidae
    .... *Macrodiplosis volvens* Kieffer

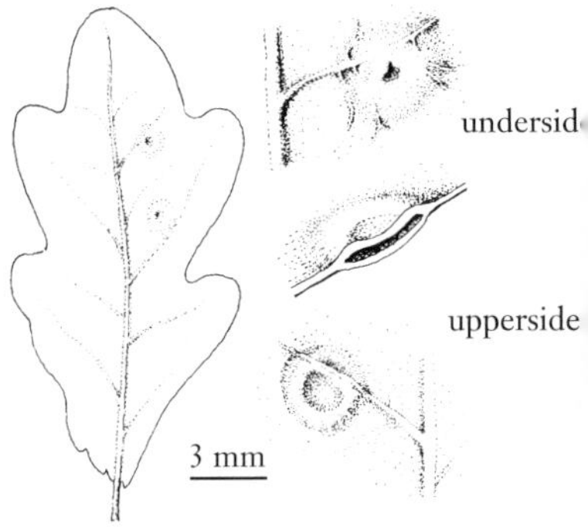

underside

upperside

3 mm

Fig. 706

10 Tight fold usually affecting lobe at tip of vein (Fig.
    709); green at first, later brown; contains a white larva
    (Fig. 707); June - September; common: **Diptera:
    Cecidomyiidae** ....*Macrodiplosis dryobia* (F. Löw)

-   Loose fold; remains green; contains aphid-like
    insects: **Hemiptera: Phylloxeridae**
    .... *Phylloxera* sp.

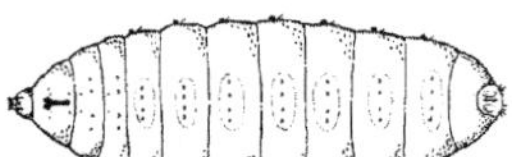

Fig. 707

11 Gall on edge of leaf, April - June **12**

-   Gall on midrib, vein or blade, usually on the
    underside **15**

12 Gall longitudinally ridged **13**

-   Gall without ridges, surface smooth or granular **14**

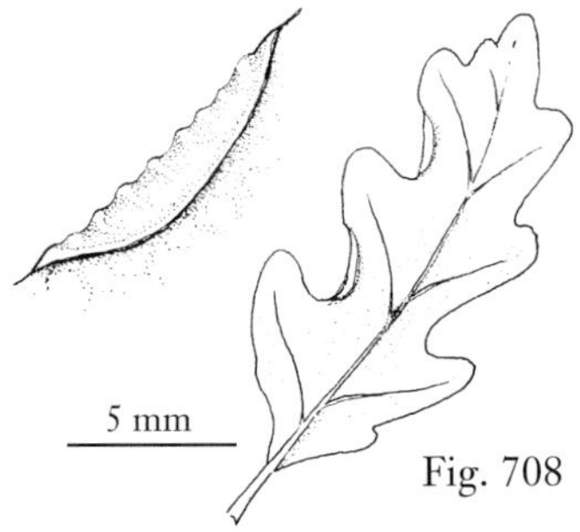

5 mm

Fig. 708

13 Stalked, spindle-shaped, 8-12 mm long including
   stalk; rare ....*Andricus seminationis* (Giraud)
                                                                    ♀♀

 -   No stalk, ovoid, 1-4 mm long; common
     .... *Andricus quadrilineatus* Hartig
     These galls also appear on catkins, see couplet E9,   ♀♀
     p.416. The sexual generations are not known.

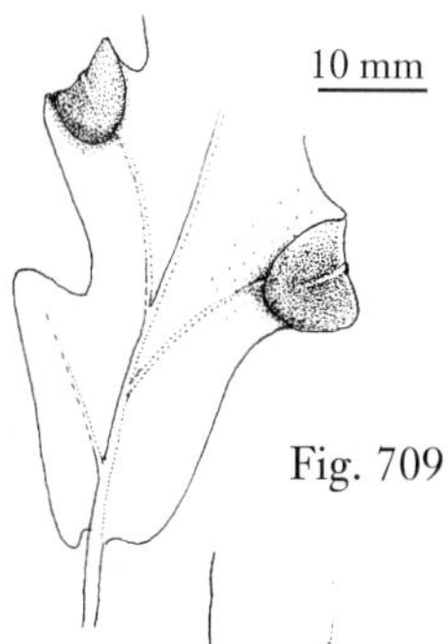

Fig. 709 ·

14 About 2 mm long, woody and smooth; attached by
   long side, often in an indentation of leaf (Fig. 710);
   common .... *Neuroterus albipes* (Schenck)
   This species also causes galls on catkins,   ♀ ♂
   see couplet E13, p. 417

 -   About 5 x 2.5 mm, slender or barrel shaped; often
     at end of main or side veins; surface covered in tiny
     liquid-filled pustules:
     Common .... *Cynips divisa* Hartig
                                        ♀ ♂ (= *verrucosa*)

     Rare .... *Cynips disticha* Hartig
                          ♀ ♂ (= *indistincta*) **red wart gall**
     These species also appear in buds, see couplet C11 and Fig. 683, p. 405. They cannot be separated in the
     field. Eady & Quinlan (1963) provide a key for identifying the adult wasps.

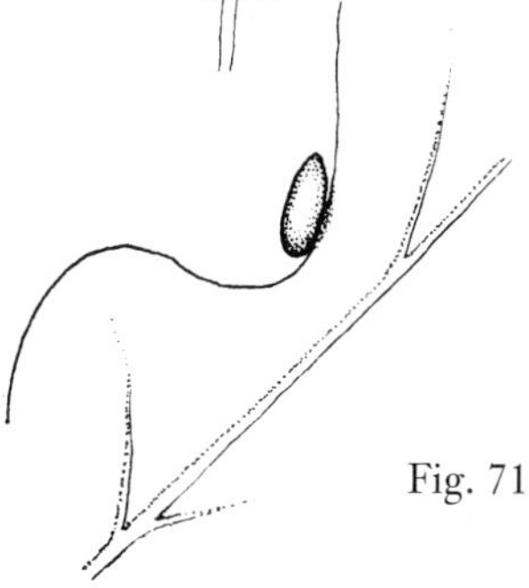

Fig. 710

15 On blade; point of attachment shows as a convex patch on upperside; May - June,
   although old galls may remain on leaf throughout the summer **16**

 -   On underside on midrib, main or side vein; point of attachment not apparent on
     upperside of blade (although occasionally galls are on the upperside) **17**

16 Spherical, smooth, succulent, berry-like; yellow,
   green, red or purple; up to 7 mm diameter (Fig. 711,
   Plate 6.1); very common
   .... *Neuroterus quercusbaccarum* (L.)
                                          ♀ ♂ **currant gall**

   This species also causes galls on catkins,
   see couplet E10, p. 416.

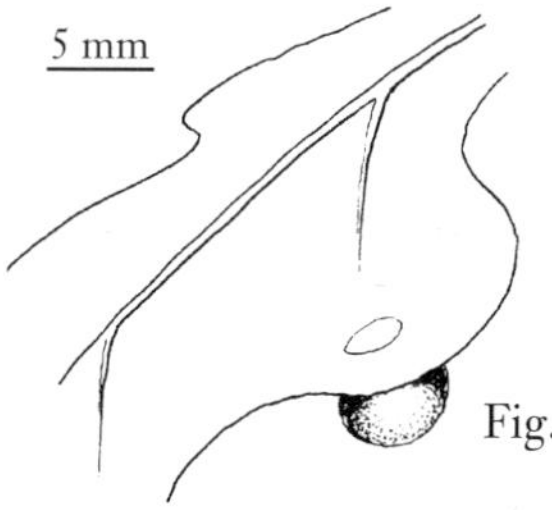

Fig. 711

 -   A flattened sphere (Fig. 712); yellow green with red
     or violet hairs; 3-5 mm diameter; several often
     coalesce; uncommon
     .... *Neuroterus tricolor* (Hartig)
                                                         ♀ ♂

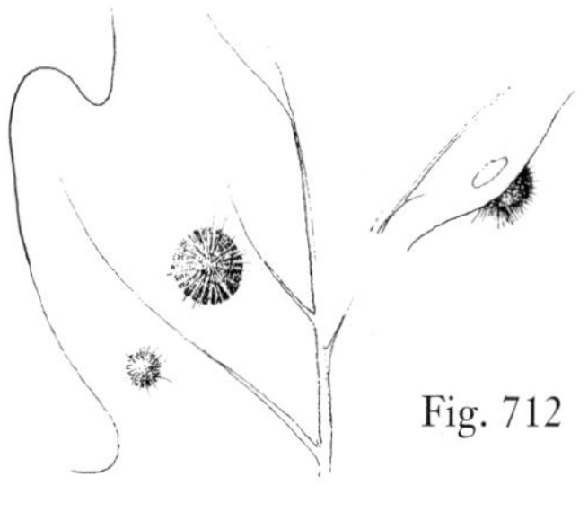

Fig. 712

10 mm

5 mm

17 Disc-like, 3-5 mm across when mature; usually attached to side vein; often numerous; appears in June, matures in September; normally falls from leaf before leaf falls from tree **18**

- Globular, egg or kidney-shaped; on midrib, main or side vein; single gall or a few on each leaf; may be found on fallen leaves **21**

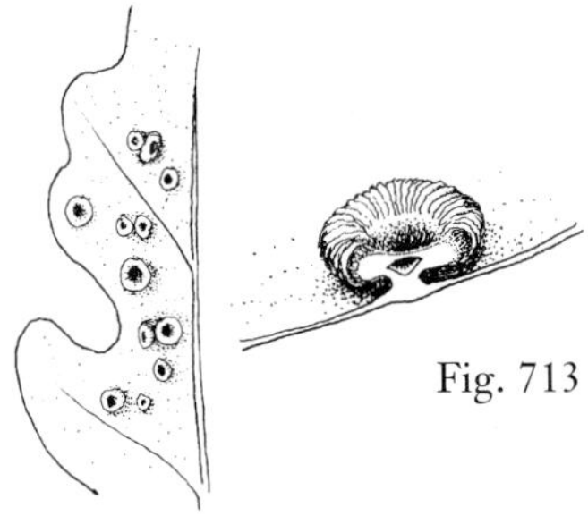

Fig. 713

18 Thick disc with deep central pit; surface hidden by flat golden hairs (Fig. 713, Plate 6.4a); very common .... ***Neuroterus numismalis*** (Geoffroy in Fourcroy)
♀♀ **silk-button gall**

- Thin disc with raised centre; smooth or with pink, red or brown hairs **19**

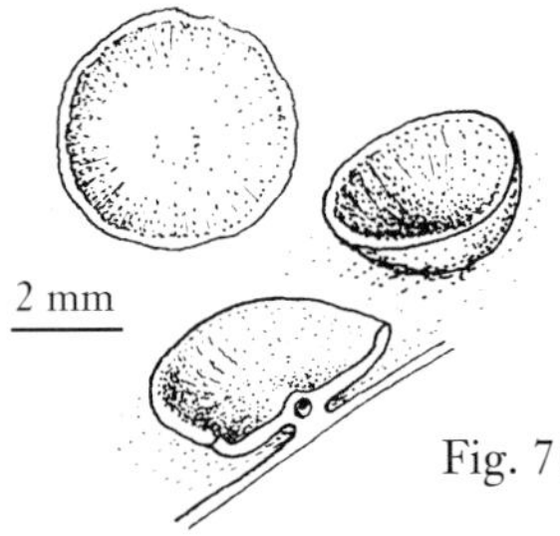

2 mm

Fig. 714

19 Smooth, hairless, although white or colourless hairs may be present while the gall develops; gall white, pale yellow or green, often with pink, red or purple patches; often has a narrow rim and may be cup-shaped (Fig. 714); never in large numbers on a leaf; common .... ***Neuroterus albipes*** (Schenck)
♀♀ (= *laeviusculus*) **smooth spangle gall**

- With tufts of hairs **20**

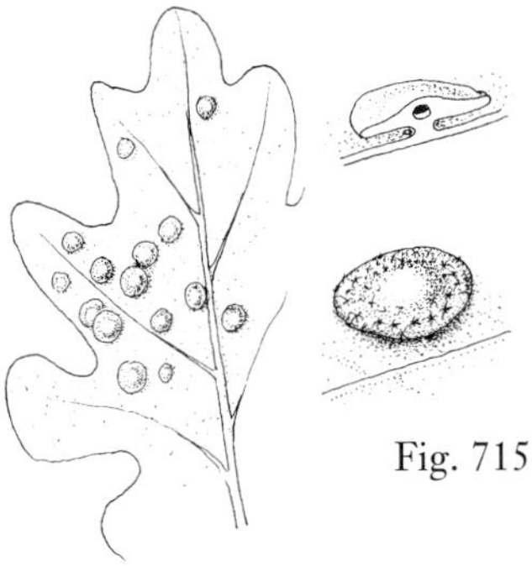

Fig. 715

20 Rimless, edges rising smoothly to central mound (Fig. 715, Plate 6.4b); very common .... ***Neuroterus quercusbaccarum*** (L.)
♀♀ (= *lenticularis*) **common spangle gall**

- Raised, hairy rim (Fig. 716); often cup-shaped and may be folded almost in half; often on Lammas leaves; uncommon............. ***Neuroterus tricolor*** Hartig
♀♀ (= *fumipennis*) **cupped spangle gall**

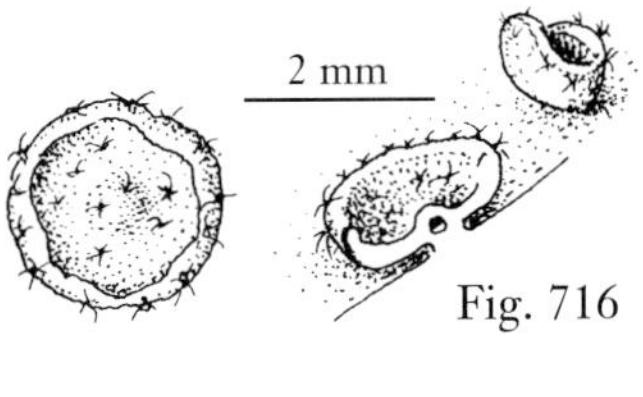

2 mm

Fig. 716

21 Kidney- or crescent-shaped, 2-4 mm long; often several along a main vein (Fig. 717); September - October; mostly found in north and west; uncommon .... ***Trigonaspis megaptera*** (Panzer)
♀♀ (= *renum*)

- Globular or egg-shaped; June - October **22**

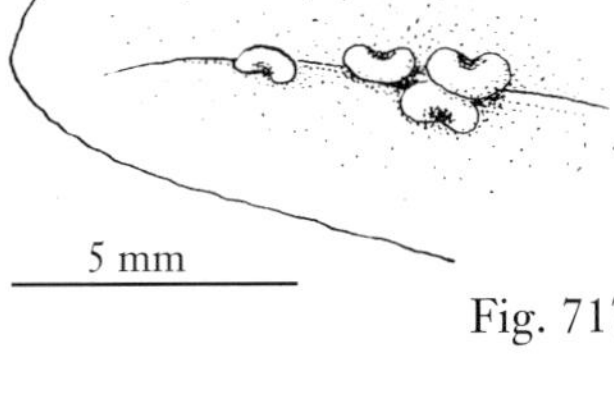

5 mm

Fig. 717

22 Egg-shaped, up to 3 mm long; flap of tissue on either side where gall is attached to midrib or main vein (Fig. 718); yellow or cream with pink, red or brown spots; usually falls from leaf before leaf falls from tree; very common

.... ***Neuroterus anthracinus*** (Curtis)

♀♀ (= *Andricus anthracina* = *ostreus*) **oyster gall**

Removed from *Andricus* and placed in *Neuroterus* by Pujade Villar *et al.* (1998).

Fig. 718

- Globular, or roughly so, usually > 4 mm across; without flaps of tissue; may be found on fallen leaves **23**

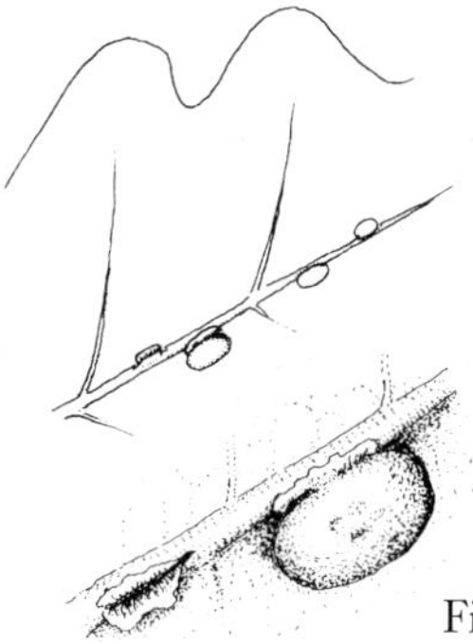

23 Hard, roughly globular with central depression; smooth or bumpy surface (Fig. 719); two chambers with larva in the one nearest the point of attachment; rare .... ***Cynips disticha*** Hartig

♀♀

4 mm

Fig. 719

- Hard or succulent; no central depression; single chamber with one larva **24**

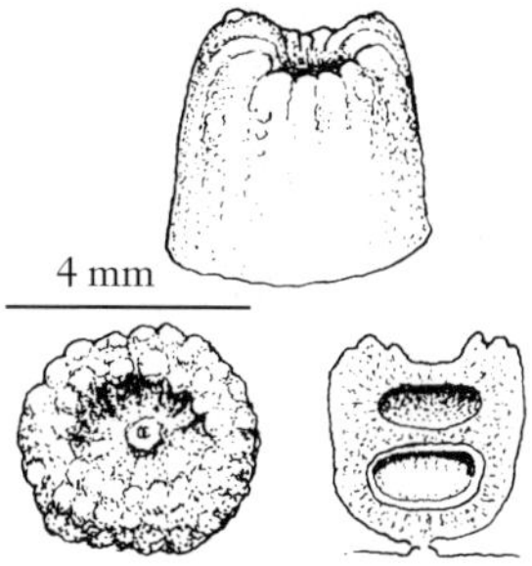

24 Diameter 10-20 mm; succulent, smooth (on *Q. robur*) or warty (on *Q. petraea*) (Fig. 720); yellow-green suffused with pink or red, later dark red then brown; thick-walled chamber; common

.... ***Cynips quercusfolii*** L.

♀♀ **cherry gall**

It is not known how the smooth / warty character manifests itself on *Q.* x *rosacea*.

- Diameter < 10 mm; hard; if surface bumpy the bumps forming lines **25**

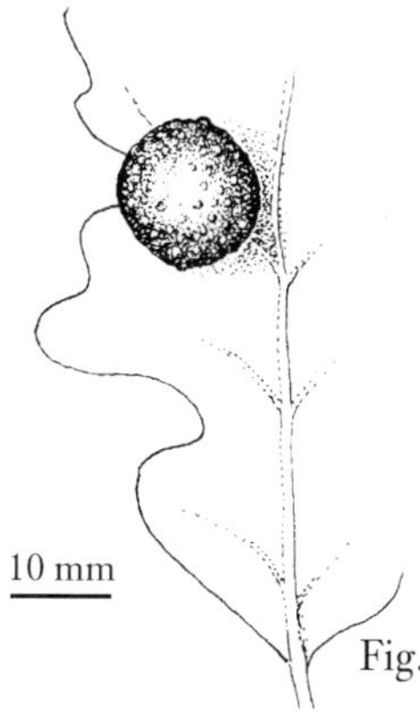

10 mm

Fig. 720

25 Surface with lines of bumps (Fig. 721); pale yellow with red or pink spots or stripes; chamber elongate; common .... *Cynips longiventris* Hartig
♀♀ **striped pea gall**

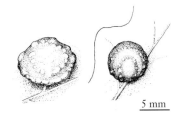

5 mm

Fig. 721

Bagnall and Harrison claimed to have found *Cynips quercus* (Fourcroy) in Britain early in the 20th century, but no other records are known. However, there are reports of galls which, whilst usually attributed to *C. longiventris* ♀♀, do not exactly fit its description. It is possible that these galls are caused by *C. quercus*, or *C. flosculi* (Giraud) as it should, apparently, now be known (Robbins, personal communication). It seems that the galls of the agamic generation are the same size as those of *C. longiventris* but lack the spots and stripes. The sexual generation gall is said to resemble that of *C. quercusfolii* (see couplet C23) but with red rather than purple or violet hairs. For firm evidence that this species exists in Britain the adult must be reared and its identity checked by an expert taxonomist. It is likely that the galls reported are caused by *C. longiventris* (or perhaps other *Cynips* species) distorted by inquilines or malformed during development.

- Surface smooth (Fig. 722); pink, red, orange or yellow at first, later brown; chamber circular **26**

Fig. 722

26 Thick-walled, hard, resists crushing, small chamber; common .... *Cynips divisa* Hartig
♀♀ **pea gall**

- Thin-walled, large chamber; uncommon
.... *Cynips agama* Hartig
♀♀

Quercus Key E: Galls on Catkins

All gall causers are **Hymenoptera: Cynipidae**, with larvae as in Fig. 723. Catkins usually appear in May and are present through June and to a varying degree into July. Galled catkins may persist for longer than normal.

1 On *Q. cerris*; often gregarious **2**

- On *Q. robur*, *Q. petraea* or *Q.* x *rosacea* **3**

1 mm

READ THREE ALTERNATIVES
2 Very small, < 1.5 mm long, cone-shaped, (Fig. 724); green at first, later light brown, not hairy; common .... *Andricus quercuscalicis* (Burgsdorf)
♀ ♂ (= *cerris*)

Fig. 723

Fig. 724

- Larger and fatter, about 6 x 3-4 mm, rounded with a distinct point (Fig. 725); green with fine hairs when young, becoming red, then dark purple or black; shiny and hard
.... ***Andricus grossulariae*** Giraud
♀♂

Walker (2002) confirms that the agamic generation of this species is *Andricus mayri* (Wachtl), which causes galls on acorns, and was first recorded in Berkshire in 2000. See couplet F4, p. 419.

10 mm

Fig. 725

- A cluster of galls attached to the catkin stalk, 10-35 mm across with many folds and indentations (Fig. 726); greenish-yellow and soft when young, becoming bright red, hard and woody; affected catkins remain attached to the tree until July or August (unaffected catkins fall earlier)
.... ***Andricus lucidus*** (Hartig)
♀♂ (= *aestivalis*)

Walker (2002) confirms that the agamic generation of this species causes galls on buds and acorns, and was first recorded in Berkshire in 2000. See couplets C4, p. 403, and F4, p. 419.

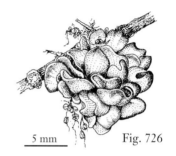

5 mm

Fig. 726

3 A mass of white cottonwool-like hairs up to 20 mm across, or small, generally hairy gall about 2 mm long **4**

- Sparsely hairy or smooth, if hairs present they are mainly at the tip **8**

4 Mass of white hairs completely obscuring chamber walls, except perhaps at the base **5**

- Gall hairy but chamber wall visible **6**

Fig. 727

10 mm

5 Up to 20 mm across, hairs completely concealing gall chambers (Fig. 727); up to 20 chambers, each with a larva; uncommon
.... ***Andricus quercusramuli*** (L.)
♀♂ **cottonwool gall**

- Up to 5 mm across, hairs not usually covering the base of the gall (Fig. 728); 1 - 6 chambers each with a larva; high on mature trees; rare
.... ***Andricus callidoma*** (Hartig)
♀♂ (= *cirratus*)

Fig. 728

6 Covered with long, dense white hairs, surface not ridged (Fig. 729); catkin usually not distorted; common .... *Andricus fecundator* (Hartig)

♀♂ (= *pilosus*)

\- Hairs more sparse; surface longitudinally ridged (Fig. 730) **7**

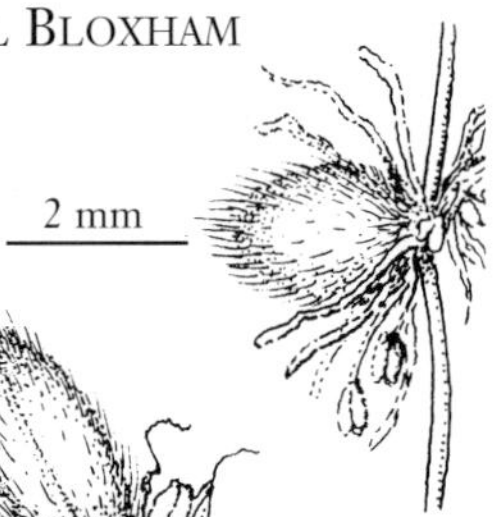

7 One ridge on each side meeting at the tip (Fig. 730); hairs red, brown or yellow; at base of stunted catkin; exit hole in the side of the tip; common ....*Andricus solitarius* (Fonscolombe)

♀♂ (= *occultus*)

\- Two ridges on each side meeting below the tip (Fig. 731); pale yellowish hairs; gall greenish yellow at first, later brown; rare .... *Andricus amenti* Giraud

♀♂

The agamic generation of this species has now been shown to be *Andricus giraudianus* DT & Kffr., although this has not yet been recorded in Britain (Walker, personal communication).

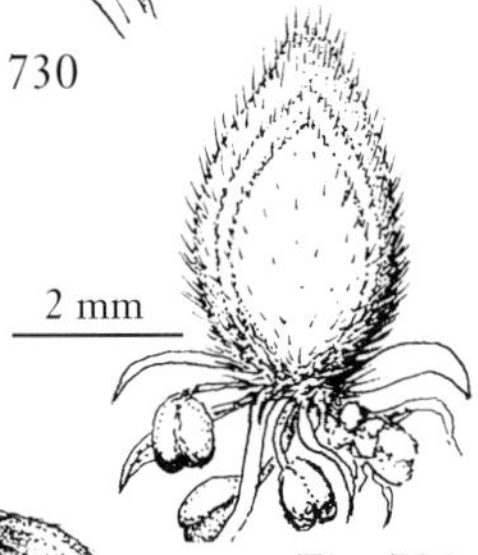

8 Gall longitudinally ridged; with or without a stalk.... **9**

\- Surface smooth or rough but without ridges **10**

The immature gall of *Neuroterus aprilinus* (couplet E13, opposite) has a broad ridge (Fig. 737) which is lost when mature.

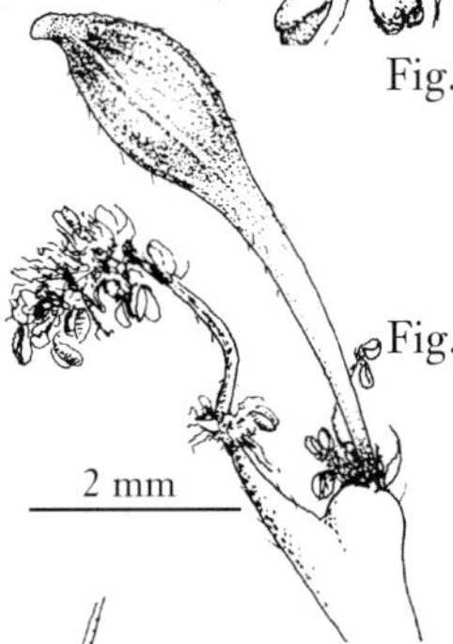

9 Spindle-shaped, stalked, up to 10 mm long; scattered hairs (Fig. 732); rare .... *Andricus seminationis* Giraud

♀♀

The gall of *Andricus nudus* ♀♂ is found very rarely on catkins (see couplet C12, p. 405, and Fig. 685).

\- Ovoid, without stalk or hairs (Fig. 733); 3-4 mm long; green or yellow at first, later dark red; common .... *Andricus quadrilineatus* Hartig

♀♀

These two species also cause galls on leaves, see couplet D13, p. 411. The sexual generations are unknown.

10 Spherical, smooth, succulent, 4-7 mm diameter (Fig. 734); yellow, green, red or purple; very common .... *Neuroterus quercusbaccarum* (L.)

♀♂ **currant gall**

This species also causes galls on leaves, see couplet D16, p. 411.

2 mm

Fig. 729

Fig. 730

2 mm

Fig. 731

Fig. 732

2 mm

Fig. 733

10 mm   Fig. 734

- Pear-shaped or ovoid, up to 2 mm long; surface smooth or rough; yellow-green or brown **11**

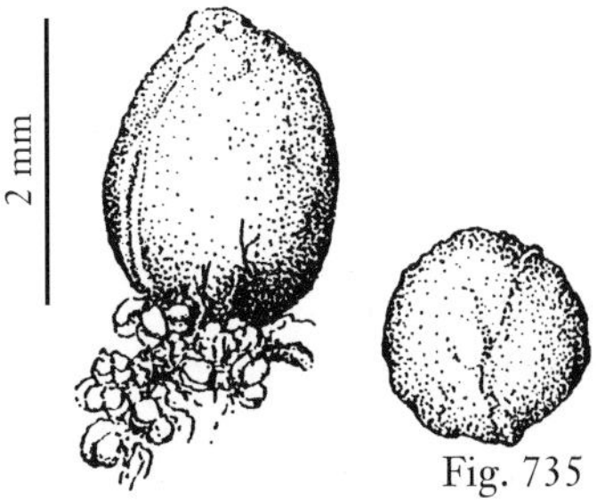

11 Pear-shaped, sometimes with a projection at the tip; surface smooth or rough **12**

- Ovoid; surface smooth or with a broad ridge when immature (Fig. 735) **13**
  This is a difficult distinction; if uncertain try both routes.

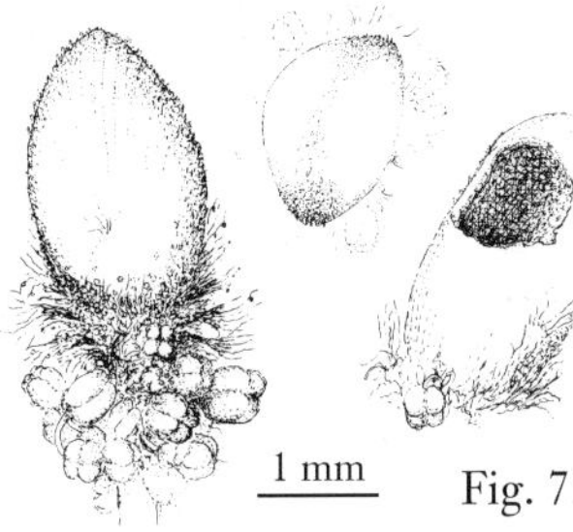

Fig. 735

12 Surface rough; tip bluntly pointed, may have a few hairs (Fig. 736); uncommon
.... ***Andricus glandulae*** (Schenck)
♀♂ (= *xanthopus*)

- Surface smooth; tip truncated (Fig. 737); rare
.... ***Andricus nudus*** Adler
♀♂

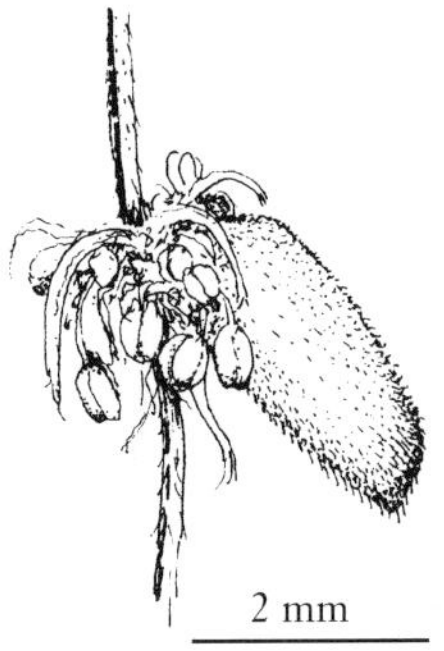

Fig. 736

13 Solitary; walls thin and woody, apex rounded
.... ***Neuroterus albipes*** (Schenck)
♀♂

This species more often causes galls on leaves, see couplet D14, p. 411.

- Gregarious; broad ridge when young disappears at maturity (Fig. 735); common
.... ***Neuroterus aprilinus*** (Giraud)
♀♀ (= *schlechtendali*)

Fig. 737

Quercus KEY F: GALLS ON ACORNS

All gall causers included here are **Hymenoptera: Cynipidae**, with larvae as in Fig. 738.

Gall midge larvae (**Diptera: Cecidomyiidae**; larva Fig. 739) are sometimes found in stunted acorns: *Dasineura squamosa* (Tavares), originally described from *Quercus lusitanica* in Spain, has been recorded in England and Scotland, but there is doubt about the accuracy of these records (Harris, personal communication).

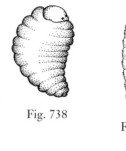

Fig. 738

Fig. 739

1   On *Q. cerris*; inside acorn which may be slightly distorted; contains several chambers (Fig. 740); larvae or pupae remain in fallen acorns for up to eight years
.... ***Callirhytis erythrocephala*** (Giraud)
♀♀ or ***C. erythrostoma*** Dettmer ♀♀

These may not be distinct species. There is a great deal of confusion relating to them, and to *C. bella* and *C. glandium*. Eady & Quinlan (1963) confirm *C. bella* as British but do not mention its gall, and report that *C. glandium* is a synonym of *C. erythrocephala*. Further confusion surrounds hosts – Dauphin & Aniotsbehère (1993) only mention *C. glandium* and state its hosts as being *Quercus suber*, *Q. ilex* and *Q. cerris*. Robbins (personal communication) suggests that *C. glandium* is now known to be restricted to *Q. ilex* and that old records from *Q. cerris* are of *C. erythrocephala*. There is evidence that *Callirhytis* spp. have an alternate sexual generation which causes galls in the twigs of *Q. cerris* and *Q. robur* (Walker, personal communication).

10 mm

Fig. 740

-    On *Q. robur*, *Q. petraea* or *Q.* x *rosacea* **2**

2   Gall inside acorn which is brown and stunted; one chamber, but galls usually attacked by an inquiline *Synergus clandestinus* Eady, which causes several chambers in the acorn (Fig. 741); common
.... ***Andricus legitimus*** Wiebes-Rijks
♀♀

The sexual generation of this species is unknown.

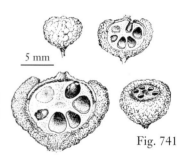

5 mm

Fig. 741

-    Gall on outside of acorn, sometimes concealing it, may be green and sticky at first, later brown and hard; either a dense mass of short (4-8 mm) spines, each tipped with a small knob, knobbly with contorted, flattened projections, or a mass of ridged tissue **3**

3   1-10 galls on acorn; ridged (Fig. 742, Plate 6.5); contains large interior cavity with small inner gall; very common .... ***Andricus quercuscalicis*** Burgsdorf
♀♀ **knopper gall**

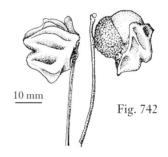

10 mm

Fig. 742

-    With spines or contorted, flattened projections; contains several chambers each with a single larva ... **4**

4 Single gall on the edge of the acorn cup; spiny,
each spine tipped with a small knob
.... ***Andricus lucidus*** (Hartig)
See also p. 403   ♀♀ **hedgehog gall**

- Gall on acorn cup, often enclosing immature
acorn; with flattened projections (Fig. 743)
.... ***Andricus grossulariae*** Giraud
See note under couplet E2   (= *mayri*) ♀♀

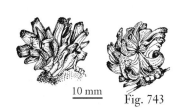

10 mm   Fig. 743

RADIOLA see *LINUM*

E133. *RANUNCULUS*

Three cecid galls (**Diptera: Cecidomyiidae**), with larvae as in Fig. 739, are found on
meadow buttercup, *R. acris* L., creeping buttercup, *R. repens* L., bulbous buttercup, *R.
bulbosus* L., and goldilocks buttercup, *R. auricomus* L.
    Fungi also cause galls (see p. 250).

1 Edge of leaflet rolled or bulged upwards and
thickened (Fig. 744), green or reddish; may affect
whole of young leaf (Fig. 745); larvae whitish when
young, later red; usually on *R. repens*, *R. acris* and
probably other species, local
.... ***Dasineura ranunculi*** (Bremi)
A narrow, upward, marginal roll, containing mites (**Acari:
Eriophyoidea**), is caused by *Epitrimerus rhyncothrix* (Nalepa); it
has not been recorded since 1928.

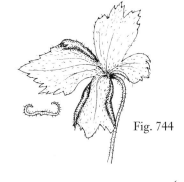

Fig. 744

2 Flower bud slightly swollen, remaining closed,
failing to develop, sometimes with a violet tint;
larvae pale yellow to pink; usually on *R. acris*
.... ***Dasineura traili*** (Kieffer)

3 Achene swollen, often several affected in a flower;
each contains a yellow larva; on *R. auricomus*; N.
England and Scotland
.... ***Dasineura auricomi*** (Kieffer)

Fig. 745

E134. *RHAMNUS*

Galls are recorded from the native buckthorn, *Rhamnus cathartica* L. and the introduced Mediterranean buckthorn, *R. alaternus* L.

A rust distorts leaves and petioles (see p. 251).

1 Flower bud swollen, club-shaped (Fig. 746); contains a white larva (Fig. 747); on *R. alaternus*, rare: **Diptera: Cecidomyiidae**
.... *Asphondylia borzi* (Stefani)

Only one unpublished record from Letchworth 1929, based on larvae in the Natural History Museum London (Harris, personal communication).

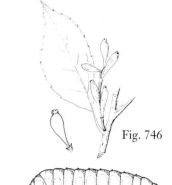

Fig. 746

- Gall in leaf blade **2**

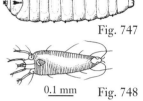

Fig. 747

2 Erineum on underside, blade thickened above; contains mites (Fig. 748); on *R. cathartica*: **Acari: Eriophyoidea** .... *Phyllocoptes annulatus* (Nalepa)
(= *Aceria*)

0.1 mm   Fig. 748

- Pit gall or marginal roll; contains nymph(s) **Hemiptera: Psylloidea** **3**

3 Leaf margin thickened, rolled upwards, 0.5-2 cm long (Fig. 749); paler than rest of leaf, or tinted red or purplish; contains several nymphs (Fig. 750); on *R. cathartica*, locally common in S. England, scarcer north to Cumbria and Yorkshire
.... *Trichochermes walkeri* Förster
(= *Trichopsylla*)

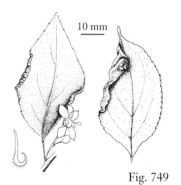

10 mm

Fig. 749

- Small bulge in upper surface, with corresponding depression below; usually several in a leaf; a flat nymph lives in each depression; on *R. cathartica*, locally common in S. England, scarcer north to Cumbria .... *Trioza rhamni* (Schrank)

Two rare *Psylla* species also cause pit galls on *Rhamnus* leaves: *P. rhamnicola* Scott on *R. cathartica* and *P. alaterni* Förster on *R. alaternus*, the second known only from Ireland. For certain determination, the psyllids should be identified (see Hodkinson & White, 1979, White & Hodkinson, 1982).

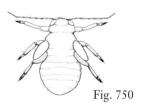

Fig. 750

RHAPHANUS see BRASSICACEAE

E135. *RHINANTHUS*

One cecid gall (**Diptera: Cecidomyiidae**) is recorded on yellow-rattle, *Rhinanthus minor* L.

Flower deformed and fleshy, covered with felt-like hairs; contains several white larvae; N. England; rare .... ***Rhopalomyia cristaegalli*** (Karsch)

E136. *RIBES*

Galls have been recorded from black currant, *Ribes nigrum* L., red currant, *R. rubrum* L., mountain currant, *R. alpinum* L. and gooseberry, *R. uva-crispa* L.

Rust galls may be found on the leaves and berries (see p. 252).

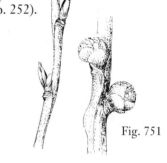

Fig. 751

1 A big bud; terminal or lateral bud swollen and rounded, up to c. 1 cm across, remaining closed (Fig. 751); contains mites (Fig. 748); **Acari: Eriophyoidea:**

On *R. nigrum*; common .... ***Cecidophyopsis ribis*** (Westwood)

C. ribis has also been recorded on *R. uva-crispa*, as has *C. grossulariae* (Collinge); it is unclear whether the latter causes big bud (see couplet 3 and references in Amrine & Stasny (1994).

On *R. rubrum* .... ***Cecidophyopsis selachodon*** Eyndhoven

- Gall on leaf 2

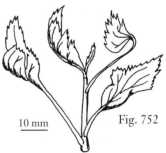

10 mm   Fig. 752

2 Young leaf tightly twisted, folded upwards and failing to open, usually affects several together (Fig. 752); contains many white or yellow larvae (Fig. 753) between May and September (there are 3 - 4 generations and each galled leaf contains larvae for a brief period only); leaf turns black after larvae have left; mainly on *R. nigrum*: **Diptera: Cecidomyiidae** .... ***Dasineura tetensi*** (Rübsaamen)
(= *ribicola*)

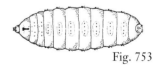

Fig. 753

D. ribicola (Kieffer) is recorded from *R. uva-crispa* and was synonymised with *D. tetensi* by Skuhravá (1989). However, Barnes (1948) found that *D. tetensi* females in captivity would not lay eggs on *R. uva-crispa*, suggesting that the two plants are galled by different species.

- Young or older leaf buckled, crumpled or otherwise distorted, often with raised patches or thickened veins 3

3 Leaf completely distorted, inrolled and twisted, with veins thickened (Fig. 754); ± hairy inside, with mites (Fig. 755); on *R. alpinum*: **Acari: Eriophyoidea** .... *Aceria scaber* (Nalepa)

Small upward bulges in leaves of *R. uva-crispa*, containing mites, are apparently caused by *Cecidophyopsis grossulariae* (Collinge)

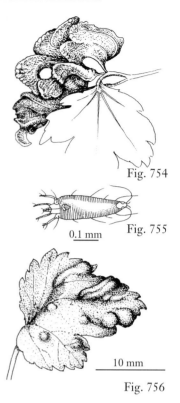

Fig. 754

Fig. 755

0.1 mm

- Raised thickened patches on upper surface, often yellowish or red (Fig. 756), leaf often curled downwards; hairy depressions below with aphids (Fig. 757): **Hemiptera: Aphididae**:

On *R. rubrum*; aphids yellow-green .... *Cryptomyzus ribis* (L.)

On *R. alpinum*; aphids pink or reddish .... *Cryptomyzus korschelti* Börner

Damage caused by aphids of other species is common. Leaves, particularly young ones, are crumpled, buckled, inrolled and misshapen, but are not usually thickened; they are not, therefore, regarded as true galls.

Fig. 757

10 mm

Fig. 756

RORIPPA see BRASSICACEAE

E137. *ROSA*

There are many species of wild roses; some are difficult to distinguish, and hybridisation is an additional problem. Common species in hedgerows and scrub are dog rose, *Rosa canina* L. and field rose, *R. arvensis* Hudson. Burnet rose, *R. pimpinellifolia* L. (= *spinosissima*) is frequent in coastal sites around Britain. These, and the uncommon native species, are galled by most of the species below; only *Diplolepis spinosissimae* is more host-specific. Cultivated roses, and the widely planted Japanese rose, *R. rugosa* Thunb. ex Murray, are rarely hosts (but see couplet 6).

Crown gall, *Agrobacterium tumefaciens*, and galls caused by nematodes are common on the roots, and orange rusts cause swellings on the leaves and stems; see pages 218, 252 and 270. Flower buds may remain closed and blacken inside; they frequently contain yellow, red or orange larvae of *Clinodiplosis cilicrus* (Kieffer) (= *rosiperda*) which are not gall-inducing.

1 Gall on stem, developed from a leaf- or flower-bud; globular, hairy or spiny, with one or more chambers each with a larva (Fig. 758) in summer and winter, a pupa in spring (adult emerges in June); old galls persist as woody masses: **Hymenoptera: Cynipidae ... 2**

Galls occasionally occur on hips.

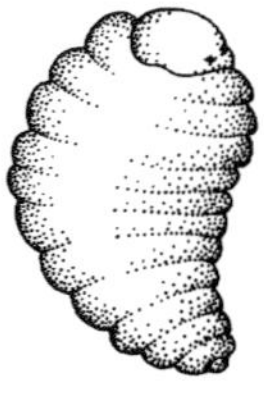

Fig. 758

A swelling in the stem of *R. pimpinellifolia* (Fig. 759), similar to the gall of *Lasioptera rubi* on *Rubus* (see Key E139) was first found in Britain in 1999. It is caused by a cecid (**Diptera: Cecidomyiidae**) that has not yet been named.

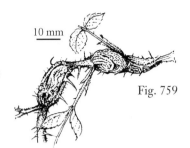

Fig. 759

- Gall on leaf: petiole, midrib or blade of leaflet **3**

Pea galls (couplet 5) occasionally occur on stems.

2 Covered with long branched wiry hairs forming a mass up to 6 cm (occasionally more) across (Fig. 760, Plate 5.6); green, often red in July - August, later brown and woody; usually with several chambers, sometimes only one; widespread and common .... ***Diplolepis rosae*** (L.)
bedeguar gall, robin's pin cushion

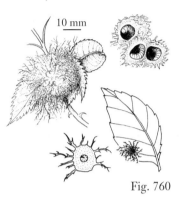

Fig. 760

- Group of spherical coalesced galls (sometimes only one), sparsely covered with short stiff unbranched spines (Fig. 761); soft, green or reddish at first, later brown and hard; in S. England, rare ....***Diplolepis mayri*** (Schlechtendal)

Tiny galls may also occur on leaflets (see Figs. 760, 761). The inquiline cynipid *Periclistus brandtii* (Ratzeburg) may cause clusters of small thick-walled chambers near surface of gall of either species, which may distort and enlarge it; it cannot, however, cause a gall on its own.

3 Spherical or ovoid gall, smooth, or with hairs or spines; on one side of leaflet or protruding from both sides; sometimes on midrib or petiole; contains one or more chambers each with one larva (Fig. 758) or pupa: **Hymenoptera: Cynipidae** **4**

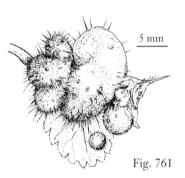

Fig. 761

- Leaflet rolled or folded, ± thickened **6**

4 Surface covered with branched hairs or stiff spines .. **2**

- Surface smooth, covered with papillae or with 2-6 spikes (Fig. 762); yellow-green or reddish, later brown; usually on blade of leaflet, or on midrib or petiole **5**

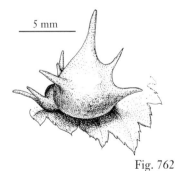

Fig. 762

READ TWO ALTERNATIVES, THE SECOND ONE SUBDIVIDED

5 Ovoid or rounded gall in midrib or petiole, 3-
10mm across, smooth, protruding from both sides
(Fig. 763); sometimes several coalesce; usually on
burnet rose, locally common in coastal sites
.... ***Diplolepis spinosissimae*** (Giraud)

- Spherical gall on blade, 2-8 mm diameter, smooth
(Fig. 764), covered with papillae or with 2-6 spikes
(Fig. 765, Plate 5.5); usually on underside
.... ***Diplolepis*** sp.
rose pea gall

Smooth or with spikes, common .. **D. nervosa** (Curtis)
(= *rosarum* = *dispar*)

Smooth, locally common .... **D. eglanteriae** (Hartig)

Usually with papillae, rare .... **D. centifoliae** (Hartig)

Smooth rose pea galls cannot be safely distinguished; rear the
adult and identify in Eady & Quinlan (1963). Gall may be
enlarged or distorted if inquiline cynipids occur in wall of
chamber.

6 Both sides of leaflet rolled downwards to main
vein, forming loose tubes, often spirally twisted
(Fig. 766, Plate 7.4); green caterpillar (Fig. 767)
present May - July; widespread and common:
Hymenoptera: Tenthredinidae
.... ***Blennocampa phyllocolpa*** (Viitasaari & Vikberg)
Common also on cultivated roses.   (= *pusilla*)

- Leaflet folded upwards along main vein, thickened
and pod-like (Fig. 768); contains many white, later
yellowish red larvae (Fig. 769) in summer and early
autumn; widespread and common: **Diptera:**
Cecidomyiidae .... ***Wachtliella rosarum*** (Hardy)
(=*Dasineura*)

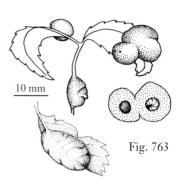

10 mm

Fig. 763

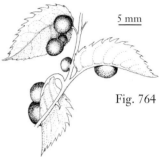

5 mm

Fig. 764

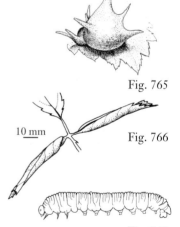

5 mm

Fig. 765

10 mm

Fig. 766

Fig. 767

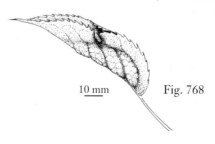

10 mm   Fig. 768

Fig. 769

E138. *RUBIA*

One mite gall (**Acari: Eriophyoidea**) occurs on wild madder, *Rubia peregrina* L.

Tip of shoot and last whorl of leaves modified into a globular gall, varying considerably in size and shape (Fig. 770); contains mites (Fig. 771) .... *Aceria rubiae* (Canestrini)
(= *Eriophyes*)

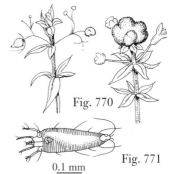

Fig. 770

Fig. 771

0.1 mm

E139. *RUBUS*

This is a large and complex genus. Galls are recorded from raspberry, *Rubus idaeus* L. and dewberry, *R. caesius* L., but mostly from blackberries or brambles, '*R. fruticosus* L.'. This is a general name for an aggregate of over 2,000 microspecies. Gall causers probably discriminate between them but specific details are not known. Cultivated as well as wild varieties may be galled.

Solid, rough, woody swellings on roots and stems are caused by crown gall (see p. 218).

READ THREE ALTERNATIVES

1 Swelling in stem; green at first, later brown and hard **2**

- Gall in leaf blade **3**

- Flower bud swollen, remaining closed **8**

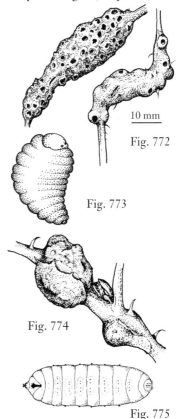

10 mm

Fig. 772

Fig. 773

2 Elongated, 2-15 x 1 cm, often curved or causing stem to bend, surface bumpy (each bump indicates a gall chamber, Fig. 772, Plate 5.7); contains many regular, spherical chambers (c. 200 in large galls), each with a white larva (Fig. 773) in summer and winter, pupa in spring; old galls, with numerous adult exit holes, persist for many years: **Hymenoptera: Cynipidae**
.... *Diastrophus rubi* (Bouché)

- More rounded, up to 5 x 2cm, surface sometimes with longitudinal fissures (Fig. 774, Plate 3.9); contains many irregular cavities with larvae (Fig. 775), white when young, later red-orange in summer and winter, pupae in spring: **Diptera: Cecidomyiidae** .... *Lasioptera rubi* (Schrank)
The cavities are lined with fungal mycelia on which the larvae feed; galls occasionally found in leaf petioles.

Fig. 774

Fig. 775

3 Erineum or small pustule, often several in a leaf; contains mites (Fig. 776): **Acari: Eriophyoidea** **4**

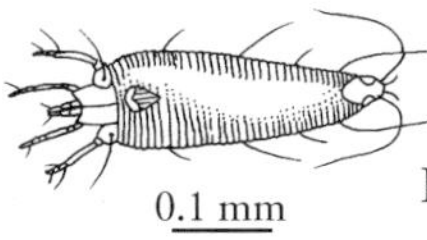

- Leaf distorted, often buckled and discoloured, sometimes with thickened veins **6**

0.1 mm   Fig. 776

4 Irregularly-shaped pustules raised on both surfaces (Fig. 777), c. 2 mm across or high; often reddish on upperside, yellow-green below with oval opening; hairy within..................... ***Aceria silvicola*** (Canestrini)
(= *Eriophyes*)

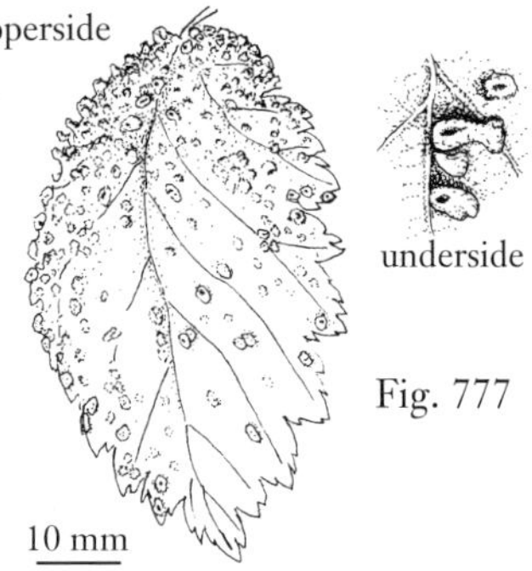

- Erineum on either surface, sometimes a corresponding bulge on opposite side **5**

upperside

underside

Fig. 777

10 mm

5 Greyish white felt along veins (Fig. 778), may extend to cover most of either surface
.... ***Phyllocoptes gibbosus*** (Nalepa)
(= *Eriophyes*)

May also occur on stems, flower stalks, flowers or fruits.

- Hairy patch in slight depression on under surface, with a slight bulge above; usually on *R. caesius*
.... ***Eriophyes rubicolens*** (Canestrini)

Fig. 778

6 Leaf crumpled, with yellowish patches, veins not obviously thickened (Fig. 779); contains mites (Fig. 776); usually on *R. idaeus*: **Acari: Eriophyoidea** .... ***Phyllocoptes gracilis*** (Nalepa)

The discolouration may be due to virus infection (Coulianos & Holmåsen, 1991). This damage may not be a true gall.

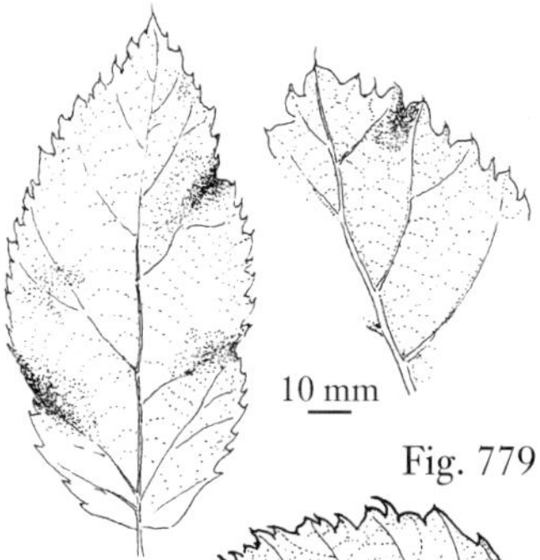

- Midrib and side veins thickened **7**

10 mm

Fig. 779

7 Leaf creased, pleated or buckled (damage very variable) (Fig. 780), often becoming black around midrib; several white larvae present in the creases briefly in late spring or early summer; common: **Diptera: Cecidomyiidae**
.... ***Dasineura plicatrix*** (Loew)

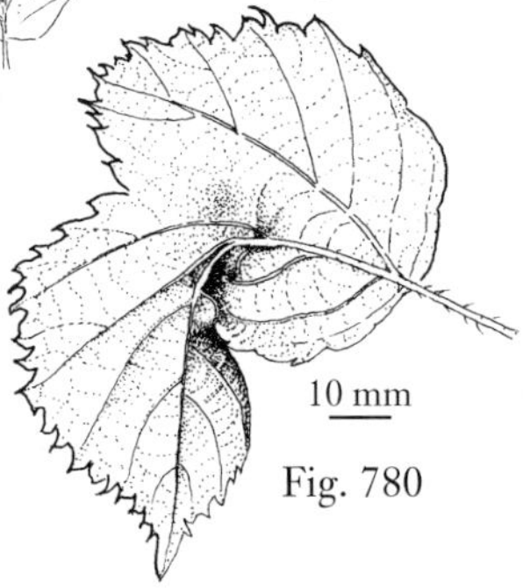

- Blade discoloured, with margins twisted and curled to underside; contains aphids (Fig. 781): **Hemiptera** .... **Aphididae**

Several aphid species have this effect, which may not be a true gall.

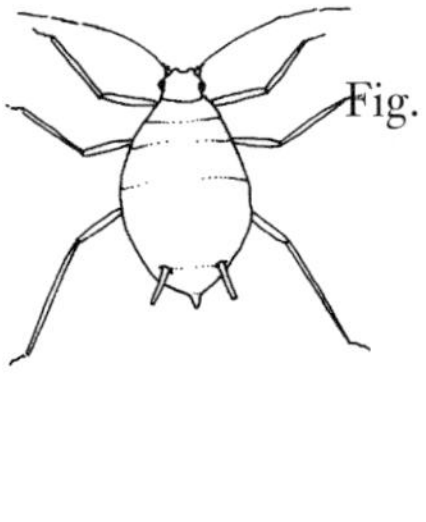

10 mm

Fig. 780

Fig. 781

8 Deformed petals crinkled and stamens blackened (Fig. 782); contains many white jumping larvae (Fig. 783) in summer; usually on *R. caesius*: **Diptera: Cecidomyiidae**
.... ***Contarinia rubicola*** Kieffer

- Contains one white larva (Fig. 784): **Coleoptera: Curculionidae** .... ***Anthonomus rubi*** Herbst
This may not be a true gall.

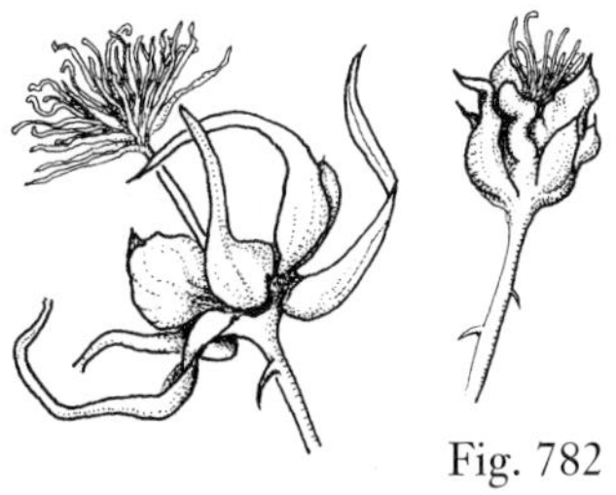

Fig. 782

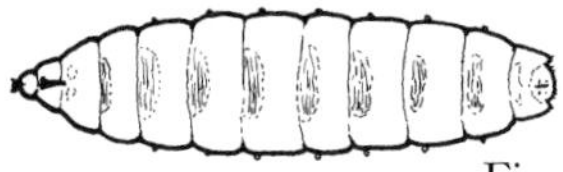

Fig. 783

E140. *RUMEX*

Rumex is divided into three subgenera. The species from which galls have been recorded are:

ACETOSELLA: R. *acetosella* L., sheep's sorrel
ACETOSA: R. *acetosa* L., common sorrel
  R. *scutatus* L., French sorrel
RUMEX: R. *obtusifolius* L., broad-leaved dock
  R. *crispus* L., curled dock
  R. *conglomeratus* Murray, clustered dock
  R. *hydrolapathum* L., water dock
  R. *pulcher* L., fiddle dock

Many gall insects on *Rumex* cause similar types of gall, but are restricted to species in the different subgenera. Most are gall midges (**Diptera: Cecidomyiidae**) or weevils (**Coleoptera: Brentidae: Apioninae**) and their biology is not well known. Identifications made using this key should be verified by rearing and identifying the adults.

READ THREE ALTERNATIVES

1 Swelling in root, root collar or stem, occasionally in petiole; contains one or more chambers, each with a larva (Fig. 784) or pupa: **Coleoptera: Brentidae: Apioninae** .. **2**

- In leaf blade, midrib or petiole **3**

- Flower bud swollen, remaining closed; containing larva(e): **Diptera: Cecidomyiidae** **4**

2 On subgenus *RUMEX*; gall in root collar or stem (sometimes in petiole), widespread and common
.... ***Apion frumentarium*** (L.)
  (= *miniatum*)

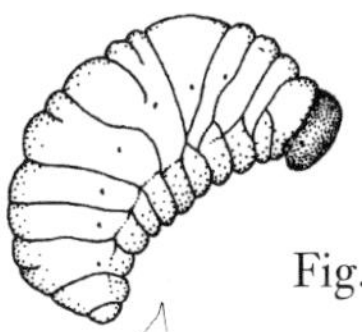

- On *R. acetosella*; irregular swelling > 1 cm long (Fig. 785):

England and Wales north to Westmorland, rare
.... ***Apion rubiginosum*** Grill
  (= *sanguineum*)

Fig. 784

5 mm

Fig. 785

Throughout Britain, locally common in south, decreasing northwards
.... ***Perapion marchicum*** (Herbst)

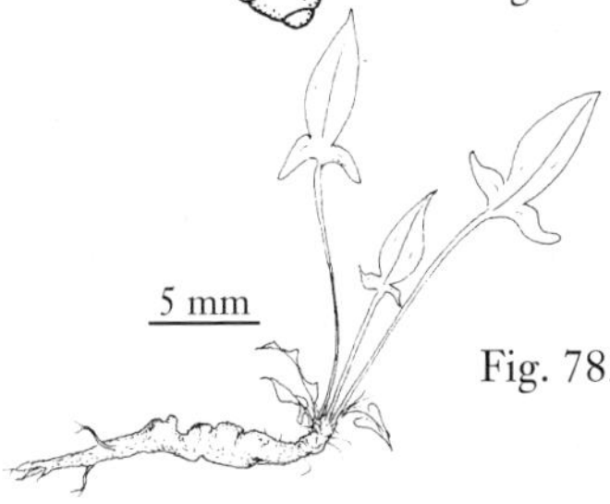

Several weevils are common stem and root borers without causing galls:

In roots of *ACETOSELLA* .... *Apion haematodes* Kirby (= *frumentarium* (Paykull))

In stems of species in all subgenera .... *Perapion curtirostre* (Germar)

In stems of *RUMEX* and *ACETOSA* .... *Perapion violaceum* (Kirby)

In lower stem or root, or base of petiole of *R. acetosa* .... *Apion cruentatum* Walton

It is essential the adults are reared and identified before records are confirmed (see Morris, 1990, Salt & Whittaker, 1998).

3   Swelling in midrib or petiole; contains a larva (Fig. 786) or pupa; on *R. acetosella*; England, Wales and S. Scotland, local: **Coleoptera: Brentidae: Apioninae** .... *Apion rubens* Stephens

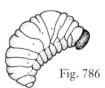

Fig. 786

-   Leaf curled downwards, discoloured; with small depressions on underside, each containing a nymph: **Hemiptera: Psylloidea**:

    On *RUMEX* ..... ***Aphalara panli*** (Weber & Mohr)

    On *R. acetosa* and *R. acetosella* .... ***Aphalara exilis*** (Weber & Mohr)

    To identify psyllids, see Hodkinson & White (1979), White & Hodkinson (1982).

4   On *RUMEX*; jumping larvae (Fig. 787) .... ***Contarinia rumicis*** (Loew)

-   On *R. acetosa* and *R. acetosella* **5**

Fig. 787

5   Several jumping, yellow-white, pinkish or orange larvae (Fig. 787) .... ***Contarinia acetosellae*** (Rübsaamen) (= *acetosae* = *Atylodiplosis*)

-   Single non jumping, reddish larva (Fig. 788); on *R. acetosella* .... ***Jaapiella rubicundula*** (Rübsaamen)

    Contarinia scutati Rübsaamen, with a white jumping larva, is found in swollen seeds and ovaries of species in *RUMEX*; its galls have been recorded in Britain (Robbins, 1995, gall only) but the identification needs confirming.

Fig. 788

E141. *SALIX*

The genus *Salix* supports more galls than any other in Britain, although individual oak (*Quercus*) species support more than individual *Salix*. Some are difficult to identify (particularly those caused by gall midges in the genus *Rabdophaga* (= *Rhabdophaga*) and mites, Eriophyoidea) because their taxonomy and biology have not been fully sorted out. For example, some taxonomists include *Rabdophaga* with *Dasineura*. However, as most gall causers are restricted to one or a few related species of *Salix*, identifying the host plant to species helps considerably; for some gall causers it is essential (eg. *Pontania* spp.). Unfortunately *Salix* species frequently hybridise, and this increases the difficulty of firm identification. These hybrids, though, are most common between *S. caprea*, *S. cinerea* and *S. aurita* (grouped together here as 'sallows'; other species are described as 'willows') and most galls found on one of the group will also be found on the others; thus identification to sallow is usually adequate. For identification of willows and sallows, see Meikle (1984).

As well as the wide variety of gall midges affecting *Salix*, there is a notable number of gall-causing sawflies in the genera *Pontania* and *Euura*.

The witches' broom on catkins, once thought to be caused by a mite, is now thought to be caused by a virus (see p. 219); a hard woody lump on stems or derived from catkins, particularly prominent in winter, may have a similar cause.

The key is divided as follows:

A GALLS IN BUDS, INCLUDING ROSETTES AND LEAF BUNCHES AT SHOOT TIPS   below

B GALLS IN TWIGS OR STEMS   page 431

C GALLS IN CATKINS   page 434

D GALLS IN LEAF BLADES AND PETIOLES   page 434

SALIX KEY A: GALLS IN BUDS, INCLUDING ROSETTES AND LEAF BUNCHES AT SHOOT TIPS

Rabdophaga spp. causing *Salix* bud galls are difficult to identify. This key should be regarded as provisional only and will be revised and improved as more information becomes available. Only the commoner or more easily identified species are included.

1   Bud swollen or elongated 2

-   Bud composed of bunched and distorted young
    leaves which may form a rosette; contains one or
    many pink or red larvae (Fig. 789) or pupae:
    Diptera: Cecidomyiidae 4

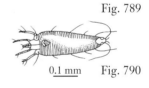

Fig. 789

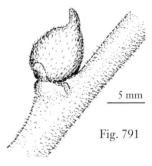

0.1 mm   Fig. 790

2   Bud swollen, hairy, containing mites (Fig. 790); on
    sallows: **Acari: Eriophyoidea**
    .... *Aculus gemmarum* (Nalepa)
                              (= *Eriophyes* = *Aceria*)

-   Bud pear-shaped or elongated 3

3   Bud about twice normal size (Fig. 791); contains a
    greenish caterpillar (Fig. 792) in June - July and frass;
    on many *Salix* spp. particularly sallows; widespread
    and common: **Hymenoptera: Tenthredinidae**
    .... *Euura mucronata* (Hartig)

-   Bud elongated up to 13 mm long, forming horny,
    reddish tubes tapering to the tip which is open when
    mature; contains orange larva (Fig. 789) at the base;
    on *S. repens*; Scotland: **Diptera: Cecidomyiidae**
    .... *Rabdophaga repenticornua* Bland
    See Bland (2001) for the description (with figures) of this new
    species.

5 mm

Fig. 791

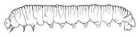

Fig. 792

4   Rosette or artichoke gall in terminal bud, > 20 mm across, not abnormally hairy (Fig. 793); central chamber with pink or red larva; old gall brown, persisting over winter; common:
On *S. alba* .... ***Rabdophaga strobilina*** Bremi
(= *rosaria*)

On sallows .... ***Rabdophaga cinerearum*** (Hardy)
These two species are generally considered to be synonymous (Barnes 1951), but Robbins (1995) claims that they are distinct species.

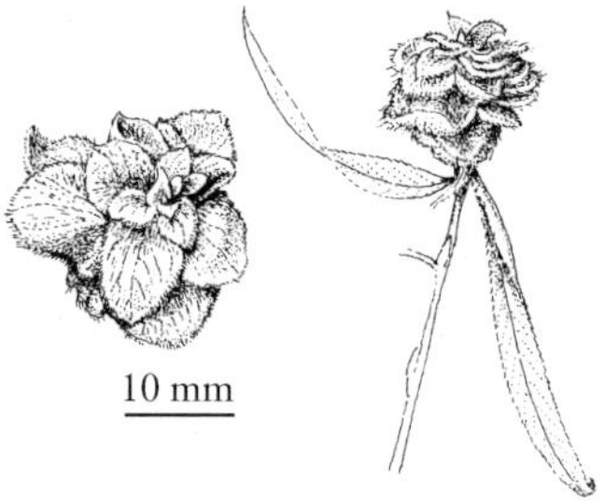

\-   Bunched and distorted leaves forming an enlarged bud or small rosette, < 15 mm across; may be hairy; usually not persisting over winter **5**

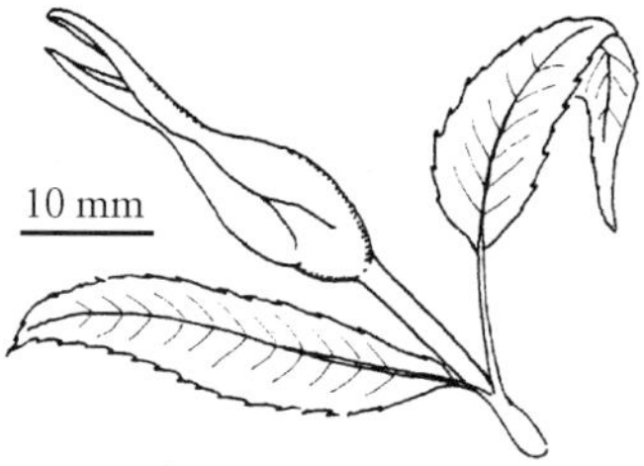

5   Leaves of terminal bud slightly thickened, not hairy, sometimes curled and crinkled, united into an elongate gall (Fig. 794), often hidden by older leaves; elongate cavity inside with many red larvae; gall green or reddish, later black; on *S. alba, S. fragilis*......................... ***Rabdophaga terminalis*** (Loew)

\-   Terminal or lateral bud enlarged and hairy, often with clustered, rosette-like leaves; contains several orange or red larvae; on *S. triandra, S. repens* and sallows **6**

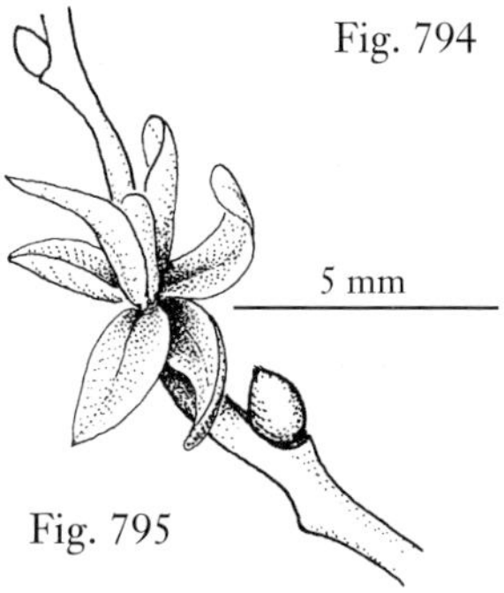

6   Enlarged bud or small rosette, 3-6 mm across:
On sallows, *S. repens* (Fig. 795)
.... ***Rabdophaga clavifex*** (Kieffer)
or ***R. pulvini*** (Kieffer) (= *rosariella* = *superna*)
For synonymy see Stelter (1977).

On *S. repens* (Fig. 796)
.... ***Rabdophaga repentis*** (Skuhravá)
(= *jaapi*)

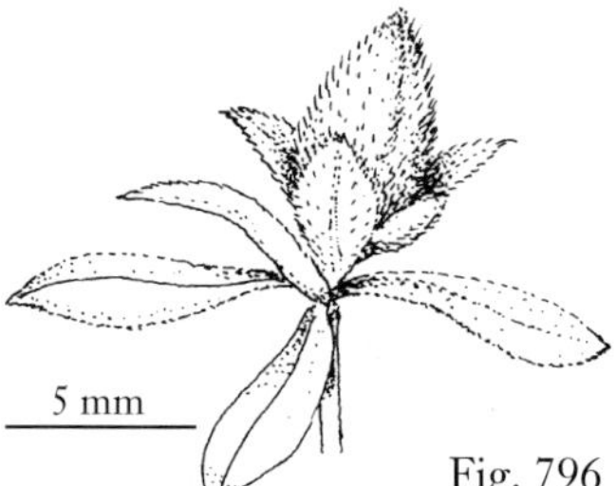

\-   Larger and very hairy, up to 15 mm across (Fig. 797):
On sallows .... ***Rabdophaga iteobia*** (Kieffer)

On *S. triandra* .... ***Rabdophaga heterobia*** (Loew)
generation 2

10 mm

Fig. 793

10 mm

Fig. 794

5 mm

Fig. 795

5 mm

Fig. 796

Fig. 797

10 mm

SALIX KEY B: GALLS IN TWIGS OR STEMS

1 Stem distinctly swollen **2**

- Stem not or hardly swollen; galls apparent when emerging adults leave 'shot holes' in bark (Fig. 798); these often appear on or just below stubs of cut shoots, or near nodes: **Diptera: Cecidomyiidae** .... **shot hole gall midges, 13**

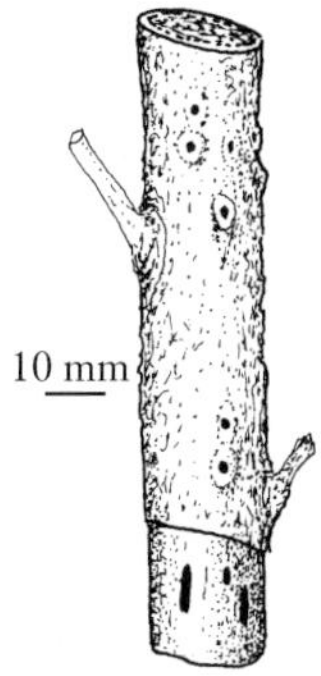

Fig. 798 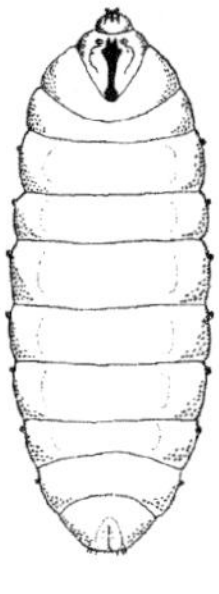   Fig. 799

2 Stem usually swollen all round; contains one or more chambers containing cecid larvae (Fig. 799), or one chamber with a moth caterpillar (Fig. 800) or beetle larva (Fig. 801) **3**

- Stem swollen mainly on one side; contains one chamber with a cecid (Fig. 799) or agromyzid (Fig. 802) larva, or with sawfly caterpillar(s) (Fig. 803) ... **11**

   Separation based on the gall alone is difficult; normally it will have to be opened. If unsure which route to follow, work through both. If larvae or pupae are not present identification cannot be confirmed.

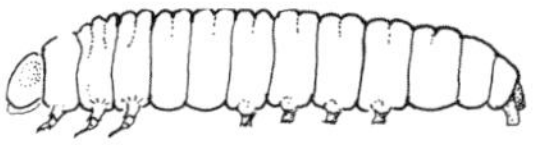

Fig. 800

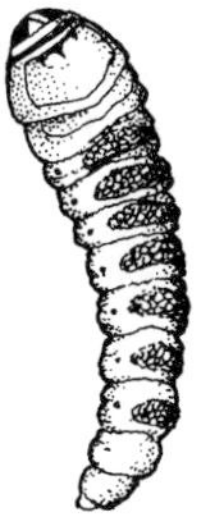

Fig. 801 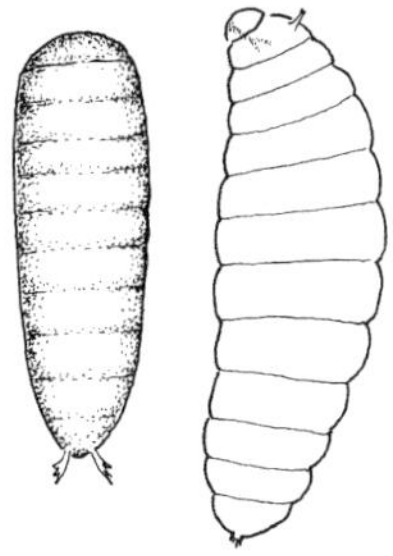   Fig. 802

3 Swelling spindle- or pear-shaped, tapering into twig; one chamber inside with one larva **4**

- Swelling irregular, globular or cylindrical, sometimes several merging (Fig. 804); contains many yellowish or red larvae (Fig. 799), or pupae in winter, in one or in separate chambers: **Diptera: Cecidomyiidae** **7**

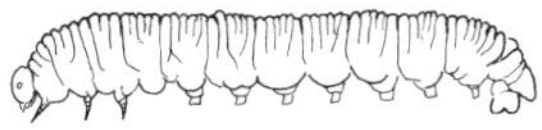

Fig. 803

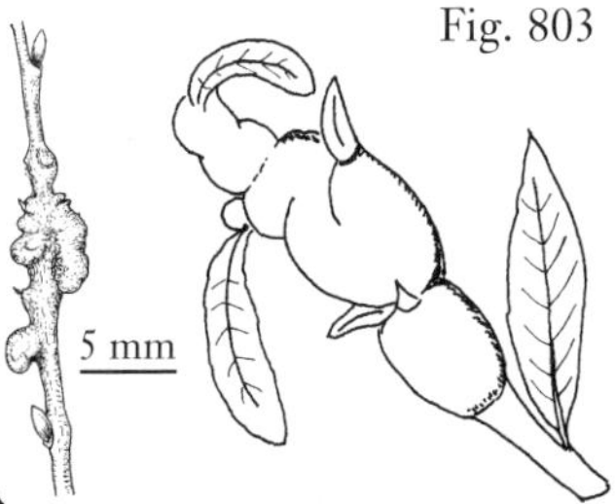

4 Swelling about 3 mm wide, with exit hole, sometimes in a bud (Fig. 805); contains a reddish larva (Fig. 799) or pupa, but no frass; on sallows: **Diptera: Cecidomyiidae** .... ***Rabdophaga karschi*** (Kieffer) (= *oculiperda*)

- Swelling larger, 6 mm wide or more; contains a beetle larva or caterpillar, and frass in elongate chamber **5**

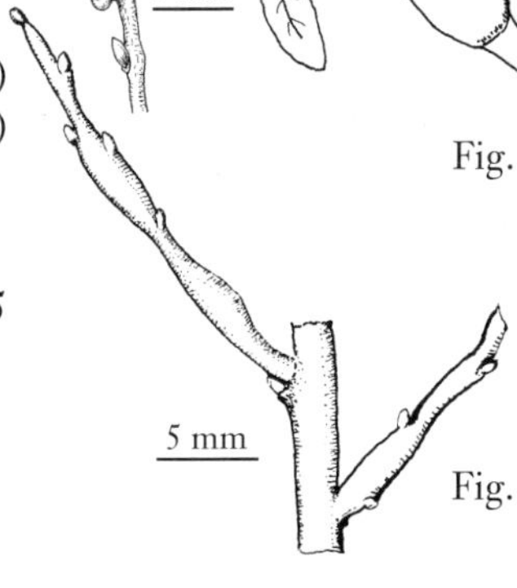

Fig. 804

Fig. 805

5 Swelling in internode (Fig. 806); inside, yellowish beetle larva (Fig. 807) or pupa; S. England, (commoner in *Populus*): **Coleoptera: Cerambycidae**
.... *Saperda populnea* (L.)

- Swelling in node or internode; inside, caterpillar (Fig. 808) in July to early spring, pupa in spring; larva prepares a capped exit hole before pupating **6**

6 Swelling spindle-shaped, 6-8 mm wide (Fig. 809); simple elongate tunnel inside; S. England and Wales, uncommon: **Lepidoptera: Tortricidae**
.... *Cydia servillana* (Duponchel)

- Swelling pear-shaped, >10 mm across at its widest; inside, the straight vertical tunnel leads to a circular horizontal one in thickest part of gall (Fig. 810); S. England, local: **Lepidoptera: Sesiidae**
.... *Synanthedon flaviventris* (Staudinger)
sallow clearwing moth

Gall apparent in second autumn of larval life; discovered in 1926 in Britain and probably under-recorded (Brough, personal communication). For more information, see Baker (1985).

7 Many chambers (occasionally only one) beneath bark or in pith, each with one larva or pupa **8**

- One chamber or several, not clearly separated in pith, with many larvae or pupae; on sallows **10**

8 Irregular gall (Fig. 811) with larval chambers just beneath bark; larvae prepare emergence windows in bark; in *S. fragilis, S. alba*
.... *Rabdophaga saliciperda* (Dufour)
(= *Helicomyia*)

- Globular or cylindrical gall (Fig. 812) with larval chambers deep in pith **9**

9 In *S. repens*, sallows and others (Plate 3.7); widespread and common
....*Rabdophaga salicis* (Schrank)
Occasionally occurs in petiole, see D7, p. 436.

- In *S. purpurea*; mainly northern, uncommon
.... *Rabdophaga degeerii* (Bremi)
(= *ramicola*)

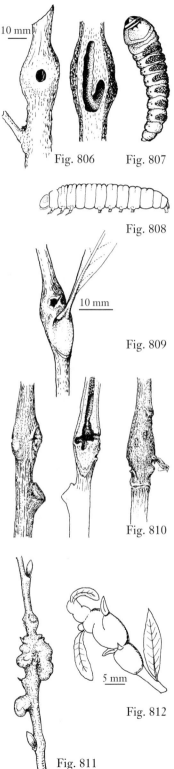

10 mm

Fig. 806   Fig. 807

Fig. 808

10 mm

Fig. 809

Fig. 810

5 mm

Fig. 812

Fig. 811

10 Several chambers running together (Fig. 813); larvae yellowish red; N. England and Scotland, uncommon ....***Rabdophaga dubiosa*** Kieffer

- One large chamber; larvae red
  .... ***Rabdophaga pierreana*** (Kieffer)

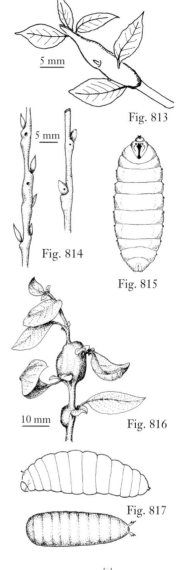

Fig. 813

11 Slight swelling in young twig below a bud, with later emergence hole in bud or stem (Fig. 814); contains one orange-red larva (Fig. 815); on *S. alba*: **Diptera: Cecidomyiidae**
.... ***Rabdophaga albipennis*** (Loew)

- More prominent swelling, at least 8 x 5 mm; contains one larva (not as in Fig. 815) **12**

Fig. 814

Fig. 815

READ THREE ALTERNATIVES
12 A globular swelling (Fig. 816) containing a larva in summer and puparium in winter (Fig. 817); several galls may coalesce round stem; on sallows, rare: **Diptera: Agromyzidae**
.... ***Hexomyza simplicoides*** (Hendel)

- Globular swelling (Fig. 818) the size of a hazelnut or larger, containing one or several sawfly caterpillars (Fig. 818a) or pupae; bark on surface becomes cracked; on *S. pentandra* and possibly other willows; N. England and Scotland: **Hymenoptera: Tenthredinidae** .... ***Euura amerinae*** (L.)

- Elongate swelling with smooth bark tapering into stem (Fig. 819), containing a sawfly caterpillar (Fig. 818a) June onwards, later a pupa (adult emerges the following May - June); on many *Salix* spp.: **Hymenoptera: Tenthredinidae**
  .... ***Euura atra*** (Jurine)

Fig. 816

Fig. 817

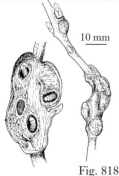

Fig. 818

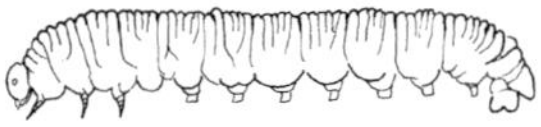

Fig. 818a

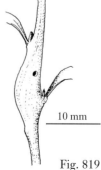

Fig. 819

13 Galls gregarious, exposed by removing bark; larvae prepare emergence windows in bark; position sometimes indicated by depressed lesions where stem is weakened (it may break); most spp. are restricted to a particular *Salix* sp. as follows (the following list is tentative; certain identification requires specialist study):

- In sallows .... ***Rabdophaga pierrei*** (Kieffer)

- In *S. viminalis* .... ***Rabdophaga viminalis*** (Westwood)

- In *S. purpurea*
  .... ***Rabdophaga purpureaperda*** Barnes or ***R. justini*** Barnes, both generations

- In *S. triandra* .... ***Rabdophaga triandraperda*** Barnes

- In *S. repens* .... ***Rabdophaga exsiccans*** Rübsaamen

- In *S. pentandra* .... ***Rabdophaga nielseni*** Kieffer & Nielsen

Salix Key C: Galls in Catkins

Distinct ovoid, downy swelling at base or tip of catkin (Fig. 820); stamens and scales thickened; contains several light red larvae (Fig. 821); on *S. triandra*, common: **Diptera: Cecidomyiidae** .... ***Rabdophaga heterobia*** (Loew) generation 1

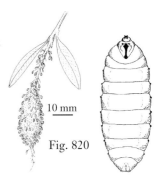

10 mm

Fig. 820

Fig. 821

- Inconspicuous; catkin distorted with thickened rachis containing a larva (Fig. 822) which leaves a brown-edged boring; on willows and sallows, common: **Coleoptera: Curculionidae** ....***Dorytomus taeniatus*** (F.)

The thickening may be wound tissue only, *ie.* not a true gall.

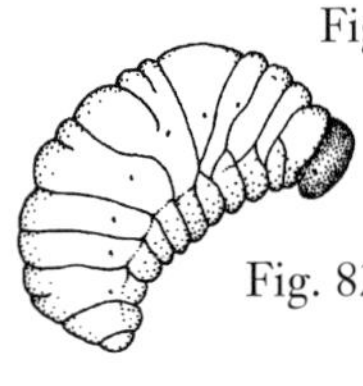

Fig. 822

Salix Key D: Galls in Leaf Blades and Petioles

1 Tight fold or roll of leaf margin, thickened and often distorted **2**

Loose folds or rolls involving the leaf margin or most of the blade, briefly containing a sawfly caterpillar (Fig. 823) in early summer, are not treated here as galls as there is no associated thickening of the leaf. They are caused by species of *Pontania*, subgenus *Phyllocolpa*, **Hymenoptera: Tenthredinidae**.

Fig. 823

- Gall in or on petiole, midrib or blade **5**

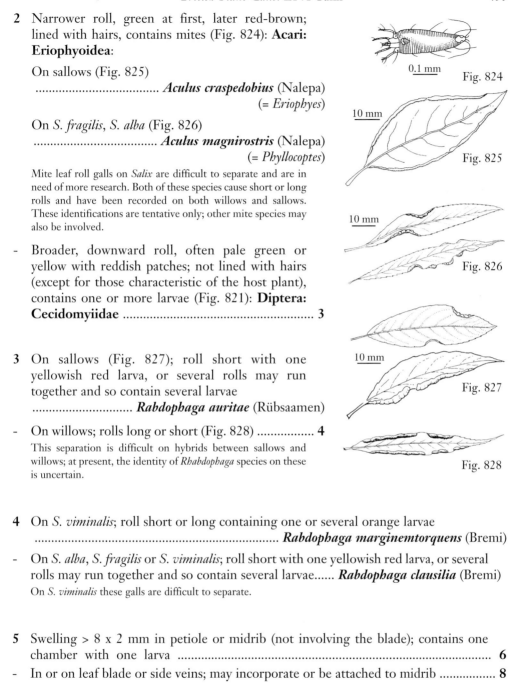

2 Narrower roll, green at first, later red-brown; lined with hairs, contains mites (Fig. 824): **Acari: Eriophyoidea**:

On sallows (Fig. 825)
.... ***Aculus craspedobius*** (Nalepa)
(= *Eriophyes*)

On *S. fragilis, S. alba* (Fig. 826)
.... ***Aculus magnirostris*** (Nalepa)
(= *Phyllocoptes*)

Mite leaf roll galls on *Salix* are difficult to separate and are in need of more research. Both of these species cause short or long rolls and have been recorded on both willows and sallows. These identifications are tentative only; other mite species may also be involved.

0.1 mm   Fig. 824

10 mm   Fig. 825

10 mm   Fig. 826

- Broader, downward roll, often pale green or yellow with reddish patches; not lined with hairs (except for those characteristic of the host plant), contains one or more larvae (Fig. 821): **Diptera: Cecidomyiidae** **3**

3 On sallows (Fig. 827); roll short with one yellowish red larva, or several rolls may run together and so contain several larvae
.... ***Rabdophaga auritae*** (Rübsaamen)

- On willows; rolls long or short (Fig. 828) **4**
This separation is difficult on hybrids between sallows and willows; at present, the identity of *Rhabdophaga* species on these is uncertain.

10 mm   Fig. 827

Fig. 828

4 On *S. viminalis*; roll short or long containing one or several orange larvae
.... ***Rabdophaga marginemtorquens*** (Bremi)

- On *S. alba, S. fragilis* or *S. viminalis*; roll short with one yellowish red larva, or several rolls may run together and so contain several larvae...... ***Rabdophaga clausilia*** (Bremi)
On *S. viminalis* these galls are difficult to separate.

5 Swelling > 8 x 2 mm in petiole or midrib (not involving the blade); contains one chamber with one larva **6**
- In or on leaf blade or side veins; may incorporate or be attached to midrib **8**

6   Gall in petiole, broadest at base (Fig. 829); contains a sawfly caterpillar (Fig. 830) and frass; in N. Britain: **Hymenoptera: Tenthredinidae:**

On sallows .... ***Euura venusta*** (Zaddach)

On *S. viminalis*, rare .... ***Euura laeta*** (Zaddach)

-   Gall in petiole or midrib, ovoid or spindle-shaped.....**7**

7   Spindle-shaped (Fig. 831); contains a sawfly caterpillar (Fig. 830) and frass; on *S. alba*, *S. fragilis*, or *S. triandra*; locally common in N. Britain: **Hymenoptera: Tenthredinidae**
.... ***Euura testaceipes*** (Zaddach & Brischke)

-   Ovoid (Fig. 832); contains an orange or red larva (Fig. 833) or pupa, without frass; on sallows: **Diptera: Cecidomyiidae**
.... ***Rabdophaga salicis*** (Schrank)

R. salicis is more common in stems, see B9, p. 432.

8   Single gall spindle-shaped or irregular, in main or side vein, or a complex of rounded coalesced galls, incorporating midrib, adjacent side veins and blade; each gall contains one larva: **Diptera: Cecidomyiidae** **9**

-   Gall in blade; or on underside attached to midrib or side vein **10**

9   Coalesced group of 2 - 10 hard round galls (Fig. 834); circular, often red-rimmed, openings on underside; larvae white when young, later orange or red; on sallows, widespread and common
.... ***Iteomyia major*** (Kieffer)

This species has been synonymised with *I. capreae*, see couplet 11; this is thought to be an error.

-   Single spindle-shaped or irregular swelling in vein; larva (Fig. 833) orange or red, or pupa present:

On sallows .... ***Rabdophaga nervorum*** (Kieffer)

On *S. purpurea* (Fig. 835)
.... ***Rabdophaga justini*** Barnes generation 2

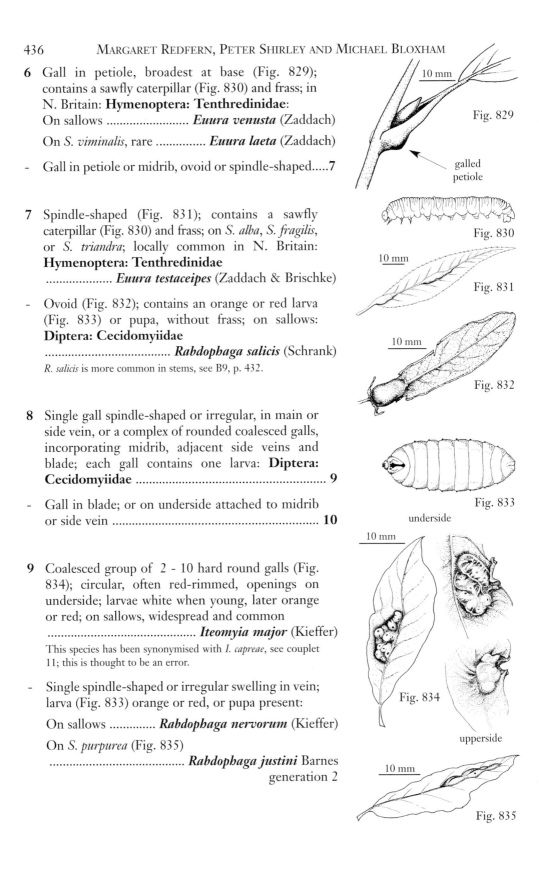

Fig. 829

galled petiole

Fig. 830

10 mm

Fig. 831

10 mm

Fig. 832

Fig. 833

underside

10 mm

Fig. 834

upperside

10 mm

Fig. 835

READ THREE ALTERNATIVES

10 Small dimple on underside, containing a flat nymph bordered with wax; on *S. alba, S. fragilis, S. triandra*; widespread and common: **Hemiptera: Psylloidea** .... ***Trioza albiventris*** Förster

- Small pustule or pouch rounded above, more obvious on underside, 1-3 mm across, with opening below; usually several to many in a leaf; each contains a cecid larva or mites **11**

- Larger, 4 mm or more, globular, ovoid or elongate; one or a few in or on a leaf; contains a sawfly caterpillar (Fig. 830) and frass: **Hymenoptera: Tenthredinidae** **13**

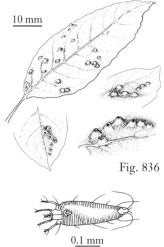

10 mm

Fig. 836

11 Hard pustule domed above and conical below, with a circular, red-rimmed, opening (Fig. 836); greenish, becoming yellow, brown, purple or red; without hairs inside; contains a larva white when young, later orange; on sallows, widespread and common: **Diptera: Cecidomyiidae** .... ***Iteomyia capreae*** (Winnertz)

I. major may be a synonym, see couplet 9.

- Pustule or pouch raised on upper surface, green or reddish, with slit-like opening below; contains hairs and mites (Fig. 837): **Acari: Eriophyoidea** **12**

0.1 mm

Fig. 837

12 Rounded pustule 1-2 mm high (Fig. 838); opening usually below with protruding hairs:

On sallows .... ***Aculus laevis*** (Nalepa)
(= *Eriophyes tetanothrix* f. *laevis*)

On *S. alba* and other willows
.... ***Aculus tetanothrix*** (Nalepa)
(= *Eriophyes*)

- Irregular pouch 2-4 mm high (Fig. 839), projecting below; hairs do not protrude through opening; on sallows .... ***Aceria iteinus*** (Nalepa)
(= *Eriophyes*)

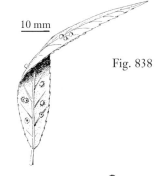

10 mm

Fig. 838

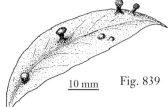

10 mm   Fig. 839

13 Attached to underside of midrib or side vein, with a scar, sometimes on a bulge, on upper surface; green or yellowish, often red-flushed **14**

\-   Within thickness of leaf and apparent on both sides, though may be more prominent on one; green or yellowish, often red or purple later **18**

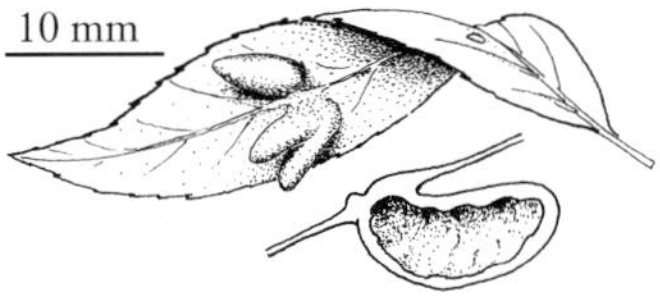

10 mm

Fig. 840

14 Pear-shaped, often with 2 or 3 lobes; about 8 mm long, at an angle to the midrib (Fig. 840); slightly hairy; on *S. myrsinifolia, S. phylicifolia*; northern Britain, uncommon........ ***Pontania arcticornis*** Konow

\-   Globular or ovoid, 4-12 mm across (more if two galls coalesce) **15**

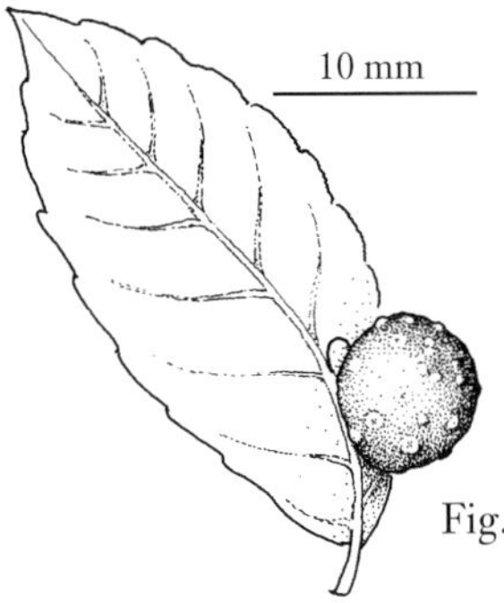

10 mm

Fig. 841

READ THREE ALTERNATIVES

15 On *S. repens*; about 7 mm across, hairless or slightly hairy, covered with small warts (Fig. 841); northern Britain and Ireland, locally common .... ***Pontania collactanea*** (Förster)

\-   On *S. purpurea* (perhaps also on *S. viminalis, S. fragilis, S. lapponum, S. myrsinifolia*); 5-12 mm across, usually hairless, often covered with small warts (Fig. 842), pointed when young (Fig. 843); throughout Britain, locally common .... ***Pontania viminalis*** (L.)

\-   On sallows or *S. phylicifolia*; 4-9 mm across, more or less hairy according to the hairiness of the host plant **16**

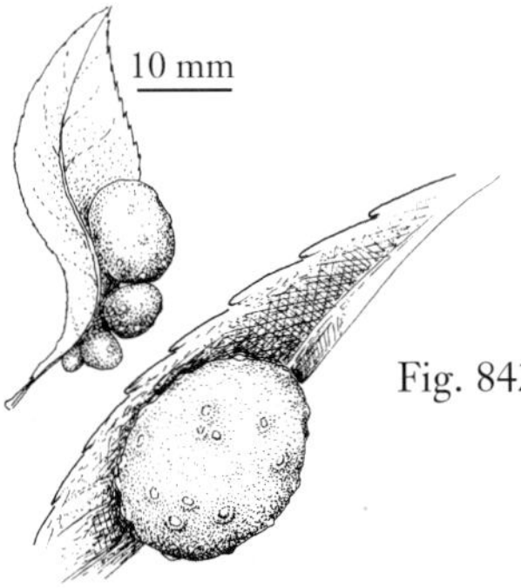

10 mm

Fig. 842

Fig. 843

10 mm

16 Gall larger, usually > 5 mm across; caterpillar grey or brownish grey; on *S. caprea, S. cinerea* or *S aurita*; scarce, commoner in northern Britain .... ***Pontania tuberculata*** Benson

\-   Gall smaller, usually 5 mm or less across; caterpillar yellowish or pale green **17**

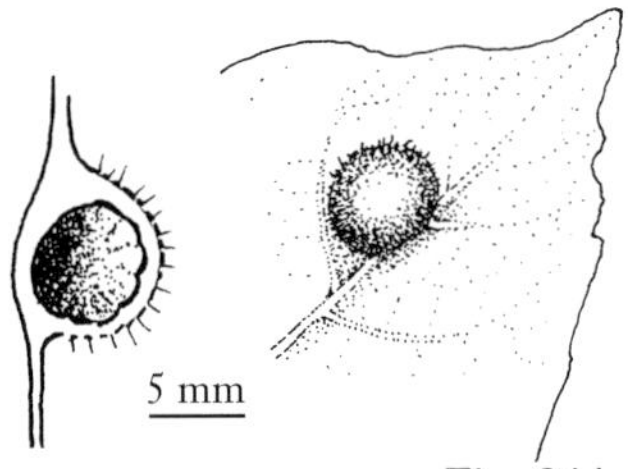

5 mm

Fig. 844

17 Gall rounded:
  On *S. cinerea*; usually not more than 4mm across; scar on upper side ± flush with leaf surface (Fig. 844); caterpillar yellowish green with a brown head; common .... ***Pontania pedunculi*** (Hartig)

  On *S. aurita* (Fig. 845); known only from one Scottish record .... ***Pontania bella*** (Zaddach)

5 mm

Fig. 845

- Gall longer than broad, c. 5 x 4 mm; scar on upper side in a bulge raised c. 1 mm above leaf surface (Fig. 846); caterpillar white with a grey or brown head; on *S. caprea*, probably less common than *P. pedunculi* .... ***Pontania gallarum*** (Hartig)

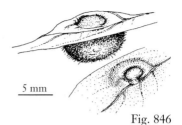

5 mm

Fig. 846

The identifications in couplets 16 and 17 are tentative only, based on Beneš (1968), Kopelke (1991) and Liston (1995). The galls vary considerable in size and shape, and the larvae, too, are difficult to separate (keys to larvae and adults are given in Beneš and Kopelke). On hybrid sallows, identification from the galls alone is not possible. For certain identification of all species, adults should be reared and identified.

18 Globular, 6-10 mm across; on *S. herbacea* (perhaps also on *S. arbuscula*, *S. myrsinites*, *S. lapponum*); N. Britain, uncommon
.... ***Pontania herbaceae*** (Cameron)
(= *crassipes*)

On *S. myrsinites*, projecting more below leaf than above (Fig. 848): *Pontania myrsiniticola* Kopelke.

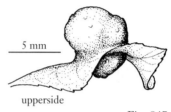

underside

5 mm

upperside

Fig. 847

- Sausage- or bean-shaped, clearly longer than wide...**19**

19 Sausage-shaped, projecting more on upper surface, about 10 x 2 mm, usually paired one each side of midrib (Fig. 848); on *S. myrsinifolia*, *S. phylicifolia* and montane and arctic species; N. Britain, locally common above 350 m
.... ***Pontania dolichura*** (Thomson)

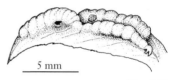

5 mm

Fig. 848

- Bean-shaped, projecting on both sides of leaf, one or several in a leaf **20**

20 Thin-walled, bladder-like, at least 11 x 5 mm, may broaden the leaf blade; on *S. purpurea*, *S. myrsinifolia*, *S. phylicifolia* **21**

- Thick-walled, often hard (but softer after caterpillar has left), about 8 x 4 mm; on *S. alba*, *S. fragilis*, *S. viminalis*, *S. triandra* or sallows **22**

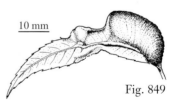

10 mm

Fig. 849

21 On *S. purpurea* and its hybrids (Fig. 849)
.... ***Pontania vesicator*** (Bremi)

- On *S. myrsinifolia*, *S. phylicifolia* (Fig. 850)
.... ***Pontania pustulator*** Forsius

10 mm

Fig. 850

READ THREE ALTERNATIVES

22 On *S. alba, S. fragilis, S. viminalis* (Fig. 851, Plate 7.5); widespread and common
..................................*Pontania proxima* (Lepeletier)

- On *S. triandra* (Fig. 852); locally common
.... *Pontania triandrae* Benson

- On sallows (Fig. 853); widespread and common
.... *Pontania bridgmanii* (Cameron)

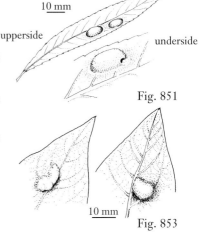

upperside   underside

Fig. 851

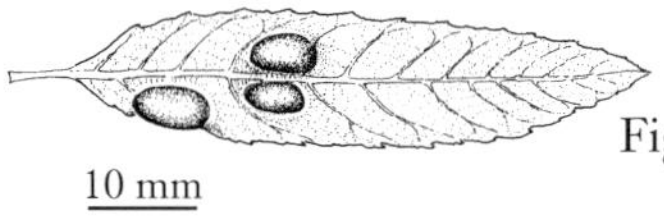

Fig. 852

10 mm

10 mm

Fig. 853

E142. *SALVIA*

One mite gall (**Acari: Eriophyoidea**) has been recorded on *Salvia*, mainly on meadow clary, *S. pratensis* L.

Leaf blade with erineum, usually on underside, with bulge on other side; hairs white at first, later brownish; often several in a leaf; may also affect petiole, stem and flowers; contains mites (Fig. 854); rare .... *Aceria salviae* (Nalepa)
(= *Eriophyes*)

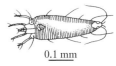

0.1 mm

Fig. 854

E143. *SAMBUCUS*

Two galls are found on elder, *Sambucus nigra* L. Whether the less common dwarf elder, *S. ebulus* L. and the introduced red-berried elder, *S. racemosa* L. are also hosts is not known.

1 Margin of leaflet rolled upwards and slightly thickened, roll 1-5 mm wide, tight or loose, short or extending around most of leaf (Fig. 855); leaf may be creased or buckled and reduced in size; contains mites (Fig. 854): **Acari: Eriophyoidea**
.... *Epitrimerus trilobus* (Nalepa)

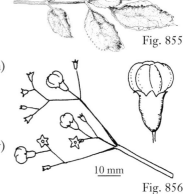

Fig. 855

2 Flower bud swollen, remaining closed, often several affected in an inflorescence (Fig. 856); contains an orange larva (Fig. 857): **Diptera: Cecidomyiidae** .... *Placochela nigripes* (F. Löw)

White larvae of the inquiline cecid *Arnoldiola sambuci* (Kieffer) may also be found in the galls; there are also records of it causing swollen flower buds. Another flower gall on *Sambucus*, caused by *Contarinia sambuci* (Kaltenbach) (Cecidomyiidae), with yellow jumping larvae, is found in mainland Europe. In Britain, however, its host plant is usually *Viburnum*.

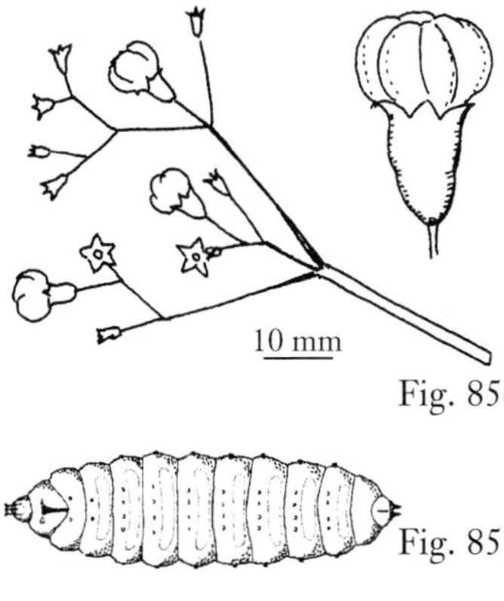

10 mm

Fig. 856

Fig. 857

E144. *SANGUISORBA (= POTERIUM)*

Two galls are found on great burnet, *Sanguisorba officinalis* L. and salad burnet, *S. minor* Scop. (= *Poterium sanguisorba*).

For rust galls on the leaves, see p. 253.

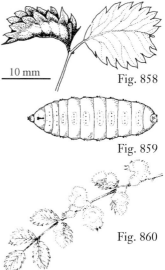

1   Leaflet thickened, folded into a pod (Fig. 858), sometimes several leaflets of a leaf affected; contains many orange-red larvae (Fig. 859); June to autumn; on *S. officinalis* (and *S. minor* abroad): **Diptera: Cecidomyiidae**
.... ***Dasineura sanguisorbae*** (Rübsaamen)
The inquiline *Dasineura peinei* (Rübsaamen) may be present in the pods; its larvae are yellow.

Fig. 858

Fig. 859

Fig. 860

2   Leaves and stems, sometimes also flower buds, covered with thick, yellow-white felt-like erinea (Fig. 860); affected parts often deformed, erinea contain mites (Fig. 854); on *S. officinalis*, *S. minor*: **Acari: Eriophyoidea**
.... ***Aceria sanguisorbae*** (Canestrini)
(= *Eriophyes*)

SAROTHAMNUS see *CYTISUS*

E145. *SAXIFRAGA*

Two galls are recorded, on meadow saxifrage, *S. granulata* L., and yellow saxifrage, *S. aizoides* L.

1   Flower bud swollen, remaining closed, ± reddened; contains several yellow larvae; on *S. granulata*: **Diptera: Cecidomyiidae** .... ***Dasineura saxifragae*** (Kieffer)
Identified from a gall only by Bagnall & Harrison; no subsequent records are known.

2   Shoot tip and flower heads deformed, internodes shortened, abnormally hairy; gall contains mites (Fig. 854); on *S. aizoides*; N.England and Scotland: **Acari: Eriophyoidea** .... ***Aculus kochi*** (Nalepa & Thomas)
(= *Eriophyes*)

E146. *SCABIOSA*

Galls are recorded from the native small scabious, *Scabiosa columbaria* L.

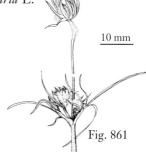

1   Terminal leaves and/or flower head swollen into a dense grey, downy mass, covered with short white hairs (Fig. 861); mites (Fig. 854) live among the hairs: **Acari: Eriophyoidea**
.... ***Aceria squalidus*** (Nalepa)
(= *Eriophyes*)

-    Gall in leaf bud, stem or flower head; contains larvae: **Diptera: Cecidomyiidae** **2**

Fig. 861

2   Leaf bud in rosette or on stem swollen, hairy; contains white (later reddened each end), non-jumping larvae (Fig. 862)
.... *Jaapiella scabiosae* (Kieffer)

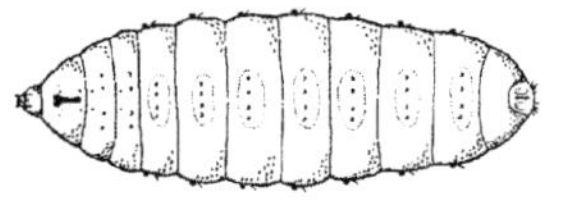

Fig. 862

-   Several florets in a flower head swollen, closed; each with one jumping larva (Fig. 863)
.... *Contarinia scabiosae* Kieffer

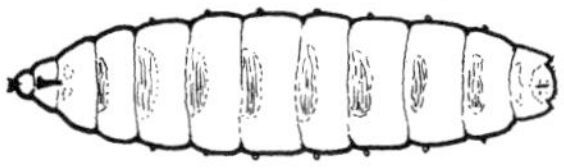

Fig. 863

SCIRPUS see *BOLBOSCHOENUS*

E147. *SCROPHULARIA*

One cecid gall (**Diptera: Cecidomyiidae**) is found in the flowers of common figwort, *Scrophularia nodosa* L. A rust gall is common on stems and leaves (see p. 254).

Flower swollen, remaining closed, often several in an inflorescence affected (Fig. 864); inside are thickened floral parts and several white to citrus-yellow, jumping larvae (Fig. 863)
.... *Contarinia scrophulariae* Kieffer

Asphondylia scrophulariae Tavares may be found in Britain but this is unconfirmed; its gall is similar but lined with fungal mycelia and contains one deep yellow larva. *Gymnetron beccabungae* (L.) (**Coleoptera: Curculionidae**) has been recorded as causing swollen ovaries of *S. nodosa* and *S. auriculata* L. These records need confirming as its normal host plants are *Veronica* spp. (Morris, personal communication.)

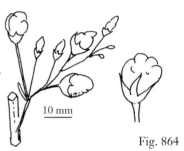

10 mm

Fig. 864

E148. *SCUTELLARIA*

One mite gall (**Acari: Eriophyoidea**) is found on skullcap, *Scutellaria galericulata* L.

Leaf deformed, slightly thickened, margins uprolled, covered with whitish or red-violet hairs; usually several leaves at shoot tip affected; may also affect petioles, stem and flowers; contains mites (Fig. 865); rare
.... *Aculus scutellariae* (Canestrini & Massalongo)
(= *Vasates*)

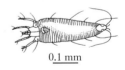

0.1 mm

Fig. 865

SECALE see POACEAE

E149. *SEDUM*

One mite gall (**Acari: Eriophyoidea**) is known on the native roseroot, *S. rosea* (L.) Scop.

Leaves and inflorescence, sometimes whole plant, deformed, with shiny wart-like swellings, up to 2 mm across; contain mites (Fig. 865) .... *Aceria rhodiolae* (Canestrini)

Other mite species may cause galls on other *Sedum* species. Colonies of the aphid *Aphis sedi* Kaltenbach infest young stems, leaves and inflorescences and, if abundant, can cause distortion of shoots. These are not thought to be true galls. The larvae of *Perapion sedi* (Germar) (**Coleoptera: Brentidae: Apioninae**) mines in the stem, petiole or midrib of *Sedum* spp., sometimes causing slight swellings not thought to be true galls. The mine has been studied in detail by Voight (1932). In Britain, local from Cornwall to Norfolk, rare in Wales and Scotland. It also occurs on house-leeks, *Sempervivum* spp.

SEMPERVIVUM see *SEDUM*

E150. *SENECIO*

Senecio is a large genus and most gall inducers are found on several species. The most commonly recorded host plants are common ragwort, *S. jacobaea* L., marsh ragwort, *S. aquaticus* Hill, hoary ragwort, *S. erucifolius* L. and groundsel, *S. vulgaris* L.

For fungi causing galls on stems and leaves, see p. 254.

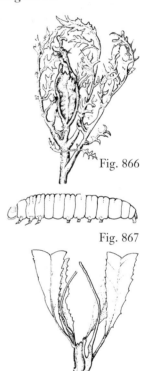

Fig. 866

Fig. 867

Fig. 868

READ THREE ALTERNATIVES
1 Young leaves at tip of main or side shoot deformed, covered with white hairs, and crowded due to shortened internodes (Fig. 866); contains mites (Fig. 865); on *S. jacobaea*; SE England: **Acari: Eriophyoidea** .... *Aceria leioproctus* (Nalepa)
(*= Phytoptus*)

- Irregular swelling in stem, usually near top; leaves crowded due to shortened internodes; tunnel inside contains a caterpillar (Fig. 867) and frass, or a pupa: **Lepidoptera** **2**

- Flower head swollen, with some or all florets aborted **3**

2 In *S. jacobaea*: **Cochylidae**
.... *Cochylis atricapitana* (Stephens)
Bradley *et al.* (1973) describe this species and include a drawing of stem damage caused by the young larva, before the stem gall is apparent.

- In *S. aquaticus* (Fig. 868): **Pterophoridae**
....*Stenoptilia isodactyla* (Zeller)
(*= Platyptilia*)

3   Flower head swollen at base, with bracts broader than normal (Fig. 869); may not open, or may produce some mature florets; contains a white larva (Fig. 870) or brown puparium: **Diptera: Tephritidae** .... *Sphenella marginata* (Fallén)

Larvae of two other tephritids and a muscid may occur in flower heads of *Senecio* spp. without causing galls. *Icterica westermanni* (Meigen) is rare, in SE. England only; *Trupanea stellata* (Fuessly) is more common and infests other composites in mainland Europe. *Phorbia seneciella* Meade (**Muscidae**) produces a cone of froth which dries around a bunch of florets which protrude above the normal florets.

-   Flower head rounded or pear-shaped, up to 15 mm diameter, often closed; bracts normal; contains larvae (Fig. 871), June - September; in *S. jacobaea* and other perennial species: **Diptera: Cecidomyiidae** **4**

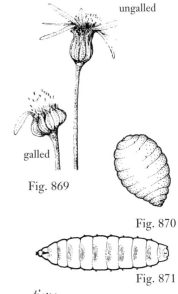

ungalled

galled

Fig. 869

Fig. 870

Fig. 871

4   Young, rounded, usually unopened flower head; one, or a few, yellow to pink larvae; local .... *Contarinia aequalis* Kieffer

-   Older, pear-shaped flower head, often with some mature florets (Fig. 872); creamy white to pale orange, jumping larvae live between aborted achenes and in hollowed receptacle; widespread .... *Contarinia jacobaeae* (Loew)

Other cecids may also gall *Senecio* flower heads.

Fig. 872

10 mm

E151. *SERRATULA*

Two galls are recorded from saw-wort, *Serratula tinctoria* L.; both are rare and poorly known. Fungi may gall the leaves (see under Asteraceae p. 226).

1   Spindle-shaped swelling in leaf petiole or midrib, c. 8 x 3 mm; contains one (or several?) larvae (Fig. 873); S. England: **Diptera: Cecidomyiidae** .... *Loewiola serratulae* Kieffer

2   Swelling and deformation of flower head; contains several (?) larvae (Fig. 874); S. England: **Diptera: Tephritidae** .... *Urophora spoliata* (Haliday)

Mite galls (identity uncertain) similar to those of *Aceria centaureae* on *Centaurea* (Fig. 189, p. 305) may occur on leaves.

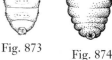

Fig. 873 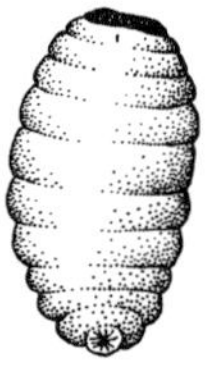   Fig. 874

E152. *SHERARDIA*

There is one species only, field madder, *S. arvensis* L., on which only one gall, caused by a psyllid (**Hemiptera: Psylloidea**), is known. *Sherardia* is closely related to bedstraws, woodruff and squinancywort, *Galium* and *Asperula* species.

Terminal leaves deformed, thickened and bunched together (Fig. 875); contains nymphs; common
.... ***Trioza galii*** Förster
(= *velutina*)

Fig. 875

SILAUM see APIACEAE

E153. *SILENE*

Galls are recorded on four native species in Britain, red campion, *Silene dioica* (L.) Clairv., white campion, *S. latifolia* (Poir.) (= *S. alba*), bladder campion, *S. vulgaris* Garcke and moss campion, *S. acaulis* (L.) Jacq.

1 Gall at shoot tip, leaves in a bunch or an artichoke; whole shoot may be deformed **2**

- Gall in flower bud, or in leaf bud at or below ground surface; contains larva(e): **Diptera: Cecidomyiidae**
.... **4**

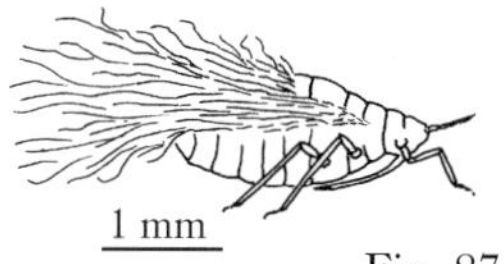

1 mm
Fig. 876

2 Leaves curled, bunched, sometimes affecting basal leaves or whole plant; contain light green woolly aphids covered with white wax (Fig. 876); on *S. vulgaris*: **Hemiptera: Aphididae**
.... ***Brachycolus cucubali*** (Passerini)
(= *Hayhurstia cadiva*)

- Artichoke gall, leaves shorter and broader than normal; contains larva(e): **Diptera: Cecidomyiidae**
.... **3**

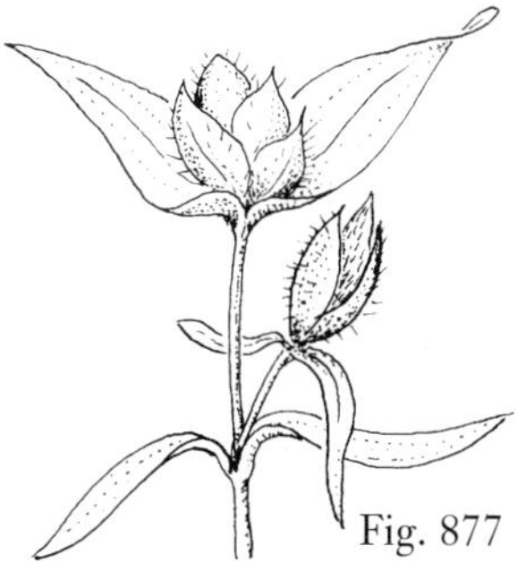

Fig. 877

READ THREE ALTERNATIVES

3 On *S. latifolia*, *S. dioica*; gall hairy (Fig. 877); larvae white, non-jumping
.... ***Neomikiella lychnidis*** (von Heyden)

- On *S. vulgaris*; larva(e) white, jumping (Fig. 871) .... ***Contarinia cucubali*** Kieffer

- On *S. acaulis*; larvae rose-red, non-jumping (Fig. 873) .... ***Jaapiella alpina*** (F. Löw)

4 Underground or ground level bud swollen, up to 5 mm across; with one white larva; on *S. vulgaris* .... ***Dasineura subterranea*** (Kieffer)

Identified in Britain from gall only (Chandler, 1998); needs confirmation by rearing and identifying adult.

- Flower bud swollen and hairy, remaining closed **5**

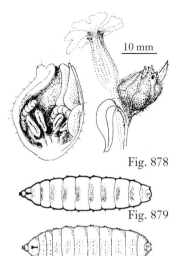

Fig. 878

5 On *S. dioica*, *S. latifolia* (Fig. 878); larvae (Fig. 879) white, later yellow, can jump .... ***Contarinia steini*** (Karsch)

- On *S. vulgaris*; larvae (Fig. 880) yellowish or red, non-jumping .... ***Jaapiella floriperda*** (F. Löw)

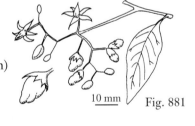

Fig. 879

Fig. 880

SINAPIS see BRASSICACEAE

SISYMBRIUM see BRASSICACEAE

E154. *SOLANUM*

There are two galls found on bittersweet or woody nightshade, *Solanum dulcamara* L. For fungal galls on potato, *S. tuberosum* L., see p. 256.

1 Flower bud swollen, closed, often several affected in an inflorescence (Fig. 881); contains white larvae (Fig. 879); SE. England: **Diptera: Cecidomyiidae** .... ***Contarinia solani*** (Rübsaamen)

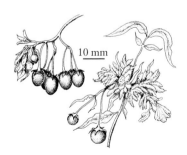

Fig. 881

2 Individual flower, or part or all of inflorescence, greened and leafy (phyllanthy), very hairy (Fig. 882); contains mites (Fig. 883): **Acari: Eriophyoidea** .... ***Aceria cladophthirus*** (Nalepa)
(= *Eriophyes lycopersicae*)

This species has been confused with *Aceria lycopersici* (Wolffenstein) which causes similar damage, normally on tomato *Lycopersicon esculentum* Mill.; separation requires expert identification of the mites (see Amrine & Stasny, 1994).

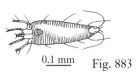

0.1 mm   Fig. 883

Fig. 882

E155. *SOLIDAGO*

Two galls are recorded from goldenrod, *Solidago virgaurea* L. and both are rare. A red-brown aphid, *Uroleucon solidaginis* (F.), may cause folding and crumpling of young leaves; this is thought not to be true gall formation.

1 Spindle-shaped gall in stem, about 1 cm long (Fig. 884); contains a white larva (Fig. 885) or brown puparium; rare: **Diptera: Tephritidae**
.... ***Campiglossa grandinata*** (Rondani)
Old records from Sussex. Found in 1984 at Horsenden Hill, Middlesex.

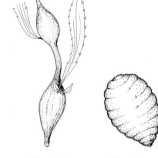

2 Margin of leaf rolled upwards, often affecting terminal leaves; contains larvae (Fig. 880), white when young, later yellow-orange; Cheshire northwards, local: **Diptera: Cecidomyiidae**
.... ***Dasineura virgaeaureae*** (Liebel)

Fig. 884   Fig. 885

E156. *SONCHUS*

Three species are common: perennial sow-thistle, *Sonchus arvensis* L., smooth sow-thistle, *S. oleraceus* L. and prickly sow-thistle, *S. asper* (L.) Hill. The following gall causers, except *Aulacidea follioti*, may be found on any of these hosts.

1 Gall in stem or leaf **2**

- Flower head swollen, remaining closed **4**

2 Circular pustule in leaf, 4-5 mm across, raised 1 mm high on upperside, slightly concave below; pale-coloured, surrounded by a dark purple zone, often several in a leaf (Fig. 886); each contains a pale yellow to pale orange larva (Fig. 880) or pupa; adult emerges from hole on under side in autumn; locally common: **Diptera: Cecidomyiidae**
.... ***Cystiphora sonchi*** (Bremi)
Fungal leaf spots are easily mistaken for this gall.

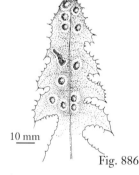

10 mm

Fig. 886

- Swelling in stem; contains yellow-white larva(e) (Fig. 887); central and southern England, rare: **Hymenoptera: Cynipidae** **3**

Fig. 887

3 Swelling distinct, gnarled
.... ***Phanacis sonchi*** (Stephani)
(= *Timaspis*)

- Swelling slight, irregular, often low down on stem
(Fig. 888); on *S. asper*........ ***Aulacidea follioti*** Barbotin

The latter species was first recorded in Britain in Essex in 1993
(Bowdrey, 1999). These two galls are similar; for certain
determination, adults must be reared and identified.

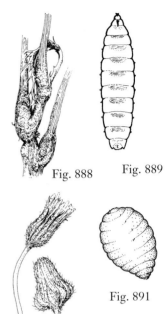

Fig. 888   Fig. 889

4 Head rounded; contains yellow, jumping larvae
(Fig. 889); rare: **Diptera: Cecidomyiidae**
.... ***Contarinia schlechtendaliana*** (Rübsaamen)
(= *sonchi*)

- Head swollen at base (Fig. 890); contains white
larvae (Fig. 891) or brown puparia; S. England and
East Anglia: **Diptera: Tephritidae**
.... ***Tephritis formosa*** (Loew)

Other tephritids may be found in *Sonchus* flower heads; they do
not cause galls.

Fig. 891

Fig. 890

E157. *SORBUS*

The three native British species are frequently galled: rowan or mountain ash, *Sorbus
aucuparia* L., common whitebeam, *S. aria* (L.) Crantz and wild service tree, *S. torminalis* (L.)
Crantz. Exotic species are rarely hosts.

For rust galls on leaves of *S. aucuparia*, see p. 256.

READ THREE ALTERNATIVES

1 Flower bud slightly swollen, remaining closed;
contains light yellow larvae (Fig. 889); on *S.
aucuparia, S. aria*: **Diptera: Cecidomyiidae**
.... ***Contarinia floriperda*** Rübsaamen

Dasineura aucupariae (Kieffer) rarely causes a similar gall on *S.
aucuparia*, with larvae as in Fig. 892. For confirmation adults
should be reared and identified. Dauphin & Aniotsbèhere
(1993, 1997) state that it causes hairy, pleated or folded leaves.

Fig. 892

- Terminal leaves deformed and clustered; aphids
(Fig. 893) present in late spring and early summer:
Hemiptera: Aphididae 2

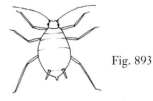

Fig. 893

- Gall in leaf 3

2 On *S. torminalis*; leaves rolled and twisted, yellowish between veins, sometimes reddened; aphids dark brown; rare
.... ***Dysaphis aucupariae*** (Buckton)
(= *Sappaphis*)

- On *S. aucuparia*; leaves crumpled and curled into tight bunches, only slightly yellowed; usually on small side shoots; aphids yellow-green or dark green
.... ***Dysaphis sorbi*** (Kaltenbach)
(= *Sappaphis*)

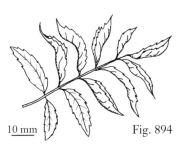

10 mm   Fig. 894

These may not be true galls; other aphids may curl, roll or distort the leaves. To identify the aphids see Blackman & Eastop (1994).

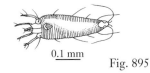

0.1 mm
Fig. 895

3 Leaflet or leaf segment folded along main vein to form a pod, not noticeably thickened (Fig. 894); contains white larvae (Fig. 889); on *S. aucuparia*: **Diptera: Cecidomyiidae**
....*Contarinia sorbi* Kieffer

- Pustule or erineum on blade of leaf or leaflet; contains mites (Fig. 895): **Acari: Eriophyoidea 4**

10 mm

Fig. 896

4 Dense felt-like erineum on under- or upperside of leaflet (Fig. 896); hairs white at first, later yellowish or pink; on *S. aucuparia*; widespread, common in N. England and Scotland, rare in south: .... ***Phyllocoptes sorbeus*** (Nalepa)
(= *Phytoptus* = *Eriophyes*)

- Rounded pustule raised on both surfaces, up to 2 mm across, sometimes coalescing; with opening on upper- or underside, often many on a leaf; light green or yellowish at first, later brown **5**

10 mm   Fig. 897

READ THREE ALTERNATIVES
5 On *S. aucuparia* (Fig. 897)
.... ***Eriophyes sorbi*** (Canestrini)
(= *Phytoptus*)

- On *S. aria* (Fig. 898) .. ***Eriophyes arianus*** (Canestrini)
(= *Phytoptus*)

- On *S. torminalis* .... ***Eriophyes torminalis*** Nalepa
This separation of species is tentative and requires further research (see Spooner & Savage, 1989, Amrine & Stasny, 1994).

Fig. 898

10 mm

E158. *STACHYS*

Most galls are recorded from hedge woundwort, *Stachys sylvatica* L., and betony, *S. officinalis* (L.) Trevis., though other species may also be galled. Three galls are known.

1 Flowers greened, leaflike (chloranthy) and abnormally hairy; contains mites (Fig. 899); on *S. officinalis*; rare: **Acari: Eriophyoidea**
.... *Aceria solidus* (Nalepa)
(= *Eriophyes*)

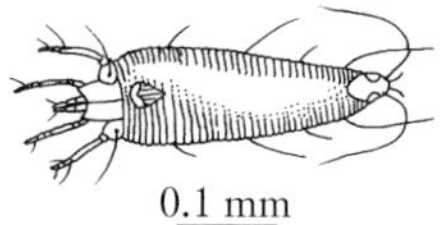

0.1 mm
Fig. 899

2 Leaves at shoot tip curled, thickened, often yellowish; adjacent flower buds closed, with enlarged calyces (Fig. 900), abnormally hairy; contain yellowish orange larvae (Fig. 901); on *S. sylvatica* and other species; England and S. Scotland, local: **Diptera: Cecidomyiidae**
.... *Wachtliella stachydis* (Bremi)

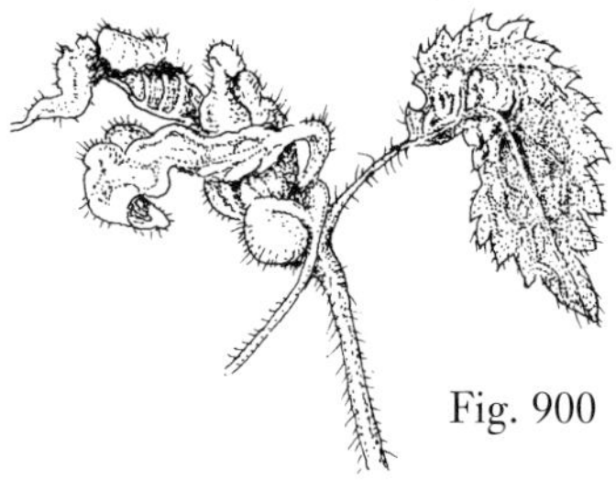

Fig. 900

3 Flower bud swollen, closed, not thickly hairy; contains white jumping larvae; on *S. sylvatica*; N. England, rare: **Diptera: Cecidomyiidae**
.... *Ametrodiplosis crassinerva* (Kieffer)

Larvae of the cecid *Clinodiplosis cilicrus* (Kieffer) (= *betonicae*) may be found in flower buds, which may remain closed and become slightly swollen if numbers are high. Larvae are white or yellowish and non-jumping, and are not thought to be gall causers.

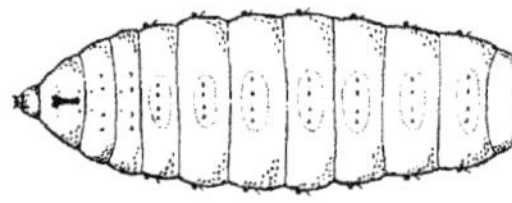

Fig. 901

E159. *STELLARIA*

Galls have been recorded on four native species, common chickweed, *Stellaria media* (L.) Vill., greater stitchwort, *S. holostea* L., lesser stitchwort, *S. graminea* L. and bog stitchwort, *S. uliginosa* Murray.

1 Seed capsule shorter than normal, swollen; contains a white larva (Fig. 901); usually on *S. holostea*: **Diptera: Cecidomyiidae**............................ *Dasineura holosteae* (Kieffer)

- Gall at shoot tip, usually involving two or more leaves **2**

2 Two terminal leaves thickened, with margins pressed together to form a small inconspicuous pouch; contains one or more larvae (Fig. 901): **Diptera: Cecidomyiidae**
.... **3**

- Leaves, especially at and near shoot tip, thickened, margins inrolled upwards, often twisted, distorted, and bunched together **4**

3 On *S. media* (Fig. 902), may be very inconspicuous; larvae white to lemon-yellow; rare
....*Macrolabis stellariae* (Liebel)

- On *S. holostea*; larvae white to creamy-yellow; gall falls soon after larvae have left
.... *Macrolabis holosteae* Rübsaamen

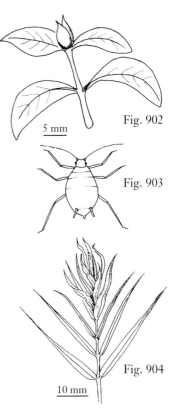

Fig. 902

5 mm

Fig. 903

4 Contain elongated green waxy aphids (Fig. 903); on *S. holostea* (Fig. 904) and *S. graminea*: **Hemiptera: Aphididae**
.... *Brachycolus stellariae* (Hardy)

- Contain mites (Fig. 899); on *S. graminea, S. uliginosa, S.media*: **Acari: Eriophyoidea**
.... *Cecidophyopsis atrichus* (Nalepa)
(= *Eriophyes*)

Fig. 904

10 mm

E160. *SYMPHYTUM*

One cecid gall (**Diptera: Cecidomyiidae**) is found on common comfrey, *S. officinale* L.

Flower bud swollen, remaining closed (Fig. 905), covered in white hairs; often several affected in an inflorescence; contains white or yellowish larvae (Fig. 901); SE England
.... *Dasineura symphyti* (Rübsaamen)

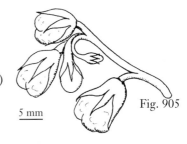

Fig. 905

5 mm

E161. *SYRINGA*

One mite gall (**Acari: Eriophyoidae**) is found on the introduced lilac, *Syringa vulgaris* L.

Bud enlarged; Kent .... *Eriophyes loewi* (Nalepa)
(= *Phytoptus*)

A species found in continental Europe, recorded in Kent (Robbins, personal communication).

E162. *TAMARIX*

One cecid gall (**Diptera: Cecidomyiidae**) is recorded on the introduced tamarisk, *T. gallica* L.

Spindle-shaped swelling in stem, c. 5 x 2 mm (Fig.
906); contains one thick-walled chamber with
several yellow larvae
....................................***Psectrosema tamaricis*** (Stefani)
Recorded in 1922 from Devon and Sussex by Bagnall and
Harrison; no subsequent records.

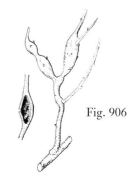

Fig. 906

E163. *TAMUS*

One cecid gall (**Diptera: Cecidomyiidae**) is found on black bryony, *Tamus communis* L.

Flower bud elongated, swollen, remaining closed; chamber lined with fungal
mycelium, contains one larva; widespread .... ***Schizomyia tami*** Kieffer
Identified from gall only (Chandler, 1998); requires confirmation by rearing adults.

E164. *TANACETUM*

There are two British *Tanacetum* species, tansy, *T. vulgare* L. and feverfew, *T. parthenium* (L)
Schultz-Bip. The following galls are recorded from tansy only.

1   Gall ovoid or flask-shaped, hard, about 8 x 5 mm,
    lobed or toothed at apex (Fig. 907, Plate 4.5); pale
    green or purplish; in flower head, leaf axil,
    occasionally on leaf; contains a pink larva (Fig.
    908) or pupa: **Diptera: Cecidomyiidae**
    .... ***Rhopalomyia tanaceticola*** (Karsch)

-   Not like this; gall in achene, leaf, apex of shoot, or
    stem **2**

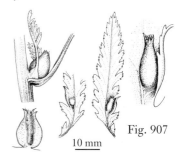

Fig. 907

10 mm

2   Achene swollen to about twice normal size (Fig.
    909), protruding above ungalled neighbours;
    contains an orange larva or pupa: **Diptera:
    Cecidomyiidae** .... ***Ozirhincus tanaceti*** (Kieffer)
    (= *Clinorhyncha*)

-   Gall in stem or leaf, sometimes at shoot apex **3**

Fig. 908

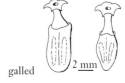

galled   2 mm   normal

Fig. 909

3 Long, slender swelling in stem; internodes may be shortened and shoot above gall stunted; contains a caterpillar (Fig. 910) in June and August - April (2 generations): **Lepidoptera: Pyralidae**
.... ***Phycitodes maritima*** (Tengstrom)
(= *carlinella* = *Homeosoma cretacella*)

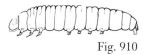

Fig. 910

May not be a true gall.

- Leaf, or several at shoot apex, with tight, slightly thickened, marginal roll, usually upward; shoot may be stunted; roll contains mites (Fig. 911): **Acari: Eriophyoidea**....*Aceria tuberculatus* (Nalepa)

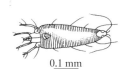

0.1 mm

Fig. 911

A. calathinus (Nalepa) may be found in Britain; it causes a hairy deformation of shoot apex. Several aphid species are common in curled, distorted leaves; they are not thought to be gall causers.

E165. *TARAXACUM*

Dandelions are a variable and difficult group. The genus is divided into eight sections, each with many microspecies whose identification is the job of a specialist. Whether gall causers discriminate between microspecies is not known; no attempt is made here to distinguish between them.

Several fungi infest the leaves, sometimes causing swellings and distortions (p. 257).

1 Swelling in leaf midrib or flower stalk **2**

- Gall in leaf blade, which may be twisted **3**

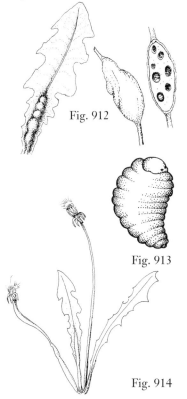

2 Rounded or ovoid, hard, smooth swelling, 2-6 mm across, often several partially or completely fused into a swelling up to 4 cm long (Fig. 912); light green to reddish; individual swellings each with one chamber, or fused galls with several, each containing a white larva (Fig. 913) or pupa; rare: **Hymenoptera: Cynipidae**
.... ***Phanacis taraxaci*** (Ashmead)

- Elongated swelling, causing flower head to abort if in flower stalk (Fig. 914); contains a larva or pupa (Fig. 915): **Diptera: Agromyzidae**
.... ***Phytomyza wahlgreni*** (Hartig)
(= *taraxacocecis*)

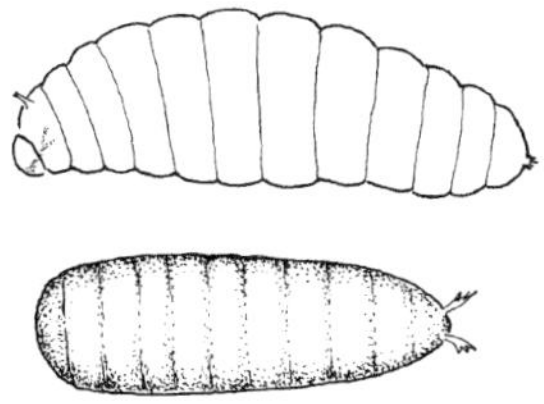

Fig. 912

Fig. 913

Fig. 914

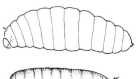

Fig. 915

3 Flat circular blister, up to 5 mm across, usually several in a leaf (Fig. 916); rim of gall becomes dark red or purple; contains a yellow-red larva (Fig. 917); N. England and Scotland **Diptera: Cecidomyiidae** .... *Cystiphora taraxaci* (Kieffer)

-   Narrow upward roll of margin, leaf often twisted; roll may be hairy; contains mites (Fig. 922); rare: **Acari: Eriophyoidea** .... *Aculus rigidus* (Nalepa)
    (= *Phyllocoptes* = *Vasates*)

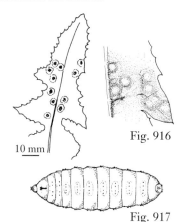

10 mm

Fig. 916

Fig. 917

E166. *TAXUS*

Yew, *Taxus baccata* L., is native in Britain and often bears galls. Several cultivated varieties may also be hosts. Only two gall causers are known in Britain, the first with two forms; both are found in terminal and axillary buds.

1a A tight cluster of leaves forming an artichoke, 1-3 cm tall (Fig. 918, Plate 3.1) sometimes the outer leaves spreading; inner leaves small, pale and delicate, enclosing an orange larva (Fig. 919) or pupa; full-sized gall July, adult emerges following May - June; old galls with brown inner leaves persist on tree; common: **Diptera: Cecidomyiidae** .... *Taxomyia taxi* (Inchbald) **yew gall midge** (2-year life cycle)

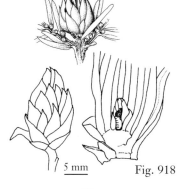

5 mm

Fig. 918

1b An enlarged bud < 6 mm tall, composed of relatively few leaves (Fig. 920), enclosing an orange larva (Fig. 919) or pupa; full-sized gall April, adult emerges May - June of same year; uncommon .... *Taxomyia taxi* (Inchbald) (1-year life cycle)

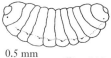

0.5 mm

Fig. 919

2 An enlarged distorted bud 3-10 mm tall, with inner leaves fleshy and thickened (Fig. 921), covered with mites (Fig. 922); full-sized gall May - July; locally common: **Acari: Eriophyoidea** .... *Cecidophyopsis psilaspis* (Nalepa)

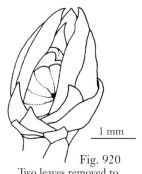

1 mm

Fig. 920
Two leaves removed to show larva inside

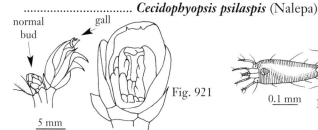

normal bud

gall

Fig. 921

5 mm

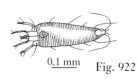

0.1 mm   Fig. 922

E167. *TEUCRIUM*

Two rare galls are known in Britain, from wood sage, *Teucrium scorodonia* L., and the very rare wall germander, *T. chamaedrys* L. A rust gall is common on leaves of wood sage (see p. 258).

1   Buds at tip of main or side shoot deformed, surrounded by crowded, hairy, slightly thickened leaves; contain one or more orange-red larvae (Fig. 917); on *T. scorodonia* (and other species abroad); S. England: **Diptera: Cecidomyiidae**
.... ***Dasineura teucrii*** (Tavares)

2   Margins of leaf rolled downwards, thickened, yellowed and abnormally hairy inside and out (Fig. 923); contain mites (Fig. 922); on *T. chamaedrys*; SE England: **Acari: Eriophyoidea**
.... ***Aculus teucrii*** (Nalepa)
(= *Phyllocoptes* = *Vasates*)

Fig. 923

E168. *THALICTRUM*

Two cecid galls (**Diptera: Cecidomyiidae**) are recorded from common meadow-rue, *Thalictrum flavum* L., and lesser meadow-rue, *T. minus* L.; they contain larvae as in Fig. 917. For smut and rust galls on stems and leaves, see p. 258.

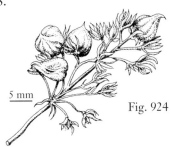

1   Small, hairy leaves bunched at shoot tip, c. 1 cm high; or flower bud swollen, remaining closed; both contain shiny red larvae
.................................***Jaapiella thalictri*** (Rübsaamen)

2   Fruit swollen, egg-shaped, ribbed and pointed, up to 5 mm across (Fig. 924); contains 1 or 2 yellow larvae .... ***Ametrodiplosis thalictricola*** (Rübsaamen)

5 mm

Fig. 924

THLASPI see BRASSICACEAE

E169. *THYMUS*

Most galls are found on wild thyme, *Thymus polytrichus* A. Kern. ex Borbás.

READ THREE ALTERNATIVES

1   Swelling in stem, 1-4 x 2 mm (Fig. 925); one chamber
    with pale yellow larva (Fig. 926) or pupa; England
    and Wales as far north as Chester, SE Yorkshire;
    common: **Coleoptera: Brentidae: Apioninae**
    .... ***Squamapion atomarium*** (Kirby)
    (= *Thymapion*)

-   Flowers ± swollen or stunted and deformed, remaining
    closed; gall may include bracts below flowers; contain
    a larva or pupa: **Diptera: Cecidomyiidae** **2**

-   Gall formed from leaves at tip of shoot, sometimes
    incorporating flower buds **3**

Fig. 925

5 mm

Fig. 926

2   Flowers swollen, not involving the bracts; gall
    chamber lined with fungal mycelium; larva (Fig.
    927) red; N. England .... ***Asphondylia serpylli*** Kieffer

-   Bracts enclose galled flowers, which are stunted
    and deformed; gall chamber without mycelium;
    larva (Fig. 928) reddish yellow; N. England, S.
    Scotland .... ***Janetiella thymi*** (Kieffer)
    Also forms a shoot tip gall, couplet 3.

Fig. 927   Fig. 928

3   Gall small, up to 5 mm tall; formed from the last
    two pairs of leaves, which are short, thickened, not
    abnormally hairy (Fig. 929); yellow-green or
    reddish; inner pair encloses the chamber
    containing reddish yellow larva (Fig. 928) or pupa;
    widespread but commoner in N. England, S.
    Scotland: **Diptera: Cecidomyiidae**
    .... ***Janetiella thymi*** (Kieffer)
    Also galls flowers, couplet 2.

-   Gall larger, at least 10 mm across; a rosette of
    many leaves covered with white cotton wool-like
    hairs **4**

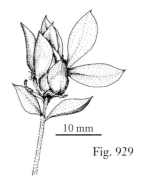

10 mm

Fig. 929

4 Rosette ± spherical, up to 10 mm across (Fig. 930); mites (Fig. 931) live amongst the long white hairs; summer and autumn; common: **Acari:Eriophyoidea** .... ***Aceria thomasi*** (Nalepa)
(= *Eriophyes*)

- Rosette up to 20 x 15 mm (Fig. 932); contains red larvae (Fig. 928) throughout the summer; English midlands northwards, common in Scotland: **Diptera: Cecidomyiidae** .... ***Bayeriola thymicola*** (Kieffer)
(= *Bayeria*)

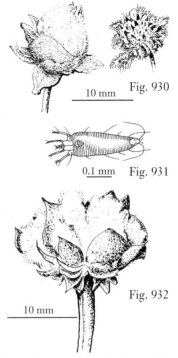

Fig. 930

0.1 mm   Fig. 931

Fig. 932

E170. *TILIA*

There are three species, all probably native and widely planted: small-leaved lime, *Tilia cordata* Mill., large-leaved lime, *T. platyphyllos* Scop., and common lime, *T.* x *europaea* Hayne, the hybrid between them. Unless stated otherwise, the following species cause galls on all three.

READ THREE ALTERNATIVES

1 Tip of shoot distorted, with terminal leaves rolled and curled round each other to form a leaf nest; contains woolly aphids (Fig. 933): **Hemiptera: Aphididae: Pemphiginae** .... ***Patchiella reaumuri*** (Kaltenbach)
(= *Schizoneura*)

If no evidence of aphids present, try couplet 11.

- Hard globular swelling 2-15 mm across, in petiole, flower stalk or young stem (Fig. 934), occasionally in bud or extending into midrib or in main vein of bracteole (Fig. 935); pale-coloured, becoming green, often reddened; contains one to many chambers each with a lemon-yellow larva (Fig. 936): **Diptera: Cecidomyiidae** .... ***Contarinia tiliarum*** (Kieffer)

Small galls are easily overlooked, see Fig. 934, arrowed.

- Gall on or in leaf blade or bracteole; often several on leaf **2**

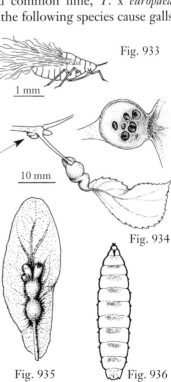

Fig. 933

1 mm

10 mm

Fig. 934

Fig. 935   Fig. 936

READ THREE ALTERNATIVES

2   Woody swelling or blister in leaf blade, raised on both sides, without hairs; contains a larva: **Diptera: Cecidomyiidae** 3

-   Pouch gall, hairy bump or erineum (hairs may be very short) on leaf blade or bracteole; contains mites (Fig. 937): **Acari: Eriophyoidea** 4

-   Margin of leaf or bracteole rolled and thickened; or young leaves of new shoot stunted and crinkled ..**11**

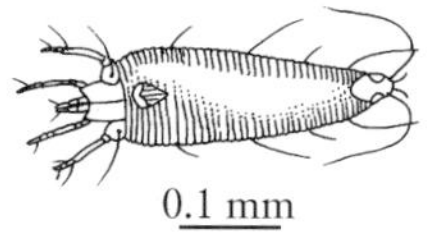

3   Woody swelling, conical on upperside, about 6 x 4 mm, hemispherical below raised about 2 mm (Figs 938, 939), sometimes reversed; in midsummer, a cylindrical inner gall containing a bright yellow larva, protrudes from cone (Fig. 939), which later falls to the ground leaving a hole in the outer gall which is gradually covered over .... ***Didymomyia tiliacea*** (Bremi) (= *reaumuriana*)

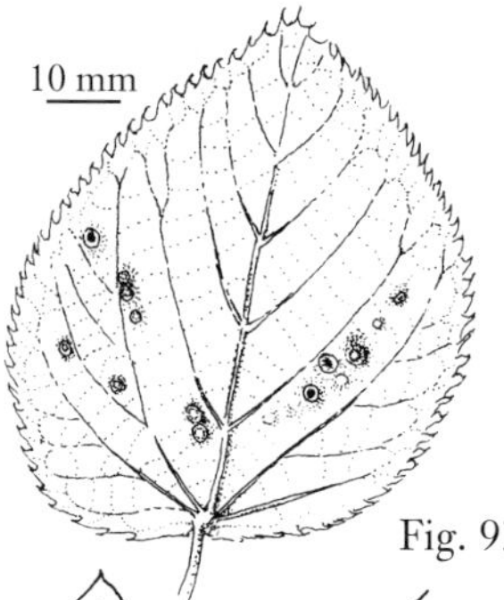

-   Slightly raised rounded blister (Fig. 940) turning brown after larva has left; larva white ....***Physemocecis hartigi*** (Liebel)

4   Pouch gall or hairy bump 1-15 mm high, usually on upperside of leaf blade, with small, often hairy, opening below 5

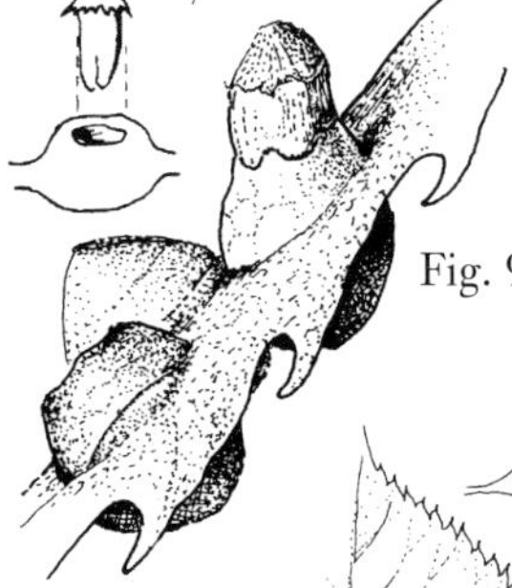

-   Erineum on or between veins, often with a raised bulge on other side 9

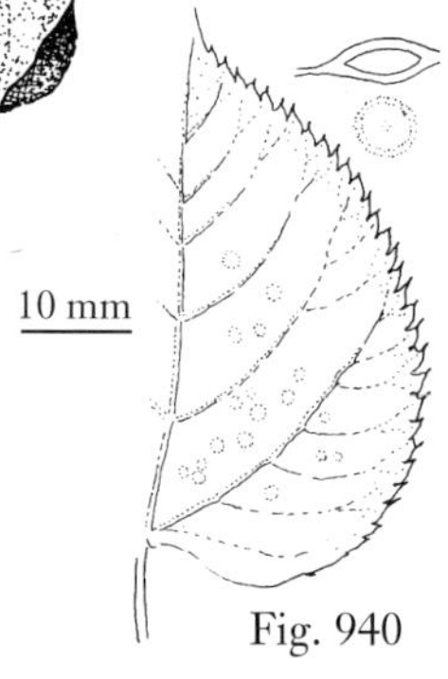

5   In angle of veins; a hairy hemispherical bump raised 2-3 mm on upperside, a hairy swelling below (Fig. 941); hairs white, later brown .... ***Eriophyes exilis*** (Nalepa) (= *Aceria*)

-   Club-shaped or elongate pouch on blade, not on main veins, often reddened 6

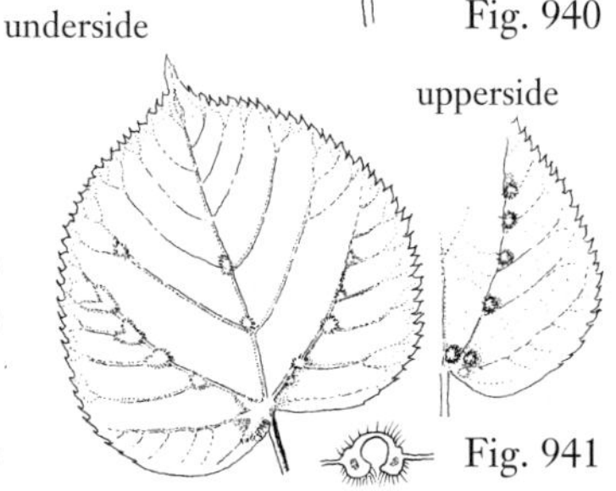

6   Pouch 1-3 mm tall, with rounded apex, with long hairs on outside particularly at base, not hairy inside (Fig. 942) 7

-   Pouch 5-15 mm tall, elongate, tapering to the tip, hairless or with short hairs on outside, hairy inside; common, **nail galls** 8

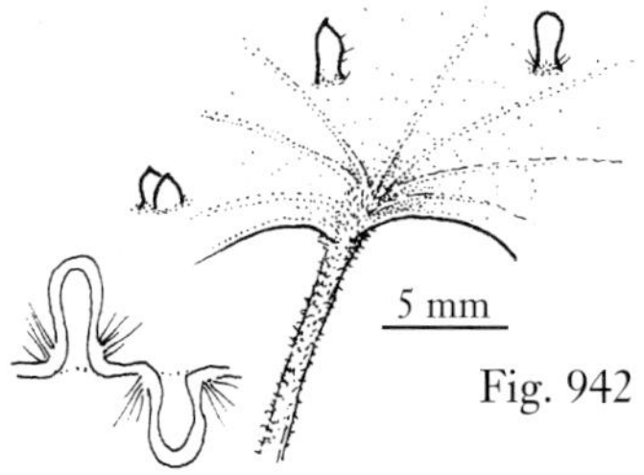

0.1 mm   Fig. 937

10 mm

Fig. 938

Fig. 939

10 mm

underside   Fig. 940

upperside

Fig. 941

5 mm

Fig. 942

7 Aperture rounded .... ***Phytoptus bursarius*** (Nalepa)

- Aperture a narrow slit.. ***Phytoptus stenoporus*** (Nalepa)

This description of the gall of *P. stenoporus* is based on Buhr (1964-65) and Dauphin & Aniotsbehère (1997); Coulianos & Holmåsen (1991) and Amrine & Stasny (1994), however, state that it causes wart-like bulges and curling of leaf margins.

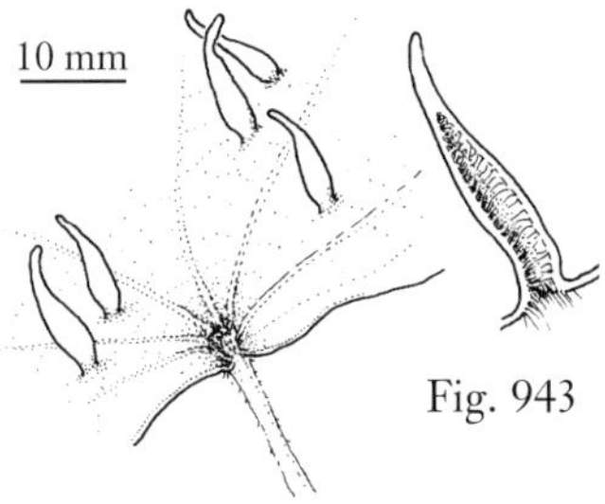

10 mm

8 On *T. platyphyllos*; galls usually > 8 mm tall, with pointed tips (Fig. 943, Plate 1.7)
.... ***Eriophyes tiliae*** (Pagenstecher)
(= *Phytoptus*)

Fig. 943

- On *T. cordata*; galls c. 5 mm tall, with rounded tips
.... ***Aceria lateannulatus*** Schulze
Both galls occur on the hybrid *T.* x *europaea*.   (= *Phytoptus*)

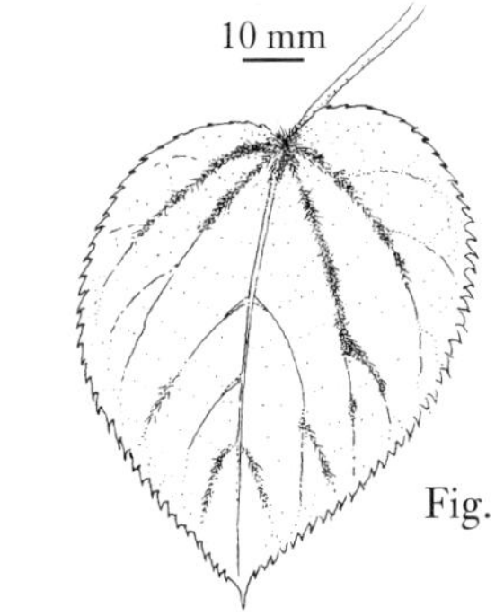

10 mm

9 Erineum along slightly thickened veins, usually on upperside (Fig. 944); hairs short and thick, white at first, later red or brown ...... ***Eriophyes nervalis*** Nalepa
(= *Phytoptus*)

- Erineum between veins, on upper- or underside, with a bulge or discoloured patch on other side; hairs transparent or white at first, later reddish or brown.. **10**

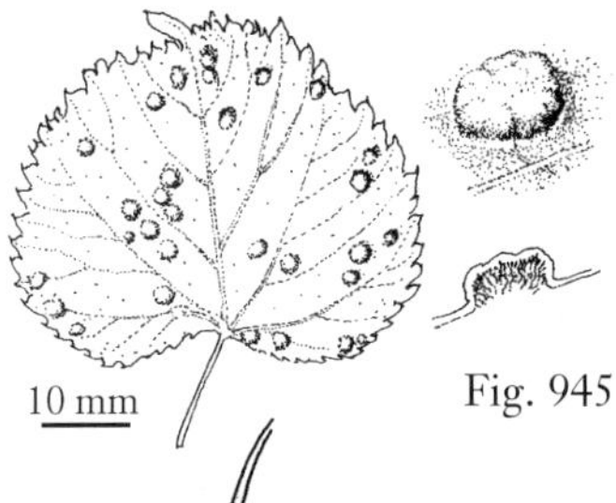

Fig. 944

10 Upward bulge distinct, up to 5 mm across (Fig. 945); hairs of erineum slender and tapering to a point .... ***Phytoptus abnormis*** (Nalepa)

- Upward bulge usually less distinct, sometimes merely a discoloured patch, usually > 5 mm across; hairs of erineum enlarged with rounded tips
.... ***Eriophyes leiosoma*** (Nalepa)
(= *Phytoptus*)
This section on mite galls is tentative only; the identity of the mites needs to be verified.

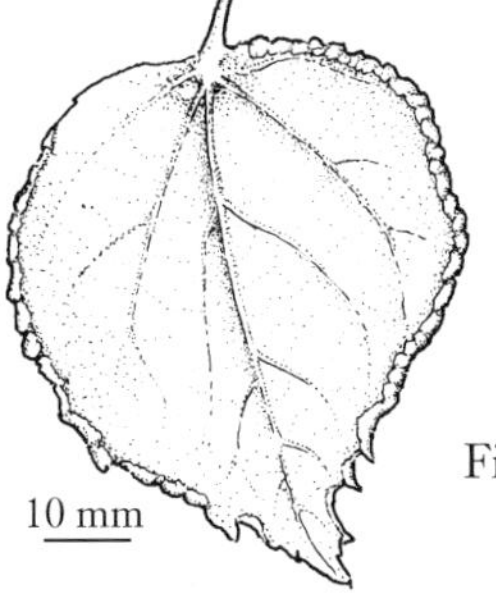

10 mm   Fig. 945

11 Narrow roll, usually downward, 1 - 2 mm wide, short or long (Fig. 946), may affect whole margin; inside hairy, with mites (Fig. 937): **Acari: Eriophyoidea**
.... ***Phytoptus tetratrichus*** (Nalepa)
(= *Phytocoptella*)

Fig. 946

- Roll less narrow, usually upward; rolls may affect whole blade of young leaf, or young leaves may be crinkled, distorted and bunched together; inside without hairs, with larvae (Fig. 947): **Diptera: Cecidomyiidae** **12**
NB See note overleaf

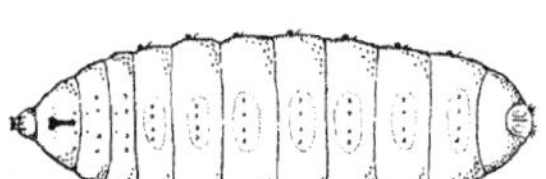

10 mm

Fig. 947

Rolled part of leaf margin may be mined by a sawfly, *Parna tenella* (Klug) (**Hymenoptera: Tenthredinidae**). Mines (not galls) appear in June, each containing one whitish larva until early July, after which the mines dry up and turn brown (Halstead, personal communication).

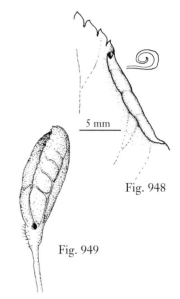

Fig. 948

12 Roll on edge of mature leaf (Fig. 948) or bracteole; larvae yellowish red, May - June
.... ***Dasineura tiliae*** (Schrank)
(= *tiliamvolvens*)

- Young terminal leaf rolled (Fig. 949), or crinkled and distorted with thickened veins; often shoot stunted with several affected leaves close together; larvae white at first, later pale orange-red, present briefly in early June (may be a second generation in late July) .... ***Dasineura thomasiana*** (Kieffer)

Fig. 949

E171. *TRAGOPOGON*

There are two galls on *Tragopogon*; they are most likely to be found on goat's-beard or Jack-go-to-bed-at-noon, *T. pratensis* L.
   Fungi may gall the shoots, see p. 259.

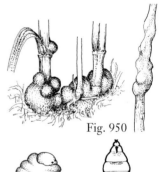

Fig. 950

1   Rounded swelling in stem, usually near base, or in root, often several partly coalescing (Fig. 950, Plate 5.3); also causes an elongated flower head; each swelling contains a chamber with a white larva (Fig. 951) or pupa; locally common: **Hymenoptera: Cynipidae**
.... ***Aulacidea tragopogonis*** (Thomson)
(= *pigeoti*)

2   Flower head swollen at base, remaining closed; contains several yellow or white larvae (Fig. 952) which jump, or pupae: **Diptera: Cecidomyiidae**
.... ***Contarinia tragopogonis*** Kieffer

Aphids may deform, crinkle or fold leaves; they are not gall causers.

Fig. 951

Fig. 952

E172. *TRIFOLIUM*

This is a large genus whose galls are not well known. Galls are usually recorded on related species as follows:

LOTOIDEA: white clover, *T. repens* L., alsike clover, *T. hybridum* L.
VESICARIA: strawberry clover, *T. fragiferum* L.
CHRONOSEMIUM: large trefoil, *T. aureum* Pollich, hop trefoil, *T. campestre* Schreb., lesser trefoil, *T. dubium* Sibth.

TRIFOLIUM: red clover, *T. pratense* L., zigzag clover, *T. medium* L., hare's-foot clover, *T. arvense* L.

Nodules caused by *Rhizobium* species are common on roots, a phytoplasma causes phyllody of shoots, and rusts are common on the leaves (see pp. 219, 259).

1 Gall a swelling in root or stem; chamber inside with a yellowish white larva (Fig. 953) or pupa: **Coleoptera: Brentidae: Apioninae** **2**

Catapion (= *Apion*) spp. on *Trifolium* are not well known; this section of the key is preliminary only.

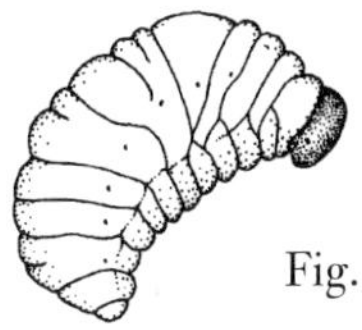

Fig. 953

- Gall in leaflet, bud or flower head **4**

2 Swelling 6 x 3 mm in root collar or root; on *T. fragiferum* and, probably, *T. repens*; coasts of South England, rare .... ***Catapion curtisii*** (Stephens)

- Swelling in stem, up to 6 x 3 mm or twice thickness of normal stem **3**

3 On *T. campestre*, *T. aureum*, *T. dubium*; Yorkshire, Westmorland southwards, locally common .... ***Catapion pubescens*** (Kirby)

- On *T. pratense*; common in S. England, rare north to S. Scotland .... ***Catapion seniculus*** (Kirby)

4 Leaflet swollen, folded upwards along midrib into a pod (Fig. 954); contains one or a few white, later orange larvae (Fig. 955) or pupae; common on *T. repens*, occasionally found on other species: **Diptera: Cecidomyiidae**
.... ***Dasineura trifolii*** (F. Löw)

Fig. 954

10 mm

This species was first described in Britain on *T. pratense* (Harris, personal communication). The mite, *Aceria trifolii*, which normally causes chloranthy of flower parts (couplet 6), may roll or fold margins of leaflets.

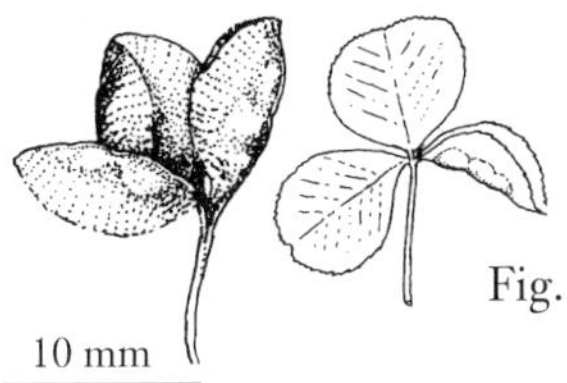

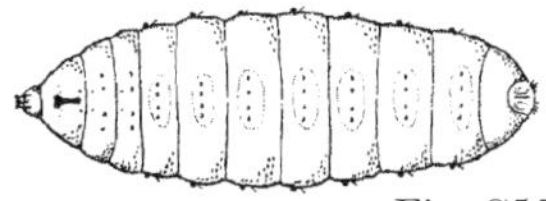

Fig. 955

- In bud or flower head **5**

5 Axillary bud enclosed by swollen stipules; contains a red larva (Fig. 955); on *T. fragiferum*, *T. medium*: **Diptera: Cecidomyiidae** .... ***Dasineura axillaris*** Kieffer

- Flower head misformed, sometimes flower parts green and leafy (chloranthy) **6**

6 Flower head rounded or cylindrical (Fig. 956), firm to touch; individual flowers have enlarged calyces and fail to set seed; contains many white, later pink, larvae (Fig. 957) or pupae in summer and early autumn; on *T. pratense*, *T. arvense*: **Diptera: Cecidomyiidae**
.... ***Dasineura leguminicola*** (Lintner)

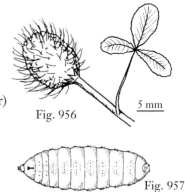

Fig. 956

5 mm

Non-galling cecid larvae may also occur in flower heads. Several Apioninae weevils are also recorded in flower heads with larvae as in Fig. 960, though they may not cause true galls: *Protapion laevicolle* (Kirby) on *T. repens*, *P. varipes* (Germar) and *P. apricans* (Herbst) on *T. pratense*. For firm identification rear adult and identify in Morris, 1990, or Gønget, 1997.

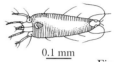

Fig. 957

- Flower parts greened and leafy (chloranthy); contain mites (Fig. 958): **Acari: Eriophyoidea**
.... ***Aceria trifolii*** (Nalepa)
(= *Eriophyes*)

0.1 mm

Fig. 958

Can be confused with phyllody caused by a phytoplasma, see Fig. 4, p. 219; certain identification requires microscopical examination. This mite may also cause inrolling of leaflet margins (see couplet 4).

TRIPLEUROSPERMUM see *ANTHEMIS*

TRITICUM see POACEAE

E173. *ULEX*

There are three species, common gorse, *Ulex europaeus* L., western gorse, *U. gallii* Planch. and dwarf gorse (or furze), *U. minor* Roth. Galls have rarely been recorded on western gorse; whether this species is an uncommon host or its galls have been overlooked is not known.

Root galls caused by *Rhizobium* species are common, see p. 218.

1 Ovoid swelling in stem, up to 10 x 6 mm (Fig. 959, Plate 7.8), particularly in young stem; inside thick-walled chamber contains a larva (Fig. 960) or pupa; common on *U. minor*, uncommon on *U. europaeus*, *U. gallii*: **Coleoptera: Brentidae: Apioninae**
.... ***Eutrichapion scutellare*** (Kirby)
(= *Apion*)

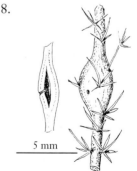

5 mm

Fig. 959

- Leaf or flower bud slightly swollen, sometimes hairy; or transformed into an artichoke gall; contains one or more larvae: **Diptera: Cecidomyiidae** **2**

A mite, *Aceria genistae* (Nalepa) (**Acari: Eriophyoidea**), has been recorded on *U. europaeus* and *U. minor* in continental Europe, but not yet in Britain. Here it is found on *CYTISUS* and *GENISTA*. Its gall is a mass of miniature, hairy leaves forming an enlarged bud with a bumpy, irregular surface (see Figs 263, 346), containing mites.

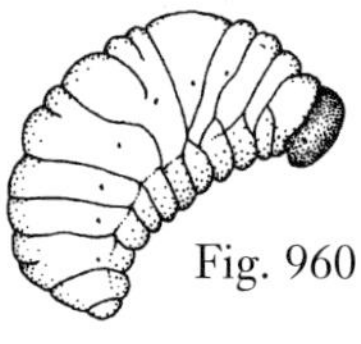

Fig. 960

2 Artichoke gall up to 5mm long, usually at shoot tip; one larva (Fig. 957); on *U. europaeus*; uncommon
.... **Dasineura ulicis** (Kieffer)

- Bud slightly enlarged; usually lateral buds affected... **3**

3 Gall hairy (Fig. 961), with a large cavity lined with fungal mycelium, white at first, later black; contains a pale orange-yellow larva (Fig. 962); on *U. europaeus*, more common in N. Britain
.... **Asphondylia ulicis** Trail

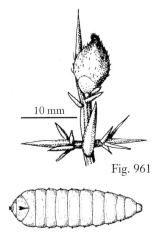

10 mm

Fig. 961

- Unopened flower slightly swollen, contains many pinkish larvae (Fig. 957); on *U. europaeus*; S. England; rare ....**Dasineura gallica** (Kieffer)

Fig. 962

E174. *ULMUS*

This is a difficult genus to identify to species. Stace (1997) recognises four species, but instructs that for identification, only leaves on the middle of short shoots in high summer should be used. Leaves on suckers, long shoots, epicormic growth and lammas growth should be ignored. The four species are: wych elm, *Ulmus glabra* Hudson, English elm, *U. procera* Salisb., *U. minor* Miller (various English names) and Plot's elm, *U. plotii* Druce.

Galls on wych elm are distinguished from those on other (small-leaved) species and their hybrids. Some pemphigid galls are similar in form especially when young; their aphids should be identified for confirmation.

1 Gall on young root; rounded nodules about 2 mm across, which may run together:
Hemiptera: Aphididae: Pemphiginae .... **Mimeuria ulmiphila** (del Guercio)
The nodules are formed from mycorrhizal fungal hyphae, see Blackman & Eastop (1994); they may not, therefore, be true galls.

- Gall on leaf or shoot **2**

2 Most or all of leaf distorted into a bladder, or leaf inrolled from margin affecting edge only or most of blade, thickened and often discoloured; contains aphids (Fig. 963) often with woolly wax and honeydew: **Hemiptera: Aphididae: Pemphiginae** **3**

1 mm

Fig. 963

- Gall a pouch, dimple, blister or pock on leaf; contains aphids, mites or a cecid larva **7**
Certain identification of aphid galls usually requires the aphids to be present, see Heie (1980).

3 Most or all of leaf forming a large bladder, 3-8 cm across (Fig. 964); pale green with waxy aphids in July and August, later brown and dry, persisting after leaf fall; usually on small-leaved elms .... ***Eriosoma lanuginosum*** Hartig

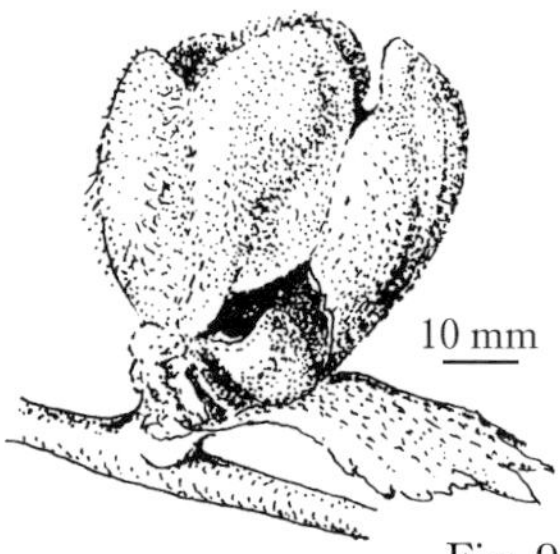

- Margins or sides of leaf inrolled downwards, affected leaves may seem bunched together; aphids present May - August **4**

4 Both sides of leaf inrolled, affecting most of leaf blade or margin only; may be only slightly thickened **5**

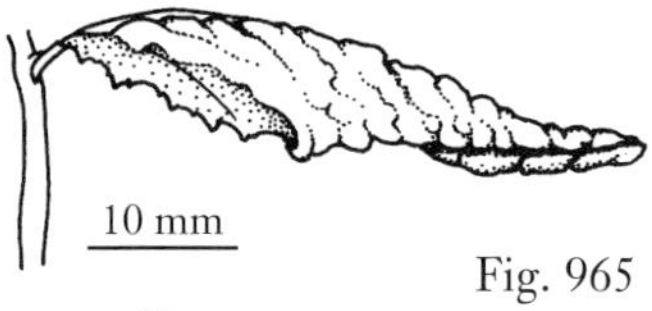

- One side of leaf inrolled and thickened, affecting all or part of blade **6**

5 Rolls affecting most of blade (Fig. 965); rose red on young trees and suckers, yellow or pale green on older branches; aphids bluish grey; on small-leaved elms ....***Eriosoma anncharlotteae*** Danielsson
Galls of this species have not yet been found in Britain; only the free-living aphids have been recorded.

- Rolls not markedly thickened and of similar colour to normal leaf; often restricted to leaf margins on *U. glabra*, affecting more of leaf on softer small-leaved elms, where several affected young leaves at tip of shoot may appear bunched together; aphids waxy, yellow-green .... ***Eriosoma patchiae*** (Börner & Blunck)

6 Leaf roll (Fig. 966, Plate 2.6) containing waxy aphids, green when small, brown when large; common and widespread............. ***Eriosoma ulmi*** (L.)

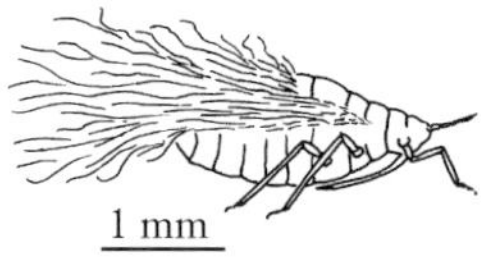

- Leaf roll containing grey-green non-waxy aphids; uncommon .... ***Eriosoma grossulariae*** (Schüle)
Both galls are found on all elms and can only be safely distinguished if aphids are present; see Carter & Danielsson (1993).

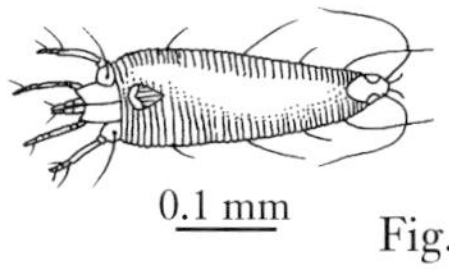

7 Gall a pouch (sometimes very small, only 1-2 mm high) **8**

- Gall a small dimple, blister or pock, < 5 mm across **13**

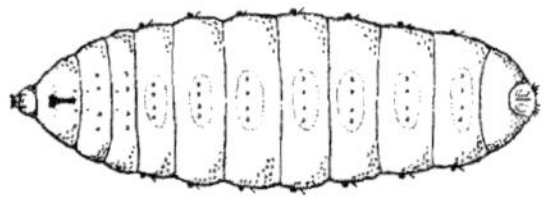

Fig. 964

Fig. 965

Fig. 966

Fig. 967

Fig. 968

Fig. 969

8 Gall ovoid or club-shaped, > 7 mm in height, usually on upperside; contains aphids (Fig. 967) in summer: **Hemiptera: Aphididae: Pemphiginae** **9**

- Gall raised, < 5 mm in height; contains mites (Fig. 968) or a cecid larva (Fig. 969) **11**

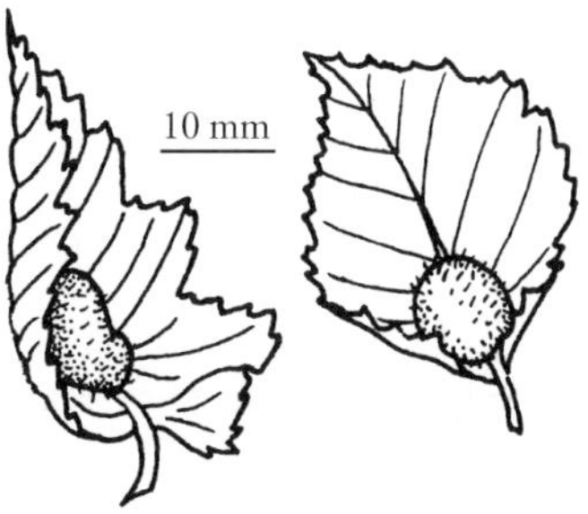

9 Globular, ± hairy swelling on midrib, 8-15 mm across, often distorting the leaf (Fig. 970); dark green aphids leave through hole in top of gall in August; rare .... ***Kaltenbachiella pallida*** (Haliday)

- Elongated or club-shaped pouch gall, not hairy, on leaf blade, usually away from midrib **10**

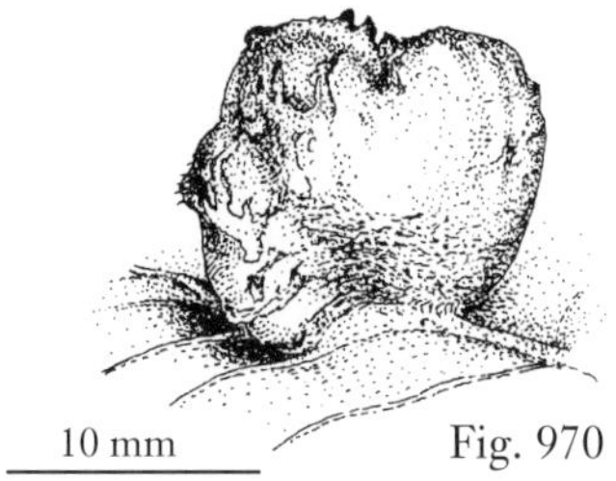

10 Stalked club-shaped gall, 7-15 mm tall, leaf thickened and yellowed around stalk (Fig. 971); usually on upper side of blade away from midrib; aphids waxy, grey-black above, grey-green below, leave through hole near base of gall on one side, in June or July; locally common .... ***Tetraneura ulmi*** (L.) **fig gall**

Partly-formed galls are irregular lumpy projections in pale yellow patches on upper surface of leaf. Young galls have an opening on underside of leaf.

- Gall elongated, laterally compressed, 'coxcomb-shaped', up to 8 mm tall (Fig. 972), alongside midrib or in blade; yellowish, often tinged with red; aphids green, not waxy; rare .... ***Colopha compressa*** (Koch)

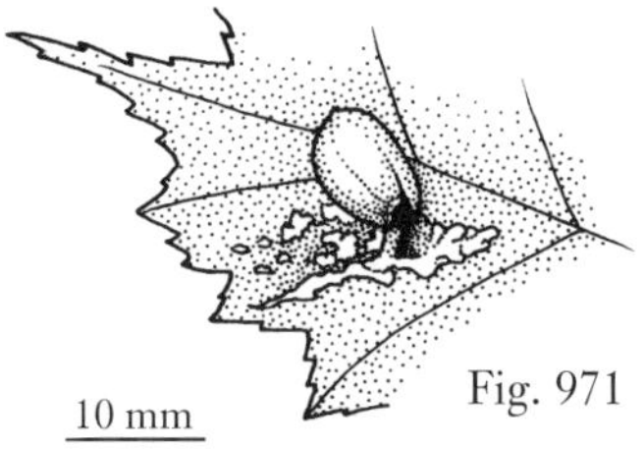

11 Width 5-8 mm, rounded above, conical, with opening below (Fig. 973); on veins, often several running together; hairless inside, with yellow larva (Fig. 969); on small-leaved and wych elms and hybrids: **Diptera: Cecidomyiidae** .... ***Janetiella leemei*** (Kieffer)

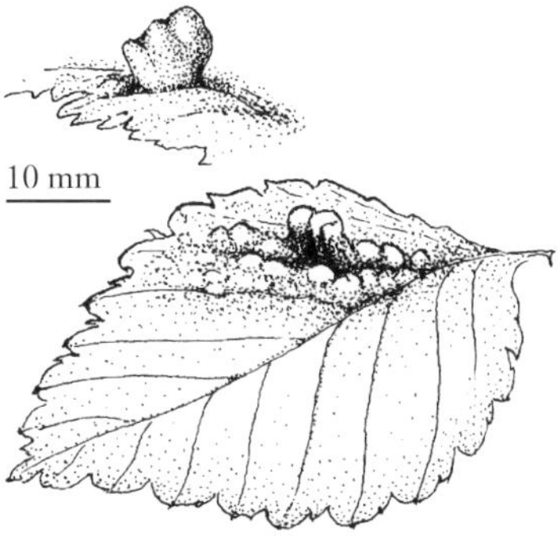

Gall sometimes on petiole or young twig.

- Width 1-2 mm, on blade or veins; hairy opening below; contains mites (Fig. 968): **Acari: Eriophyoidea** **12**

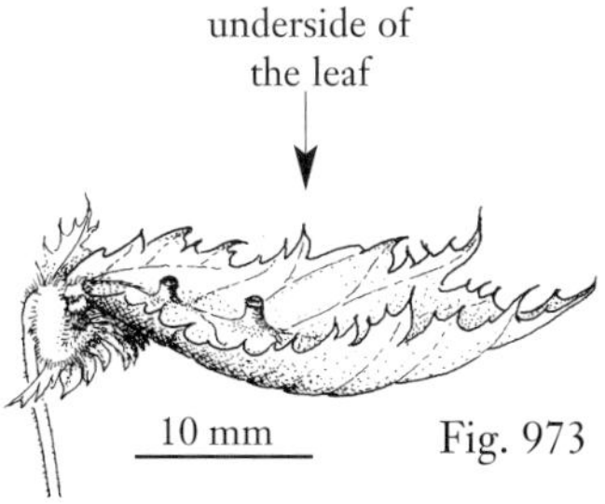

10 mm

10 mm   Fig. 970

10 mm   Fig. 971

10 mm

Fig. 972

underside of the leaf

10 mm   Fig. 973

12 Pimple 2 mm across, projecting only from upperside, with narrow hairy opening below (Fig. 974); on side veins
.... *Aceria brevipunctatus* (Nalepa)
(= *Aculus* = *Eriophyes*)

- Rounded above with conical projection below, 1 mm across (Fig. 975, Plate 1.1); on blade, often very numerous; probably only on small-leaved elms .... *Aceria ulmicola* (Nalepa)
(= *Aculus* = *Eriophyes ulmi* = *campestricola*)

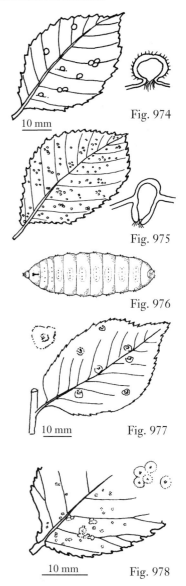

Fig. 974

10 mm

Fig. 975

Fig. 976

13 Small dimple on underside, surrounded by discoloured area < 5 mm across, with a corresponding bulge on upperside; briefly contains a white larva (Fig. 976) in early summer: **Diptera: Cecidomyiidae**
.... *Dasineura ulmicola* (Kieffer)

- Small circular blisters or thickened pocks **14**

14 Blister gall 3-4 mm across, raised on upperside; indistinct yellow patch below with central opening (Fig. 977); contains a white larva (Fig. 976) until July or August, then blister turns brown **Diptera: Cecidomyiidae** .... *Physemocecis ulmi* (Kieffer)

- Tiny thickened pocks 1-3 mm across, raised scab-like on underside with opening, upper surface with roughened discoloured spots (Fig. 978); pale green, later brown; contain long thin mites: **Acari: Eriophyoidea** .... *Aceria filiformis* (Nalepa)
(= *Eriophyes*)

Erinea caused by mites are sometimes found on the leaves; no attempt is made to identify them here.

10 mm   Fig. 977

10 mm   Fig. 978

E175. *URTICA*

Two nettle species are native in Britain, the common nettle (or perennial stinging nettle), *Urtica dioica* L. and the small annual stinging nettle, *U. urens* L. The commoner *U. dioica* is more often galled, but both species may be hosts to all the gall causers included here.

An orange rust galls stems, petioles and leaf veins (see p. 260).

READ THREE ALTERNATIVES

1 Irregular, thickened, pouch-like swelling, 3-8 mm across, often several together in leaf blade, petiole or flower stalk, occasionally in stem (Fig. 979, Plate 4.8), with slit-shaped opening usually on upperside; pale green to purplish; contains several (occasionally one) white larvae (Fig. 980) in summer and early autumn; very common: **Diptera: Cecidomyiidae**

.... ***Dasineura urticae*** (Perris)

Galls often also contain pink, orange or red cecid larvae; these are inquilines or predators.

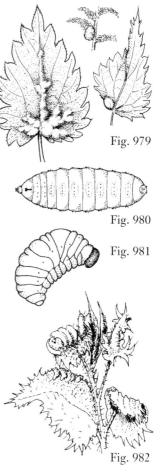

Fig. 979

Fig. 980

Fig. 981

- Slight swelling in stem at a node; contains a larva (Fig. 981); locally common: **Coleoptera: Brentidae: Apioninae** .... ***Taeniapion urticarium*** (Herbst)
(= *Apion*)

The adult weevil is 2 mm long, dark red or reddish brown, and feeds on leaves and the outside of the stem (Morris, 1991).

- Leaf margin curled; sometimes several young leaves of terminal or side shoots stunted, distorted, thickened and bunched together **2**

2 Leaf margin slightly thickened and curled loosely upwards, whitish or reddish (Fig. 982); contains yellowish white larvae (Fig. 980) in summer: **Diptera: Cecidomyiidae**

.... ***Dasineura dioicae*** (Rübsaamen)

- Shoot with stunted, curled, distorted leaves, often bunched together, containing aphids or psyllids **3**

Fig. 982

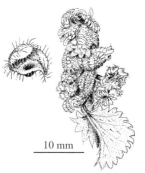

3 Individual leaf curled, dark green and hairy with depressions (Fig. 983); each depression contains a flat psyllid; affects young leaves in August - September; common: **Hemiptera: Psylloidea**
.... ***Trioza urticae*** (L.)

10 mm

Fig. 983

- Shoot tip with bunched, curled, compressed leaves; covered with a dense colony of dark green to black aphids (Fig. 984) which exude wax; early summer, often attended by ants: **Hemiptera: Aphididae** .... ***Aphis urticata*** Gmelin

This may not be a true gall.

Fig. 984

E176. *VACCINIUM*

Galls are found on three native species, bilberry, *Vaccinium myrtillus* L., bog bilberry, *V. uliginosum* L. and cowberry, *V. vitis-idaea* L.

Fungal galls may be found on leaves and stems (see p. 260).

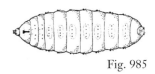

Fig. 985

1   Leaves bunched at shoot tip, due to shortened internodes; leaves concave, ± thickened, unusually small, outer leaves enclosing inner; contain larvae (Fig. 985): **Diptera: Cecidomyiidae** **2**

\-   Leaf margin inrolled, ± thickened; blade may also be folded or wrinkled **4**

2   On *V. myrtillus*, gall (Fig. 986) up to 8 x 5 mm, leaves often reddened; larvae red; June - August .... ***Jaapiella vacciniorum*** (Kieffer)

\-   On *V. vitis-idaea* **3**

Fig. 986

3   Leaves shiny, dark reddish purple; larvae yellow .... ***Dasineura anglica*** (Kieffer)

\-   Larvae white .... ***Dasineura vitisidaea*** (Kieffer)

<small>Little is known about these species, identified from larva and gall only (Chandler, 1998); they may not be distinct. This needs to be confirmed by rearing adults.</small>

Fig. 987

4   Margin thickened, rolled downwards (Fig. 987), often yellowish or reddish; contains pale yellow larvae; on *V. uliginosum* (and other species abroad): **Diptera: Cecidomyiidae** .... ***Hygrodiplosis vaccinii*** (Kieffer)

\-   Very narrow upwards roll, not noticeably thickened; leaf sometimes folded or wrinkled; contains mites (Fig. 988); on *V. myrtillus*, *V. uliginosum*: **Acari: Eriophyoidea** ....***Phyllocoptes vaccinii*** (Flögel & Goosman)

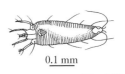

0.1 mm

Fig. 988

E177. *VALERIANA*

Three galls are found on common valerian, *Valeriana officinalis* L. or marsh valerian, *V. dioica* L. All are uncommon or rare.

Fungal galls may affect the leaves (see p. 261).

Fig. 989

1 Sections of leaf folded or inrolled upwards, thickened, twisted and discoloured, sometimes hairy; each contains several white jumping larvae (Fig. 989); on *V. officinalis*: **Diptera: Cecidomyiidae** .... ***Contarinia crispans*** Kieffer

2 Flower swollen, distorted, remaining closed; often several crowded together in a compact inflorescence, with shortened flower stalks; each contains several white jumping larvae (Fig. 989); on *V. officinalis*: **Diptera: Cecidomyiidae** .... ***Contarinia valerianae*** (Rübsaamen)

3 Inflorescence with flowers greened and leafy (phyllanthy), bunched together into a rounded mass due to shortened flower stalks; contains mites (Fig. 988); on both *Valeriana* spp.: **Acari: Eriophyoidea** .... ***Aceria macrotuberculatus*** (Nalepa)
(= *Eriophyes*)

E178. *VALERIANELLA* and *CENTRANTHUS*

One gall (**Hemiptera: Psylloidea**) is recorded on native cornsalads, *Valerianella* species and the introduced red valerian, *Centranthus ruber* (L.) DC.

Leaves at shoot tip broader than normal, with margins thickened and rolled upwards (Fig. 990); inflorescence also sometimes affected, flowers a tangled leafy mass (phyllanthy), pale green (Fig. 991); contains flat nymphs; widespread but rare .... ***Trioza centranthi*** (Vallot)

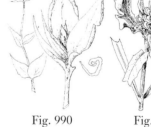

Fig. 990   Fig. 991

E179. *VERONICA*

Gall causers on speedwells may be restricted to one species or attack several. Arthropod galls are recorded from germander speedwell, *Veronica chamaedrys* L., thyme-leaved speedwell, *V. serpyllifolia* L., heath speedwell, *V. officinalis* L., brooklime, *V. beccabunga* L., marsh speedwell, *V. scutellata* L., water-speedwell, *V. anagallis-aquatica* L., pink water-speedwell, *V. catenata* Pennell and, occasionally, other species.
    Fungi gall stems, leaves and roots (see p. 261) and may cause stunting of the plants.

1 Gall in flower or fruit; ovary swollen (may not be apparent from the outside), containing a white larva (Fig. 992) or pupa: **Coleoptera: Curculionidae** **2**

- Gall in stem or leaf, often involving several young leaves at tip of shoot **4**

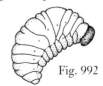

Fig. 992

2 Swollen ovary up to 8 x 5mm, causing distinct
   enlargement of flower (Fig. 993); adult weevil 2.5-
   3 mm long; in *V. anagallis-aquatica*, *V. catenata*, *V.
   scutellata*, *V. beccabunga*
   .... ***Gymnetron villosulum*** Gyllenhal

- Swollen ovary less pronounced, flower normally
   remaining closed; adult weevil 1.8-2.2 mm long **3**

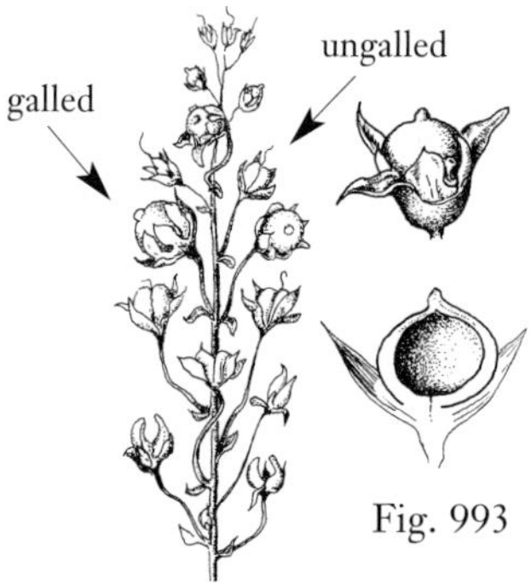

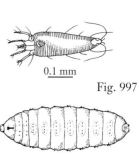

galled   ungalled

Fig. 993

Fig. 994

3 Adult weevil 1.8-2.0 mm long; gall in *V. scutellata*
   or *V. beccabunga* .... ***Gymnetron beccabungae*** (L.)

- Adult weevil 2.0-2.2 mm long; gall in *V. anagallis-
   aquatica*, *V. beccabunga* or *V. catenata*
   .... ***Gymnetron veronicae*** (Germar)
   There is considerable overlap in host plants of *Gymnetron*
   species and their galls are very similar. For firm identification,
   rear the adult and use the key to *Veronica* weevil species in
   Dauphin & Aniotsbehère (1993, 1997). Host plants in Britain
   may be more restricted than is indicated here.

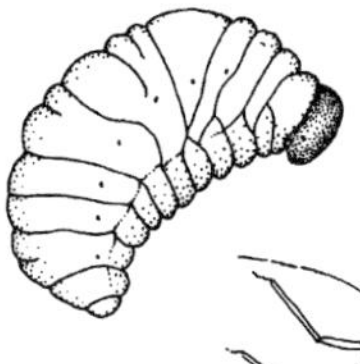

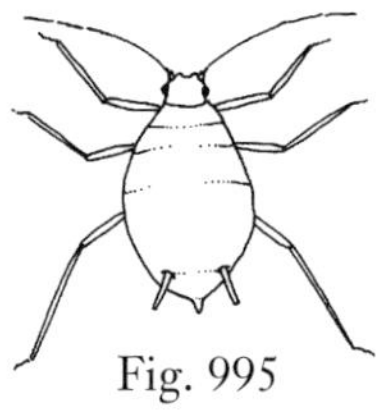

Fig. 995

4 Swelling in stem, 3-7 mm long, with 1-2 chambers
   each containing a white larva (Fig. 994) or pupa;
   gall may be low down with shoot above stunted; in
   V. serpyllifolia: **Coleoptera: Curculionidae**
   .... ***Gymnetron melanarium*** (Germar)

- Gall in leaf or several leaves at shoot tip; adjacent
   stem and flowers may be involved (but without a
   weevil larva as in Fig. 994) **5**
   Several aphid species (**Hemiptera: Aphididae**, Fig. 995) are
   found in young rolled or crumpled leaves at shoot tip; these are
   not considered to be true galls.

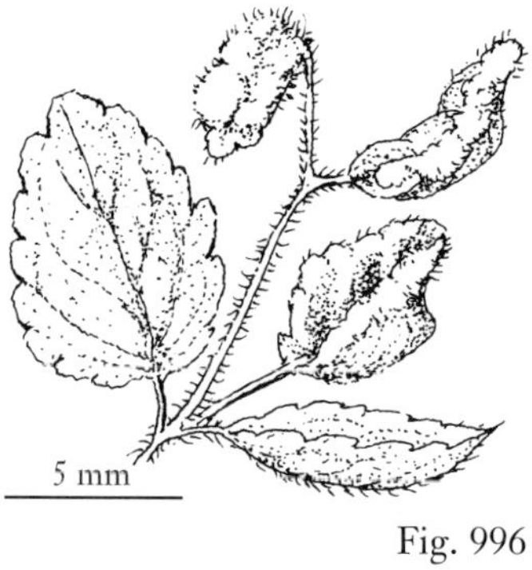

5 mm

Fig. 996

5 Leaves blistered or margin rolled, hairy (Fig. 996);
   contain mites (Fig. 997); on *V. chamaedrys*: **Acari:
   Eriophyoidea**
   .... ***Aceria anceps*** (Nalepa)
   (= *Eriophyes*)
   Gall can resemble a distorted pouch if several young leaves at
   shoot tip are affected.

- Leaves thickened, the edges of the two terminal
   pairs pressed together to form a pouch, often very
   hairy; contains many orange or red larvae (Fig.
   998) or pupae: **Diptera: Cecidomyiidae** **6**

0.1 mm

Fig. 997

Fig. 998

6 Pouch broader, 5-10 mm across (Fig. 999, Plate 4.9); larvae orange-red; mainly on *V. chamaedrys*; common .... *Jaapiella veronicae* (Vallot)

White larvae of the inquiline *Macrolabis incolens* Rübsaamen may also be present.

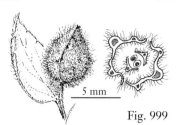

- Pouch more slender; larvae yellow-orange; mainly on *V. scutellata* .... *Dasineura similis* (F. Löw)

Fig. 999

E180. *VIBURNUM*

Galls are found on the two native species, guelder-rose, *Viburnum opulus* L. and wayfaring-tree, *V. lantana* L.

1 Flower bud swollen, closed (Fig. 1000); contains 1 to 3 jumping larvae, white at first, later yellow (Fig. 1001): **Diptera: Cecidomyiidae** ....*Contarinia viburnorum* Kieffer or *Contarinia sambuci* (Kaltenbach)

Separation of these two species is not possible at present. *C. sambuci* occurs on *Sambucus* (Key E144, p. 440) and other Caprifoleaceae as well as on *Viburnum*. Their status has not been clearly established; they may not be distinct. Their identity and range of host plants needs clarification.

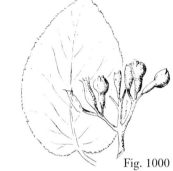

Fig. 1000

- Pustule or pouch gall in leaf blade, usually several on a leaf **2**

The identity of mites causing erinea on leaves is unknown. Black aphids live on underside of leaves, which may be reduced in size, shrivelled, curled downwards and bunched together; leaves on young shoots in spring and early summer are most commonly affected. Common species are *Aphis viburni* Scopoli and *Ceruraphis eriophori* (Walker); they are not thought to cause true galls.

Fig. 1001

2 Pustules 3-4 mm across, raised more on upper surface, with opening below (Fig. 1002); red, not hairy; each contains an orange-yellow larva; on *V. lantana*; S. England: **Diptera: Cecidomyiidae** .... *Sackenomyia reaumurii* (Bremi) (= *Phlyctidobia solmsi*)

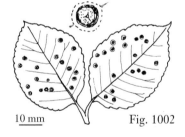

10 mm   Fig. 1002

- Pouch galls, c. 3 mm wide and high, usually on upper surface (Fig. 1003); covered with fine velvety hairs; green in May, becoming pink or red, brown by August; hairy opening below; contains mites (Fig. 997); usually on *V. lantana*; widespread and common: **Acari: Eryphyoidea** .... *Eriophyes viburni* (Nalepa)

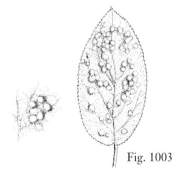

Fig. 1003

E181. *VICIA*

Vicia is a large genus and includes the cultivated broad bean. Most gall causers are restricted to groups of closely related species as follows (names grouped as in Clapham *et al.*, 1987):

ERVUM: hairy tare, *V. hirsuta* (L.) Gray, smooth tare, *V. tetrasperma* (L.) Schreb.

CRACCA: tufted vetch, *V. cracca* L., wood vetch *V. sylvatica* L.

VICIA: bush vetch, *V. sepium* L., common vetch *V. sativa* L. (+ subspecies)

FABA: broad bean, *V. faba* L.

Root nodules are common and swellings may occur at the base of the stem (see p. 219).

1   Gall in pod or flower bud; contains one or more larvae: **Diptera: Cecidomyiidae** 2

-   Gall in stem or leaf (petiole or leaflet), may be bunched at tip of shoot 4

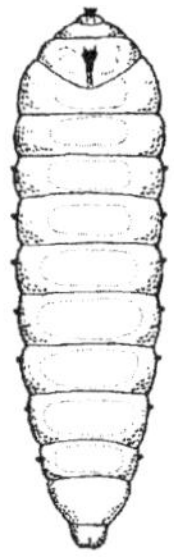

Fig. 1004 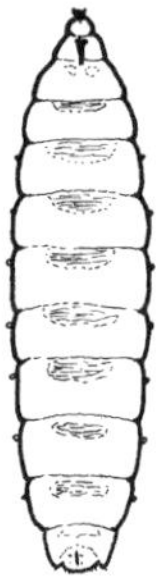   Fig. 1005

2   Swelling in pod, usually near base; cavity lined with fungus; larva (Fig. 1004) yellow, non-jumping; on *V. hirsuta*, *V. tetrasperma*; rare .... ***Asphondylia ervi*** Rübsaamen

Contarinia pisi (Winnertz) has been reported galling pods, with white jumping larvae (Fig. 1005); probably only on *Pisum sativum* (Key E120, p. 379) in Britain.

-   Flower bud swollen, failing to open, often several buds affected in an inflorescence 3

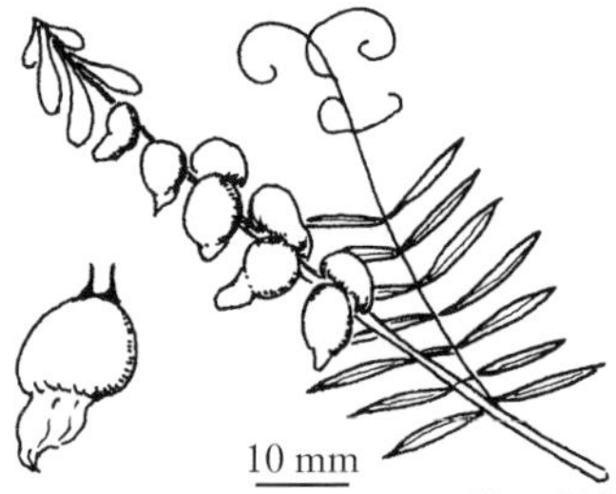

3   Each gall with one non-jumping, orange-yellow larva; on *V. sepium* .... ***Anabremia viciae*** Kieffer

-   Each gall with several jumping, white, later yellow-orange larvae; on *V. cracca* (Fig. 1006) ....***Contarinia craccae*** Kieffer

The identity of cecids in flower buds is confused; *A. viciae*, for example, may be an inquiline (Harris, personal communication) and not a gall causer. *Contarinia loti* (De Geer) has been recorded on *V. cracca*; recent authors consider it attacks *Lotus* only (Key E98, p. 362).

10 mm

Fig. 1006

4   Swelling in stem or petiole 5

-   In blade of leaflet, or leaves at tip of shoot 7

5 Stem swelling c. 2 cm long; contains a larva (Fig. 1007); on *V. cracca*; rare: **Diptera: Agromyzidae** .... *Agromyza erythrocephala* Hendel

Fig. 1007

- Slender thin-walled swelling in stem, 5-15 mm long, occasionally in petiole; single cavity with a yellow-white larva (Fig. 1008) or pupa; on *Vicia* spp.: **Coleoptera: Brentidae: Apioninae** **6**

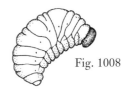

Fig. 1008

6 Gall up to 15 mm long; usual host probably *V. cracca* in Britain; uncommon .... *Cynapion gyllenhali* (Kirby)

- Gall 7 x 2 mm; usual hosts probably *V. sativa* or *sepium* in Britain .... *Holotrichapion aethiops* (Herbst)

Catapion seniculus (Kirby) has been recorded causing similar galls on *V. cracca*. In Britain, it normally feeds in stems of *Trifolium* (Key E172) and, possibly, *Medicago* (Key E102) in mainland Europe. Adults need to be reared to confirm identity of galls.

7 Leaves, usually at tip of shoot, crumpled and rolled; contains dark green aphids (Fig. 1009) with black cauda and siphunculi; on *V. sativa*, *V. sepium*, *V. faba*: **Hemiptera: Aphididae** .... *Megoura viciae* Buckton

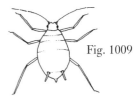

Fig. 1009

Two other aphids cause similar damage, both forming dense colonies at shoot tip when abundant, and often attended by ants. *Aphis craccae* L. is blackish green, 1.9-2.8 mm long, covered with powdery wax so that colonies appear greyish, on *Vicia* spp. (but not *V. faba*). *Aphis fabae* Scopoli is black, 1.7-2.8 mm long, without wax, on *V. faba* (and many other plants). It may be that none of these aphids are true gall causers.

- Leaflet folded into a pod, or margin rolled, often several affected together at tip of shoot **8**

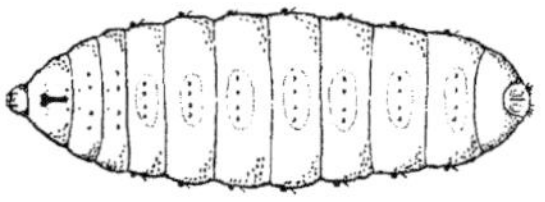

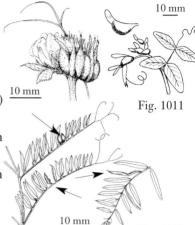

Fig. 1010

8 Leaflet swollen and stunted, folded upwards to form a pod, green, yellowish or reddened; often many crowded together forming a mass up to 40mm across; each contains larvae (Fig. 1010) or pupae: **Diptera: Cecidomyiidae**:

Usually on *V. sepium*, *V. sativa* (Fig. 1011)
.... ***Dasineura viciae*** (Kieffer)

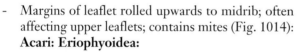

Fig. 1011

On *V. cracca* (Fig. 1012)
.... ***Dasineura spadica*** Rübsaamen

On *V. tetrasperma* and other spp. (Fig. 1013)
.... ***Dasineura loewiana*** Rübsaamen

Identifications are provisional only; *D. viciae* may represent more than one species. Larval colour of both gall causers and inquilines varies and is not a useful diagnostic character. Until more research is done the host plant provides the best guide to identification.

Fig. 1012

-    Margins of leaflet rolled upwards to midrib; often affecting upper leaflets; contains mites (Fig. 1014): **Acari: Eriophyoidea**:

Usually on *V. cracca* (Fig. 1015): rare
.... ***Aculus retiolatus*** (Nalepa)
                                  (= *Vasates*)

On *V. hirsuta*, *V. tetrasperma* (Fig. 1016)
.... ***Aceria trifolii*** (Nalepa)
                                  (= *Eriophyes*)

A. trifolii normally affects *Trifolium* (E172, p. 462); whether or not it occurs on *Vicia*, needs confirmation.

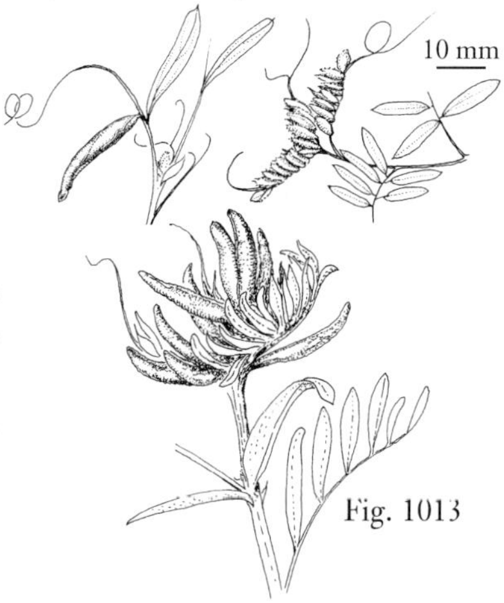

Fig. 1013

0.1 mm

Fig. 1014

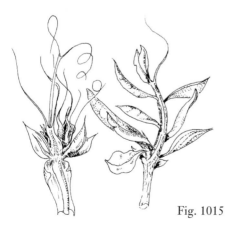

Fig. 1015

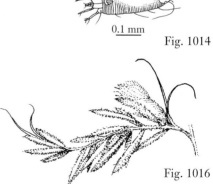

Fig. 1016

E182. *VIOLA*

This is a large and complex genus, divided into two distinct subgenera, violets and pansies, each with many subspecies, and hybridisation is common within each group. The complex taxonomy of the host plants is reflected in the confusion of identification within *Dasineura* (Cecidomyiidae), the main genus of arthropod gall causers. The host associations suggested here are tentative only, and should be regarded as preliminary until rigorous host preference tests have been carried out. Violets recorded as hosts are common dog-violet, *V. riviniana* Reichenbach, early dog-violet, *V. reichenbachiana* Jordon ex Boreau, heath dog-violet, *V. canina* L., sweet violet, *V. odorata* L., and hairy violet, *V. hirta* L. Host plants amongst pansies are wild pansy, *V. tricolor* L., field pansy, *V. arvensis* Murray, mountain pansy, *V. lutea* Hudson, and the garden escape horned pansy, *V. cornuta* L. Cultivated varieties may also be affected.

Leaves and stems may be galled by rusts and a smut (see p. 262).

1   Margin of leaf rolled tightly upwards, colour similar to rest of leaf, not obviously thickened nor abnormally hairy; contains mites (Fig. 1014); probably on *V. tricolor*, *V. cornuta* and *V. lutea*; widespread: **Acari: Eriophyoidea** .... *Cecidophyes violae* (Nalepa)
(= *Phyllocoptes*)

-   Margin of leaf rolled upwards, loose or tight, thickened and usually pale-coloured, sometimes reddened, often hairy; whole plant may be dwarfed, with flowers and stems as well as leaves affected; contains many larvae (Fig. 1010) or pupae: **Diptera: Cecidomyiidae** **2**

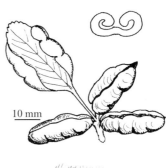

2   Roll on one or both sides of leaf (Fig. 1017), often hairy, with several adjacent leaves affected; rolls affect all of young leaf but only part of blade of older leaf; larvae white when young, later orange-yellow; on violets:

10 mm

On *V. riviniana*, *V. reichenbachiana* and, perhaps, *V. canina*; widespread
   .... *Dasineura affinis* (Kieffer)

On *V. odorata*; S. England and E. Anglia
   .... *Dasineura odoratae* Stelter

Fig. 1017

On *V. hirta*; rare .... *Dasineura hirtae* Stelter

These host associations are suggested by Stelter (1982) and require confirmation. He provides a key enabling separation of male cecids, necessary for firm identification.

-   Whole plant dwarfed with affected leaves forming a rosette; leaf rolls very hairy; petals and sepals and stems may also be affected; larvae orange; on pansies *V. tricolor*, *V. arvensis*; rare .... *Dasineura violae* (F. Löw)

Marginal rolls of leaves on many *Viola* species may also be caused by aphids. These are probably not true galls.

E183. *VITIS*

Two galls have been found on the cultivated grape-vine, *Vitis vinifera* L., both of them pests abroad.

1   Leaf blade with felt-like erineum on under side, with a corresponding bulge above, often several in a leaf (Fig. 1018); hairs white in early summer, later rust-red; contains mites (Fig. 1019): **Acari: Eriophyoidea** .... ***Colomerus vitis*** (Pagenstecher)
(= *Eriophyes*)

See Hancy & Hancy (1997). Established in Britain at least since the 1970s.

2   Leaf blade with pouch galls on underside, a slight bulge above; or swellings on roots; with aphids inside or on surface of galls; in Cornwall: **Hemiptera: Phylloxeridae**
......................................***Daktulosphaira vitifolia*** Fitch
(= *vitis*)

For figures of galls and further details see Dauphin & Aniotsbehère (1997). This species, the scourge of the European wine industry, is not established in Britain but is sometimes introduced on imported vines, when it can become a temporary pest (Halstead, personal communication).

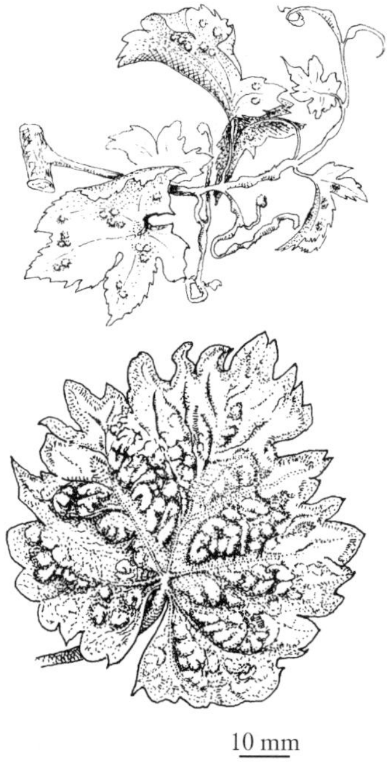

10 mm

Fig. 1018

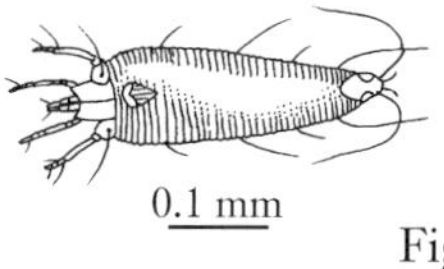

0.1 mm

Fig. 1019

GLOSSARY
(plural in brackets; **bold** defined elsewhere in glossary)

achene: dry fruit containing a single seed, *e.g.* Asteraceae (daisies), thistles, dandelions etc.

aecium (aecia): **sorus,** in a **rust fungus,** which produces aeciospores.

agamic: without sexual cells (gametes), reproducing asexually; all-female, agamic, generations are common amongst Aphidoidea (Hemiptera) (**aphids**) and Cynipidae (gall wasps).

alate: winged, hence alata (alatae) winged **aphid(s)** (cf. **apterous**).

angiosperm: flowering plant (cf. **gymnosperm**, fern).

annual: a life cycle which lasts one year or less (cf. **biennial, perennial**).

anther: male part of flower, produces pollen.

aphid: insect, adult or **nymph,** of the superfamily Aphidoidea (Hemiptera); includes greenfly and (garden) blackfly.

apterous: wingless; hence aptera (apterae) wingless adult **aphid**(s) (cf. **alate**).

artichoke gall: leafy gall originating from a bud, formed from overlapping leaves caused by the failure of **internodes** to lengthen; length longer than width (cf. **rosette gall**).

ascospore: a spore formed within an **ascus,** following nuclear fusion and meiosis, in ascomycete fungi.

ascus: the structure within which **ascospores** form in ascomycete fungi.

asexual generation (♀♀): all-female generation reproducing asexually.

axil: angle between a stem and a lateral leaf stalk or smaller stem, hence **axillary** bud (cf. **terminal**).

axillary: within, or associated with, an **axil.**

basidiospore: a spore formed outside a **basidium,** following nuclear fusion and meiosis, in basidiomycete fungi.

basidium: a structure outside which **basidiospores** form in basidiomycete fungi.

biennial: a life cycle which lasts two years (cf. **annual, perennial**).

blade: (leaf blade) surface of a leaf either side of the main vein (**midrib**).

blister: rounded thin-walled swelling, with a cavity, raised on one or both sides of a leaf.

bracteole: leaf-like wing of a fruit *e.g.* in *Tilia* (a restricted meaning applicable for these keys only).

bracts: scale-like modified leaves, often green, enclosing a flower head, especially in the Asteraceae (daisy family).

callous tissue / callus: wound tissue; plant reaction caused by feeding by a generalised herbivore, or by an unspecialised gall causer, *e.g.* stem borer or flower head feeder.

calyx (calyces): the **sepals** of a flower.

cambium (cambium layer): layer of dividing and growing cells in plant stems and roots; responsible for increases in girth (and sometimes in length).

canker: solid growth or swelling on a woody branch or the trunk of tree, caused by bacteria or fungi.

caterpillar: **larva** of a moth or butterfly (Fig. 1020), or of a sawfly (Fig. 1021), with jointed legs on thorax and fleshy prolegs on abdomen.

Fig. 1020

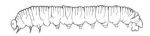
Fig. 1021

catkin: erect or pendulous spike of petal-less flowers produced by some trees, *e.g.* hazel, birch, oak, poplar, willow.

cecid: gall midge, belonging to family Cecidomyiidae (Diptera).

chloranthy: transformation of petals and sepals, and sometimes other flower parts, into leaf-like structures (also **phyllanthy, phyllody,** which mean the same).

cocoon: silken pupal case spun by an insect **larva**, especially that of a moth, butterfly, **cecid** or beetle.
concave: hollowed, like the inside of a bowl.
coppice: trees or shrubs cut to ground level to encourage multi-stemmed growth.
corolla: the petals of a flower which may be separate or fused into a tube.
culm: the stem of a grass (Poaceae).

depression: a hollow on one side of a leaf, with a corresponding thickened bulge on the other side, larger than a **dimple**.
dicotyledon: plant which germinates with two seed leaves; normal leaves usually with a **midrib** and a network of minor veins (cf. **monocotyledon**).
differentiated tissues: groups of cells of different types with different functions, forming distinct patches or layers in a gall.
dimple: a shallow hollow on one side of leaf, with a corresponding thickened bulge on the other side, smaller than a **depression**.
distal: part of a structure farthest from the base or point of attachment (cf. **proximal**).
dormant bud: undeveloped bud on trunk, branch or in an **axil**.

epidermis: outermost layer of cells in a plant.
ergot: black or purple growth replacing grain of grasses (Poaceae) and some sedges (Cyperaceae), caused by the fungus *Claviceps*.
erineum (**erinea**): a patch of hairs, usually on a leaf or stem, caused by gall mites which live amongst them.

fasciation: abnormal multiplication of plant parts, often with flattening and thickening, due to bacteria or viruses or to physiological malformation.
floret: a small individual flower, a number of which make up a compound flower head or **inflorescence**, *e.g.* in Asteraceae (daisies etc.) and Poaceae (grasses).
frass: dry granular faeces produced by **caterpillars**, beetle **larvae** etc.
frond: leaf of a fern (Fig. 1022).

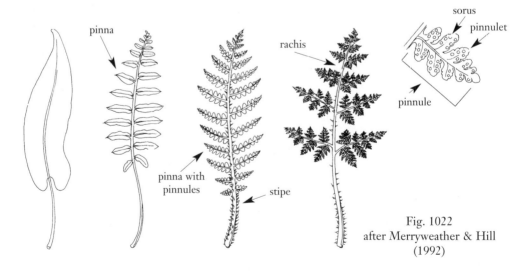

Fig. 1022
after Merryweather & Hill
(1992)

fruit: ovary of a plant containing fertilised seed(s).
fruiting body: part of fungus which carries the spores.
fundatrix (**fundatrices**): the female (stem-mother) **aphid** which lays eggs to start a new generation in spring.

gill lamellae: structures on underside of **fruiting body** of certain basidiomycete fungi (mushrooms and toadstools) which carry the spores.

glume: outer bract in a grass **spikelet** (Fig. 1023), containing one or more **florets.**

grain: fruit (containing the seed) of a grass.

gymnosperm: conifer (cf. **angiosperm**).

haustorium (haustoria): swelling at point of attachment of gall-causing plant to its host, formed from tissues of both organisms.

honeydew: sweet liquid produced from anus of **aphids, psyllids** and **scale insects**, often collected by ants.

host: plant or fungus (including lichenised fungus) which is parasitised by a gall causer (a restricted meaning applicable for these keys only).

hybrid: a plant resulting from crossing of two species (written as *Genus* x *species* names, see Stace, 1997).

hyperparasite: a parasite of a parasite.

hyperplasy: abnormal growth caused by multiplication of cells.

hypertrophy: abnormal growth caused by enlargement of cells.

hypha (hyphae): thread-like strucure(s) which make up the body of a fungus (the **mycelium**).

inflorescence: flower head composed of two or more (often many) **florets,** *e.g.* in Asteraceae (daisies, etc.), Apiaceae (umbellifers), Poaceae (grasses), Cyperaceae (sedges), Juncaceae (rushes); or flowering shoot bearing many flowers, *e.g.* in *Chamerion, Epilobium* etc. (cf. **panicle**).

inquiline: a mite or insect which lives in and feeds on the tissue of a gall caused by another species, and which may itself distort the gall.

instar: the stage of development of an arthropod between two moults.

internode: portion of stem between two joints (**nodes**).

lamina: leaf blade.

lammas leaves or **lammas growth**: second flush of leaves, produced by some trees in summer (July - August).

larva (larvae): juvenile feeding stage of an insect with a **pupa** in the life cycle (cf. **nymph**), *e.g.* of Diptera (flies), Lepidoptera (butterflies and moths), Coleoptera (beetles), Hymenoptera (ants, bees and wasps).

lateral bud: bud on side of stem, in **axil** of a leaf (cf. **terminal**).

lateral vein: side vein of leaf (cf. **midrib**).

leaflet: separate section of a compound leaf, attached to **rachis**, *e.g.* in *Fraxinus, Rosa, Pisum.*

lemma: inner **bract** in a grass **spikelet** (Fig. 1023).

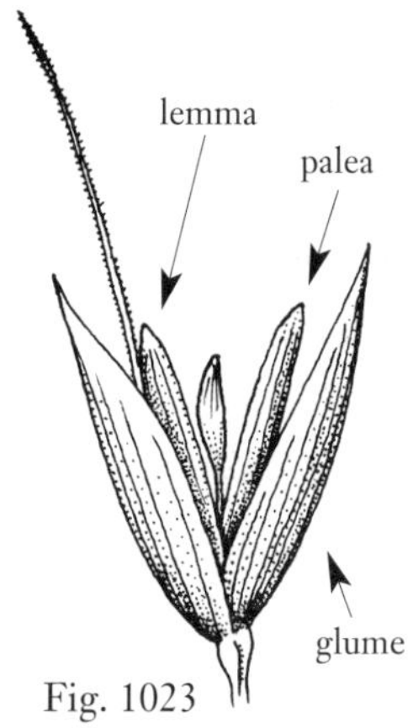

Fig. 1023

meristem: part of plant containing undifferentiated cells, able to divide rapidly and develop into a variety of structures, found at root and shoot tips, in the **cambium** and (in grasses) at the base of stems and leaf sheaths.

midrib: main, central vein of a leaf.

mine: excavation in thickness of leaf or stem, caused by a feeding insect **larva**.

monocotyledon: plant which germinates with one seed leaf; normal leaves usually with parallel veins, sometimes without a distinct **midrib**, *e.g.* Poaceae (grasses), Liliaceae (lilies) (cf. **dicotyledon**).

monophagous: an animal which feeds on one species of plant only (cf. **oligophagous, polyphagous**).

mycelium: the body of a fungus, made up of **hyphae**.

native: an organism indigenous in Britain (cf. **naturalised**).

naturalised: an organism which is not **native** to Britain, but which now occurs and reproduces here.

node: position on stem where a leaf or lateral stem arises; scar marking one year's growth of a woody stem (cf. **internode**).

nodule: small swelling, without internal chambers, caused by bacteria on roots of legumes and other plants.

nymph: juvenile stage of an insect without a **pupa** in the life cycle, e.g. of **aphids**, **psyllids**, **scale insects** (cf. **larva**).

oligophagous: an animal which feeds on a few species of related plants only, *e.g.* in one genus or family (cf. **monophagous**, **polyphagous**).

ovary: female part of flower containing **ovule(s)** (cf. **fruit**).

ovoid: egg-shaped.

ovule: female gamete which will become the seed after fertilisation (enclosed in **ovary**).

palea: inner bract in a grass **spikelet** (Fig. 1023).

panicle: branched **inflorescence**, *e.g.* of grasses.

parasitoid: an insect which feeds on only one host animal and invariably kills it, displaying behaviour between that of a parasite and a predator.

parthenogenesis: production of eggs or young by female without fertilisation. A species that reproduces in this way is parthenogenetic.

pedicel, peduncle: flower stalk (a restricted meaning applicable for these keys only).

perennial: life cycle of more than two years (cf. **annual**, **biennial**).

petiole: leaf stalk.

phyllanthy: transformation of petals and sepals, and sometimes other flower parts, into leaf-like structures (also **chloranthy**, **phyllody**, which mean the same).

phyllody: see **phyllanthy**; phyllody is used particularly for the condition on *Trifolium* (clover) plants.

pimple: very small rounded **pouch** gall, raised on one side of leaf, with opening on other side.

pinna (pinnae): first division of a divided **frond** of a fern (Fig. 1022).

pinnule: second division of a divided **frond** of a fern, division of a **pinna** (Fig. 1022).

pinnulet: third division of a divided **frond** of a fern, division of a **pinnule** (Fig. 1022).

pit gall: a small deep **depression** usually in stem, often with a raised rim; if in leaf, a sharp upward bulge occurs on other side.

pith: tissue forming core of non-woody stem, also called the medulla.

plasmodium: stage in the life cycle of slime moulds, Plasmodiophoraceae.

pocks: small scab-like spots raised on both sides of leaf, with an opening developing on one side.

polyphagous: an animal which feeds on many species of plants from unrelated families (cf. **monophagous**, **oligophagous**).

polypore fungus: basidiomycete species belonging to the Aphyllophorales, in which the undersurface of the cap of the fruiting body has pores instead of gills.

pouch: elongate finger-shaped gall raised on surface of leaf, or a sac-like gall formed from part or all of leaf; inside surface is usually the undersurface of leaf, with an opening connecting with the outside (cf. **pimple**).

proximal: part nearer to the stem or point of attachment (cf. **distal**).

psyllid: insect belonging to superfamily Psylloidea (Hemiptera).

pupa (pupae): stage in life cycle of some insects, between **larva** and adult stages, *e.g.* of Diptera (flies), Lepidoptera (butterflies and moths), Coleoptera (beetles), Hymenoptera (ants, bees and wasps).

puparium: hardened skin of last larval stage of some flies (Diptera), **pupa** develops inside.

pustule: thick-walled rounded swelling, with a cavity, raised on one or both sides of leaf, or on one side of stem (cf. **blister**).

raceme: an **inflorescence** bearing stalked flowers, those nearest the base opening first.

rachis (rachides): central stalk or stem of compound leaf, **inflorescence** or **frond** of fern (Fig. 1022).

receptacle: swollen tip of **peduncle** which bears the flower parts or, in the Asteraceae (daisies etc.), the **florets** and **bracts**.

recurved: curved down or back.

rhizome: horizontal, underground or ground level stem, often thickened.

root collar: base of stem at junction with root, often thickened.

rosette: (i) leafy gall originating from a bud, formed from a bunch or tuft of overlapping leaves; width greater than length (cf. **artichoke gall**).

(ii) basal leaves of plant growing flat on the ground, with a central growing point.

rust fungus: a basidiomycete fungus belonging to the order Uredinales.

sapling: young tree.

scale insect: insect belonging to superfamily Coccoidea (Hemiptera).

sepals: leaf- or bract-like outer parts of flowers, usually green, enclosing the rest of the flower when in bud.

septum (septa): dividing partition, *e.g.* in a poppy seed capsule.

sessile: without a stalk (as in sessile oak where the acorns are closely attached to the stem).

sexual generation (♀♂): generation with both females and males.

sheath: part of leaf enclosing stem of Poaceae (grasses) and Cyperaceae (sedges), or enclosing **inflorescence** of Apiaceae (umbellifers).

smut fungus: a basidiomycete fungus belonging to the order Ustilaginales.

sorus (sori): a fruiting structure, producing a powdery mass of spores, especially the spores which occur in the life history of **rusts**, **smuts** and other fungi (see introduction to Section B, p. 220).

spikelet: one or a group of flowers in **panicle** of Poaceae (grasses) or Cyperaceae (sedges) (Fig. 1023).

sporangium (sporangia): an organ occurring in various classes of fungi, within which sporangiospores are produced.

sternal spatula

sternal spatula: structure on underside of thorax of the final (third) larval **instar** of Cecidomyiidae (Fig. 1024), important in identification (it is absent in some species).

stipule: small, often paired, appendage, sometimes leaf-like, at base of **pedicel** or **petiole**.

synonym: previously-used name for a genus or species, included in these keys in brackets after current name.

telium (telia): **sorus**, in **rust fungi**, which prduces teliospores.

terminal: at tip of shoot, hence terminal bud (cf. **lateral**).

tubercle: a small, hard, thick-walled **pouch** gall, often pointed at tip.

umbel: a nearly flat **inflorescence** of Apiaceae (umbellifers), with **pedicels** arising from the same points, forming primary and secondary groups of flowers.

Fig. 1024

uredinium (uredinia): **sorus**, in **rust fungi**, which produces urediniospores.

ustilospores: spores of **smut fungi** analogous to the teliospores of **rust fungi** (see introduction to Section B, p. 220).

window pit

vector: an organism which transports a pathogen between hosts.

wart: small solid bump on surface of a gall.

whorl: ring of three or more leaves, petals etc., arising from the same point of a stem.

window: small patch in wall of gall covered by a thin skin, through which adult insect emerges.

window-pit: **window** in wall of galled fruit in a birch catkin (see Fig. 1025).

witches' broom: cluster of twigs or distorted leaves forming an untidy growth, on trunks or branches of trees.

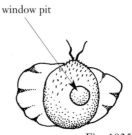

Fig. 1025

ABBREVIATIONS

agg.	aggregate species, composed of many microspecies
c.	circa, approximately
cf.	compare
f.	form of a species, a sub-specific taxon
F.	Fabricius
L.	Linnaeus
sp., spp.	species (singular and plural)
ssp.	subspecies
var.	variety of a species
<	less than
>	more than
±	more or less
♀♀	asexual generation
♀♂	sexual generation
µm	micrometres (1µm = 0.001mm, one-thousandth of a millimetre)

ACKNOWLEDGEMENTS

Several people have given us unvaluable help and advice. Patrick Dauphin and Jean-Claude Aniotsbehère allowed us to use their illustrations as a basis for some of our drawings; photographs in other works (marked with an asterisk in the References) have been used as a basis for others. Tom Preece and Brian Spooner have written the sections on viruses, bacteria, phytoplasmas and fungi, and John Southey the nematode section. John Southey would like to thank Safia Siddiqi of CAB International, Wallingford, for help with literature searches. Keith Harris and Mike Morris provided advice and checked details of cecidomyiid galls (KMH); weevil and other beetle galls (MGM); Keith also has drawn many of the illustrations of cecid galls. Philip Entwistle, Andrew Halstead, John Ismay, Brian Mitchell, Craig Slawson, Kenneth Spencer, Brian Wurzell and many members of the British Plant Gall Society have commented on and improved particular keys or illustrations, and collected or photographed specimens of galls used for the illustrations. We are grateful, too, for the many constructive comments made by people organised by AIDGAP to test the keys. Finally, thanks are due to Steve Tilling and Rebecca Farley of the Field Studies Council. We thank them all; we could not have completed the work without them.

In addition, we thank various members of our families for their help, patience and forbearance during the long gestation of these keys.

PLATE 1. **Galls caused by mites (Acari: Eriophyoidea)**
1.1 *Aceria ulmicola* on English elm, *Ulmus procera*, 1.2 *Acalitus longisetosus* on downy birch, *Betula pubescens*, 1.3 *Eriophyes convolvens* on spindle-tree, *Euonymus europaeus*, 1.4 *Eriophyes prunispinosae* on blackthorn, *Prunus spinosa*, 1.5 *Aceria fraxinivorus* on ash, *Fraxinus excelsior*, 1.6 *Acalitus calycophthirus* on silver birch, *Betula pendula*, 1.7 *Eriophyes tiliae* on large-leaved lime, *Tilia platyphyllos*, 1.8 *Aceria fagineus* on beech, *Fagus sylvatica*, 1.9 *Aceria aceriscampestris* on field maple, *Acer campestre*.

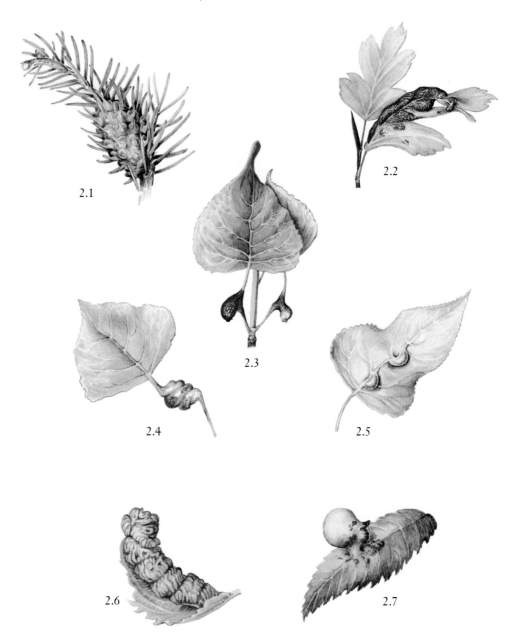

PLATE 2. Galls caused by aphids (Hemiptera: Aphididae and Adelgidae, 2.1)
2.1 *Adelges abietis* on Norway spruce, *Picea abies*, 2.2 *Dysaphis crataegi* on hawthorn, *Crataegus monogyna*, 2.3 *Pemphigus bursarius* on Lombardy poplar, *Populus nigra* var. *italica*, 2.4 *Pemphigus spyrothecae* on Lombardy poplar, *Populus nigra* var. *italica*, 2.5 *Pemphigus populinigrae* on black poplar, *Populus nigra*, 2.6 *Eriosoma ulmi* on wych elm, *Ulmus glabra*, 2.7 *Tetraneura ulmi* on wych elm, *Ulmus glabra*.

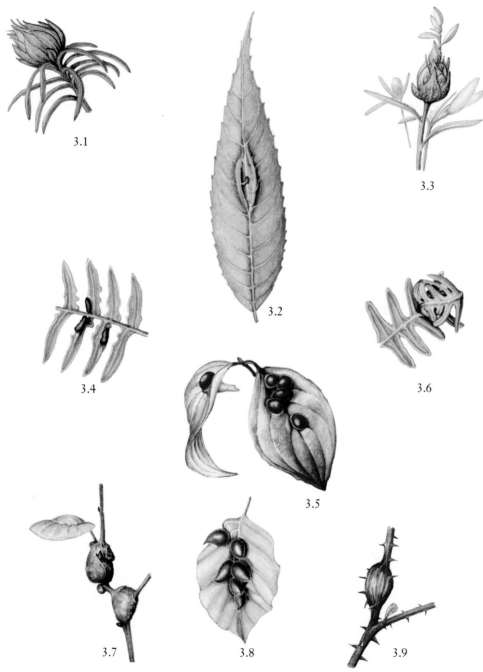

PLATE 3. Galls caused by gall midges (Diptera: Cecidomyiidae) and an anthomyiid fly (Diptera: Anthomyiidae, 3.6) on trees, shrubs and ferns

3.1 *Taxomyia taxi* on yew, *Taxus baccata*, 3.2 *Dasineura fraxini* on ash, *Fraxinus excelsior*, 3.3 *Jaapiella genisticola* on dyer's greenweed, *Genista tinctoria*, 3.4 *Dasineura filicina* on bracken, *Pteridium aquilinum*, 3.5 *Craneiobia corni* on dogwood, *Cornus sanguinea*, 3.6 *Chirosia grossicauda* on bracken, *Pteridium aquilinum*, 3.7 *Rabdophaga salicis* on goat sallow, *Salix caprea*, 3.8 *Mikiola fagi* on beech, *Fagus sylvatica*, 3.9 *Lasioptera rubi* on bramble, *Rubus 'fruticosus'* agg.

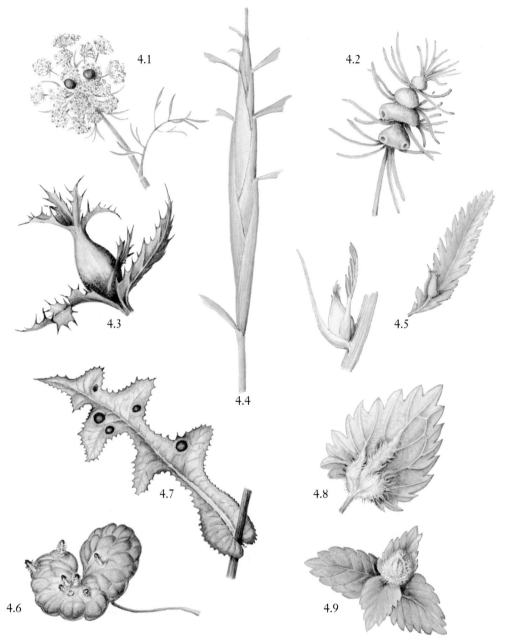

Plate 4. Galls caused by gall midges (Diptera: Cecidomyiidae), a gall fly (Diptera: Tephritidae, 4.3) and a gout fly (Diptera: Chloropidae, 4.4) on herbaceous plants

4.1 *Kiefferia pericarpiicola* on wild carrot, *Daucus carota*, 4.2 *Geocrypta galii* on hedge bedstraw, *Galium mollugo*, 4.3 *Urophora cardui* on creeping thistle, *Cirsium arvense*, 4.4 *Lipara lucens* on common reed, *Phragmites australis*, 4.5 *Rhopalomyia tanaceticola* on tansy, *Tanacetum vulgare*, 4.6 *Rondaniola bursaria* on ground ivy, *Glechoma hederacea*, 4.7 *Cystiphora sonchi* on perennial sow-thistle, *Sonchus arvensis*, 4.8 *Dasineura urticae* on stinging nettle, *Urtica dioica*, 4.9 *Jaapiella veronicae* on germander speedwell, *Veronica chamaedrys*.

PLATE 5. **Galls caused by cynipids (Hymenoptera: Cynipidae) and a chalcid (Hymenoptera: Eurytomidae, 5.1) on plants other than oak *Quercus* spp.**
5.1 *Tetramesa hyalipennis* on couch grass, *Elytrigia repens*, 5.2 *Liposthenes glechomae* on ground-ivy, *Glechoma hederacea*, 5.3 *Aulacidea tragopogonis* on goat's beard, *Tragopogon pratensis*, 5.4 *Aylax papaveris* on field poppy, *Papaver rhoeas*, 5.5 *Diplolepis nervosa*, smooth and spiked forms, on dog rose, *Rosa canina*, 5.6 *Diplolepis rosae* on dog rose, *Rosa canina*, 5.7 *Diastrophus rubi* on bramble, *Rubus 'fruticosus'* agg.

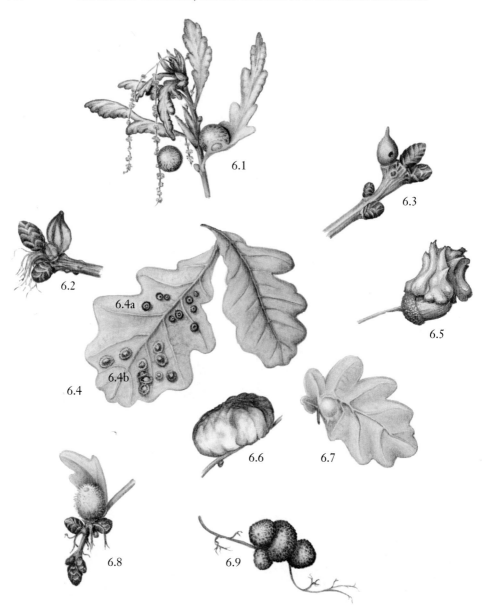

Plate 6. Galls caused by cynipids (Hymenoptera: Cynipidae) on pedunculate and sessile oak, *Quercus robur* **and** *Q. petraea* **(♀ ♂ or ♀ ♀ generations are indicated)**

6.1 *Neuroterus quercusbaccarum* ♀♂; when on a young leaf, the gall is normally on the underside, 6.2 *Andricus nudus* ♀♀; the red stripes shown in this specimen are unusually distinct, 6.3 *Andricus solitarius* ♀♀, 6.4a *Neuroterus numismalis* ♀♀, 6.4b *Neuroterus quercusbaccarum* ♀♀, 6.5 *Andricus quercuscalicis* ♀♀, 6.6 *Biorhiza pallida* ♀♂, 6.7 *Andricus curvator* ♀♂, 6.8 *Andricus glandulae* ♀♀, 6.9 *Biorhiza pallida* ♀♀.

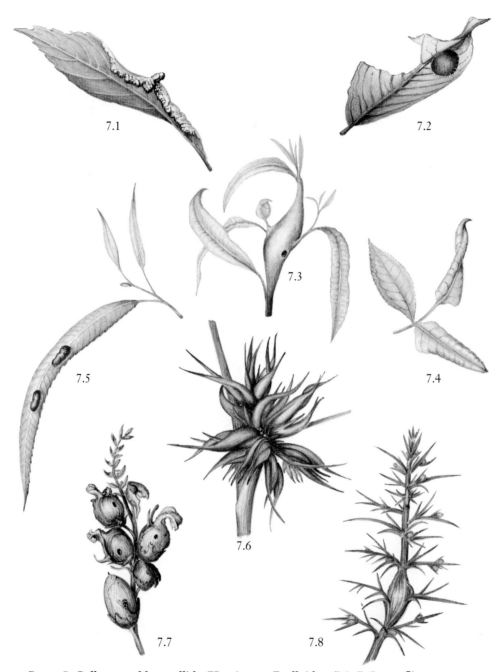

PLATE 7. **Galls caused by psyllids (Hemiptera: Psylloidea, 7.1, 7.6), sawflies (Hymenoptera: Tenthredinidae, 7.2, 7.4, 7.5), weevils (Coleoptera: Curculionidae, 7.7, and Brentidae, 7.8) and a moth (Lepidoptera: Momphidae, 7.3)**

7.1 *Psyllopsis fraxini* on ash, *Fraxinus excelsior*, 7.2 *Pontania pedunculi* on grey sallow, *Salix cinerea*, 7.3 *Mompha nodicolella* on rosebay willowherb, *Chamerion angustifolium*, 7.4 *Blennocampa phyllocolpa* on dog rose, *Rosa canina*, 7.5 *Pontania proxima* on crack willow, *Salix fragilis*, 7.6 *Livia juncorum* on heath rush, *Juncus squarrosus*, 7.7 *Gymnetron antirrhini* on common toadflax, *Linaria vulgaris*, 7.8 *Eutrichapion scutellare* on dwarf gorse, *Ulex minor*.

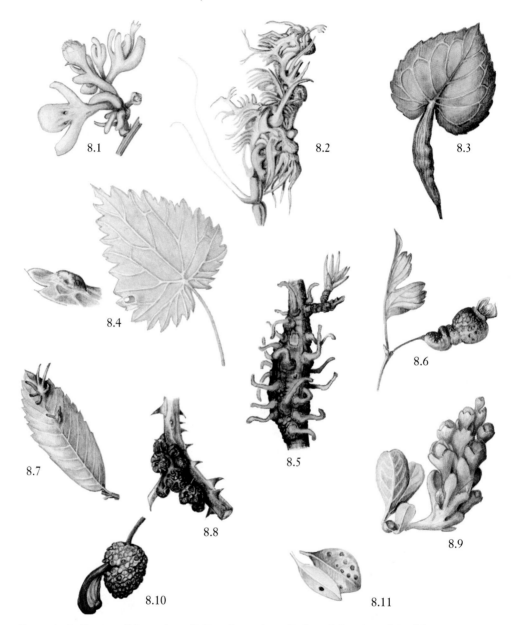

PLATE 8. **Galls caused by a virus (8.2), a bacterium (8.8) and fungi: a white blister (Peronosporales: Albuginaceae, 8.1), an ascomycete (Taphrinales: Taphrinaceae, 8.10), and basidiomycetes: Exobasidiales: Exobasidiaceae, 8.9, rusts (Uredinales: Pucciniaceae, 8.4-8.7, 8.11) and a smut (Ustilaginales: Tilletiaceae, 8.3)**

8.1 *Albugo candida* on shepherd's-purse, *Capsella bursa-pastoris*, 8.2 virus on willow, *Salix* sp., 8.3 *Urocystis violae* on common dog-violet, *Viola riviniana*, 8.4 *Puccinia urticata* on stinging nettle, *Urtica dioica*, 8.5 *Gymnosporangium clavariiforme*, on juniper *Juniperus communis*, 8.6 *Gymnosporangium clavariiforme* on hawthorn, *Crataegus monogyna*, 8.7 *Gymnosporangium cornutum* on rowan, *Sorbus aucuparia*, 8.8 *Agrobacterium tumefaciens* on bramble, *Rubus 'fruticosus'*, 8.9 *Exobasidium myrtilli* on bilberry, *Vaccinium myrtillus*, 8.10 *Taphrina alni* on alder, *Alnus glutinosa*, 8.11 *Puccinia buxi* on box, *Buxus sempervirens*.

REFERENCES

* Illustrations from these works have been used as a basis for some of the figures included.

ADLER, H. & STRATON, C. R., (1894). *Alternating Generations. A Study of Oak Galls and Gall Flies.* Oxford, Clarendon Press.

ALEXOPOULOS, C. J., MIMS, C. W. & BLACKWELL, M., (1996). *Introductory Mycology.* 4th edition. New York, John Wiley & Sons.

ALFORD, D. V., (1984). *A Colour Atlas of Fruit Pests, their Recognition, Biology and Control.* London, Wolfe Publishing.

ALFORD, D. V., (1995). *A Colour Atlas of Ornamental Trees, Shrubs and Flowers.* London, Manson Publishing.

*AMBRUS, B., (1974). Cynipida-Gubacsok=Cecidia Cynipidarum. *Magyarország Állatvil-ga Fauna Hungariae.* Budapest, Académiai Kiadó.

AMRINE, J. W. & STASNY, T. A., (1994). *Catalog of the Eriophyoidea of the World.* Michigan, Indira Publishing House.

ANANTHAKRISHNAN, T. N., (ed.) (1984). *The Biology of Gall Insects.* London, Edward Arnold.

BAGNALL, R. S. & HARRISON, J. W. H., (1918). A preliminary catalogue of British Cecidomyiidae (Diptera) with special reference to the gall-midges of the North of England. *Transactions of the Royal Entomological Society of London,* **65**, 346-426.

BAKER, B., (1985). Sesiidae. In; Heath, J. & Emmett, A. M. (eds), *The Moths and Butterflies of Great Britain and Ireland* Vol. 2. Great Horkesley, Colchester, Essex, Harley Books.

BARNES, H. F., (1948-1956). *Gall Midges of Economic Importance.* Vols I-VII. London, Crosby Lockwood.

BENĔS, K., (1968). Galls and larvae of the European species of genera *Phyllocolpa* and *Pontania* (Hymenoptera: Tenthredinidae). *Acta Entomologica Bohemslovaca,* **65**, 112-137.

*BEVAN, D., (1987). *Forest Insects. A Guide to Insects Feeding on Trees in Britain.* Handbook 1. Forestry Commission, London, H.M.S.O.

*BLACKMAN, R. L. & EASTOP, V. F., (1994). *Aphids on the World's Trees. An Identification and Information Guide.* London, CAB International and Natural History Museum.

BLAND, K. P., (2001). *Rabdophaga repenticornua* sp. nov. (Diptera: Cecidomyiidae) galling *Salix repens* in Scotland. *Entomologist's Gazette,* **52**, 195-198.

BORATYNSKI, K., (1961). A note on the species of *Asterolecanium* Targioni-Tozzetti 1869 (Homoptera, Coccoidea, Asterolecaniidae) on oak in Britain. *Proceedings of the Royal Entomological Society of London (B),* **30**, 1-14.

*BOWDREY, J., (1999). New gall wasp discovered at Fingringhoe Ranges, Essex. *Cecidology,* **14**, 12-13.

BRADLEY, J. D., TREMEWAN, W. G. & SMITH, A., (1973). *British Tortricoid Moths. Cochylidae and Tortricidae: Tortricinae.* London, Ray Society.

*BRADLEY, J. D., TREMEWAN, W. G. & SMITH, A., (1979) *British Tortricoid Moths. Tortricidae: Oleuthreutinae.* London, Ray Society.

BRZESKI, K M. W., (1998). *Nematodes of Tylenchida in Poland and Temperate Europe.* Warsaw, Museum: Institute zoologii Polska Academia Nank Warsawa.

*BUHR, H., (1964-65). *Bestimmungstabellen der Gallen (Zoo- und Phytocecidien) an Pflanzen Mittel- und Nordeuropas.* Vols. I & II. Jena, Fischer Verlag.

*CARTER, C. I., (1971). Conifer woolly aphids (Adelgidae) in Britain. *Forestry Commission Bulletin,* **42**, 1-49.

CARTER, C. I. & DANIELSSON, R., (1993). New and additional records of gall-forming aphids of the family Pemphigidae in Britain. *The Entomologist,* **112**, 99-104.

CHANDLER, P., (ED.) (1998). Checklists of insects of the British Isles (new series). Part I: Diptera. *Handbooks for the Identification of British Insects,* **12**, 256pp. London, Royal Entomological Society.

CHINERY, M. & SPOONER, B., (1998). The galling of sea firs (Hydrozoa) and other coelenterates by larval sea spiders (Pycnogonida). *Cecidology,* **13**, 24-27.

CLAPHAM, A. R., TUTIN, T. G. & MOORE, D. M., (1987). *Flora of the British Isles*. 3rd edition. Cambridge, Cambridge University Press.

*CLARIDGE, M. F. & DAWAH, H. A., (1994). Assemblages of herbivorous chalcid species and their parasitoids associated with grasses – problems of species and specificity. In Williams, M. A. J. (ed.) *Plant Galls. Organisms, Interactions, Populations*. Systematics Association Special Volume 49. Oxford, Clarendon Press. pp. 313-329.

CLEMENT, E. J. & FOSTER, M. C., (1994). *Alien Plants of the British Isles*. London, Botanical Society of the British Isles.

CMID (see International Mycological Institute (IMID) below).

COLES, J. W., (1958). Nematodes parasitic on sea weeds of the genera *Ascophyllum* and *Fucus*. *Journal of the Marine Biological Association, UK*, **37**, 145-155.

Commonwealth Institute of Helminthology, (1972-1975). *C.I.H. Descriptions of plant-parasitic Nematodes*.

    FRANKLIN, M. T., (1973). *Meloidogyne naasi*. Set 2, No. 19.

    HOOPER, D. J., (1972). *Ditylenchus dipsaci*. Set 1, No. 14.

    ORTON WILLIAMS, K. J., (1972). *Meloidogyne javanica*. Set 1, No. 3.

    ORTON WILLIAMS, K. J., (1973). *Meloidogyne incognita*. Set 2, No. 18.

    ORTON WILLIAMS, K. J., (1974). *Meloidogyne hapla*. Set 3, no. 31.

    ORTON WILLIAMS, K. J., (1975). *Meloidogyne arenaria*. Set 5, No. 62.

    PITCHER, R. S., SIDDIQI, M. R. & BROWN, D. J. F., (1974). *Xiphinema diversicaudatum*. Set 4, No. 60.

    SIDDIQI, M. R., (1974). *Aphelenchoides ritzemabosi*. Set 3, No. 32.

    SOUTHEY, J. F., (1972). *Anguina tritici*. Set 1, No. 13.

    SOUTHEY, J. F., (1973). *Anguina agrostis*. Set 2, No. 20.

    SOUTHEY, J. F., (1974). *Anguina graminis*. Set 4, No. 53.

CONNOLD, E. T., (1901). *British Vegetable Galls*. London, Hutchinson.

CONNOLD, E. T., (1908). *British Oak Galls*. London, Adlard & Sons.

CONNOLD, E. T., (1909). *Plant Galls of Great Britain*. London, Adlard & Sons.

*COULIANOS, C-C. & HOLMÅSEN, I., (1991). *Galler*. Stockholm, Interpublishing AB.

COURTECUISSE, R. & DUHEM, B., (1995). *Collins Field Guide to Mushrooms and Toadstools of Britain and Europe*. London, Harper Collins.

*CSÓKA, G., (1997) *Plant Galls*. Forest Research Institute. Budapest, Agroinform.

CSÓKA, G., MATTSON, W. J., STONE, G. N. & PRICE, P. W., (eds.) (1998) *The Biology of Gall-Inducing Arthropods*. St. Paul, Minnesota, US Department of Agriculture.

*DARLINGTON, A., (1968). *The Pocket Encyclopaedia of Plant Galls in Colour*. London, Blandford.

*DAUPHIN, P. & ANIOTSBEHÈRE, J-C., (1993, revised 1997). *Les Galles de France*. Mémoires de la Société Linnéenne de Bordeaux, Tome 2.

*DOCTERS VAN LEEUWEN, W. M., (1957, revised and enlarged by Wiebes-Rijks, A.A. & Houtman, G., 1982). *Gallenboek*. Zutphen, Thieme & Cie.

DREGER-JAUFFRET, F. & SHORTHOUSE, J. D., (1992) Diversity of gall-inducing insects and their galls. In; Shorthouse, J. D. & Rohfritsch, O. (eds.) (1992). *Biology of Insect-Induced Galls*. Oxford, Oxford University Press. pp. 8-33.

DUDMAN, A. A. & RICHARDS, A. J., (1997). *Dandelions of Great Britain and Ireland*. Handbook No. 9. London, Botanical Society of the British Isles.

*EADY, R. D. & QUINLAN, J., (1963). Hymenoptera: Cynipoidea. *Handbooks for the Identification of British Insects*. **8**, 1(a), 1-81. London, Royal Entomological Society.

ELLIS, H. A., (2000). Fungus-induced galls on alder catkins. *Field Mycology*, **1**, 78-80.

ELLIS, M. B. & ELLIS, J. P., (1985), *Microfungi on Land Plants. An Identification Handbook*. London, Croom Helm.

ENTWISTLE, P. F., (2001). *Polystepha malpighii* (Kieffer) – a neglected gall. *Cecidology*, **16**, 6-12.

EVANS, K., TRUDGILL, D. L. & WEBSTER, J. H. (EDS), (1993). *Plant Parasitic Nematodes in Temperate Agriculture*. Wallingford, CAB International.

EVANS, L., (1986). Norfolk records of two gall midges (Diptera: Cecidomyiidae) derived from fungi. *Cecidology*, **1**, 31.

EVANS, L., (1992). Midge galls on fungi. *Cecidology*, **7**, 95.

EVANS, R. E., (1970). Observations on the development of *Mycocecis ovalis* (Diptera: Cecidomyiidae) on the fungus *Hypoxylon rubiginosum* Pers. ex Fr. *Proceedings of the Royal Entomological Society of London* (A), **45**, 156-159.

FELT, E. P., (1940) *Plant Galls and Gall Makers.* Ithaca, New York, Comstock Publishing Company.

FITTER, R., FITTER, A. & BLAMEY, M., (1974). *The Wild Flowers of Britain and Northern Europe.* London, Collins.

FITTER, R., FITTER, A. & FARRAR, A., (1984) *Collins Pocket Guide to Grasses, Sedges, Rushes and Ferns of Britain and Northern Europe.* London, HarperCollins.

FOWLER, W. W., (1887-1891). *The Coleoptera of the British Islands.* London, Reeve.

GAGNÉ, R. J., (1989). *The Plant-feeding Gall Midges of North America.* Ithaca, New York, Cornell University Press.

GAGNÉ, R. J., (1990). Gall midge complex (Diptera: Cecidomyiidae) in bud galls of Palaearctic *Euphorbia* (Euphorbiaceae). *Annals of the Entomological Society of America*, **83**, 335-345.

GAGNÉ, R. J., (1994). *The Gall Midges of the Neotropical Region.* Ithaca, New York, Comstock Publishing Company.

GØNGET, H., (1997). The Brentidae (Coleoptera) of Northern Europe. *Fauna Entomologica Scandinavia*, **34**, 289pp.

GOODEY, T., (1933). *Plant Parasitic Nematodes and the Diseases They Cause.* London, Methuen.

GRAHAM, G. G. & PRIMAVESI, A. L., (1993). *Roses of Great Britain and Ireland.* London, Botanical Society of the British Isles.

GRATWICK, M., (ed.) (1992). *Crop Pests in the U.K.* London, Chapman & Hall.

HALSTEAD, A. J. (1995). The *Hemerocallis* gall midge (*Contarinia quinquenotata*): where is it now? *Cecidology*, **10**, 16-17.

HANCY, R. & HANCY, B., (1997). Galled vine leaves from a stately home. *Cecidology*, **12**, 70.

HARRIS, K. M., (1975). The *Chondrilla* gall midge, *Cystiphora schmidti* (Rübsaamen) comb. n. (Diptera: Cecidomyiidae). Taxonomy and description. *Bulletin of Entomological Research*, **65**, 51-54.

*HARRIS, K. M. & EVANS, R. E., (1979). Gall development in the fungus *Peniophora cinerea* (Fr.) Cooke induced by *Brachyneurina peniophorae* sp. n. (Diptera: Cecidomyiidae). *Entomologists' Gazette*, **30**, 23-30.

HAWKSWORTH, D. L., KIRK, P M., SUTTON, B. C. & PEGLER, D. N., (1995). *Ainsworth and Bisby's Dictionary of the Fungi* (8th. edition). International Mycological Institute, Wallingford, CAB International.

*HEIE, O. E., (1980) The Aphidoidea (Hemiptera) of Fennoscandia and Denmark. I. General part: the families Mindaridae, Hormaphididae, Thelaxidae, Anoeciidae and Pemphigidae. *Fauna Entomologica Scandinavica*, **9**, 236 pp., Klampenborg, Denmark, Scandinavian Science Press.

HENDERSON, D. M., (2000). *A Checklist of the Rust Fungi of the British Isles.* British Mycological Society.

HODGE, P .J. & JONES, R. A., (1995). *New British Beetles. Species not in Joy's Practical Handbook.* London, British Entomological and Natural History Society. (Contact address: BENHS, Pelham-Clinton Building, Dinton Pastures Country Park, Davis Street, Reading, Berkshire RG10 0TH.)

HODKINSON, I. D. & WHITE, I. M., (1979). Homoptera, Psylloidea. *Handbooks for the Identification of British Insects*, **2** (5a), 1-98. London, Royal Entomological Society.

HOUARD, C., (1908-1913). *Les Zoocécidies des Plantes d'Europe et du Bassin de la Mediterranée.* Paris, Hermann.

ING, B., (1994). European Exobasidiales and their galls. In Williams, M. A. J., (ed.) *Plant Galls. Organisms, Interactions, Populations.* Systematics Association Special Volume 49. Oxford, Clarendon Press. pp. 67-76.

ING, B., (1998) *Exobasidium* in the British Isles. *Mycologist*, **12**, 80-82.

INGRAM, D. & ROBERTSON, N., (1999). *Plant Disease: a Natural History.* London, HarperCollins.

INTERNATIONAL MYCOLOGICAL INSTITUTE (IMID) (1964 onwards) *Descriptions of Fungi and Bacteria*. Bakeham Lane, Egham, Surrey TW20 9TY.

ISMAY, J. W., (1999). The British and Irish genera of Chloropinae (Diptera, Chloropidae). *Entomologists' Monthly Magazine*, **135**, 1-37.

JACKSON, E., (2000). *Taphrina amentorum* in Cornwall. *Cecidology* **15**: 78.

JOY, N. H., (1932). *A Practcal Handbook of British Beetles*. 2 vols. London, Witherby.

*KAPLAN, F., (1977). *The Chloropidae of Israel*. Unpublished MSc Thesis, Department of Zoology, Tel-Aviv University.

*KIR'YANOVA, E. S. & KRALL, E. L., (1971) *Plant-parasitic Nematodes and Their Control*. Leningrad, Nauka. (English translation of Vol. II published by Amerind, New Delhi, 1980.)

KLOET, G. S. & HINCKS, W. D., (1964-1978). A check list of British insects. Part 1: Small orders and Hemiptera 2nd ed. (1964); Part 2: Lepidoptera (1972); Part 3: Coleoptera (1977); Part 4: Hymenoptera (1978). *Handbooks for the Identification of British Insects*. **12**. London, Royal Entomological Society.

KOPELKE, J. P., (1991). Die Arten der *viminalis*-Gruppe, Gattung *Pontania* O. Costa 1859, Mittel- und Nordeuropas (Insecta: Hymenoptera, Symphyta: Tenthredinidae). *Seckenbergiana Biologica*, **71**, 65-128.

*KRALL, E. L., (1991). Wheat and grass nematodes: *Anguina, Subanguina*, and related genera. In;Nickle, W. R., (ed.) *Manual of Agricultural Nematology*. New York, Marcel Dekker.

LAREW, H. G., (1992). Fossil galls. In; Shorthouse, J. D. & Rohfritsch, O., (1992) (eds.) *Biology of Insect-Induced Galls*. Oxford, Oxford University Press. pp. 50-59.

LEATHER, S. R. & BLAND, K. P., (1999). *Insects on Cherry Trees*. Naturalists' Handbooks, **27**. Slough, Richmond Publishing Company.

LISTON, A. D., (1995). *Compendium of European Sawflies*. Gottfrieding, Germany, Chalastos Forestry.

LUCAS, J. A., (1988). An outbreak of *Mahonia* rust, *Cumminsiella miribilissima*. *The Mycologist*, **2**, 163.

MANI, M. A., (1964). *Ecology of Plant Galls*. Hague, Dr. W. Junk.

MEIKLE, R. D., (1984). *Willows and Poplars of Great Britain and Ireland*. BSBI Handbook **4**. London, Botanical Society of the British Isles.

*MERRYWEATHER, J. & HILL, M., (1992). The fern guide. An introductory guide to the ferns, clubmosses, quillworts and horsetails of the British Isles. *Field Studies*, **8**, 101-188.

*MEYER, J., (1987). *Plant Galls and Gall Inducers*. Berlin & Stuttgart, Borntraeger.

*MEYER, J. & MARESQUELLE, H. J., (1983) *Anatomie des Galles*. Berlin & Stuttgart, Borntraeger.

MITCHELL, A., (1974). *A Field Guide to the Trees of Britain and Northern Europe*. London, Collins.

MIX, A. J., (1949, English translation from the German 1969) *A Monograph of the Genus* Taphrina. Codicote, Wheldon & Wesley. Also in *University of Texas Science Bulletin*, **23**, 3-167.

MORDUE, E. M. & AINSWORTH, G. C., (1984). Ustilaginales of the British Isles. IMID (see above).

MORRIS, M. G., (1990). Orthocerous weevils. Coleoptera: Curculionoidea (Nemonychidae, Anthribidae, Urodontidae, Attelabidae and Apionidae). *Handbooks for the Identification of British Insects*, **5** (16), 1-108. London, Royal Entomological Society.

MORRIS, M. G., (1991) A taxonomic check list of the British Ceutorhynchinae, with notes, particularly on host plant relationships (Coleoptera: Curculionidae). *Entomologists' Gazette*, **42**, 255-265.

MORRIS, M. G., (1993). British orthocerous weevils: corrections and new information (Coleoptera: Curculionoidea). *Entomologists' Monthly Magazine*, **129**, 23-30.

MORRIS, M. G. & BOOTH, R. G., (1997). Notes on the nomenclature of some British weevils (Curculionoidea). *Coleopterist*, **6**, 91-99.

NIJVELDT, W., (1969). *Gall Midges of Economic Importance* Vol. VIII. London, Crosby Lockwood.

*PAQUETTE, L. C., BAGATTO, G. & SHORTHOUSE, J. D. (1993) The distribution of mineral nutrients within the leaves of common dandelion (*Taraxacum officinale*) galled by *Phanacis taraxaci* (Hymenoptera: Cynipidae). *Canadian Journal of Botany*, **71**, 1026-1031.

*PREECE, T. F., (1993). Maize cob galls caused by the smut fungus *Ustilago zeae*. *Cecidology*, **8**, 88-90

PREECE, T. F., (1996). *Guides for the Amateur Mycologist* No. 5. *Downy Mildews, Powdery Mildews, Smuts and Rusts*. British Mycological Society.

PREECE, T. F., (2000). The strange story of box rust, *Puccinia buxi*, in Britain. *Mycologist*, **14**, 104 – 106.

PREECE, T. F., CLEMENT, J. A. & GRAMSHAW, A., (1999). *Entyloma chrysospleni* rediscovered on *Chrysosplenium alternifolium* in Yorkshire. *Mycologist*, **13**, 86-87.

PREECE, T. F. & HICK, A. J., (1990). *An Introductory Scanning Electron Microscope Atlas of Rust Fungi*. London, Farrand Press.

PREECE, T. F. & HICK, A. J., (2001). An introduction to the Protomycetales: *Burenia inundata* on *Apium nodiflorum* and *Protomyces macrosporus* on *Anthriscus sylvestris*. *Mycologist*, **15**, 119-125.

PREECE, T. F., MORDUE, E. M. & HICK, A. J., (1994). Recent finds of an unusual rust fungus in the leaves of *Arum maculatum* in Shropshire - is it a smut? *Mycologist*, **8**, 68-70.

PREECE, T. F., PETTIT, P. R. & BIGGS, D. T., (1994). *Fusarium heterosporum* growing on ergots (*Claviceps purpurea*) in spikelets of common cord-grass (*Spartina anglica*) in the Isle of Wight. *Mycologist*, **8**, 9-11.

PREECE, T. F., WEBER, R. W. S. & WEBSTER, J., (2000). Origin and spread of the daisy rust epidemic in Britain caused by *Puccinia distincta*. *Mycological Research*, **104**, 576-580.

PRICE, P. W., MATTSON, W. J. & BARANCHIKOV, Y. N. (eds.), (1994). *The Ecology and Evolution of Gall-forming Insects*. St. Paul, Minnesota, US Department of Agriculture.

PUJADE-VILLAR, J., ROS-FARRE, P. & ARNEDO, M. A., (1998). Phylogenetic position of *Neuroterus anthracinus* (Curtis1838) comb. nov. (Hymenoptera: Cynipidae). *Gea, Flora et Fauna*, **1998**, pp. 111-114.

*REDFERN, M. & ASKEW, R. R., (1992, updated reprint 1998). *Plant Galls*. Naturalists' Handbook **17**. Slough, Richmond.

ROBBINS, J., (1995). *A Provisional Atlas of the Gall Midges of Warwickshire (Insects: Diptera: Cecidomyiidae)*. Warwickshire Museum Service, 19pp.

ROHFRITSCH, O. (1992) Patterns in gall development. In; Shorthouse, J. D. & Rohfritsch, O., (1992) (eds.) *Biology of Insect-Induced Galls*. Oxford, Oxford University Press. pp. 60-86.

ROSE, F., (1981). *The Wild Flower Key: British Isles - N.W. Europe*. London, Warne.

ROSKAM, J. C., (1992). Evolution of the gall-inducing guild. In; Shorthouse, J. D. & Rohfritsch, O., (1992) (eds.) *Biology of Insect-Induced Galls*. Oxford, Oxford University Press. pp. 34-49.

SALT, D. T. & WHITTAKER, J. B., (1998). *Insects on Dock Plants*. Naturalists' Handbooks **26**. Slough, Richmond Publishing Company.

SCOTT, A. C., STEPHENSON, J. & COLLINSON, M., (1994). The fossil record of leaves with galls. In; Williams, M. A. J., (ed.) *Plant Galls. Organisms, Interactions, Populations*. Systematics Association Special Volume **49**. Oxford, Clarendon Press. pp. 447-470.

SHORTHOUSE, J. D. & ROHFRITSCH, O., (1992) (eds.) *Biology of Insect-Induced Galls*. Oxford, Oxford University Press.

SIDDIQI, M. R., (2000). *Tylenchida: Parasites of Plants and Insects*. 2nd. edition. Wallingford, CABI.

*SIDDIQI, M. R. & HAWKSWORTH, D. L., (1982). Nematodes associated with galls on *Cladonia*, including two new species. *Lichenologist*, **14**, 175-184.

SKUHRAVÁ, M., (1989). Taxonomic changes and records in Palaearctic Cecidomyiidae (Diptera). *Acta Entomologica Bohemoslovaca*, **86**, 202-233.

*SKUHRAVÁ, M., (1991) The plant-feeding gall midges (Cecidomyiidae, Diptera) of the Palearctic region. Part 1. *Cecidologica Nationale* **12**: 1-12.

SKUHRAVÁ, M. & SKUHRAVÝ, V., (1986). Outbreak of two gall midges, *Harrisomyia* n. gen. *vitrina* (Kieffer) and *Drisina glutinosa* Giard (Cecidomyiidae, Diptera) on maple *Acer pseudoplatanus* L. in Czechoslovakia, with descriptions of the two genera and species. *Zeitschrift für angewandte Entomologie* **101**: 256-274.

*SKUHRAVÁ, M. & SKUHRAVÝ V., (1992a). Biology of gall midges on common reed in Czechoslovakia. In; Shorthouse, J. D. & Rohfritsch, O., (1992) (eds.) *Biology of Insect-Induced Galls*. Oxford, Oxford University Press. pp. 196-207.

*Skuhravá, M. & Skuhravý, V., (1992b). *Atlas of Galls Induced by Gall Midges.* Czechoslovakia, Academia Praha.

*Skuhravá, M. & Skuhravý, V., (1993). *Die Gallmücken (Diptera: Cecidomyiidae) des Fürstentums Liechtenstein.* Praha, Vaduz.

*Southey, J. F., (1969). A gall-forming nematode (*Anguina* sp.) parasitic on cocksfoot grass. *Plant Pathology* 18: 164-166.

*Southey, J. F., (ed.) (1978, reprinted 1982). *Plant Nematology.* Ministry of Agriculture, Fisheries and Food Reference Book 407. London, HMSO.

Southey, J. F., Topham, P .B. & Brown, D. J. F,. (1990). Taxonomy of some species of *Anguina* Scopoli, 1777 (*sensu* Brzeski, 1981) forming galls on Gramineae: value of diagnostic characters and present status of nominal species. *Revue de Nématologie* 13: 127-142.

*Spencer, K. A., (1972). Diptera: Agromyzidae. *Handbooks for the Identification of British Insects,* **10** (5g): 1-136. London, Royal Entomological Society.

Spooner, B. M., (1985). *Melanopsichum* (Ustilaginales), a genus new to the British Isles. *Transactions of the British Mycological Society,* **85**, 540-544.

Spooner, B. M., (1994a). *Thalestris rhodymeniae* – a gall-causing copepod. *Cecidology,* **9**, 39-41.

Spooner, B. M., (1994b). *Proales werneckii*: a gall-causing rotifer. In; Williams, M. A. J., (ed.) *Plant Galls. Organisms, Interactions, Populations.* Systematics Association Special Volume **49**. Oxford, Clarendon Press. pp. 99-117.

Spooner, B. M., (1997). Galls on echinoderms: true animal galls? *Cecidology,* **12**, 7-8.

Spooner, B. M., (1999). Checklist of British galls and gall-causing organisms. 3. Nematoda: preliminary list. *Cecidology,* **14**, 63-79.

Spooner, B. M., (2002). Mycocecidia of larger fungi in Britain. *Cecidology,* **17**, 38-42.

Spooner, B. & Bowdrey J. P., (1993) Checklist of British gall-causing organisms: progress report 1992. *Cecidology,* **8**, 31-35.

Spooner, B. M. & Savage, D. P., (1989). Gall-mites (Eriophyidae) on *Sorbus* species in Britain. *Cecidology,* **4**, 18-20.

Stace, C., (1997). *New Flora of the British Isles.* 2nd edition. Cambridge, Cambridge University Press.

Stelter, H., (1977). Die Knospengallen der Wollweiden (*Salix aurita, S. cinerea, S. caprea*). *Reichenbachia,* **16**, 241-256.

Stelter, H., (1982). Europaische Gallmücken der Gattung *Dasineura* an *Viola*-Arten. *Entomologische Mitteilungen aus dem Zoologischen Museum, Hamburg,* **116**, 253-268.

Stone, G. N. (2001). It is not *Andricus corruptrix* after all. *Cecidology,* **16**, 18-19.

Stone, G. N. & Sunnucks, P. J., (1992). The hedgehog gall *Andricus lucidus* (Hartig 1843) confirmed in Britain. *Cecidology,* **7**, 30-35.

Stroyan, H. L. G., (1984). Aphids - Pterommatinae and Aphidinae (Aphidini). Homoptera, Aphididae. *Handbooks for the Identification of British Insects.* 2 (6): 1-232. London, Royal Entomological Society.

Stubbs, F. B., (ed.) (1986). *Provisional Keys to British Plant Galls.* British Plant Gall Society.

Swanton, E. W., (1912). *British Plant Galls.* London, Methuen.

Trail, J. W. H., (1888). The gall-making Diptera of Scotland. *Scottish Naturalist,* **3**, 281-288, 309-328, 373-382.

Vánky, K., (1994). *European Smut Fungi.* Stuttgart, Gustav Fischer Verlag.

Voigt, G., (1932). Galle oder Blattmine? Beitrag zur Histologie der vergallten Mine von *Apion sedi* Germ. (Curculion.) und anderer *Sedum*-Minen. *Anzeiger für Schädlingskunde,* **8**, 135-143.

Walker P., (2002). Two new records for cynipid Oak Galls (Cynipidae: Hymenoptera) in Britain. *Cecidology,* **17**, 64-67.

Weber, R. W. S., Webster, J. Wakley, G. E. & Al-Gharabally, D. H., (1998) *Puccinia distincta*, cause of a devastating rust disease of daisies. *Mycologist,* **12**, 87-90.

Wehrmaker, A. & Kwast, E., (2002). Sticking up for *Andricus corruptrix*: Schlechtendal's first new gall wasp was first. *Cecidology,* **17**, 43-47.

*WEIDNER, H..E. & SCHREMMER, F., (1962). Zur Erforschungsgesichte, zur Morphologie und Biologie der Larve von *Aganthomyia wankowiczi* Schnabl, einer an Baumpilsen gallenerzeugenden Dipterenlarve. *Entomologische Mitteilungen aus dem Zoologischen Staatinstitut und Zoologischen Museum, Hamburg* **2 (40)**: 11pp.

WELCH, R. C., (1993). Colonisation of introduced oaks by Cynipidae. *Cecidology*, **8**, 58-76.

WESTPHAL, E. & MICHLER, P., (1975). Mise en évidence de particules bacilliformes dans les malformations du type Wirrzopf apparaissant sur certaines Saules. *Comptes Rendus des Séances l'Academie des Sciences, Paris*, **281**, 403-405.

*WHITE, I. M. & HODKINSON, I. D., (1982). Psylloidea (nymphal stages). Hemiptera, Homoptera. *Handbooks for the Identification of British Insects*. **2 (5b)**, 1-50. London, Royal Entomological Society.

WHITE, I. M., (1988). Tephritid flies. *Handbooks for the Identification of British Insects*. **10 (5a)**: 1-134. London, Royal Entomological Society.

WILLIAMS, M. A. J., (ed.) (1994). *Plant Galls. Organisms, Interactions, Populations*. Systematics Association Special Volume **49**. Oxford, Clarendon Press.

WILSON, M. & HENDERSON, D. M., (1966). *British Rust Fungi*. Cambridge, Cambridge University Press.

WURZELL, B., (2002). The maple bladder gall of the gall mite *Vasates quadripedes* new to Britain. *Cecidology*, **17**, 31-35.

INDEX

TO HOST PLANTS AND FUNGI

INDEX

TO THE ORGANISMS THAT CAUSE GALLS
AND TO THOSE THAT MAY BE CONFUSED WITH THEM